W9-CPM-735

AIA Guide to the Architecture of Washington, DC

SIXTH EDITION

AIA GUIDE
to the Architecture of
Washington, DC

G. Martin Moeller, Jr., Assoc. AIA
for the Washington Chapter,
American Institute of Architects, Inc.
(AIA | DC)

Johns Hopkins University Press

Baltimore

Johns Hopkins University Press
2715 North Charles Street
Baltimore, Maryland 21218-4363
www.press.jhu.edu

Library of Congress Cataloging-in-Publication Data

Names: Moeller, Gerard Martin, author. | American Institute of Architects.
Title: AIA guide to the architecture of Washington, DC / G. Martin Moeller, Jr.
Description: 6th edition. | Baltimore : Johns Hopkins University Press, 2022. |
    Includes bibliographical references and index.
Identifiers: LCCN 2021036190 | ISBN 9781421443843 (hardcover) |
    ISBN 9781421443850 (paperback) | ISBN 9781421443867 (ebook)
Subjects: LCSH: Architecture — Washington (D.C.) — Tours. | Washington
    (D.C.) — Buildings, structures, etc. — Tours. | Washington (D.C.) — Tours.
Classification: LCC NA735.W3 M64 2022 | DDC 720.9753 — dc23
LC record available at https://lccn.loc.gov/2021036190

A catalog record for this book is available from the British Library.

The photo of the National Museum of African American History and Culture and the Washington Monument (pages ii–iii) is courtesy of NMAAHC / Alan Karchmer.

Special discounts are available for bulk purchases of this book. For more information,
please contact Special Sales at specialsales@jh.edu.

Contents

Preface   vii

Acknowledgments   xi

Notes to the Reader   xiii

INTRODUCTION

The Architecture of Washington, DC, 1791–2021   1

TOURS

A Governmental Capitol Hill   24

B The Mall   40

C Near Southwest   68

D Capitol Riverfront   80

E Residential Capitol Hill   88

F NoMa / Union Market   98

G Judiciary Square / Mount Vernon Square / Penn Quarter   110

H Pennsylvania Avenue   130

I Downtown—East End   146

J White House / Lafayette Square   172

K Downtown—West End   186

L Foggy Bottom   200

M Georgetown   220

N Foxhall   246

O Sheridan-Kalorama / Massachusetts Avenue Heights   252

P Dupont / Logan   270

Q Shaw / U Street   298

R Meridian Hill   316

S Woodley Park / Cleveland Park / Van Ness   328

T Other Buildings of Interest   344

Index   365

Photo Credits   381

Preface

This is the sixth edition of a guidebook first published in 1965 under the auspices of the Washington Metropolitan Chapter of the American Institute of Architects (AIA). The first version, written by architects Warren J. Cox, Hugh Newell Jacobsen, Francis D. Lethbridge, and David R. Rosenthal, contained brief descriptions of significant buildings in the District of Columbia, northern Virginia, and suburban Maryland. The second edition, incorporating modest revisions and additions, appeared in 1974. For the third edition, written by Maryland-based historian Christopher Weeks and published in 1994, the leadership of the Washington Chapter / AIA, as it was then called, decided to narrow the scope of the book to the District of Columbia proper (an exception was made for Arlington National Cemetery).

AIA | DC, as the chapter is now known, approached me in the early 2000s to "revise and update" the Weeks edition, but we soon agreed that a fresh start was in order because the architectural character of the city had changed so dramatically during the intervening years. In addition to researching and writing dozens of new entries, I reinvestigated and rewrote all entries carried over from the previous version. The result was an almost entirely new text that was published as the fourth edition in 2006.

I also wrote the fifth edition, released just six years after the fourth, in time for the 2012 AIA National Convention, which was held in Washington that year. For that edition, 44 new entries were added, while 27 were either deleted or incorporated into other entries. That brought the total number of featured buildings to more than 400 for the first time.

Over the past decade, Washington's growth has only accelerated. Areas of the city that were largely unknown to many locals have been redeveloped with astonishing speed. DC government agencies have embarked on ambitious building and renovation campaigns, and major new institutional, commercial, and residential buildings have appeared. AIA | DC decided it was time for another edition and invited me back as author.

I took the opportunity to rethink many aspects of the guidebook's content, including the criteria for inclusion, the arrangement of suggested tours, and the objectives of my commentary for each featured building. I concluded that quite a few older buildings that had not appeared in previous editions deserved to be included in this one. (Some of these buildings were in areas that previously seemed out of the way but no longer do. In other cases, I simply couldn't figure out why they hadn't been included before but determined to correct those oversights.)

Coupled with the existing entries carried over from the previous edition and the dozens of new buildings that were clearly worthy of inclusion, the incorporation of these overlooked historic buildings made for a *very* long list of potential entries. To help me whittle it down (and subsequently to review the draft text for the book), I relied on a specially appointed advisory committee composed of Emily Hotaling Eig, Bradford C. Grant, NOMAC, David Metzger, FAIA, FCSI, Mary L. Oehrlein, FAIA, and Amy Weinstein, FAIA (who are credited more fully in the acknowledgments). AIA|DC's executive director, Mary Fitch, also provided vital counsel throughout the process.

In the end, we settled on 80 entirely new entries for this edition. Thirty-six entries from the previous edition were either incorporated into others or deleted because the buildings had been altered, were demolished, or seemed less significant with the passage of time. Inevitably, many interesting and worthy buildings had to be omitted in order to meet the target length for the book.

Once again, all of the entries carried over from the previous edition have been researched anew, and the vast majority were revised for various reasons. In some cases, the buildings have been altered, requiring updated descriptions; in others, continuing research has unearthed interesting facts that warranted revisions to the text. In some instances, my opinions about the buildings had simply changed.

Writing guidebooks is a tricky business. Accuracy and currency can be elusive goals, as buildings are constantly being built, renovated, enlarged, demolished, renamed, or sold. Even seemingly pedigreed landmarks can pose challenges, as historians sometimes disagree about basic facts such as dates of construction. In preparing this guide, I sought credible sources for all data, relying heavily on the documents of the Historic American Buildings Survey, the National Register of Historic Places, specific institutional archives, local governmental agencies, and authoritative articles and books. To the extent possible, all essential information in a given entry was verified with the building's owner or architect, or in the case of a historic building, a person presumed to have relevant knowledge such as a curator, archivist, or historian. If, despite this diligence, an error has slipped through, I would welcome a correction, which may be submitted through the AIA|DC chapter.

This guide is not intended to serve as a purely factual historical record; much of the content, in fact, is subjective and often includes positive or negative criticism. The reader should remember that the opinions expressed herein are just that—opinions—and are solely those of the author. Reasonable people may disagree as to whether a given work of architecture is good, bad, gorgeous, or hideous—a negative comment about a particular building is not intended to give offense to the architects or any others involved in its creation.

Most of the research and writing for this edition took place between May 2020 and February 2021, as the COVID-19 pandemic raged, civil unrest swept the country after police officers killed George Floyd in Minneapolis, and false claims of voter fraud caused turmoil following the 2020 presidential election. The culmination of an already gut-wrenching era in our country's history came on January 6, 2021, when right-wing extremists stormed the Capitol Building, some of them clearly intent on capturing or possibly assassinating members of Congress. I, like so many others, watched in disbelief as the chief architectural symbol of American democracy was breached and vandalized.

Though I had already written almost all of the entries for this book by then, I realized that I had to revisit some of them in the light of recent events. Ultimately, I did not change much text at that late stage, though I added a paragraph addressing the siege of the Capitol to the end of that entry. Frankly, I am not sure that I have adequately or appropriately addressed any of the recent incidents that took place in or near sites included in this book—the memories are too raw, making objectivity difficult.

Every nonfiction book is a snapshot of a point in time. While working on this edition of the guide, I've tried to keep in mind that many people will still be reading it years after the text goes to the publisher, and that some events that seem significant now may seem trivial later on. I hope so! As I write these words, the COVID-19 pandemic continues (though vaccinations are being delivered rapidly, raising hopes for an end to the public health crisis), and the nation's political environment is as fractious as ever. It is my fervent hope that, by the time this guide is published, things will have calmed down, and that readers will be able to comfortably and peacefully take a walk or a drive and enjoy some lovely architecture.

G. M. M.

Acknowledgments

O n behalf of the AIA | DC Chapter, I extend my thanks to all the individuals and firms who helped to prepare this sixth edition. First and foremost is our author, G. Martin Moeller, Jr., Assoc. AIA. We are also incredibly thankful to the group of advisors Martin assembled to help him determine the makeup of the book to tell the full story of Washington, DC. The committee members were Emily Hotaling Eig, Founder and CEO, EHT Traceries; Bradford C. Grant, NOMAC, Professor, Department of Architecture, Howard University; David Metzger, FAIA, FCSI, retired Vice President, Heller & Metzger PC; Mary L. Oehrlein, FAIA, Historic Preservation Officer, Architect of the Capitol; and Amy Weinstein, FAIA, Principal, Weinstein Studio. Overall, 80 buildings were added—not only structures and places that are new since our last edition in 2012, like the Wharf, but also older structures that might have been overlooked in previous editions but help to fill out a complete picture of where the city is today.

Grateful acknowledgments are also due to the generous sponsors of this edition:

- Skidmore, Owings & Merrill
- Robert and Arlene Kogod
- StudioHDP: Anice Hoachlander, Judy Davis & Allen Russ

And to the following firms through their Sustaining Affiliate Membership:

- AECOM
- Balodemas Architects
- BarnesVanze Architects Inc
- Christian Zapatka Architect
- cox graae + spack architects
- Eric Colbert & Associates PC
- Hickok Cole
- HKS Inc.
- Moseley Architects
- MV+A Architects
- Page/
- Quinn Evans
- SK+I Architecture
- SmithGroup
- Square 134 Architects
- Studio Twenty Seven Architecture
- WDG Architecture, PLLC

While we are at it, let's thank all the photographers in this guide, including Alan Karchmer, Assoc. AIA, and Boris Feldblyum, with additional photography by Peter Aaron, Chris Ambridge, Richard Barnes, Bryan Becker, Robert Benson, Dana Bowden Photography, John Cole, Ty Cole, George A. Cott, Robert Creamer, Dan Cunningham, Bruce Damonte, Judy Davis, John DeFerrari, Michael Dersin, Philip A. Esocoff, Debi Fox, Scott Frances, Jeff Goldberg, Jim Hedrich, Julia Heine, Mark Herboth Photography, Carol M. Highsmith, Anice Hoachlander, Wolfgang Hoyt, Tim Hursley, Alex Jamison, Sam Kittner, Andrew Lautman, Robert Lautman, Hon. AIA, Bill Lebovich, Nic Lehoux, Larry M. Levine, Maxwell

MacKenzie, David Madison Photography, Robert H. McNeill, G. Martin Moeller, Jr., Assoc. AIA, Michael Moran, Ronald O'Rourke, Donald Paine, Prakash Patel, Devon Perkins, Ema Peter Photography, Robert Polidori, Kevin G. Reeves, Paúl Rivera, Joseph Romeo, Alan Schindler, Dan Schwalm, Sean Shanahan, Ron Solomon, Fred Sons Photography, Nicole Sorg, Ezra Stoller, Eric Taylor Photography, Michael Ventura, Paul Warchol, and Kenneth M. Wyner.

Thanks also to KUBE architecture and Jim Hicks for working hard to make sure our maps are as accurate as they are handsome and to Greg Britton and his team at Johns Hopkins University Press.

Our author, Martin, would like to add his personal thanks to the roughly 1,000 people (yes, really!) who provided information or images, or otherwise contributed to the content of this project, and especially to his husband, Steven K. Dickens, AIA, for helpful advice—and occasional reality checks—during the research and writing of the book.

And last, we are very grateful to the members of the Washington Chapter of the American Institute of Architects, who not only underwrote a substantial part of the production of this publication but who are also its real stars.

Mary Fitch, AICP, Hon. AIA
Executive Director
AIA | DC

Notes to the Reader

- The year listed in the architectural credits for a given project is intended to indicate the date of the project's completion. When a project was the result of an unusually drawn-out period of design and/or construction, a range of years may be listed. (Engraved cornerstones, for buildings that include them, tend to list the years in which construction began, and therefore those dates will probably differ from the ones listed in this book.)

- The primary name listed for each entry is generally the one that seems to be the most commonly used for that building or site. Former names, official names, or other alternative names may be listed parenthetically.

- Most of the entries in this book are grouped as walking tours, some of which are quite compact, while others might take several hours to complete. The order of entries within each tour suggests one possible path (taking into account terrain and other factors that could enhance or hinder the walk) but is not intended to be prescriptive.

- Preferred descriptors for people of color shift over time, of course. In this edition, in accordance with increasingly common practice, I use the terms *Black* and *Indigenous* in lieu of *African American* and *Native American*, respectively, which were used in previous editions.

AIA Guide to the Architecture of Washington, DC

Introduction:
The Architecture of Washington, DC, 1791–2021

Washington, DC, owes its existence—fittingly enough—to a political deal.

In the summer of 1790, the fledgling American republic remained quite fragile, and Congress was deadlocked on two key issues: the proposed assumption of individual states' debts by the federal Treasury and the selection of a site for the young nation's permanent capital. One evening that June, Secretary of State Thomas Jefferson hosted what must have been a tense little dinner party attended by Secretary of the Treasury Alexander Hamilton and US representative (and future president) James Madison—bitter rivals who embodied the opposing factions. Jefferson ultimately convinced Madison, his fellow Virginian, not to block the assumption of debts favored by most northerners, while Hamilton, a New Yorker, agreed to siting the permanent capital in a relatively southerly location where slavery was entrenched. This "dinner table bargain" led to passage of the Residence Act of 1790, which authorized a new seat of government within a territory "not exceeding ten miles square" on the banks of the Potomac River, somewhere upstream of the Eastern Branch, to be carved from portions of the states of Maryland and Virginia.

The area had been a center of trade since before the colonial era. In the 17th century, a portion of the land was occupied by the Nacotchtank, an Algonquian people whose principal village stood near the confluence of the two rivers, not far from the fall line (the abrupt rise from the coastal plain that marked the limit of navigable water before the invention of mechanical locks). The name Nacotchtank, in fact, derives from the word *anaquashatanik*, meaning "a town of traders." The word is memorialized in the modern name of the Eastern Branch: the Anacostia River.

The Spanish had explored the Chesapeake Bay and adjacent rivers before the end of the 16th century, but the first formal documentation of the region by Europeans came after English captain John Smith sailed up the Potomac River in 1608. Smith's *The Generall Historie of Virginia, New England & the Summer Isles*, first published in England in 1627, was accompanied by a detailed map that served as a cartographical template for nearly a century. He described the Potomac in florid terms (and with the now-curious spellings common at the time):

> The fourth river is called Patawomeke, 6 or 7 myles in breadth. It is navigable 140 myles, and fed as the rest with many sweet rivers and springs, which fall from the bordering hils. These hils many of them are planted, and yeeld no lesse plentie and varietie of fruit, then the river exceedeth with abundance of fish. It is inhabited on both sides.[1]

In 1632, the first Baron Baltimore, a Roman Catholic, applied for a royal charter for the land between the existing English colony of Virginia to the south and the Dutch colony of New Netherland to the north. His goal was to create a haven in the "New World" for fellow Catholics fleeing religious persecution in their homeland. Lord Baltimore died shortly before the charter was granted, but in 1634 his son Leonard Calvert arrived in the new colony—named Maryland in honor of Queen Henrietta Maria, the Catholic wife of King Charles I, and not the Virgin Mary as many assume—with two shiploads of settlers, including both Protestants and Catholics. The group established St. Mary's City, near the mouth of the Potomac, which became the fourth permanent English settlement in what is now the United States. As the Maryland colony grew over the next seven decades, the Indigenous people were gradually killed off—whether by violence or by infectious diseases introduced by the settlers—or forced out of the expanding English territory by those same settlers.

It was only eight years after the founding of St. Mary's City that enslaved Africans were first brought to the Maryland colony. Slavery was already well established in neighboring Virginia, where captive Africans had been forced into labor since 1619—the year that is now widely regarded as the starting point for Black enslavement in the American colonies. Most of the area's slaves worked in the cultivation of tobacco, which was the cornerstone of the regional economy throughout the colonial era.

English settlement continued at a steady pace throughout the mid-Atlantic region over the next century. By the mid-1700s, the most successful planters, continuing to reap vast profits from their slavery-dependent enterprises, had built some impressive houses, such as Gunston Hall, George Mason's home on the Virginia bank of the Potomac, completed in 1759. The most famous mansion of the era is undoubtedly George Washington's at Mount Vernon, initially built around 1734 and expanded in stages over the following decades.

The region's flourishing tobacco trade necessitated ever-expanding shipping infrastructure, which led to the founding of the ports of Alexandria, Virginia, in 1748, and Georgetown, Maryland, in 1751. Accounts by travelers in the late 18th century depict both ports as thriving towns with some elegant houses, large commercial structures, and gritty wharves. It is safe to assume that, even if the new national capital had not been built in their midst, Alexandria and Georgetown would have grown into important cities on their own.

The Residence Act of 1790, which had authorized the creation of a new governmental district, delegated the selection of the district's exact site to President George Washington, though many people assumed that Georgetown, which was squarely within the initial area specified in the legislation, was a shoo-in to become the capital city. After poking around the area a bit, President Washington settled on a site centered between Georgetown and the Eastern Branch. At his request, the original legislation was modified to allow the new federal district to extend slightly farther south to incorporate nearby Alexandria.

Meanwhile, Washington and Jefferson had engaged surveyor Andrew Ellicott, who was assisted by free Black astronomer Benjamin Banneker, to assess the (literal) lay of the land. Once the exact location for the new federal territory had been decided, Ellicott's team began placing a series of engraved stones at one-mile intervals to demarcate its official borders. These boundary stones, most of which remain in place today, defined a perfect square, tilted so that its

This 1795 aquatint print by George Isham Parkyns depicts a portion of the new Territory of Columbia overlooking the Potomac River.

corners pointed in the four cardinal directions, with roughly two-thirds of its area on the Maryland side of the Potomac and the rest on the Virginia side. (The portion south of the river, including the town of Alexandria, would be retroceded to Virginia in 1846.)

In September 1791, the presidentially appointed commissioners overseeing the surveying effort declared that the new federal precinct would be called the Territory of Columbia—a slightly fanciful name derived from the feminization of "Columbus" (as in Christopher)—and the capital city within its borders would be named Washington in honor of the first president. Georgetown remained a separate jurisdiction within the territory until 1871. That same year, the Territory of Columbia was renamed the District of Columbia.

To prepare a plan for the city to be named for him, Washington hired a young French artist and engineer, Pierre Charles L'Enfant, who had arrived in the American colonies in 1777 at the age of only 23. L'Enfant, whose father had been a painter in the court of King Louis XV and was thus thoroughly entrenched in the *ancien régime*, had abandoned his privileged position in order to join the revolutionary Continental army, rising to the rank of major. He became so enamored of the American cause that he soon adopted the anglicized version of his given name: Peter.

L'Enfant, who had studied art at the Royal Academy in Paris, met Washington when the Marquis de Lafayette commissioned him to paint a portrait of the general and future president during the Valley Forge campaign. L'Enfant also drew portraits of other officers and painted scenes of military encampments.

Pierre (Peter) Charles L'Enfant's 1791 "Plan of the City, intended for the Permanent seat of the Government" called for a "Grand Avenue" running westward from the "Congress house," which appears as a green band lined by buildings in red. The drawing reproduced here is a facsimile of L'Enfant's badly faded original, prepared by the United States Coast and Geodetic Survey in 1887.

After the war, he established himself as a civil engineer in New York City, which became the interim capital of the newly independent United States from 1785 to 1790. He oversaw the conversion of the City Hall there into Federal Hall, the seat of the first US Congress under the Constitution and the site of George Washington's first presidential inaugural.

The Frenchman had grand designs for the new American capital. Inspired at least in part by the work of André Le Nôtre, the landscape architect who created the gardens at the Palace of Versailles, L'Enfant devised a plan featuring broad diagonal avenues superimposed over an orthogonal street grid. He adjusted the exact spacing of the streets and the alignments of the avenues in response to significant topographical features. More than a half century before Baron Georges-Eugène Haussmann transformed Paris into a masterpiece of urban design, L'Enfant employed some of the same compositional devices and strategies in the design of Washington.

At the core of L'Enfant's plan was the Capitol Building—the "Congress house," he called it—which was to be perched atop a hill about a mile inland from the river. Extending westward from the Congress house toward the Potomac would be a greensward, which he labeled a "Grand Avenue, 400 feet in breadth," culminating in an equestrian statue of George Washington located near the water line. A second major axis, forming a right angle to the first and extending northward from the statue, led to the "President's house," set behind its own park. The Congress house and the President's house were connected—yet simultaneously separated—by one of the diagonal avenues, a gesture that reflected the separation of legislative and executive powers enshrined in the US Constitution. Sprinkled across the plan were various public plazas of differing shapes and sizes, some labeled and some not, linked by other diagonals.

The graphic plan that L'Enfant drew was a work of art in itself. The distinctive outline of the city's core, bounded by the Potomac River to the southwest, the Eastern Branch (Anacostia River) to the southeast, and the fall line to the northwest and northeast, reflected the careful surveying work on which the plan was based. The juxtaposition of the orthogonal street grid and the diagonal avenues yielded an intricate web-like pattern, accented by the various public buildings and squares. Fundamentally rational yet picturesque, informed by the natural topography of the site, and reflecting key democratic principles, the plan was in many ways an expression of the ideals of the Age of Enlightenment.

L'Enfant was truly a visionary, but sadly, like many a visionary, he was haughty and temperamental. He bristled at the authority of the presidentially appointed commissioners overseeing his work and maintained—inaccurately—that he was responsible to the president alone. In February 1792, after L'Enfant had failed to make a drawing of his plan available for reproduction as ordered, Washington reluctantly fired him. In the aftermath of L'Enfant's dismissal, surveyor Andrew Ellicott, assisted by his brother Benjamin Ellicott and by Benjamin Banneker, the astronomer who had participated in the original survey of the territorial boundaries, re-created the plan as closely as possible (supposedly from memory). Ellicott's version regularized the shapes of public squares and realigned some segments of the diagonal avenues, among other changes. Despite these discrepancies, the brilliant, instantly recognizable plan that defines Washington's core to this day can appropriately be credited to L'Enfant.

In 1800, when the federal government moved from Philadelphia, which had succeeded New York as the temporary capital, to Washington, the nascent city was, quite bluntly, a mess. The Capitol Building was incomplete, the Executive

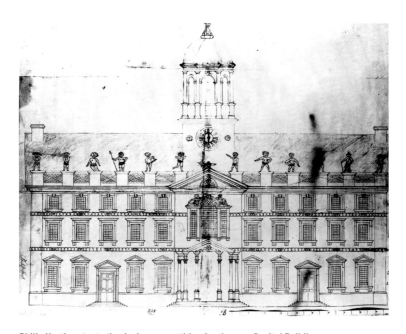

Philip Hart's entry to the design competition for the new Capitol Building would have had a collegiate character were it not for the cartoonish finials.

Mansion, as it came to be called, was largely unfurnished, and the "avenue" connecting them was a swath of mud. Many officials, upon arriving in the city for the first time, could be excused for doubting that it would ever amount to much. Nonetheless, real estate speculators, anticipating the inevitable attraction of humans to power, were already busily scheming, buying, selling, and building.

Fortunately, the new capital attracted a number of talented building designers in its early years, now labeled as the Federal period in architectural history. These included amateurs, such as William Lovering, several of whose houses still stand; self-taught "gentleman architects," such as Dr. William Thornton, who had won the competition for the design of the Capitol; and formally trained architect-engineers, such as Benjamin Henry Latrobe, whom President Thomas Jefferson appointed surveyor of public buildings—the de facto lead architect for the federal government—in 1803. Perhaps inevitably, in an era in which there were no widely accepted professional credentials, these men—and they were all men in those days—developed personal rivalries and often criticized each other's work. George Hadfield, the young English architect who supervised construction of the Capitol from 1795 to 1798, once wrote the following of Thornton and other entrants to the design competition for that project: "This premium [for the best design of the Capitol] was offered at a period when scarcely a professional architect was to be found in any of the United States; which is plainly to be seen in the pile of trash presented as designs for said building."[2]

By the time British invaders sacked and burned the city of Washington in 1814, frankly, there wasn't that much to burn: the Capitol was still far from finished, and private development was spotty. Even so, the sight of the Capitol, the

Published in London, this engraving marks the day the British took Washington during the War of 1812 and, according to the original caption, "burnt and destroyed their Dock Yard, . . . Senate House, Presidents [*sic*] Palace, War Office, Treasury and the Great Bridge."

This engraving, published in Robert Dale Owen's *Hints on Public Architecture* of 1849, exaggerates the scale of James Renwick's Smithsonian Institution Building but vividly conveys its picturesque composition.

Executive Mansion, and other major structures in ruins only added to the already rampant speculation that this experiment in building a new capital city might not stick. After fleeing to safety in the suburbs, President James Madison and First Lady Dolley Madison, who had bravely saved an iconic full-length portrait of George Washington (a copy of painter Gilbert Stuart's original) before the Executive Mansion was torched, took up temporary residence in Colonel John Tayloe's town house, the Octagon, which was among the few buildings spared by the British. It was there, in a second-floor parlor, that Madison signed the Treaty of Ghent, formally ending the War of 1812. (The Octagon later became the headquarters of the American Institute of Architects and is now open to the public as a house museum.)

After the war, architects began the work of resurrecting the charred city. The Executive Mansion was rebuilt and got a fresh, thick coat of white paint (the building was previously covered with lime-based whitewash, which gave rise to its popular moniker: the White House). The Capitol finally reached a point resembling completion in 1829 (only to be substantially expanded a couple of decades later). Large new buildings for various governmental departments and agencies—including the Treasury Building and the Patent Office, each initially designed by Robert Mills and later expanded by various architects—adhered to the classical revival styles popular at the time and added to the sense of grandeur expected in a national capital. And near the spot where L'Enfant had specified an equestrian statue of George Washington, a great obelisk, also designed by Robert Mills, rose instead (though the monument would not be finished until the 1880s).

As the country grew westward, local commercial interests backed the construction of the Chesapeake and Ohio (C&O) Canal, intended to link the Potomac to the headwaters of the Ohio River. Unfortunately, the canal soon became obsolete as the Baltimore and Ohio (B&O) Railroad, which covered essentially the same route, proved to be more efficient. Meanwhile, the Potomac and Ana-costia rivers began to silt up, which hampered the local shipping industry and further diminished commercial activity in Washington. The once-thriving ports of Georgetown and Alexandria entered a slow but steady decline.

The federal government continued to grow, however, bringing steady demand for new buildings. Classical revival styles remained popular for public architecture through the mid-19th century, when things began to get murky. James Renwick's design for the home of the new Smithsonian Institution, con-structed beginning in 1847, exemplified the move away from buttoned-down neoclassicism. Quickly dubbed the "Castle," it was a picturesque, turreted fantasy in a style usually described as *Norman* for lack of a better word. In 1849, Robert Dale Owen, a congressman and son of Robert Owen, founder of the utopian colony of New Harmony, Indiana, published *Hints on Public Archi-tecture*, which included a defense of Renwick's design. Owen criticized what he considered the false qualities of the Greek and Roman Revival buildings that had long been accepted not only as paragons of good taste but also as appropriate exemplars of democratic ideals. Owen went so far as to propose that Renwick's design, exemplifying "the style of the twelfth century," should be a model for "a National Style of Architecture for America."[3] (Owen's proposal did not catch on, and even Renwick himself, in his subsequent works, switched to the trendy French Second Empire style, among others.)

The urban planning and landscape architecture of the period also exhibited an increasingly Romantic bent. Before his death in a Hudson riverboat explosion in 1852, Andrew Jackson Downing had laid out the grounds of the Smithsonian and the White House with asymmetrical meandering paths and naturalistic plantings. Unfortunately, all that informality thwarted some critical features of L'Enfant's plan, most notably the axial promenade that was supposed to connect the Capitol to the monument honoring George Washington and the riverbank beyond.

The outbreak of the Civil War soon transformed the city of Washington into an armed camp. The capital, which had been sited so carefully to be near the line between the North and South, suddenly found itself just across the river from Confederate territory (the Virginia portion of the federal district having been retroceded to that state more than a decade earlier). Union forces soon built a ring of defensive forts on the hills surrounding the city, and although in 1864 a Confederate army led by Jubal Early reached the outskirts of the Territory of Columbia at Fort Stevens, the city's defenses were never breached.

Washington's population grew rapidly during the war, but aside from the ongoing work on the Capitol's new dome and extended wings, little permanent construction took place until the end of hostilities. The postwar era marked the beginning of a local construction boom as a strengthened and expanded federal government required an array of new offices and other facilities. Prominent players in this period included the Office of the Supervising Architect of the Treasury—the federal government's chief architect—and the US Army Corps of Engineers, which moved beyond infrastructure projects to oversee the con-struction of major public buildings.

American architecture of the post–Civil War era is often broadly labeled *Vic-torian*—adopting, oddly enough, a term associated with the queen of a country

As evident in this photograph from the Capitol dating to around 1863, L'Enfant's vision of a Grand Avenue stretching toward the Potomac had not been realized. The area that would become the National Mall was still marred by haphazard residential and commercial development (*center left*), a disused canal, and temporary government office buildings (*center background*).

that had been at war with the United States only a few decades earlier. The period was characterized by stylistic eclecticism and yielded a curious array of public and private buildings. Often highly ornamented, asymmetrically composed, and incorporating elements of diverse precedents, many buildings of the era can be read as purposeful rebukes to the aesthetic chastity of the Federal period.

One such example is the former National Museum (now the Smithsonian Arts and Industries Building), which was designed by Adolf Cluss and Paul Schulze based on a plan by Montgomery C. Meigs and finished in 1881. Its pointy towers seem like neighborly gestures toward the original Smithsonian Castle next door, but with its polychrome brick façades, round-arched windows, central rotunda, and exposed interior trusses, the Arts and Industries Building took stylistic and organizational cues from many other sources. Constructed in the aftermath of Philadelphia's Centennial Exposition of 1876, the building initially housed displays transferred from that exposition, and its design evokes the festive spirit of such temporary fairs.

Meigs, who had prepared the initial plan of the Arts and Industries Building, was one of the most fascinating figures of the era. He served as quartermaster general of the Union army during and after the Civil War but had made his mark on Washington even before the war while acting as supervising engineer for the Capitol expansion of the 1850s, implementing the designs of architect Thomas U. Walter. He also designed and oversaw the construction of the Washington Aqueduct, which provides water to parts of the city of Washington to this day.

The Center Market, which stood between Constitution and Pennsylvania Avenues and between 7th and 9th Streets, NW, from 1872 to 1931, was one of numerous important municipal buildings designed by Adolf Cluss. The market was demolished to make way for the National Archives Building.

Meigs's crowning achievement, however, was the enormous Pension Building (now the National Building Museum), completed in 1887, housing the offices of the US Pension Bureau, which had grown exponentially as it processed benefits for Union veterans of the Civil War and their families. Although built in a Renaissance Revival style, the building's formidable red-brick façades stood in marked contrast to the white and cream-colored stone that prevailed among the city's federal landmarks.

The State, War, and Navy Building (now the Eisenhower Executive Office Building), built next to White House between 1871 and 1888, took yet another stylistic direction for federal architecture. With its dense granite walls and soaring mansard roofs, the Second Empire design seemed lavish in comparison to the relative modesty of the neighboring Executive Mansion and most other public buildings. In fact, it *was* lavish—it cost more than $10 million, an almost inconceivable sum at the time, and while its great expense was roundly criticized, its completion signified that Washington really was going to remain the national capital despite the persistent doubts about the city's viability (not to mention the lingering hopes of some partisans that the capital might be relocated to a site nearer to their constituencies).

By the 1880s, the Romanesque Revival style closely associated with Boston architect H. H. Richardson was becoming predominant in Washington as elsewhere. Richardson himself designed several large houses in the capital, including those for John Hay and Henry Adams, which overlooked Lafayette Square until they were demolished to make way for the hotel that now bears both their names. Washington's most prominent building in the neo-Romanesque vein, however, is the Old Post Office Building on Pennsylvania Avenue, designed by Willoughby J. Edbrooke and completed in 1899. Its clock tower remains the third-tallest occupiable structure in the District of Columbia.

The local firm of John L. Smithmeyer and Paul J. Pelz exemplified the eclecticism of the late Victorian era. Their completed works included the neo-Gothic Healy Hall at Georgetown University and the Renaissance Revival main building of the Library of Congress. Some of the firm's most startling designs, however, were never built. Among them were a medieval-looking multitowered bridge across the Potomac, a palatial new Executive Mansion spanning 16th Street at Meridian Hill, and merchant Franklin Webster Smith's proposed National Galleries of History and Art, a sort of permanent world's fair that would have stretched from the west side of the White House grounds all the way to the Potomac.

As the government continued to grow in the late 19th century, so did the local population, which needed new schools, shops, and, of course, housing. Several of Washington's great row house neighborhoods were initially developed during this period, including those surrounding Logan Circle and Dupont Circle. The city also gained its first large apartment buildings, such as the approximately 160-foot-tall Cairo, on Q Street, NW, whose construction led to the passage of the District's first building height limit in 1894.

It was during this period that the city of Washington truly began to develop its own local architectural character, complementing—but distinct from—the federal presence. Adolf Cluss, who had codesigned the Arts and Industries Building, also designed numerous innovative municipal buildings, including Eastern Market, which is still a focal point of the Capitol Hill neighborhood. His design for the Franklin School, now home to Planet Word in downtown Washington, attracted international recognition and acclaim following its completion in 1869.

Among the most significant local developments of the late 19th century were the ambitious infrastructure projects overseen by Alexander Robey "Boss" Shepherd, the most powerful member of the District of Columbia Board of Public Works from 1871 to 1873, who was subsequently presidentially appointed governor for less than a year from 1873 to 1874. Shepherd transformed the still-underdeveloped city into a modern capital by introducing its first horse-drawn streetcar system, paving and regrading many miles of streets, filling in a fetid canal, and planting thousands of trees. The costs for all these improvements were astronomical, not to mention well beyond the amounts budgeted, leading to the District of Columbia's bankruptcy and Shepherd's removal from office.

Shepherd's efforts, while fiscally ruinous, laid the groundwork for Washington's Gilded Age. In the late 19th and early 20th centuries, the capital became popular as a seasonal home for many of the country's richest families. Spectacular mansions, such as the Townsend House (now the Cosmos Club), the Patterson House (now the Oakwood Suites & Studios), and the Anderson House (now the Society of the Cincinnati), were erected along Massachusetts Avenue and nearby streets, bringing an air of glamour—and more than a whiff of cultural decadence—to a city that had long been derided as merely a government town.

While the broader cityscape of Washington was finally coming into its own by the turn of the 20th century, L'Enfant's magnificent design for the city's governmental core had never been fully realized. His proposed Grand Avenue—the

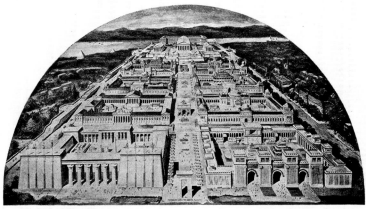

PAUL J. PELZ,) Advisory Architects.   FRANKLIN WEBSTER SMITH, Architect.   HARRY DODGE JENKINS, Pinxit.
HENRY IVES COBB,)

DESIGN FOR NATIONAL GALLERIES OF HISTORY AND ART.

Beginning in the 1890s, Boston merchant Franklin Webster Smith proposed building a vast cultural complex called the National Galleries of History and Art, which would have stretched from the White House grounds to the Potomac River. He engaged prominent architects, including James Renwick Jr., Paul J. Pelz, and Henry Ives Cobb, to design elements of the scheme, which garnered significant support in Congress but never came to fruition.

east-west axis between the Capitol and the river—was instead a mélange of mismatched buildings, haphazard paths, and inconsistent plantings, with a variety of streets and small private buildings encroaching upon the perimeter and sooty train tracks cutting right across it. Several of the adjacent neighborhoods were dangerously seedy, and the city's riverfronts were grungy and prone to flooding.

This sorry state of affairs appalled Glenn Brown, who was the secretary (chief executive officer) of the American Institute of Architects (AIA) at the time. Under Brown's leadership, the AIA held its annual convention in Washington in 1900 with its principal focus being the status of the city's monumental core. The papers and design proposals presented at the convention directly led to the formation in March 1901 of the Senate Park Commission, commonly called the McMillan Commission after Senator James McMillan of Michigan, chairman of the Senate Committee on the District of Columbia and the driving force behind the initiative. The commission's purpose was to suggest improvements to the monumental core and other areas in order to bring order to the prevailing chaos and establish an aesthetic framework for future development.

On the advice of the AIA, McMillan appointed architect Daniel H. Burnham and landscape architect Frederick Law Olmsted Jr. to serve on the commission. Burnham had led the design and planning team for the World's Columbian Exposition in Chicago in 1893, while Olmsted's father was chief landscape architect for that project. This world's fair was the first major expression of the ideals of the City Beautiful movement, which advocated the improvement of cities both for beauty's sake and as a means of inspiring "civic virtue," and thus served as direct inspiration for McMillan and other political leaders concerned about Washington's urban character. Burnham and Olmsted, in turn, successfully petitioned McMillan to add architect Charles Follen McKim, of the prominent firm

McKim, Mead & White, and sculptor Augustus Saint-Gaudens to the commission. Both had worked intimately with Burnham on the planning and execution of the Columbian Exposition.

The commission's report, published in 1902, was an ambitious and persuasive document. Rather than simply advocating the belated execution of the L'Enfant Plan, it called for an entirely new conception of the city's monumental core, taking inspiration not only from L'Enfant but also from many of the great capitals of Europe (several of which the commission members visited and carefully studied). The commission re-envisioned L'Enfant's "Grand Avenue" as a broad green mall lined by major public buildings and memorials, all to be designed in styles derived from classical antiquity. The Washington Monument, which stood isolated at the top of a shallow hill, was to be given an imposing architectural base, with wide steps and terraces spanning the greensward. Clumps of stone-clad governmental offices would surround the Capitol Grounds and Lafayette Square. The unruly riverbank would be tamed, and an elegant neoclassical bridge would extend across the Potomac to Arlington. The commission also presented its suggestions for other significant green spaces in the city, most notably Rock Creek.

Although the group's recommendations took decades to implement, and many of them were never realized, the Senate Park Commission had a profound impact on Washington, helping to transform it into one of the world's most majestic cities. The commission ultimately gave us the National Mall as we know it today (even if the buildings bracketing it are far more varied than Burnham and his colleagues would have preferred), and laid the conceptual groundwork for the redevelopment of adjacent areas of the city. Indeed, the work of the Senate Park Commission has achieved near-mythic status—perhaps just a notch

The Senate Park Commission of 1901–2 produced an ambitious plan for Washington's monumental core. Key elements of the plan, as seen in this bird's-eye rendering by Francis L. V. Hoppin, included rows of neoclassical buildings flanking the National Mall, new memorials at the ends of the axes emanating from the Capitol and the White House, and a grand bridge linking the Mall to Arlington.

below that of L'Enfant's original plan—among generations of local architects, planners, and public officials.

In 1910, Congress once again exerted its influence over the District of Columbia by passing the Height of Buildings Act, which superseded the earlier height limits imposed by the District commissioners in the 1890s. Contrary to popular belief, the restrictions outlined in this legislation were not directly related to the heights of the Washington Monument or the Capitol Dome. Rather, they were based on the width of the streets abutting a given site and were intended to ensure access to ample sunlight and fresh air throughout the city. The 1910 act, which remains in effect today despite a few minor modifications, has yielded the famously low-rise skyline that makes Washington unique among modern American cities.

Washington's architectural history in the first half of the 20th century reflected the emergence of the United States as a global power, and of the city itself as a major center of commerce and culture. New row house neighborhoods sprang up across DC, many of them developed by Harry Wardman, who also commissioned a number of apartment buildings (it is estimated that, at one point, fully 10 percent of the population of the District of Columbia lived in a structure built by Wardman). The F Street corridor in downtown Washington was lined with major department stores and other shops, complementing more neighborhood-oriented shopping strips around the city. Vaudeville theaters, nickelodeons, and, later, full-fledged movie theaters and concert halls provided places for amusement. Although such facilities were racially segregated at the time, the U Street entertainment corridor offered leisure opportunities for Black people unmatched by any other American city save New York.

The most significant governmental project of the period was the Federal Triangle, which entailed the redevelopment of the wedge-shaped area bounded by Pennsylvania Avenue, Constitution Avenue, and 15th Street, NW, between 1926 and 1937. Under the direction of Secretary of the Treasury Andrew W. Mellon, who oversaw a specially appointed Board of Architectural Consultants, the initiative built on the ideas of the Senate Park Commission, creating an enclave of large-scale neoclassical buildings housing governmental offices, a public auditorium, and the central facility of the National Archives. Although each constituent building was designed by a different architecture firm, the overall enclave is elegant and harmonious, though today the area is far from lively thanks to the buildings' daunting scale and lack of retail uses.

The Great Depression extinguished the last flickering lights of the Gilded Age, as the ultra-rich families that had reveled in Washington's "social season" sold, rented, or donated their mansions to nonprofit organizations, federal agencies, or foreign governments. Nonetheless, the capital weathered the economic crisis far better than most American cities thanks to the rapid growth in the federal workforce during the New Deal. Private development slowed, of course, but never fully dried up, since all those new workers needed housing (not to mention schools for their children, shops, and so on). As one of the few places where significant construction occurred during the 1930s, Washington became a hotbed of stripped classicism—a hybrid neoclassical-modern style that emerged as the Depression ground on. Paul Philippe Cret's Folger Shake-

The National Archives Building, seen here under construction in 1933, was part of the Federal Triangle project, which transformed the area between Pennsylvania and Constitution Avenues from Capitol Hill to the White House in the 1920s and '30s.

speare Library of 1932 and main Federal Reserve Building of 1937 exemplify this trend in both the private and public sectors.

By the end of the 1930s, there were several signs that Washington was poised for something of an architectural revolution. The first was the 1939 competition-winning design by the team of Eero Saarinen, his father, Eliel Saarinen, and brother-in-law, J. Robert F. Swanson, for the proposed Smithsonian Gallery of Art, which was to have been located on the site now occupied by the National Air and Space Museum. Their abstract, asymmetrical scheme would have offered a radical contrast to the polite neoclassicism that had prevailed among federal buildings of the previous four decades, though given the Saarinens' demonstrated talent for deft composition and thoughtful integration of decorative motifs in otherwise spare designs, it is likely that the project would have become a beloved landmark had it been built. The design attracted predictable outrage from some conservative forces, though it was the impending entry of the United States into World War II that definitively killed the project.

Around the same time, Frank Lloyd Wright made waves with his proposal for Crystal Heights, a mammoth mixed-use development on the site now occupied by the Washington Hilton Hotel, at the corner of Connecticut and Florida Avenues. The project comprised a chain of slender, glassy residential towers situated atop a vast plinth containing parking, theaters, and retail facilities. Wright was still quibbling with planning officials over the height of the proposed towers when, again, the prospect of imminent global conflict thwarted the project for good.

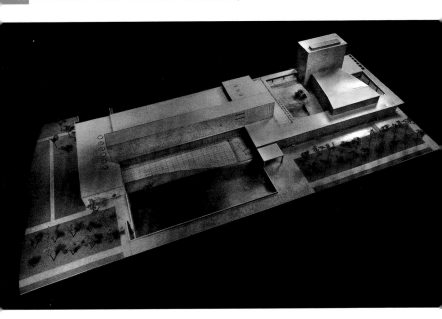

The firm of Eliel Saarinen, Eero Saarinen, and J. Robert F. Swanson won the 1939 design competition for the proposed Smithsonian Gallery of Art. With its asymmetrical massing and spare ornament, the design would have been a significant departure from the prevailing neoclassicism of Washington's monumental core, but the onset of World War II doomed the project.

Few permanent structures were built in Washington during the war, even though the population boom that began in the 1930s continued and even accelerated. Motivated by patriotism, the opportunity to make a little extra money, or both, many Washingtonians rented rooms in their houses and apartments to strangers who had no place else to live. The situation even inspired a popular 1943 comedy film, *The More the Merrier*, directed by George Stevens, about a young single woman who sublets half of her apartment to a man who has just arrived in town. Inevitably, hilarious high jinks ensue.

By 1950, the District of Columbia reached its population peak (as estimated in the decennial census) of roughly 802,000. Soon, a combination of factors, including the GI Bill, which provided low-cost mortgage loans to veterans, and the construction of the Interstate Highway System, which also facilitated intracity automobile travel, began to attract residents to new suburban neighborhoods. This trend was exacerbated by the practice of redlining—a form of institutionalized discrimination in which mortgages and business loans were routinely denied to applicants in lower-income, usually majority-Black, neighborhoods across the country. The great suburban shift would become one of the defining aspects of late 20th-century American society, ultimately bringing substantial, persistent hardships to Washington and many other cities.

Despite the urban disinvestment that resulted from suburbanization, when the first edition of this guide was published in 1965, Washington was in the early stages of an especially fertile period in its architectural history. During the 1960s and '70s, internationally recognized architects, including Marcel Breuer, I. M. Pei, Philip Johnson, and Gordon Bunshaft, were designing prominent governmental and institutional buildings in what might be called a "High Modernist" vein that celebrated pure, abstract geometry. Nathaniel Owings was leading a presidentially appointed advisory council that proposed an audacious, if terribly flawed, plan for the redevelopment of Pennsylvania Avenue. Talented local firms, such as Chloethiel Woodard Smith & Associated Architects and Keyes Lethbridge & Condon, were producing in Southwest Washington some of the most convincingly livable "urban renewal" projects in the country. At the same time, years before the preservation movement took root nationally, John Carl Warnecke was devising a scheme that saved Lafayette Square from demolition, and Arthur Cotton Moore was turning an old industrial facility in Georgetown into a model of architectural recycling known as Canal Square.

While Washington was still a small city at the time compared to New York, Chicago, and the great European capitals, and was not exactly a mecca for newly minted architects, the city's architectural scene during this period certainly seemed poised to shed its humdrum reputation. Particularly during the early 1960s, when the Kennedy administration infused the city with an air of youthful exuberance, the capital was viewed by many architects as an up-and-coming, modern metropolis.

Even so, the population of the city proper was already declining steadily. When the last DC streetcar disappeared from the tracks on January 27, 1962, long-standing assumptions about civic scale, neighborhood viability, and urban density evaporated. The prevalence of the private automobile, which both government and industry went to great lengths to accommodate, dictated subsequent urban planning and development. Downtown retailers were already struggling to hold their own against new suburban shopping malls when riots in the wake of the 1968 assassination of Martin Luther King Jr. laid waste to once-thriving commercial thoroughfares along 7th Street and 14th Street, NW, and H Street, NE. Urban emigration accelerated into the 1970s and even the 1980s amid a classic vicious cycle of crime, poverty, failing schools, and deteriorating infrastructure, initially exacerbated by Congress's direct control over the District of Columbia, subjecting the city's budgets and policies to outside political posturing (DC finally achieved home rule again in 1973).

In this increasingly desperate urban context, the bold and sometimes heroic architectural gestures that had made Washington a poster city for High Modernism began to look stale and barren to many designers and clients alike. Of course, a reaction to the puristic tendencies of the modern movement was not unique to Washington, nor was it a new phenomenon—Robert Venturi had published his postmodern manifesto, *Complexity and Contradiction in Architecture*, in 1966, and the two most widely heralded (and derided) early works of postmodern architecture were not in Washington but in Portland, Oregon (Michael Graves's Portland Building), and in New York (Philip Johnson's AT&T Building, now known as 550 Madison Avenue). But by the mid-1980s, Washington-area architects were firmly on board with the counter-revolution, creating buildings such as 1300 New York Avenue (now the Inter-American Development Bank), which moved away from modern abstraction in favor of a more traditional hierarchy of forms, articulated windows, and allusions to historical architectural motifs.

The postmodern movement essentially developed as two different, if sometimes overlapping, strains: a playful "Mannerist," often jokey school, as exemplified by Charles Moore's Piazza d'Italia in New Orleans, and a quite serious, unabashedly historicist school that celebrated specific "styles," traditional materials, and contextualism, as seen in New Urbanist communities designed by Andrés Duany and Elizabeth Plater-Zyberk. In Washington especially, the former strain never took hold, but the latter quickly became predominant. The ideals of the City Beautiful movement, of course, had never really fallen out of favor here. In retrospect, even during the heyday of modernism, most of the capital's official and commercial architecture had always adhered to a monumental purity that never seriously challenged the fundamental precepts of Daniel Burnham and his cohort, even though the strictly classical vocabulary they favored had been abandoned. So a return to historicism—especially but not exclusively a kind of classicism—was an easy transition for many Washington architects. Soon, downtown was becoming filled with superficially neoclassical buildings, each with a clearly articulated base, middle, and top, typically with punched windows, and generally respectful of the street line. The better ones had well-controlled proportions and carefully conceived ornament, but many others were ponderous, formulaic, and ultimately quite dreary.

Washington may have avoided most of the silly postmodern excesses that now tend to engender embarrassed throat-clearing at cocktail parties, but with pastiches of Greco-Roman columns, pediments, and ornament lining more and more of its streetscapes, the city soon turned into something of a caricature of itself. In the late 1980s, one Washington architect quipped that his local colleagues constituted "the avant-garde of the rear guard." The monotony of the glass curtain wall "K Street boxes" of the 1960s and '70s had been supplanted by the monotony of faux-classical boxes dutifully clad in granite, limestone, or cast stone.

The tide began to turn again in the waning years of the 20th century as modernism saw a resurgence around the world. A new generation of architects took many lessons from the postmodern era, however, creating buildings that were clearly contemporary in their materials and compositions but which responded more sensitively to their contexts—whether natural or architectural—than did most of their mid-20th-century predecessors. The new wave of modernism also reflected the growing awareness of architecture's role as both a cause and a potential mitigator of climate change. In Washington, one of the harbingers of this modernist revival was the Embassy of Finland on Massachusetts Avenue, NW, completed in 1994. Built largely of locally sourced materials and incorporating abundant natural light and passive solar shading devices, the embassy set a new benchmark for green design in civic buildings. At the same time, its sleek façades and interiors relied on the inherent beauty of fine materials to create a fresh and contemporary aesthetic.

The Washington area has enjoyed an astonishing economic boom over the last quarter century, interrupted only relatively briefly by the Great Recession of 2008. The District of Columbia itself reversed a decades-long population decline, growing by more than 22 percent since 2000. The demographic ramifications have been staggering: Millennials—mostly white and single—flocked to the city, often living in group houses in order to afford rapidly rising rents.

In 1966, architect Chloethiel Woodard Smith proposed the Washington Channel Bridge, a modern version of Florence's Ponte Vecchio containing a mix of shops and restaurants. It would have spanned the channel between the Southwest urban renewal area and East Potomac Park.

Gentrification swept neighborhoods across the District, in some cases displacing families that had lived in the same houses for generations. As of 2011, for the first time in a half century, Black people no longer constituted a majority of the DC population—the place that locals had proudly called "Chocolate City" was increasingly a swirl, causing something of an identity crisis for many longtime residents.

The area's economy has also diversified as major corporations—from Hilton Hotels to Nestlé USA—have moved their headquarters to the region. This trend reached a climax with the announcement that Amazon was to build its "HQ2" in Crystal City—er, that's "National Landing" now—just across the Potomac River from Washington. That news has set off a frenzy of real estate speculation perhaps unmatched since the early days of the District of Columbia, when would-be developers flocked to the city's riverfronts to buy up prime lots on which to build. Promising tens of thousands of jobs with salaries allegedly averaging $150,000, Amazon's arrival could have vast socioeconomic implications for the entire metropolitan area.

Meanwhile, a parade of new glass boxes—some of them no more interesting than those of a couple of generations ago—has popped up all over the city. Fortunately, there has also been a spate of compelling new architecture, including major cultural projects such as the National Museum of African American History and Culture, and a series of extraordinary new or renovated DC public schools and libraries. Even more impressive has been the comprehensive rede-

Rendering of Phase 2 of the District Wharf, now under construction.

velopment of several previously industrial or commercial areas into flourishing mixed-use neighborhoods. These include the District Wharf, the Yards / Capitol Riverfront area, and the Union Market district. Quite a few recent Washington-area projects, ranging from cutting-edge single-family houses to innovative corporate interiors, have garnered national and international recognition. Even some hardened skeptics of Washington's architectural scene observed that the city's reputation for cultural conservatism seemed seriously outdated.

Then, in 2020, came the news that the Trump administration, taking a page from Robert Dale Owen's 1849 book, *Hints on Public Architecture* (mentioned earlier in this introduction), was preparing to issue an executive order mandating an official style for governmental architecture in DC and elsewhere. Whereas Owen preferred "the style of the twelfth century," Trump's proposal would just as arbitrarily make classicism "the preferred and default style" for federal building. Most architects were appalled. At a time when thoughtful practitioners and academics were reckoning with the profession's obligations to combat climate change, address long-standing social inequities, and strengthen communities buffeted by sweeping technological changes, along came a proposal crafted by an outside, nonprofessional group calling for federal buildings to look a certain way because, well, they *liked* it (the proponents expressly railed against the horrors of Brutalism, seemingly oblivious to the fact that that movement drew its last breath roughly four decades ago). The promised executive order was issued in December 2020, near the end of Trump's term, in slightly diluted form—it allowed for nonclassical solutions necessitated by "exceptional factors." Fortunately, the new Biden administration promptly overturned that executive order in early 2021.

Federal architecture will likely remain something of a punching bag for advocates of various ideologies, but for now, corporate and institutional clients throughout the area seem to be largely committed to modern and sustainable, if not necessarily cutting-edge, design. Interestingly, in a survey of readers of *ArchitectureDC*, the quarterly magazine of AIA | DC, conducted about 10 years ago, more than 80 percent of respondents indicated that they, too, were primarily interested in modern design. Since then, the most innovative projects published in the magazine have consistently generated the most positive feedback from readers, the vast majority of whom are nonarchitects.[4]

Of course, few DC residents spend their days fretting and fuming about competing stylistic ideologies. More critical to them are quality-of-life issues, such as safety, affordability, convenience, and recreational and cultural opportunities. Like all thriving cities these days, Washington struggles with the first two of those issues: while crime rates have declined significantly over the past couple of decades, they remain worrisome, and the lack of affordable housing has reached a critical stage. On the last two points, however, the city continues to score well. Washington is consistently ranked among the most walkable major metropolitan areas in the country, and the city's bike-sharing and other alternative transportation networks have helped to support vibrant and accessible neighborhoods. Few cities can match Washington's bounty of museums, theatrical and musical performances, and other cultural programming, and its varied parks and streetscapes offer plenty of attractive places for a jog, casual stroll, or picnic. Hip new restaurants and bars have popped up in (almost) every part of the city, and although many such businesses have struggled during the COVID-19 pandemic, as of this writing others are scheduled to open in the near future.

Way back in 1842, the visiting British novelist Charles Dickens snidely labeled Washington—then only a few decades old and largely undeveloped—the "City of Magnificent Intentions." Today, many of those intentions have been realized in stone, brick, steel, and concrete. What the city may lack in sheer quantity of truly avant-garde works of architecture, it makes up in thriving neighborhoods, cohesive streetscapes, and surpassing civic order. Given that solid urbanistic foundation, augmented by an ever-growing number of beautiful and engaging individual buildings, it seems likely that Mr. Dickens, were he able to visit Washington again today, would be suitably impressed.

Notes

1. John Smith, *The Generall Historie of Virginia, New England & the Summer Isles: Together with the True Travels, Adventures and Observations, and a Sea Grammar* (Glasgow: J. MacLehose; New York: Macmillan, 1907), Jay I. Kislak Reference Collection (Library of Congress), https://www.loc.gov/resource/lhbcb.0262a/?sp=88&st=text, images 88 and 89 (accessed April 12, 2021).
2. George Hadfield, *The Washington Guide* (Washington, DC: S. A. Elliott, 1826), p. 22.
3. Robert Dale Owen, *Hints on Public Architecture* (New York: G. P. Putnam, 1849), pp. 104, 109.
4. The author of this book has served as the editor of *ArchitectureDC* since 2008.

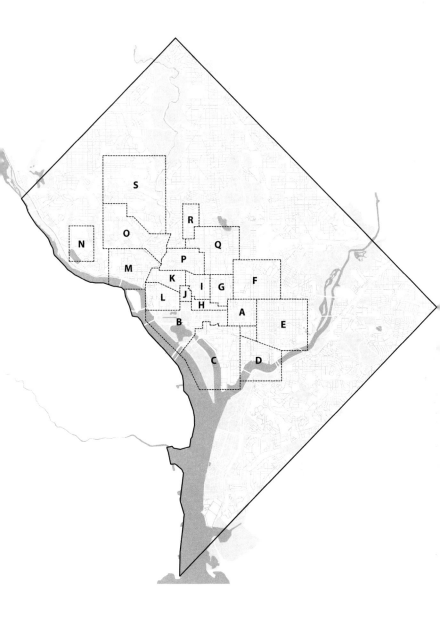

Governmental Capitol Hill

The Washington Monument may be taller, and the White House the more potent symbol of political power, but the primary architectural icon of Washington, DC —and, by extension, of American democracy—is undoubtedly the Capitol. Standing at the intersection of the cardinal axes in Pierre (Peter) Charles L'Enfant's city plan, it is both the conceptual center of the city and one majestic terminus of the Mall. Refined and, in some places, lavish in its materials and details, and surrounded by well-landscaped grounds, the Capitol is simultaneously urbane and bucolic, making it the perfect emblem of a capital city forged out of a compromise between northern urban and southern agrarian interests.

Its primacy notwithstanding, the Capitol today is just one element of a sizeable complex accommodating the US Congress and related functions. The jurisdiction of the architect of the Capitol, in fact, extends to the House and Senate office buildings that bracket the Capitol Grounds, the three major buildings of the Library of Congress, the US Supreme Court Building, and the US Botanic Garden, among other structures. Various private institutions, such as the Folger Shakespeare Library, are interspersed among these landmarks.

This chapter explores the public and private buildings at the core of the Capitol Hill neighborhood, the site of so many workings of the national government, from the petty and mundane to the noble and momentous.

TOUR A

An aerial view of Capitol Hill from 1935 showing (*clockwise from lower left*) the Russell Senate Office Building, the US Supreme Court, the Library of Congress, the Cannon House Office Building, the Longworth House Office Building, and the Capitol.

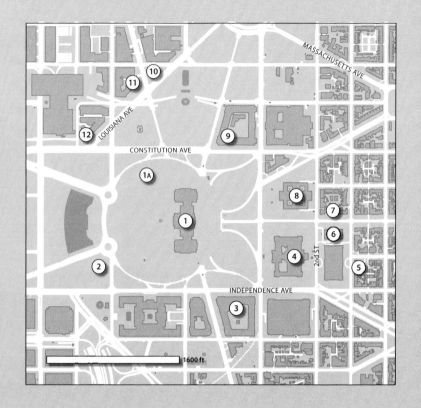

A1

The Capitol

1793–1802 — William Thornton, with Stephen Hallet, George Hadfield, and James Hoban

1803–17 — Benjamin Henry Latrobe

1818–29 — Charles Bulfinch

1836–51 — Various modifications: Robert Mills et al.

1851–65 — Extensions and new dome: Thomas U. Walter, with Montgomery C. Meigs

1949–50 — Remodeling of House and Senate chambers: David Lynn; Associate architect: Francis P. Sullivan; Consulting architects: Harbeson, Hough, Livingston & Larson

1958–62 — East Front extension: J. George Stewart; Associate architects: Roscoe DeWitt & Fred L. Hardison; Alfred Poor & Albert Swanke

1976 — Restoration of old Senate and Supreme Court chambers: George White; Associate architects: DeWitt, Poor & Shelton

1987 — West Front restoration: George White; Associate engineers: Ammann & Whitney

1993 — Infill of West Terrace courtyards: George White; Associate architect: Hugh Newell Jacobsen

2008 — Capitol Visitor Center: Alan Hantman; Associate architects: RTKL Associates Inc.

2016 — Restoration of dome: Stephen T. Ayers; Architects of record: Hoffmann Architects

Now that it is surrounded by a 21st-century metropolis, Capitol "Hill" seems little more than a mound. But in 1791, the 88-foot rise then known as Jenkins Hill impressed L'Enfant, who described it in a letter to George Washington as "a pedestal waiting for a monument." L'Enfant considered this the logical site for the principal building of the new capital city, and the rest of his plan was organized around the placement of the "Congress house" here.

The original design for the Capitol was the result of a competition, albeit only indirectly. None of the submissions received by the deadline in July 1792 fully pleased either President Washington or Secretary of State Thomas Jefferson. They decided to invite two entrants, including a French immigrant builder named Étienne (Stephen) Sulpice Hallet, to redevelop their proposals for further consideration. After the deadline had passed, William Thornton, a physician from the British West Indies, submitted a proposal that impressed the president. The design by Thornton was ultimately selected. Thornton's lack of applicable experience worried Washington and Jefferson, however, so they hired Hallet to supervise the construction of Thornton's design.

President Washington laid the cornerstone on September 18, 1793. The spirit of optimism that prevailed on that auspicious day soon faded, however, as conflicts arose among the project's principal players. Hallet was fired and replaced by George Hadfield, a young English architect, who was replaced in turn by Irish American architect James Hoban, who already had won the design competition for the President's House.

Construction of the Capitol proceeded slowly due to fiscal limitations and political bickering. As Irish journalist Isaac Weld noted in 1799, "numbers of people . . . particularly in Philadelphia" tried to sabotage work on the Capitol by withholding funds. Given this penny-pinching and intrigue-filled atmosphere, Jefferson and Washington directed the workers (who included both enslaved and free Black laborers) to concentrate on the north wing, which was finished in 1800, just in time for the government's official move to the new city. Looking at the present building from the east, one can see a small dome (to the right) that crowns the earliest part of the structure.

The small dome to the left, atop the House of Representatives wing, dates to a section completed in 1807 under architect and engineer Benjamin Henry Latrobe, whom then-president Jefferson had appointed surveyor of public buildings in 1803. Latrobe refined Thornton's design, introducing uniquely American elements to a building largely based on European precedents. His signature "corncob" column capitals, for example, were conceived as a truly American successor to the acanthus-leafed capitals of ancient Greece and Rome. Frances Trollope wrote in 1832 that "the beautiful capitals . . . composed of the ears and leaves of Indian corn" were "the only instance I saw in which America has ventured to attempt national originality; the success is perfect." Latrobe later added column capitals featuring tobacco leaves.

The War of 1812 brought British invaders to Washington, with devastating results for the Capitol. On August 24, 1814, British admiral Sir George Cockburn torched "this harbor of Yankee democracy," leaving what Latrobe called "a most magnificent ruin." After the war, Congress moved

Among Latrobe's signature design motifs were columns in which corncobs replaced the traditional acanthus leaves in the capital and the shafts were sculpted to resemble bundles of cornstalks.

temporarily to what later came to be called the "Old Brick Capitol," on the site of the present-day Supreme Court, and Latrobe was brought back to reconstruct the original Capitol. When he resigned in 1817 over a contract dispute, Latrobe left behind a curious structure—the Senate and House wings were complete, but with only a walkway connecting them, creating a fragile U in plan. President James Monroe then brought in Boston architect Charles Bulfinch to continue work on the building, and specifically to fill the void between the wings. Bulfinch's link was topped by a copper-clad dome of wood, stone, and brick, modeled on the one he had designed for the Massachusetts State House in the 1790s. Under his supervision, the project crawled to what everyone assumed was completion in 1829.

As the nation and its government grew, however, the Capitol began to bulge, so in 1850 Congress launched a competition for an expansion. Once again, this competition produced no clear winner, but Pres-

When Latrobe resigned as architect of the Capitol in 1817, the Senate
and House wings were connected only by a wooden walkway.

This daguerreotype by John Plumbe, taken circa 1846, shows the East
Front of the Capitol after it was "completed" by Charles Bulfinch,
only to be enlarged significantly in the 1850s and '60s.

ident Millard Fillmore selected entrant Thomas U. Walter, a Philadelphia architect, to undertake the work. The project was supervised by Montgomery C. Meigs, an engineer who would later serve as quartermaster general of the Union army during the Civil War. Together, they were responsible for the huge south and north extensions—the outermost elements of the building today—accommodating new House and Senate chambers. The House extension was finished in time for that body to convene there in 1857. The Senate moved into its completed quarters in 1859.

Walter and Meigs's tour-de-force, however, was the enlargement of the Capitol's dome. The 1850s extensions had more than doubled the building's length to 751 feet, thus reducing Bulfinch's dome to visual insignificance. So, in 1855, Walter designed a soaring replacement consisting of two trussed cast iron shells, one inside the other, with the exterior painted to resemble the marble of the extensions. The dome was still under construction as the Civil War began, and work continued so as to avoid breaching a favorable contract with a foundry that was committed to fabricating and installing the cast iron for only seven cents a pound. The construction came to a climax on December 2, 1863, when Thomas Crawford's 19-foot bronze statue, *Freedom*—created using slave labor, incredibly enough—was lifted into place at the peak of the cast iron dome.

The Capitol's interiors are a hodgepodge, reflecting the tastes of the various eras during which they were built. The principal ceremonial space is the Rotunda, beneath the great dome, which is 180 feet high and profusely decorated. At its apex is Constantino Brumidi's fresco, *The Apotheosis of Washington*, in which the Father of Our Country hobnobs with various allegorical figures. Because the fresco is applied to the inside of the *outer dome*, it appears to float above a hole at the top of the *inner dome*, creating the illusion that the figures in the fresco are hovering in the sky. Closer to eye level, the rotunda's walls are embellished with eight large historical paintings, including four by John Trumbull, known as the "Artist of the Revolution," which were installed between 1819 and 1824, and

four others by different artists depicting great moments in exploration, which were added between 1840 and 1855.

Beyond the Rotunda, the building contains a dizzying warren of rooms, punctuated by three major semicircular spaces: the Old Hall of the House (now the National Statuary Hall), the Old Senate Chamber (surprisingly intimate in scale), and the Old Supreme Court Chamber (the judicial branch did not have its own separate quarters until 1935). The sprawling extensions are full of delightfully excessive Victorian elements, from elaborate fireplaces to intricate cast iron grilles. While most of these are tucked away in suites that are not accessible to the general public, several of the corridors in the Senate wing boast extravagant frescos and other paintings by Brumidi and his associates, as well as richly colored encaustic floor tiles. The current House and Senate chambers are rather bland by comparison, having been stripped of their original grandeur in 1949–51.

Between 1958 and 1962, the center of the East Front was extended outward roughly 32 feet. This single stroke added 102 rooms and provided a deeper base for

This cross section through Thomas U. Walter's design for the enlarged Capitol Dome reveals its complex structure.

the dome. The stonework was changed from fragile Aquia Creek sandstone to Georgia marble in the process, but the old sandstone columns were preserved and now stand starkly and rather hauntingly on an open lawn at the National Arboretum [see T18]. A similar expansion scheme for the West Front arose in the 1970s, but this time public outcry led Congress to scrap the plans in favor of restoration. This façade was stripped of dozens of layers of paint and reinforced with steel rods, while roughly 40 percent of the crumbling sandstone was replaced with limestone. An ongoing exterior restoration of the building, begun under Architect of the Capitol Stephen T. Ayers in 2015, with Oehrlein & Associates Architects as associate architects, is expected to be completed in 2025.

The most recent major addition is the Capitol Visitor Center. Located beneath the East Plaza, it was conceived to help manage the flow of visitors and assumed new urgency after the terrorist attacks of September 11, 2001, led to more rigorous security screening. The architects had the unenviable job of responding to the conflicting demands of 535 members of Congress, coupled with changing security expectations, substantial increases in space requirements, and concomitant escalations in the budget. Completed in 2008, the 580,000-square-foot facility, which includes space for congressional offices and meeting rooms, has a generic convention center quality in some areas, but it does seem to fulfill its function and offers a few exhilarating moments, such as the glimpse of the Capitol Dome through one of the center's huge skylights.

The political, cultural, and emotional significance of the Capitol was starkly illuminated on January 6, 2021, when a riotous mob laid siege to the building in an attempt to stop the counting of Electoral College votes from the 2020 presidential election. Some of the insurgents carried Confederate flags—the very symbol of treason—into the House and Senate chambers, as members of Congress hid in fear for their lives. Damage to the building was ultimately modest—but several Capitol Police officers died directly or indirectly as a result of the assault. As of this writing, there are disheartening proposals afoot to erect a permanent barrier to thwart future attacks. Long considered an icon of transparent governance, the Capitol is now at risk of becoming a fortress.

A1a
Capitol Grounds
1st Street, NW/SW, to 1st Street, NE/SE, between Constitution and Independence Avenues

1874–92—Edward Clark; Landscape architect: Frederick Law Olmsted

It was perhaps inevitable that Frederick Law Olmsted, whose name is virtually synonymous with the profession of landscape architecture in America, would be called on to redesign the Capitol Grounds. Congress commissioned him to do so in 1874, and he responded with a bold and comprehensive plan, ranging from lampstands to tree-lined walkways to the cascading terraces that created a more impressive visual foundation for the Capitol's West Front. Largely intact after nearly a century and a half, Olmsted's design includes such entertaining elements as the cast iron waiting stations once known as "Herdics," after the Herdic Phaeton Company, whose line of horse-drawn, plushly upholstered trolleys they served.

The highlight of the northwestern part of the grounds is the Summerhouse, a hexagonal grotto with brick and terra cotta walls and a red tile roof, which Olmsted envisioned as a "cool retreat during hot summer." It originally sheltered a natural spring, which soured and had to be diverted; its fountains now flow with city water. The nearby stone tower, also designed by Olmsted, initially served both aesthetic and functional purposes: its upward thrust balanced the declivity of the grotto, while a now-closed vent within carried fresh, cool air into the Capitol through a series of underground tunnels.

At the bottom of the hill to the west is a memorial to Ulysses S. Grant, completed in 1922. The central sculpture of Grant atop his horse, Cincinnati, is one of the largest equestrian statues in the world. It is the work of Henry M. Shrady, with a base designed by Edward Pearce Casey, the architect responsible for the original interiors of the Jefferson Building of the Library of Congress [see A4].

A2

United States Botanic Garden

100 Maryland Avenue, SW

1933 — David Lynn; Associate architects: Bennett, Parsons & Frost
2001 — Restoration: Alan Hantman; Associate architects: DMJM Design
2006 — National Garden: Alan Hantman; Associate architects: SmithGroup in association with EDAW
2019 — Restoration of headhouse: Stephen T. Ayers; Associate architects: KCCT

For much of its history, the US Botanic Garden, established in 1820, occupied a site at the foot of Capitol Hill, not far off the centerline of the Mall. The Senate Park Commission Plan of 1901–2, however, demanded a clear vista along the Mall's central swath, and the garden's facilities were in the way. Although it took decades, the government eventually demolished the fanciful Victorian structure that had housed the institution since 1850 and built this Beaux-Arts conservatory at the edge of the Mall.

The rusticated north façade, evocative of a 17th-century French *orangerie*, relates the Botanic Garden to the neo-classical buildings of Capitol Hill. Behind this formal front stands an exuberant conservatory, now restored and incorpo-

rating sophisticated systems to maintain humidity and temperature levels. The structure's tall ribcage, manufactured by the venerable greenhouse firm of Lord & Burnham, is made of noncorroding aluminum, and when built it was the largest such structure in the world.

The Botanic Garden complex also includes the adjacent National Garden and a small triangular park across Independence Avenue, which features a fountain created for the Philadelphia Centennial Exhibition of 1876 by Frédéric Auguste Bartholdi (who later sculpted the Statue of Liberty). The fountain audaciously juxtaposed fire and water in a single work, with gas flames flickering amid spouting jets of liquid. When the exhibition closed, the federal government bought the fountain and moved it to Washington, where it initially occupied a different site. Electric lights eventually replaced the gas flames.

Across Washington Avenue from the little park is the American Veterans Disabled for Life Memorial, designed by Michael Vergason Landscape Architects in association with Shalom Baranes Associates and dedicated in 2014.

A3

Cannon House Office Building

27 Independence Avenue, SE

1908 — Elliott Woods; Consulting architects: Carrère & Hastings
1913 — Addition: Elliott Woods; Consulting architects: Carrère & Hastings
1932 — Renovation: David Lynn; Associate architects: Allied Architects

The commission to design freestanding office buildings for the Senate and the House was divided between the two principals of one architectural firm: Thomas

Hastings was responsible for the House Office Building (pictured here), later named for Speaker Joseph Cannon; John Carrère took the lead on the design of its Senate counterpart [see A9]. The result was a set of fraternal Beaux-Arts twins that, with their giant columns and gleaming white marble, visually merged to form a unified backdrop for the Capitol, at least until the more sober Longworth Building and the irredeemably hideous Rayburn Building came along and spoiled the view.

A major renovation of the Cannon House Office Building, begun in 2014 under Architect of the Capitol Stephen T. Ayers with Shalom Baranes Associates as associate architects, is expected to be finished in 2024.

A4

Library of Congress, Thomas Jefferson Building

10 1st Street, SE

1888–97 — John L. Smithmeyer and Paul J. Pelz; Interiors: Edward Pearce Casey

1910–65 — Renovations and additions: Various architects

1986–97 — Restoration: George White; Associate architects: Arthur Cotton Moore / Associates

As the government was preparing to move to the new federal city in 1800, Congress approved an expenditure of $5,000 to buy books and create a library for its own use. Housed within the Capitol, these original tomes were destroyed during the British invasion of 1814. To replace them, former

president Thomas Jefferson, who declared that "there is, in fact, no subject to which a Member of Congress may not have occasion to refer," sold his remarkably broad-based private library of precisely 6,487 volumes to the government. From this core, the Library of Congress has evolved into the largest library in the world, containing more than 170 million items.

The institution's growth was slow and steady until Congress passed the Copyright Act of 1870, which required that the library receive two copies of every book, drawing, photograph, map, or other item submitted to the government for copyright protection. The legislation resulted in a flood of new acquisitions — some 20,000 in the first year alone — exceeding the capacity of the library space inside the Capitol. So, in 1873, Congress authorized a competition for a new stand-alone facility. The team of John L. Smithmeyer and Paul Pelz won first place with a sedate Italian Renaissance Revival design that did not inspire much enthusiasm. Over the following 13 years, the architects continued to tinker with the design like teenagers trying on different outfits before a date, exploring a wide variety of styles, including French Renaissance, German Renaissance, and "Victorian Gothic." Congress finally agreed to a specific proposal and authorized construction in 1886, but the library was not completed until 1897, 24 years after the original competition.

The executed design is, at least on the exterior, a rather stodgy Beaux-Arts affair that combines aspects of the architects'

French and Italian schemes but ultimately is pervaded by a baronial Germanic aura. The main entrance pavilion, nonetheless, was almost certainly inspired by the elegant Paris Opera House designed by Charles Garnier. Key similarities include the arched doorways on the main level; the five central bays above, framed by paired columns; and the projecting bays on either side, topped by arched pediments. While Garnier's original conveys a kind of delicate grandeur, Smithmeyer and Pelz's interpretation seems over-wrought and bombastic. One significant difference is that the Opera House is set right at street level, while the Library of Congress is raised on a podium, contributing to a sense of aloofness. Architect and critic Russell Sturgis lambasted the library's entrance as representing "that false idea of grandeur which consists mainly in hoisting a building up from a reasonable level . . . in order to secure for it a monstrous flight of steps which must be surmounted before the main door can be reached."

The library's exterior may be awkward, but once inside, even the most skeptical visitor is likely to be dazzled. The principal interior spaces, which were overseen by Edward Pearce Casey after both Smith-meyer and Pelz were dismissed from the project, are among the most regal rooms in Washington. A team of more than 50 sculptors and painters brought the archi-tecture to life through an artistic program of appropriately encyclopedic propor-tions. The heroic Great Hall is replete with mosaics and statuary set amid a sea of marble, stained glass, and bronze. Paired columns support arches that seem to spring effortlessly into the air.

The Main Reading Room, topped by a 160-foot-high dome, is the grand finale. The room's octagonal shape was dictated by Ainsworth Spofford, the librarian of Congress during the building's construc-tion, to reflect a new system for organiz-ing books into eight categories. A mind-boggling assortment of allegorical sculptures and paintings provides intel-lectual inspiration for the reader, should any be needed. Here, the opening of a book becomes a noble rite.

The Library of Congress complex includes two other major buildings: the John Adams Building at 120 2nd Street, SE (1938—David Lynn; Associated architects: Pierson & Wilson; Consulting architect: Alexander Buel Trowbridge), and the James Madison Memorial Building at 101 Independence Avenue, SE (1980—J. George Stewart; Associated architects: DeWitt, Poor & Shelton Architects).

A5

St. Mark's Episcopal Church
301 A Street, SE

1889—T. Buckler Ghequier
1894, 1930—Additions: architects unknown
1926—Addition: Delos Smith
1966—Interior alterations: Kent Cooper & Associates
1991—Undercroft and interior alterations: Muse-Wiedemann Architects
2014—Renovation and expansion of Parish Hall wing: Bonstra | Haresign Architects

From 1896 to 1902, this beautifully composed church served as the "pro-cathedral"—in effect, an acting cathe-dral—for the Episcopal Diocese of Wash-ington. It is ostensibly in the Romanesque Revival style, but not as bulky and stern as that label might suggest. Inside the sanctuary, abundant stained-glass win-dows and slender cast iron columns con-tribute to a sense of lightness. The glass in the main baptistery window came from the studio of Louis Comfort Tiffany, while most of the other stained-glass windows were created by Franz Mayer of Munich. Fixed pews were removed in the 1960s in favor of flexible seating in the round, better to accommodate the parish's progressive style of services, as well as its ambitious arts programming.

A6
Folger Shakespeare Library
201 East Capitol Street, SE

1932 — Paul Philippe Cret; Consulting architect: Alexander B. Trowbridge
1982 — Addition and renovation: Hartman-Cox Architects
2019 — Exterior restoration: MTFA Design + Preservation

When he wasn't raking in money, oil tycoon Henry Clay Folger was, along with his wife, Emily Jordan Folger, busy amassing the world's largest collection of Shakespeare's printed works and related material. Once Henry retired as chairman of the Standard Oil Company of New York in 1928, he turned his attention to establishing a library to house their collection. Emily saw the project to completion following her husband's death in 1930.

The building, designed by Paul Philippe Cret, is one of the city's premier examples of the modernist-classical hybrid sometimes called "Stripped Classicism," "Greco-Deco," or, more wittily, "Stark Deco"—a severe yet elegant style that became popular in Depression-era Washington. The exterior is a tightly controlled composition, with only minimal recesses and projections from the principal planes of the façades. Tall windows on the north and west façades are divided by fluted pilasters—hints of pilasters, really, since the fluting is the only remnant of the traditional form. Sculptural panels below the windows on the main façade depict scenes from Shakespeare's plays.

Cret's design appears to be a perfectly exemplary building of the period until one ventures inside. Within that fashionable 1930s book jacket is an astounding neo-Elizabethan fantasy in dark, heavy wood. Cret defended the juxtaposition by explaining that the Folgers wanted a place that was "reminiscent of England," but the architect realized that "the site selected, facing a wide, straight avenue in one of the most classical of cities . . . would be inappropriate for an Elizabethan building."

The reading room at the rear of the library, added by Hartman-Cox, is a modern reinterpretation of the Great Hall that runs along the front of the original building, but it also suggests the inspiration of French visionary architect Étienne-Louis Boullée's hypothetical *Bibliothèque nationale*, with its semicircular-vaulted ceiling. While examining original drawings by Cret's office for the building, the architects of the addition noticed that several of the documents bore the initials "LK." It is safe to assume that these drawings were produced by none other than Louis Kahn, the great modernist architect who had worked for Cret during the period that this project was on the boards.

KieranTimberlake is overseeing the latest renovation of the building, with completion expected in 2022.

A7
Lutheran Church of the Reformation
212 East Capitol Street, NE

1934 — Porter & Lockie
1951 — Parish House addition: Irwin S. Porter and Sons
1993 — Elevator addition: architect unknown
2019 — Renovation and sanctuary ceiling restoration: MTFA Design + Preservation

Like the roughly contemporary Folger Shakespeare Library across the street, the Lutheran Church of the Reformation has a split personality. In this case, a Greco-Deco façade contrasts with an Arts-and-Crafts interior, replete with oak paneling and heavy wood beams connected by king posts. The design of the sanctuary reflects the influence of Scandinavian ecclesiastical traditions, which favored a simple, column-free "hall" for

the congregation with a modest, rectangular chancel. While far from ornate, the church does have a rich decorative program, including depictions of fleurs-de-lis, the tree of life, and at least 15 different versions of the Christian cross.

A8

Supreme Court Building

1 1st Street, NE

1935 — Cass Gilbert; completed by Cass Gilbert Jr. and John R. Rockart
2010 — Renovation: Alan Hantman; Associate architects: Hillier Architecture
2021 — Exterior stone restoration: Stephen T. Ayers / J. Brett Blanton; Associate architects: Oehrlein & Associates Architects

Generations of American schoolchildren have been taught that the judiciary is one of the three branches of the federal government, of equal importance to the executive and legislative components. Many people are therefore surprised to learn that the Supreme Court did not have a home of its own until 1935. Before that year, the court had occupied a succession of chambers within the Capitol, an arrangement that not only muddled the separation of powers but also caused a good deal of harrumphing among jurists who had to compete for space with members of Congress and their staffs.

In 1929, Chief Justice (and former president) William Howard Taft convinced Congress to commission a new building exclusively for the court. The government selected a site occupied by the remnants of the "Old Brick Capitol," which had served as the temporary seat of Congress while the Capitol itself was being rebuilt following the British invasion of 1814. The property, then owned by the National Woman's Party (NWP), was acquired through eminent domain and razed (the NWP received compensation and moved to what is now the Belmont-Paul Women's Equality National Monument at 144 Massachusetts Avenue, NE). Cass Gilbert, architect of the Woolworth Building in New York, which had reigned as the world's tallest building since 1913, was hired to design the court's new home.

Gilbert's design was one of the last major works of Beaux-Arts classicism

in Washington. Conceived as a temple of justice, the building draws heavily on Roman precedents. The entire structure is raised on a plinth, which extends to the front of the building proper to create a broad entry plaza. A central spine, bracketed by porticoes with sculpted pediments, contains the principal interior spaces—including the Court Chamber at the east end—and completely dominates the two side wings. Four courtyards within the wings bring natural light into adjacent offices and other spaces.

A9

Russell Senate Office Building

2 Constitution Avenue, NE

1909—Elliott Woods; Consulting
architects: Carrère & Hastings
1933—Addition: David Lynn; Associate
architects: Nathan C. Wyeth and
Francis P. Sullivan

This building was conceived as the senatorial companion piece to the Cannon House Office Building [see A3] on the opposite side of the Capitol. An ongoing exterior restoration led by the architect of the Capitol is expected to be completed in 2023.

Just down Constitution Avenue are two other Senate facilities: the stripped classical Dirksen Senate Office Building (1958—Eggers & Higgins) and the monumentally modern Philip A. Hart Senate Office Building (1982—John Carl Warnecke & Associates), whose tall, narrow windows are framed by a deeply projecting marble *brise-soleil*, or sunscreen.

A10

National Japanese American Memorial

Louisiana and New Jersey Avenues
at D Street, NW

2000—Davis Buckley Architects and
Planners; Landscape architects: James
Urban, FASLA, Landscape Architecture;
Sculptors: Nina Akamu and Paul
Matisse

This monument, officially known as the Japanese American Memorial to Patriotism During World War II, recognizes both the service of Japanese American veterans and the US government's shameful internment of more than 100,000 people of Japanese descent during the war. The most compelling feature of the memorial is a long tubular bell created by sculptor Paul Matisse (grandson of Henri, the famous painter), which visitors may ring by pumping a lever that lifts and releases a clapper. The bell emits a profound and sustained tone—actually a pair of tones that gradually merge, symbolizing the healing of emotional wounds.

A11

Acacia Building /
300 New Jersey Avenue

51 Louisiana Avenue, NW /
300 New Jersey Avenue, NW

1936—Shreve, Lamb & Harmon; Sculptor:
Edmond Romulus Amateis
1953—Addition: Shreve, Lamb & Harmon
1999—Restoration: Hartman-Cox
Architects
2009—300 New Jersey Avenue: Rogers
Stirk Harbour + Partners; Architects of
record: HKS; Associated architects for
lobby interior: Lehman Smith McLeish

The Acacia Building, built for an insurance
company, was designed by the architects
of the Empire State Building and shares
a stripped classical aesthetic with its
more famous cousin. The façades of the
Washington building are undeniably austere, relieved only by a projecting central
doorway with a hint of a scroll above it,
simple fluting on the tall pilasters, and a
few medallions below the primary cornice. Most passersby barely even glance
at the building, however, as they are too
entranced by the pair of limestone griffins
that fiercely guard its entrance.

After the insurance company moved
in 1997, the building's new owner hired
the firm of Richard Rogers, one of the
architects of the famed Pompidou Center in Paris, to design an addition and
integrate it with the original building and
a wing added to the rear in the 1950s. A
simple curtain-walled block now lines
the northern edge of the site, with an
atrium spanning the irregularly shaped
space between the three structures.
Tying the disparate blocks together is
the "Tree"—a bright yellow mast that
supports a web of bridges and stairs and
an elevator. A large branch of the Tree,
resting on a secondary mast outside the
atrium, extends toward Louisiana Avenue
to support a louvered triangular canopy
that marks the primary entrance to the
complex. Although the new block itself
is rather staid, the atrium space, with
its colorful Tree, myriad bridges, and
intricate details, recalls the sometimes
startlingly high-tech work of Rogers's
early career.

A12

101 Constitution Avenue, NW

2002 — Shalom Baranes Associates
2013 — Renovation of entry, common
    areas, and terrace: Hickok Cole

If real estate is all about location, then this property — the closest commercial office building to the Capitol — was destined for success. Fortunately, the design of the structure befits its prominent setting. The cylindrical tower serves as something of a landmark in an area that is otherwise rather nebulous in urban design terms, with ill-defined park spaces to the east and south and the monstrously banal Department of Labor building to the west (the tower also works in concert with the similarly shaped element of the Prettyman Courthouse annex [see H1] to provide a visual frame for the Labor building when seen from the Mall). The long Louisiana Avenue façade is composed of two basic forms: a tall slab with a shallow curve in plan and a rectilinear gridded block that holds the line of the street. An open colonnade at the street level creates a pleasant, quasi-public space and helps to shade the all-glass walls of the adjacent restaurant.

At the rear of this new building, along 2nd Street, is a surprising little enclave of surviving 19th-century buildings — reminders of how this part of town looked before the Senate Park Commission of 1901–2 imposed its will on the city's core.

The Mall

L'Enfant's own drawing of his plan for the city of Washington, dating to 1791, has faded almost to the point of illegibility, but on a colorized facsimile traced from the original in 1887, one area leaps out to the viewer: a linear swath of green, bracketed by parallel rows of buildings shown in red, with a street running down the middle, linking the "Congress house" to the Potomac River. The key to the plan labels this axis as a "Grand Avenue, 400 feet in breadth, and about a mile in length, bordered with gardens, ending in a slope from the houses on each side." Although L'Enfant's vision for the area as the city's most prominent residential boulevard never came to fruition, it served, of course, as the basis for what later became known as the National Mall.

For much of the city's history, the formal, museum-lined greensward that visitors and locals alike now take for granted was haphazardly occupied and often quite scruffy. In the mid- to late 19th century, trains chugged in and out of a railroad station near the center of the Mall, generating smoke that frequently obscured the view of the Capitol. An open sewer, built as a canal, ran along the Mall's northern edge, while the marshy western end along the Potomac was prone to flooding. Some of the leftover space was landscaped in a "romantic" manner, with winding paths and what designer A. J. Downing intended as a "public museum of living trees and shrubs," but this picturesque layout contributed to the perception of disorder. The ruddy turrets of the Smithsonian "Castle," then starkly isolated in the middle of the Mall, added a somber touch, and for a considerable interval, the incomplete shaft of the Washington Monument loomed near the Mall's western terminus, as if to mock the chaos of it all.

In 1901, the Senate Park Commission, often called the McMillan Commission after the Michigan senator responsible for its formation, launched a campaign to transform the Mall from a civic embarrassment to a national treasure. The commissioners sought inspiration in L'Enfant's original design, but their plan was no mere revival—rather, it reflected the spirit of the time, and in particular, the tenets of the City Beautiful movement that was strongly associated with the 1893 World's Columbian Exposition in Chicago. Following much deliberation (and a lengthy tour of European capitals offering models for outstanding urban design), the commission produced a majestic, classically inspired plan for Washington's monumental core. Over time, the railroad agreed to relocate, the marshes and canals were drained and filled in, and the Lincoln and Jefferson memorials rose in marble splendor in the reclaimed marshlands. The commission's imperially scaled plan was never fully realized—the decidedly nonclassical Smithsonian Castle successfully held its ground, for instance, and the broad, imposing terrace proposed for the base of the Washington Monument was not built—but the essence of the 1902 plan largely came to fruition over the ensuing decades.

The present two-mile-long Mall is almost incomprehensibly grand; it is also one of the most audacious urban landscapes in the world—an impressive

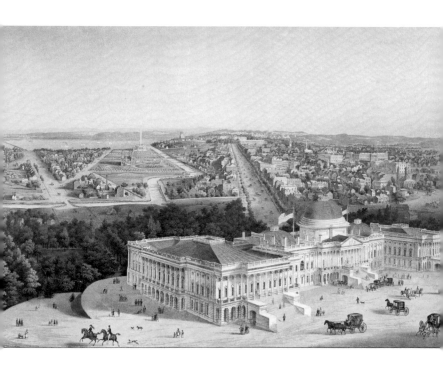

rebuke to the *horror vacui* that has engendered so many overwrought public and quasi-public spaces in America (think Disney). Christopher Knight of the *Los Angeles Times* praised the Mall's "sublime emptiness," which he defended as an important symbol of the nation's democratic, open society. Interestingly, his comments appeared in an article decrying a great threat to this important space: a proliferation of new monuments and memorials, with countless other groups already clamoring for their own causes to be recognized on this highly symbolic tract. The Mall is thus in danger of becoming a victim of its own civic success. At the same time, the space is notably lacking in many of the amenities typically associated with an urban park, such as outdoor cafés, children's play areas, and locally oriented programming. As the various stakeholders work to address these issues, for now the Mall can be safely enjoyed for its myriad museums, its often-inspiring monuments, and, above all, its gloriously improbable openness.

(*Above*) Although titled *View of Washington*, this engraving published by E. Sachse & Co. around 1852 reflected a good deal of wishful thinking. In the left background, the Mall is inaccurately depicted as a clean grassy swath, and the Washington Monument, which in fact was nowhere near finished, is shown at full height and surrounded by the circular colonnaded base that was never built.

SEE TOUR L

SEE TOUR J

CONSTITUTION AVE

23rd ST

7 7

10

11

12

9

8

13

14

15

16

17

2000 ft

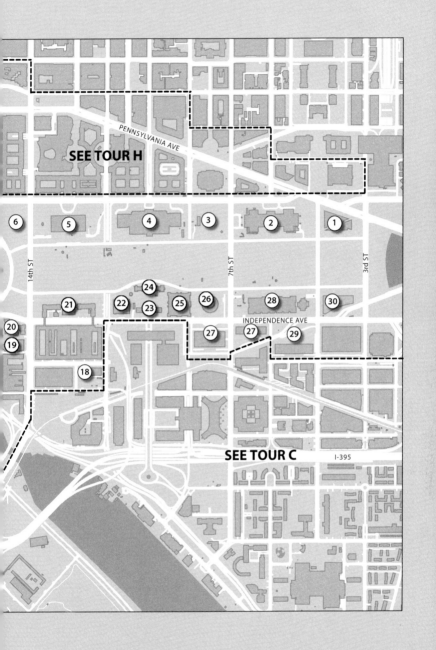

B1

National Gallery of Art, East Building

4th Street between Constitution Avenue and Madison Drive, NW

1978 — I. M. Pei & Partners; Landscape architect: Dan Kiley

2016 — Renovation and expansion: Hartman-Cox Architects; Concept architect: Perry Y. Chin, Architect

The East Building of the National Gallery of Art is widely regarded as the pinnacle of what might be termed "High Modernist" architecture in Washington, and it is arguably one of the finest such works anywhere in the country, despite its slavish reliance on a geometrical regimen that may have caused as many problems as it solved.

I. M. Pei's planning strategy was to split the potentially awkward trapezoidal site into two triangles, with a larger isosceles triangle containing gallery space and a smaller right triangle on the Mall side accommodating offices and a study center. Large chunks have been excised from these two basic forms, creating voids that reduce the structure's bulk and introduce dramatic shadows (while also yielding some obviously orphaned nooks and crannies on the interior). At the core of the building is a brightly skylit atrium, which appears in plan as a second isosceles triangle slightly offset from the main block. The triangular theme is carried through obsessively at various scales, including the shape of the floor tiles in the atrium. A huge, colorful mobile by Alexander Calder—the artist's last major work—rotates languorously in this space, providing a sensuous counterpoint to the prevailing geometrical precision.

Pei carefully related the building to its neighbors without stooping to imitation. The East Building's principal forms are of two different heights, with the lower blocks corresponding to the scale of the original gallery, now known as the West Building [see following entry], and the towers addressing the more bureaucratic structures across Pennsylvania and Constitution Avenues. Pei's building is clad in the same pink marble as the older gallery and is physically connected to its sibling by an underground tunnel whose design now seems dated, though in a rather amusing 1970s space-age way (a light installation by artist Leo Villareal enhances the effect). At the western end of the tunnel awaits a modern cafeteria, fronting a glass wall startlingly holding back a torrential cascading fountain.

The building underwent major façade repairs in 2014 after the exterior stone veneer anchors began to fail due to a construction error. Most of the stone blocks were cleaned and reinstalled in their original locations—only a couple required replacement. Ongoing interior renovations by Hartman-Cox Architects in collaboration with gallery staff include improvements to the main skylight and public spaces.

B2

National Gallery of Art, West Building

Between Constitution Avenue and Madison Drive, and 4th and 7th Streets, NW

1941 — John Russell Pope / Eggers & Higgins

1983 — Reorganization and renovation: Keyes Condon Florance Architects

2003 — Renovation of northwest quadrant: Vitetta with National Gallery of Art staff; East and west façade renovations: Vitetta

2004 — Renovation of southwest quadrant: Vitetta; Hayes Seay Mattern and Mattern

2009 — Renovation of southeast quadrant: Ewing Cole

2012 — Renovation of northeast quadrant: Hartman-Cox Architects

2013 — North façade restoration: Vitetta

Founded in 1937, the National Gallery of Art owes its existence to Andrew Mellon, who donated both his own art collection and a sizeable pile of cash to establish the institution. Mellon directly engaged John Russell Pope, an unapologetic classicist during the early years of the modern movement, to design a home for the collection on a site set aside by Congress. Visitors unaware of the late date of the gallery's construction—it was finished just before the United States entered World War II—generally assume that the building is much older than it is. As with the Jefferson Memorial [see B17], completed a few years later, the historicist design vexed many contemporary critics. Joseph Hudnut, dean of the School of Architecture at Harvard, called it "the final disaster on the Mall," while architect Philip Goodwin dismissed it as "a costly mummy."

Conservative though the building may be, it incorporates some subtle gestures that add interest. Note, for instance, the very shallow pilasters, barely articulated against the otherwise nearly blank walls flanking the central portico of the north façade. Also, look closely at the color of the pink Tennessee marble—in just the right light, one can see that it is not monochromatic, but graduated from a somewhat darker color at the bottom of the façade to a lighter shade at the top.

Regardless of one's opinion about the building's historicism, there is little debate about the high quality of its execution, particularly on the interior. The rotunda, which so easily could have been just another cold, formal, neoclassical Washington chamber, is instead a warm, visually rich space, thanks to its dark green marble columns, elegant floor patterns, and perfectly scaled fountain. Major corridors are well proportioned and beautifully skylit, and some of the grand staircases are outstanding works of sculpture in their own right.

B3

National Gallery of Art Sculpture Garden

Between Constitution Avenue and Madison Drive, and 7th and 9th Streets, NW

1988—Pavilion: Skidmore, Owings & Merrill
1999—Sculpture Garden: Olin Partnership
2000—Renovation of pavilion: National Gallery of Art staff; Architects of record: SmithGroup

A national sculpture garden was first formally proposed for this site in 1966. In 1974, an ice-skating rink was built here, and then in 1988 came the little green pavilion—a modern take on Art Nouveau motifs—that now houses a café. (Right next to the pavilion is an actual Art Nouveau artifact: an early 20th-century Paris Métro entrance portal designed by Hector Guimard and installed here in 2003.) The full Sculpture Garden finally came to fruition in 1999, when the original skating rink was removed and reconstructed.

The somewhat staid landscape design, incorporating cast iron and steel fences, as well as the same marble used on the National Gallery's two buildings, is offset by a dynamic fountain (in warm weather) and some excellent modern sculptures. On the Mall side is Roy Lichtenstein's *House I*, which seems to shift its shape as one walks by. Near the corner of Constitution Avenue and 9th Street is *Orphée*, a mosaic designed by Marc Chagall as a gift for his friends John U. and Evelyn Stefansson Nef, in whose Georgetown garden it was installed before being bequeathed to the National Gallery.

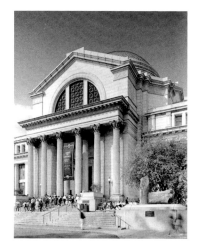

B4

National Museum of Natural History

Between Constitution Avenue and Madison Drive, and 9th and 12th Streets, NW

1911 — Hornblower & Marshall (with Daniel Burnham and Charles McKim)
1964, 1965 — Additions: Mills, Petticord & Mills
1990 — Upgrades: HSMM
1994 — Enclosure of East Court: Mariani & Associates
1995 — Enclosure of West Court: Designtech East
1999 — Renovations (including new Discovery Center, theater, and restaurant): Hammel, Green and Abrahamson with SmithGroup
2000–17 — Various interior restorations: architrave, p.c., architects
2003 — Restoration of West Exhibit Hall: HSMM
2009 — Renovation of Sant Ocean Hall: Quinn Evans Architects
2013 — Q?rius Learning Center: EwingCole
2019 — West Court Dining Hall and renovation of Hall of Fossils: EwingCole
2021 — Restoration of central portico and renovation of north entry: Quinn Evans; Landscape architects: AECOM

The National Museum of Natural History was the first structure on the north side of the Mall erected in accordance with the Senate Park Commission Plan. A branch of the Smithsonian, this museum contains a hodgepodge of artifacts that might be regarded as a microcosm of the parent institution. Highlights include the "striding" bull elephant that greets visitors in the building's octagonal rotunda, countless other stuffed critters of varied size and ferocity, and a pretty little hunk of rock known as the Hope Diamond.

The early designs for the museum, by the local firm of Hornblower & Marshall, were sumptuous compositions evoking turn-of-the-century Parisian buildings such as the Petit Palais. Unfortunately, the continuing conservative influence of former Senate Park Commission members Daniel Burnham and Charles McKim doomed these flights of fancy. An impatient McKim ultimately sent the local architects a sketch of a more modest, Roman-inspired design, along with a directive saying, in effect, "Just do it this way." It's a pity. The result, while dignified, is much less interesting than it could have been, at least on the exterior — Hornblower & Marshall was largely left to its own devices for the inside of the building. The façades of the symmetrical office wings, added in the 1960s, are dumbed-down versions of the original.

The museum's greatest interior space is the Baird Auditorium on the ground floor, which is capped by a shallow dome constructed of Guastavino tile. The recent enclosure of the two first-floor courtyards on either side of what is now the Sant Ocean Hall introduced some airy modern spaces to the building. Of particular note is the new staircase in the west court, the design of which was inspired by the anatomy of vertebrate animals.

B5

National Museum of American History, Behring Center

Between Constitution Avenue and Madison Drive, and 12th and 14th Streets, NW

1964 — Steinman, Cain & White; Associated architects: Mills, Petticord & Mills

2009 — Interior modernization: Skidmore, Owings & Merrill

2012 — Addition and adaptive reuse of South Wing: Beyer Blinder Belle Architects & Planners

2015 — Renovation of West Wing: EwingCole

If the Smithsonian is "the nation's attic," then the National Museum of American History is the hulking chest in that attic, stuffed with America's collective mementos — some precious, some odd, some a bit embarrassing. These artifacts range from Dorothy's ruby slippers from *The Wizard of Oz*, to the clichéd but irresistible collection of First Ladies' gowns, to the original flag that inspired *The Star-Spangled Banner*, to cars, locomotives, and even a chunk of the first iron railroad bridge in America (the latter few items serving as reminders that this was initially the Museum of History and Technology before it was renamed in 1980). There's even Horatio Greenough's bizarre 1841 statue of George Washington, depicted bare-chested and in sandals as if he were an ancient Roman god.

If only the building erected for the display of these curious objects were equally intriguing. Designed by the professional heirs of McKim, Mead & White, and conceived as a modern reinterpretation of the classical temples that inspired many Washington landmarks, it is neither convincingly modern nor credibly neoclassical. It's just a box. After the museum opened, columnist Russell Baker lamented, "Our own generation is unable to build a shelter worthy of housing what the old people left us."

Upon entering the museum, visitors may feel as if they are, in fact, inside a giant storage chest. The interior was, for decades, a befuddling warren of exhibition galleries, corridors, and support functions, making orientation difficult and exhaustion easy. Fortunately, a comprehensive interior renovation by Skidmore, Owings & Merrill, completed in 2009, brought much-needed hierarchy to the principal spaces and clarified the building's confusing circulation patterns. A similar rethinking of the boxy exterior would now be welcome.

B6

National Museum of African American History and Culture

Between Constitution Avenue and Madison Drive, and 14th and 15th Streets, NW

2016 — Freelon Adjaye Bond / SmithGroupJJR; Landscape architects: Gustafson Guthrie Nichol

The design of the National Museum of African American History and Culture (NMAAHC) both questions and confronts the prevailing architectural ethos of the National Mall, much as the museum itself challenges prevalent political and social narratives. Instead of white or cream-colored stone, the new museum is encased in a shimmering bronze-toned filigree, its three tiers canted outward to form a series of inverted truncated pyramids. Enigmatic voids of different sizes punctuate this screen. The building's main entrance, on the south side, is marked not by a neoclassical portico but by a broad canopy — a modern, civically scaled take on the traditional domestic porch. Inside, in lieu of the discrete galleries found in typical museums, the NMAAHC offers a more choreographed experience, in which architecture and exhibitry are often inseparable, helping to tell a complex, difficult, yet ultimately uplifting story.

The building's signature element—the tiered, filigreed screen—was inspired by the crown-like pinnacles of carved posts found on vernacular buildings of the Yoruba people in what is now Nigeria. Lead designer Sir David Adjaye, a Tanzanian-born architect based in London, dubbed it the "corona," and explained that "despite the passage of time, it represents the aesthetic world [that] the Africans brought to America as slaves." The museum's then-director (now secretary of the Smithsonian), Lonnie G. Bunch III, suggested that the metalwork on the corona be modeled after wrought iron grills fabricated by slaves in the antebellum South. The architects adapted Bunch's idea, creating a geometrical design that is historically evocative yet undeniably contemporary. From a distance, the screen appears to be composed of identical panels, but in fact, there are eight different versions, with varying densities of metalwork, positioned strategically so as to modulate the sunlight entering the building. The architects initially intended the screen to be bronze but that proved too heavy, so they devised an alternative made of bronze-toned aluminum.

The location of the museum generated controversy, due in part to general trepidations about the proliferation of buildings on the Mall, along with the specific worry that the new building might encroach on views of the Washington Monument. These concerns, coupled with the fact that the museum occupies a substantially smaller site than most of its neighbors, led the architects to place much of the structure underground. The architects turned this to advantage by devising a circulation strategy that reinforces the museum's fundamental narratives. The typical visit begins at the lowest level, where the exhibition focuses on the earliest days of the slave trade. At strategic points, depressions in the concrete floor accommodate quasi-archaeological displays that add literal and figurative depth to the narrative. Following a chronological path, visitors ascend through the three floors of history galleries via gently sloping ramps. The final ramp leads to the Concourse level, site of the Contemplative Court, which lies just below the building's north lawn. The centerpiece of the court is a fountain in which water falls from an oculus, or circular opening in the ceiling, to a pool below.

Above the main floor are three more public levels containing education facilities, the Community Galleries, and the Culture Galleries. The circulation spine along the northern edge of each floor affords views through the glass curtain wall and the corona, with dappled city vistas beyond. From this vantage point, the purpose of the curious external voids in the ornamental screen becomes clear: they judiciously frame broad lines of sight toward nearby landmarks.

The design team for the museum included four well-established architecture firms—the Freelon Group (now part of Perkins&Will), Adjaye Associates, Davis Brody Bond, and SmithGroupJJR (now simply SmithGroup)—in what appears to have been a remarkably successful collaboration despite its complexity.

B7

Capitol Gatehouses

Constitution Avenue at 15th and 17th Streets, NW

ca. 1828—Charles Bulfinch
1860—Dismantled
1880—Installed in current location
1939—Restoration: Thomas T. Waterman

The observant reader will notice that these are the *Capitol*, not *Capital*, Gatehouses. That is because they formerly guarded the US Capitol itself, and they are made of the same soft sandstone found in the original building. They were dismantled in 1860 to make room for the north and south extensions to the Capitol Building and moved here in 1880. (There are also several *gateposts* from the Capitol that now mark three of the four corners of 15th and Constitution, plus a wayward one at the southwest corner of 7th and Constitution.)

B8

The Washington Monument

Between Independence and Constitution Avenues, and 15th and 17th Streets, NW

1848–58—Robert Mills
1876–84—Completion, with modifications to original design: Thomas L. Casey

1935—Masonry restoration: architect unknown
1962—Exterior restoration: Don Myer / National Park Service
2000—Preservation architects for exterior restoration and interior renovation: Oehrlein & Associates Architects; Interior renovation: Michael Graves & Associates
2005—Landscape perimeter security improvements: Olin Partnership
2014—Post-earthquake restoration: Wiss, Janney, Elstner Associates
2019—New entrance and Visitor Screening Facility: Beyer Blinder Belle Architects & Planners

At 555 feet, 5⅛ inches, the Washington Monument was the tallest structure in the world when completed and remains the tallest made of stone. It now seems so obvious, so perfect, so timeless, that it is hard to imagine when this symbol of Washington—both the president and the city—was far from a certainty.

The monument's tumultuous history goes back to 1783, when the Continental Congress voted to build an equestrian statue of General George Washington "at the place where the residence of Congress shall be established." L'Enfant proposed placing that statue on the Mall at the point where the axes of the Capitol and the President's House crossed. Washington died in 1799 before that sculpture was executed, however, and in 1800, congressional leaders jettisoned the plan in favor of a "mausoleum of American granite and marble, in pyramidal form," to be built inside the Capitol. The Senate rejected this scheme, and several subsequent plans faced opposition from Washington's family.

In 1832, the centenary of Washington's birth revived interest in creating some sort of memorial to him. The Washington National Monument Society was formed in 1833, and in 1836 its members launched a national design competition, which was won by architect Robert Mills. His design called for an obelisk slightly taller (at 600 feet) and blunter than the present shaft, with a circular Greek-inspired temple at the base. Lack of funds caused more delay, but ground was finally broken for this design in 1848.

The site for the construction was not exactly where L'Enfant had intended. Soil tests indicated that the planned position, forming a right triangle with the President's House and the Capitol, was too marshy, so the foundation was instead placed well east, and slightly south, of the original spot. This decision had major ramifications for the Mall, forcing a slight southward kink in the axis emanating from the west portico of the Capitol and leaving its obvious intersection with the cross-axis through the White House strangely vacant.

Construction sputtered along for eight years despite a near-farcical series of delays and complications. Members of the anti-Catholic Know-Nothing party stole a stone donated by Pope Pius IX, and then they wrested control of the Washington National Monument Society, effectively bringing construction to a halt in 1856. The Know-Nothings eventually relented, but by then the country was on the brink of the Civil War and finishing the monument was not a priority. The ensuing hiatus in construction ultimately lasted nearly two decades and is evident in a slight shift in the color of the marble about a third of the way up the monument, owing to the fact that the stone from the original quarry was no longer available when the project resumed.

During the 1870s, amid a growing clamor to do *something* about the mammoth stone stump on the Mall, a spate of revisionism nearly derailed the whole effort. Architects and artists submitted various proposals for the completion of the monument, ranging from Montgomery Meigs's design for an Italian *campanile* to several bizarre and seemingly random proposals, including one modeled after "the better Hindu pagodas." After heated discussion, all these ideas were tossed aside, and the simple shaft continued its fitful rise, following a revised design

This photo of the unfinished Washington Monument was taken around 1860 by Mathew Brady. The monument would not be completed until 1884.

One of the many fanciful proposals from the 1870s for the completion of the Washington Monument, this elaborate tiered design is attributed to Arthur Mathews.

that omitted the circular colonnade at the base. On December 6, 1884, the aluminum capstone was finally set and the monument was dedicated in February of the following year. The result, despite all the drama, is a noble, superbly unpretentious memorial that remains the tallest structure (excepting telecommunications towers) in DC.

The obelisk suffered significant damage during the earthquake that struck the mid-Atlantic region in 2011. Following a restoration, it reopened to visitors in 2014, only to close two years later for elevator repairs. It opened again in 2019, this time boasting a crisp, glassy new entry pavilion, which replaced the embarrassingly perfunctory little shack that had long marred the base of the monument.

B9

World War II Memorial

17th Street between Constitution and Independence Avenues, NW

2004—Friedrich St. Florian; Architects of record: LEO A DALY; Associated architects: Hartman-Cox Architects; Landscape architects: Oehme, van Sweden & Associates; Sculptor: Raymond Kaskey

The World War II Memorial was mired in controversy as soon as it was proposed for this location. The biggest concern was that a large new structure here might interrupt the views between the Washington Monument and the Lincoln Memorial. The competition-winning design called for a plaza surrounding a reconstructed version of the existing Rainbow Pool, flanked by two roughly semicircular arcs with tall columns backed by grassy berms, with enclosed exhibition and program spaces below. Federal design review agencies insisted that the scope of the project be reduced—eliminating, for example, the berms and interior exhibition spaces—but approved the fundamental plan concept. As built, the pared-down design, with a sunken plaza at the center and taller structures kept well off of the main axis, essentially preserves the view corridor.

The lingering questions are ones of architectural expression. The two flanking arcs are defined by parades of identical, blocky piers, each adorned by a pair of bronze wreaths. At the midpoint of each arc is an equally blocky, overscaled pavilion that, sadly, largely conceals a much more interesting *baldacchino*-like sculpture with four slender columns supporting a quartet of spread-wing eagles holding another wreath. Throughout the memorial, in fact, captivating sculptural elements are overwhelmed by the overall design, which is simultaneously mundane and oppressive, and—ironically enough—uncomfortably reminiscent of the overbearing architectural forms associated with the mid-20th-century fascist regimes in Germany and Italy. (In fairness, such forms were not unknown in the United States at that time and experienced something of a revival in the

postmodern era in the 1980s and '90s, but here the symbolism seems particularly unfortunate.)

Then there is the problem of the memorial's iconography. The names of individual states are called out on separate piers, for instance, and each pier stands in a hemicycle labeled either "Atlantic" or "Pacific." This scheme not only suggests an inaccurate connection between each state and a particular theater of war but also implies that state identity was prominent in the public consciousness during a period that was in fact marked by remarkable national unity.

Ultimately, in its stiff classicism, its arbitrary symbolism, and its lack of compelling expressive gestures, the World War II Memorial's impression is not so much fascist as it is merely generic.

B10

Old Canal Lockkeeper's House

Southwest corner of Constitution Avenue and 17th Street, NW

1837—Architect unknown
1915–16—Relocation and restoration: architect unknown
2018—Relocation and restoration: Davis Buckley Architects and Planners

This building is a reminder that, for much of the 19th century, the north side of the Mall was lined by a canal (which was a de facto open sewer in its later years). The canal included locks that allowed boats to negotiate changes in level. The lockkeeper, who collected tolls and operated the lock machinery, lived in this small house.

In 1902, the house was transferred to the Army Corps of Engineers Office of Buildings and Grounds, which later became part of the National Park Service. In 1915–16, the structure was moved about 40 feet to the west when 17th Street was widened. It was subsequently used variously as a watchman's lodge, a tool shed, a "comfort station," and the headquarters of the Park Police. The building was moved again in 2018—this time farther west and slightly south—and restored. It now serves as a welcome center for Constitution Gardens, a subsidiary park within the National Mall, designed by Skidmore, Owings & Merrill and landscape architect

Dan Kiley, which was built in the 1970s and '80s.

About 150 feet south of the Lockkeeper's House is a curving stone-covered wall, mirrored on the other side of 17th Street. The walls are part of the flood-control system that protects the city's core from infrequent but severe Potomac deluges. Movable panels are inserted between the arcs to block rising water.

B11

Vietnam Veterans Memorial

5 Henry Bacon Drive, NW

1982—Designer: Maya Ying Lin; Architects of record: Cooper-Lecky Partnership

One of the most beautiful and moving memorials anywhere, this black granite slash in the Mall is inscribed with the names of Americans killed or missing in the undeclared war in Southeast Asia. Maya Lin, who was still an architecture student when she won the international competition for the memorial, envisioned it as a symbol of regeneration: "Take a knife and cut open the earth," she explained, "and with time the grass will heal it."

Lin's design was revolutionary not only in its simplicity but also in the way that it directly engages visitors. The egalitarian listing of casualties, arranged chronologically by the dates they were killed or reported missing rather than alphabetically or by rank, instantly personalizes the message of the memorial. The texture of the inscribed names compels most visitors to touch the wall, while the reflectivity of the black granite turns each visitor's own image into a virtual part of the sur-

face. (One wing of the memorial is aligned with the Washington Monument and the other with the Lincoln Memorial, and from certain vantage points, the reflections of those two white structures can be seen in the black stone.) The procession from one end to the other—approaching with the top of the wall at one's feet, descending to a point where the wall is over one's head, and then gradually ascending again to ground level—serves as a poignant metaphor for so many aspects of war, grief, and remembrance.

The wall's brilliant minimalism confounded many critics after the design was revealed, and even after it was completed. Various proposals to "heroify" the memorial with more traditional sculptural installations were, fortunately, either dismissed or relegated to a nearby spot out of immediate view. So far, the original has survived intact.

B12

Lincoln Memorial

2 Lincoln Memorial Circle, NW

1922—Henry Bacon; Sculptor: Daniel Chester French; Muralist: Jules Guerin
1995–2000—Restoration: Einhorn Yaffee Prescott; Hartman-Cox Architects
2006—Security upgrades and stone restoration: McKissack & McKissack; Preservation consultants: John Milner Associates

Built on land that did not exist when L'Enfant devised his plan for Washington—or even when Lincoln was president—the Lincoln Memorial is a worthy counterpoint to the Capitol at the other end of the Mall. To some extent, the memorial's dignity defies analysis, but it probably relates as much to Americans' continuing reverence for Lincoln and the structure's incomparable site as it does to the architecture itself.

A movement to erect a monument to Lincoln began almost immediately after his assassination, but there were no significant developments until the Senate

Park Commission of 1901–2 proposed a site at the western end of the Mall, which by then had been extended through landfill. The proposal was controversial: Illinois congressman (and later Speaker of the House) Joseph Cannon bellowed, "I'll never let a memorial to Abraham Lincoln be erected in that God-damned swamp." Around 1908, Daniel Burnham, despite having served on the commission that recommended the Mall site, sketched designs for memorials in front of Union Station and along Delaware Avenue. A few years later, John Russell Pope produced at least seven different proposals, including Greek-inspired temples on Meridian Hill and at the US Soldiers' and Airmen's Home and several uncanny schemes for stepped pyramids on the Mall.

In the end, the commission went to Henry Bacon, whose final design was loosely based on the ancient Parthenon in Athens but different in two key respects: first, he replaced the gabled roof with a flattened and recessed attic, and second, he rotated the plan 90 degrees, abandoning the traditional longitudinal orientation in favor of a transverse position (he also moved the entrance from the short side to the long side). Much of the memorial's emotional power derives from Daniel Chester French's iconic statue of the seated Lincoln, which compellingly portrays the president's anguished resolve. The lateral walls on either side of the sculpture are engraved with the text of two of Lincoln's most eloquent speeches: the Gettysburg Address and his second inaugural address. Light enters the space from above through panels made not of glass but of marble soaked in beeswax in order to enhance its translucence (to understand the rationale for this technique, think of a piece of paper stained with oil and imagine how much more light passes through the greasy spot—the concept behind the beeswax bath is essentially the same). Beneath the memorial is a crypt-like space where visitors could once examine the foundations and substructure, but which is now closed to the public.

The memorial, like Lincoln himself, is a symbol of freedom and has therefore become a popular place for public demonstrations in favor of civil rights and related causes. It was here that Marian Anderson sang after she was turned away from Constitution Hall [see L9], and it was on the steps in front of the memorial that Martin Luther King Jr. matched Lincoln's eloquence with his "I Have a Dream" speech.

B13

Korean War Veterans Memorial

Independence Avenue at Daniel French Drive, SW

1995 — Cooper-Lecky Architects;
Sculptor: Frank Gaylord

The Korean War of 1950–53 has been called "the Forgotten War," at least from the US perspective, overshadowed as it was by World War II and the Vietnam War. An initiative to compensate for the nation's collective oversight and to honor the thousands of Americans who died in the conflict led to the creation of this memorial. The design is based on a competition-winning scheme by a team of faculty members from Pennsylvania State University, but due to controversies that arose during the review process, it was executed without their direct involvement.

Sadly, as built, the memorial itself is also easily forgotten, in part because the design is derivative of more famous projects and suffers by comparison. The black granite mural wall along the southern edge of the site, for instance, obviously evokes the Vietnam Veterans Memorial across the Mall, but it is used to lesser effect here — the collage of sandblasted photographic images lacks the gravitas of Maya Lin's roster of engraved names. The acute angle formed by the Korean memorial's walkways recalls the striking knife-edged prow of I. M. Pei's East Building of the National Gallery of Art, but here the apex is anticlimactic, falling at a seemingly random spot amid the circular Pool of Remembrance. Meanwhile, the 19 overscaled stainless steel statues, which depict soldiers on a routine march, deliberately avoid the heroic sculptural depictions common in war memorials — to some visitors they are more moving as

a result, while to others they assume an unfortunate cartoonish aspect.

As of this writing, efforts are under way to add a Wall of Remembrance, listing names of members of the armed forces who died in the conflict, around the perimeter of the circular pool.

B14

District of Columbia War Memorial

Independence Avenue, SW, between the Korean War Veterans Memorial and the World War II Memorial

1931 — Frederick H. Brooke; Associated architects: Nathan C. Wyeth and Horace W. Peaslee; Landscape architects: Benjamin Franklin Cheatham and James L. Greenleaf
2011 — Restoration: National Park Service, National Mall and Memorial Parks, with Oehrlein & Associates Architects, HCM, and VITETTA

Easily overlooked amid the much larger and more famous memorials that line the Mall, this exquisite neoclassical *tempietto* honors the citizens of the District of Columbia who served in what the inscription calls simply "the World War" — that is, World War I. Designed to double as a stand for commemorative performances by the United States Marine Band, it was the first memorial on the Mall to list the names of Black and female servicemembers alongside those of white men.

B15

Martin Luther King Jr. Memorial

1964 Independence Avenue, SW

2011 — ROMA Design Group; Executive architect: Ed Jackson Jr.; Architects of record: McKissack & McKissack; Landscape architects: Oehme, van Sweden & Associates; Sculptor: Lei Yixin

In his oratorical masterpiece, the "I Have a Dream" speech delivered at the March on Washington for Jobs and Freedom in 1963, Martin Luther King Jr. stated his faith that racial justice would ultimately prevail, adding, "With this faith, we will be able to hew out of the mountain of despair a stone of hope."

That line inspired the competition-winning design for the Martin Luther King Jr. Memorial, sited along the bank of the Tidal Basin on the axis between the Lincoln and Jefferson memorials. Although the specifics of the proposal changed as it went through the official design review process, the fundamental concept remained intact: visitors pass through a cleft "mountain" of white granite, emerging into a crescent-shaped plaza of which the centerpiece is the displaced "stone of hope," which bears a sculpture of King facing the water and the Jefferson Memorial beyond. The land side of the plaza is bordered by an arc of dark granite inscribed with quotations from King's speeches and writings.

The overall concept is powerful, but the design, which was ultimately executed by the memorial's administrative foundation without the input of the original architects, falters in some of its details. Most problematic is the sculpture of King himself, by Chinese artist Lei Yixin (whose selection generated controversy among Black artists and others), which is partially embedded in the block of stone. Besides the boxy, unnatural rendering of King's business suit, the face is not a particularly good likeness. Meanwhile, the sculpting of the "mountain of despair" is a bit amateurish, though the striations on the cleft faces successfully evoke the conceptual tectonic shift of the "stone of hope." Those flaws aside, the completed project is a compelling memorial to Dr. King, and a poignant setting for contemplation.

B16

Franklin Delano Roosevelt Memorial

1850 West Basin Drive, SW

1997 (based on design of 1974) — Lawrence Halprin; Sculptors: Leonard Baskin, George Segal, Robert Graham, and Neil Estern

Franklin Delano Roosevelt supposedly once told Supreme Court justice Felix Frankfurter that if the nation ever wished to erect a monument to him, it should be no larger than his desk. He got that — a

simple marble block by the National Archives—but that seemed inadequate for such a widely revered figure, and in 1955, a special commission was established to bring about a larger memorial on a site near the Mall. An open design competition in 1960 produced a winning project by the New York firm of Pedersen and Tilney, consisting of towering pylons inscribed with quotations from FDR's speeches. It was widely ridiculed as an "instant Stonehenge," however, and rejected by the US Commission of Fine Arts. The same commission conducted another competition, selecting a proposal by Marcel Breuer and Herbert Beckhard, but their design, featuring a pinwheel of granite-clad triangular shards, fared no better.

The third time was a charm—and maybe a curse. Yet another competition, administered by the US Department of the Interior, culminated in 1974 with the selection of a design by landscape architect Lawrence Halprin. His proposal was soon revised, yielding a scheme that was perhaps the opposite of what FDR wanted—an expansive composition of four outdoor "rooms," one for each of Roosevelt's terms as president, spreading across some seven and a half acres. Although this design received all necessary approvals, its scale and estimated cost engendered bitter criticism that raged off and on for 16 years. It was not until 1991 that construction finally began on a scaled-back version of that design. The memorial was dedicated in 1997, more than four decades after Congress formed the commission charged with creating it.

Considering the time that elapsed between the design and its execution, the project turned out surprisingly well. Yes,

it's overscaled and heavy-handed, but the memorial as *landscape* is pleasant, with varied water features, abundant trees, and a balance of material textures. The memorial also features some engaging sculptural elements, including the evocative George Segal piece representing a breadline during the Great Depression. One particularly clever work is the sculpture that shows Roosevelt seated in what appears to be a simple wooden chair, but just beneath his cape one can see the small casters on the chair's legs—an accurate depiction of one of the disabled president's preferred mobility devices. Unfortunately, some detractors decried the fact that the president's disability was not portrayed sufficiently overtly, and an uninspiring sculpture of Roosevelt in a wheelchair was added as an obvious afterthought.

B17

Thomas Jefferson Memorial

16 East Basin Drive, SW

1938–43—John Russell Pope / Eggers & Higgins; Sculptors: Rudulph Evans and Adolph A. Weinman
1995–2000—Restoration: Einhorn Yaffee Prescott; Hartman-Cox Architects
2006—Security upgrades and stone restoration: McKissack & McKissack; Preservation consultants: John Milner Associates
2021—Restoration architects of record: GWWO Architects

Perhaps the culmination of City Beautiful classicism in official Washington, finished 50 years after the World's Columbian Exposition in Chicago launched the movement, the Jefferson Memorial was the subject of intense debate after John Russell Pope's plans were revealed in late 1936. Frank Lloyd Wright and other prominent architects were scandalized by the retrograde design and argued that the famously erudite Jefferson would have preferred a memorial that reflected the technology and ethos of its era. Meanwhile, nonarchitects were upset about the memorial's siting, which would require the removal of many of the famous Japanese cherry trees surrounding the Tidal Basin. Journalists decried the expenditure of vast sums on an "imperial" monument while the country was mired in the Great Depression. Congress revoked the funding for the project, but President Franklin D. Roosevelt eventually pushed it through, and by the time the memorial was nearing completion in 1943, few Americans were worried about the loss of some trees donated by a country with which they were at war.

Pope's design was based on the ancient Roman Pantheon—which had also inspired Jefferson's Rotunda at the University of Virginia—but Pope took liberties with the prototype. In both the Pantheon and the Rotunda, a nearly solid cylinder is attached to a deep Corinthian portico in contrasting materials. At the Jefferson Memorial, the cylinder is instead an open colonnade, and the relatively shallow portico is seamlessly integrated with the cylinder through consistent color and shared column heights. Pope used the Ionic order, which is less formal than the Corinthian order used on the memorial's predecessors.

The result, while anachronistic, has proved to be popular with tourists despite being stranded on the far shore of the Tidal Basin, cut off from the core of the Mall. The best aspect of the memorial is its setting at the edge of the water, especially when the nearby cherry trees—of which the vast majority remain—are in bloom. The second best may be the glimpse of Jefferson's statue through one of the side openings, silhouetted against the sky.

B18
Central Heating Plant
325 13th Street, SW

1934—Paul Philippe Cret

Although it cannot compete with, say, London's Battersea Power Station for

awesome industrial beauty, Paul Philippe Cret's Art Deco–inspired heating plant is remarkably elegant considering its mundane purpose. Note the small sculptural limestone panels flanking the main entrance on 13th Street, which depict the machinery of power production.

B19
United States Holocaust Memorial Museum
100 Raoul Wallenberg Place, SW

1993—Pei Cobb Freed & Partners;
    Associated architects: Notter Finegold
    + Alexander

This haunting structure is America's living memorial to the millions of Jews, homosexuals, prisoners of war, and others murdered by the Nazis in the 1930s and '40s. The brilliance of the architecture lies in its evocation of the veneer of normalcy that cloaked so many aspects of the Holocaust. The exterior of the museum, by virtue of its materials, scale, and simple forms, is disarmingly harmonious with the governmen-

tal buildings surrounding it, as if to remind visitors of the insidious integration of the Holocaust's administrative mechanisms into broader society. The interior is more strongly referential, with blank brick walls, steel bridges, and stark lighting suggesting the industrial architecture of concentration camps. Beneath the ostensible banality there lurks a sinister quality that powerfully frames some of the most affecting exhibitions to be found in any museum.

"You cannot deal with the Holocaust as a reasonable thing," explained architect James Ingo Freed; this "wholly un-American subject" can only be treated in "an emotional dimension." In designing this building, he successfully created an environment in which visitors are inexorably drawn into the personal stories of Holocaust victims and engaged in an intensely emotional experience from which few emerge unmoved.

B20

Sidney R. Yates Federal Building
(former Auditors Main Building)

201 14th Street, SW

1880 — James G. Hill
1902 — Addition: James Knox Taylor
1915 — Renovation: architect unknown
1989 — Renovation: Notter Finegold +
    Alexander Inc. / Mariani, Architects
2014 — Rehabilitation: RTKL Associates

Along with the Smithsonian Castle, the Arts and Industries Building, and the National Building Museum, this is one of the major remnants of the red-brick and -sandstone era in federal architecture. Like its few remaining siblings, the building survived even though its craggy asymmetrical forms soon fell out of favor

with the advent of the City Beautiful movement. Built for the Bureau of Engraving and Printing, it now houses offices of the US Forest Service. The clocks on the tower, which were included in the original design but omitted due to budget constraints, were installed by the US General Services Administration in 2017.

B21

Jamie L. Whitten Federal Building
(US Department of Agriculture main building)

Between Independence Avenue and Jefferson Drive, and 14th and 12th Streets, SW

1908 — Wings: Rankin, Kellogg & Crane
1930 — Central section: Rankin, Kellogg
    & Crane

This federal office building was the first project sited on the south side of the Mall in accordance with the Senate Park Commission Plan of 1901–2. It superseded the earlier Agriculture Department headquarters designed by Adolf Cluss, which was a brick building that stood closer to the Mall's central axis, aligned more or less with the Smithsonian Castle. Controversy raged as to the best location for the new building — it took the direct intervention of President Theodore Roosevelt to stop the department from putting it smack in the middle of the Mall — but the cornerstone was eventually laid here in 1905, on a site previously occupied by greenhouses.

Congress had appropriated funds for a relatively utilitarian building of brick and terra cotta, but Secretary of Agriculture James Wilson favored a stone-clad neoclassical design compatible with the Senate Park Commission's recommendations. Wilson gamed the system by ordering construction to begin on the two wings—which included the most critically needed laboratories—with the central administrative block to come later, funded through a separate appropriation. On the side facing the Mall, within the four pediments on the wings, are rather odd sculptures depicting pairs of naked youths holding escutcheons labeled "Forests," "Cereals," "Flowers," and "Fruits."

B22

Freer Gallery of Art

1050 Independence Avenue, SW

1923—Charles Adams Platt
1990—Interior renovations: Shepley, Bulfinch, Richardson & Abbott; E. Verner Johnson and Associates; and Smithsonian staff architects
1993—Renovations of interiors and courtyard: Cole & Denny / BVH
2014—Renovation of auditorium: Quinn Evans Architects

Charles Lang Freer made a fortune manufacturing railroad cars, but his real interest always lay in art. His collecting focused on the work of contemporary Americans, such as James McNeill Whistler, and on the ancient painting and sculpture of Asia. Freer eventually donated his collection to the Smithsonian along with money to build a museum to house it. He personally hired Charles Adams Platt to design the building and worked closely with him throughout the process.

Freer's art may have been mostly American and Asian, but Platt's building is decidedly European in spirit. Firmly committed to the precepts of the Senate Park Commission Plan of 1901–2, Platt produced an infallibly polite low-rise palazzo sited along Independence Avenue (he surely shared the common assumption that the Smithsonian Castle, which intruded into the central swath of the Mall

declared sacrosanct by the commission, would eventually be demolished). The building's heavy rustication, arches, and pronounced balustrade reflect Platt's interest in Italian Mannerism, most notably the work of the 16th-century Venetian architect Michele Sanmicheli. The Freer is, in fact, the most faithfully derivative of all the buildings on the Mall.

Most of the gallery spaces are austere, though well proportioned and perfectly suited to the display of Freer's art. A highlight of the museum is the Peacock Room, which was designed by architect Thomas Jeckyll and decorated by Whistler for the London house of shipbuilder Frederick Leyland. The room was dismantled and reconstructed in Freer's Detroit mansion, only to be moved again later to its current location in the museum. At the core of the building is a rather intimate courtyard, surrounded by an open loggia.

B23

Quadrangle Museums Project

(Arthur M. Sackler Gallery, National Museum of African Art, and S. Dillon Ripley Center)

Independence Avenue, SW, between the Freer Gallery of Art, the Castle, and the Arts and Industries Building

1987—Shepley, Bulfinch, Richardson & Abbott, based on initial concept by Junzo Yoshimura; Landscape architect: Lester Collins

Designing a new museum complex adjacent to the revered Smithsonian Castle—and nestled between the Victorian Arts and Industries Building and the neoclassical Freer Gallery of Art—would be a challenge under any circumstances. Given that the project also had to accommodate several distinct programmatic components, including new galleries for Asian and African art, a conference center, and offices, this was surely one of the most difficult architectural commissions of the late 20th century.

The conceptual design by Japanese architect Junzo Yoshimura understandably called for placing the bulk of the new facilities underground. After Yoshimura suffered a stroke, the venerable Boston firm of Shepley, Bulfinch, Richardson & Abbott assumed full control of the proj-

ect. For the aboveground structures, lead architect Jean-Paul Carlhian responded to the blizzard of competing styles and functions he faced by using a kind of generic, classically inspired vocabulary. Unfortunately, the resulting buildings are stiff and excessively self-conscious, incorporating blocky granite trim, awkwardly large spherical finials, and a profusion of pyramidal and domed roofs, though the garden itself is a pleasant public space thanks to its changing flora, elegant fountains, and a few relatively engaging works of sculpture.

The most intriguing architectural elements of the complex are the two vertiginous atria, with spiraling stairs, which connect the ground-level pavilions to the facilities below. Once inside the bowels of the museums, however, the visitor is likely to feel a bit claustrophobic and disoriented, faced with a labyrinth of corridors, galleries, and shops. To add to the confusion, the Sackler Gallery is connected underground to the Freer, as the two museums share a single administrative structure.

B24
The Smithsonian Institution Building ("The Castle")

1000 Jefferson Drive, SW

1847–55—James Renwick Jr.
1867, 1884, 1888—Reconstruction and alterations: Adolf Cluss
1970—Restoration: Chatelain, Samperton and Nolan Architects
1999—Exterior restoration and window replacement: Oehrlein & Associates Architects

When James Smithson, a British scientist and son of the first Duke of Northumberland, died in 1829, he left his estate to his nephew. Smithson's will, however, included an odd stipulation: if the nephew should die without heirs, which he did in 1835, then the bulk of the fortune would go to the United States of America—a country Smithson had never visited—for the purpose of founding in Washington "an Establishment for the increase & diffusion of knowledge among men."

Smithson was something of a political radical, who had dismissed the British monarchy as a "contemptible encumbrance" and publicly declared that the future lay with the new democracy across the Atlantic. Nonetheless, American politicians were highly suspicious of Smithson's gift. After a good deal of deliberation and anti-British posturing, Congress finally accepted Smithson's posthumous largesse in 1836, and in 1838, the government received funds totaling

more than $500,000, an enormous sum at the time. The Smithsonian Institution— the exact name was also stipulated in the benefactor's will—was formally established in 1846.

A young James Renwick was soon chosen over more established architects in a competition for the design of the new institution's home. Renwick produced a picturesque "Norman"-style structure with a dramatically asymmetrical skyline that belies its balanced, orderly plan. The Castle, as it came to be called for obvious reasons, originally contained the entire institution, including the residence of the secretary, the Smithsonian's chief executive. It now houses the Smithsonian's Visitor Center, displaying items from the collections of the institution's constituent museums. Notable interior spaces include the airy Great Hall, with its neo-Romanesque faux-stone columns; the elegant Commons, with soaring groin vaults and diamond-shaped skylights; and a small chamber holding the sarcophagus of Smithson himself, whose corporeal remains belatedly followed his money to Washington in 1904.

Like many of its stylistic siblings, the Castle almost fell victim to changing tastes when the Senate Park Commission proposed its plan for the Mall in 1902. The plan called for both the Castle and the neighboring Arts and Industries Building to be razed in favor of Beaux-Arts classical buildings that would toe a rigid line in terms of both architectural style and the physical boundaries of the Mall. They survived, though, and are now beloved for their exceptional (in the true sense of the word) character—bastions of the old brick Washington that survived the classical marble onslaught.

B25

Arts and Industries Building

900 Jefferson Drive, SW

1881—Adolf Cluss and Paul Schulze, with Montgomery C. Meigs; Sculptor: Caspar Buberl

1897–1903—Modifications: Hornblower & Marshall

1976—Restoration: Hugh Newell Jacobsen

1985—Exterior restoration: MMM Design Group / PUDI; Oehrlein & Associates Architects

2014—Restoration: Ennead Architects / SmithGroup

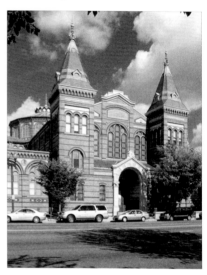

Covering more than two acres, the Arts and Industries Building is one of the largest extant Victorian-era structures in Washington. Initially known as the National Museum building (not to be confused with the National *Building Museum* [see G2]), it was built to house the Smithsonian's growing collection, which had recently expanded with the addition of artifacts from the 1876 Centennial Exposition in Philadelphia.

Montgomery C. Meigs prepared a conceptual plan for the building, calling for a large square structure with a central rotunda. Adolf Cluss and Paul Schulze subsequently won a competition for the actual commission. Their plan was similar to Meigs's, but with an overlaid Greek cross that divided the building into quadrants, which were in turn subdivided into smaller spaces. Both schemes were likely inspired by a well-known "ideal" museum plan developed in the early 1800s by J.-N.-L. Durand, a teacher of architecture at the École polytechnique in Paris.

The polychrome brick building was touted as the least expensive major structure erected by the federal government up to that time, costing less than $3 per square foot (ignoring the costs of mechanical systems and marble floors that were pushed into the following year's budget). Work began in April 1879, some offices were occupied by the end of 1880, and the building was sufficiently finished to host President James Garfield's inaugural ball in March 1881, though temporary floors and furniture had to be installed for the occasion.

Inside, the great trusses, meandering iron balconies, and complex roofing system have a character that is simultaneously industrial and old-timey. Cluss had a seemingly limitless faith in the possibilities of technology, which may help to explain why so many aspects of the structure suggest settings from a Jules Verne novel. Unfortunately, the building gradually lost its raison d'être as its collections were moved to newer, more specialized Smithsonian museum facilities over the course of the 20th century, and it was closed in 2004. Following a restoration, it reopened in 2015 as a venue for special programs and events. The building has been discussed as the possible site of a future museum of Latino history and culture, but as of this writing, its fate remains uncertain.

B26

Hirshhorn Museum and Sculpture Garden

Independence Avenue at 7th Street, SW

1974—Skidmore, Owings & Merrill
1981—Redesign of Sculpture Garden:
Lester Collins

1993—Redesign of plaza: James Urban
2005—Restoration of fountain: architrave, p.c., architects

At the opening of the Hirshhorn Museum, the legendary S. Dillon Ripley, secretary of the Smithsonian, declared that if the building "were not controversial in almost every way, it would hardly qualify as a place to house contemporary art." If that was Ripley's wish, it certainly came true. For decades, Washingtonians and visitors alike have scoffed at the museum's blank façade and its disregard for the Mall's prevailing rectilinear classicism. Indeed, it is easy to dismiss the Hirshhorn as a glorified bunker—especially considering the dark horizontal slit on the Mall side that looks as though it might produce 16-inch gun barrels at any moment—but a more careful consideration of the building reveals a number of things to like.

Designed by Skidmore, Owings & Merrill partner Gordon Bunshaft, the Hirshhorn is actually a doughnut in plan, with a central courtyard focused on an eccentric (in the geometrical sense) bronze fountain. In contrast to the almost completely solid perimeter, the internal façade is a grid of windows behind which are corridor-like galleries—mostly for sculpture—that hug the inside of the doughnut on the second and third levels. This arrangement makes for a circulation pattern that is both clear (since visitors

easily return to where they started) and pleasant (since the corridors are naturally lit and punctuated by art). The window-less perimeter galleries are well suited to paintings and other artworks that are sensitive to light. While the gently curving walls can be awkward for hanging large works, the upside is that they lend a sub-tle panoramic quality to art installations.

Across Jefferson Drive is the Hirsh-horn's sunken garden for large-scale modern sculptures, one of the finest such collections in the United States. The gar-den was originally designed by Bunshaft to span the Mall but was scaled back following a public outcry. As reworked by Lester Collins, it is a handsome enclave in which the landscape design and the sculptures complement each other. The Hirshhorn is currently seeking the approval of design review agencies for another makeover of the garden, this time by artist Hiroshi Sugimoto. S. Dillon Ripley would not be surprised to learn that the proposal is controversial in almost every way.

B27

Orville and Wilbur Wright Federal Buildings
(former Federal Office Buildings 10A and 10B)

800/600 Independence Avenue, SW

1962 — Holabird & Root; Associated architects: Carroll, Grisdale, and Van Alen; Design for Business

It would be easy to walk by these two boxy, buttoned-up buildings without giving them a second glance, dismiss-ing them as typical mid-20th-century bureaucratic architecture. But look again. Note the almost perfectly planar façades,

which could have been quite dull if not for the lustrous white marble cladding, the natural veining of which adds subtle organic patterns to the rigidly geometrical surfaces. Also consider the windows, which appear from afar to be monotonous squares, but in fact are each composed of three different-size panes that modulate their scale. The contrasting treatments of the two buildings' ground floors also add a little variety.

Containing offices of the Federal Avia-tion Administration, the two buildings were renamed for the Wright brothers in 2004. Before 1850, a portion of the site on which the Orville Wright Building now sits was occupied by William H. Williams's notorious "Yellow House"—a holding pen for slaves—which Solomon Northup described in his 1853 memoir *Twelve Years a Slave*.

B28

National Air and Space Museum

Between Independence Avenue and Jefferson Drive, and 7th and 4th Streets, SW

1976 — Hellmuth, Obata + Kassabaum
1988 — Addition: Hellmuth, Obata + Kassabaum

This blandly monumental building is laudable mostly for staying out of the way and allowing the museum's awe-inspiring artifacts to speak for themselves. From the Wright brothers' "Flyer" of 1903, to Charles Lindbergh's *Spirit of St. Louis*, to the *Apollo 11* command module, the hangar-like halls brim with historic air-planes, spacecraft, and related objects. The idea of hanging airplanes from the trusts now seems obvious, but it was an innovative design move when employed here for the first time at a significant scale.

The museum's exterior subtly plays off of nearby buildings. For example, Gyo Obata designed the north façade as a series of projecting and recessed bays, geometrically complementing the pattern of bays on the National Gallery of Art's south façade across the Mall—a kind of abstracted version of the yin and yang. The two buildings also shared a distinctive pinkish Tennessee marble (now being replaced with a gray granite on this structure). Meanwhile, the dark, horizontal recesses near the tops of the Air and Space Museum's stone-faced blocks recall the similar slit in the Hirshhorn next door.

In 1988, a glassy restaurant was appended to the east end of the building, with a sloping, stepped roof that offsets the chunky quality of the main structure. As of this writing, a comprehensive renovation of the museum by Quinn Evans Architects is under way. The most significant exterior change will be the addition of a swoopy entrance canopy, evocative of a bird in flight, facing the Mall.

B29

Dwight D. Eisenhower Memorial
540 Independence Avenue, SW

2020 — Gehry Partners / AECOM Joint Venture; Sculptor: Sergey Eylanbekov; Tapestry: Tomas Osinski

To the casual observer, the public squabble that ensued after the announcement of Frank Gehry's competition-winning design for the Dwight D. Eisenhower Memorial pitted the awesome forces of radical modernism against equally formidable advocates of reactionary neoclassicism. Um . . . no.

Eschewing his signature metallic squiggles, Gehry's proposal called for a flat plaza surrounded by a parade of colossal cylindrical columns supporting scrim-like "tapestries" of perforated metal. Within the plaza would be masonry blocks and panels with figural sculptures and the usual carved inscriptions. Except for the audacious metal tapestries, the overall effect was actually quite conservative . . . even classical.

Some members of the Eisenhower family expressed concerns about the design, including specific depictions of the former president and the potential

for wind-borne debris to be caught in the perforated metal screens—legitimate questions that did not necessarily entail a wholesale rejection of Gehry's approach. Meanwhile, in an attempt to promote a more overtly classical alternative, an unrelated organization sponsored its own alternative competition, the winner of which was a ludicrous triumphal arch. Some news outlets devoted unwarranted coverage to the counterproposal, often without critiquing the use of an architectural form associated with some of history's most ruthless emperors to honor a 20th-century American general and president.

Gehry's design underwent numerous changes through years of official design review, but the core concepts are still evident in the built memorial. The columns surrounding the plaza were retained but reduced in number, and the metal screens were scaled back. The sculptural elements within the plaza were simplified.

By day, unfortunately, the finished memorial appears overscaled and underwhelming. The imagery embedded in the one remaining "tapestry" is unintelligible, making the huge screen appear to be a purely practical device to obscure the view of the building behind it. The two isolated columns on the Independence Avenue side, which now support nothing, look like unfinished, under-designed monumental pedestals awaiting their statues. The sculptural blocks within the plaza are crudely composed and uninteresting.

By night, however, the memorial comes alive. The image in the screen—a depiction of the coast of Normandy, where Eisenhower led the invasion that changed the course of World War II—is both legible and visually stunning. The weaknesses of the memorial's design fade away amidst the entrancing glow of this decidedly modern tapestry.

B30
National Museum of the American Indian

Between Maryland Avenue and Jefferson Drive, and 4th and 3rd Streets, SW

2004—Architect and project designer: Douglas Cardinal; Design architects: GBQC Architects and Johnpaul Jones; Project architects: Jones & Jones Architects and Landscape Architects, and SmithGroup, in association with Lou Weller and the Native American Design Collaborative, and Polshek Partnership Architects; Landscape architects: Jones & Jones Architects and Landscape Architects, and EDAW

2020—National Native American Veterans Memorial: Harvey Pratt in association with Butzer Architects and Urbanism

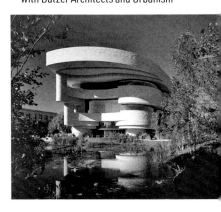

The National Museum of the American Indian (NMAI) stands out among the buildings on the Mall thanks to its organic form and evocative symbolism. The museum's curvilinear façades, covered in rough-hewn Kasota limestone, were designed to suggest natural rock formations sculpted by wind and rain over millennia—an allusion to the importance of the natural landscape in Indigenous cultures. The coarse curves also establish a dramatic contrast to the intensely angular, impeccably honed East Building of the National Gallery of Art directly across the Mall.

The original design for the NMAI was by Douglas Cardinal, a Canadian of Indigenous descent, whose substantial portfolio contains many equally sculptural buildings. Cardinal was removed from the project, however, following a dispute with the Smithsonian administration. Polshek Partnership then took over, working with many of the original team members, but not without controversy. Cardinal claimed that his design was hijacked, though the exterior as executed seems generally true to his intentions. The interior is less successful—the domed atrium space, called simply "the Potomac," is vacuous and a little disorienting, while the galleries and peripheral spaces are generally unmemorable.

The landscape immediately surrounding the NMAI captures a portion of the vast and largely undifferentiated Mall, gently appropriating it for the museum's own identity and programming. The informal arrangement of indigenous plants in the garden is another nod to naturalism. Nestled within the garden are several paved plazas of various scales and uses, including an outdoor amphitheater and the new National Native American Veterans Memorial.

Near Southwest

During the early years of the District of Columbia, when both the Potomac River and the Eastern Branch (later named the Anacostia River) seemed ripe for commercial and military navigation, the land along the riverbanks attracted the interest of real estate speculators. James Greenleaf, who gave his name to the point of land at the convergence of the two rivers (previously known as Turkey Buzzard Point), struck a particularly advantageous deal with the federal commissioners overseeing the newly established District: he was allowed to purchase 3,000 city lots on the cheap in exchange for agreeing to build at least 70 houses on the lots before 1800 and lending the municipal government funds to be used for construction of major public buildings. A development known as Wheat Row resulted from this cozy arrangement, but little else did, since Greenleaf overextended himself and went bankrupt in 1797.

Railroads gradually supplanted shipping as the primary means of transporting goods and people, and the once-thriving Potomac and Anacostia riverfronts entered a long, steady decline. Conditions in DC's inner Southwest quadrant, in particular, deteriorated rapidly in the early 20th century — by World War II, it had degenerated into the city's most notorious slum, in which half the dwellings lacked plumbing. In the 1950s, the District and federal governments took action, embarking on a vast modernization campaign resulting in the demolition of more than 6,000 dwellings.

Urban renewal was a national buzz phrase during that period, as America's struggling cities went under the knife for experimental surgery intended to cure a variety of social maladies. Decades later, many cities are still recuperating from these generally well-intentioned initiatives, and that once-optimistic term — urban *renewal* — has come to symbolize indiscriminate destruction of neighborhoods (squalid though they may have been) in favor of drab, soulless superblocks. Fortunately for Washington, much of the redevelopment in the Southwest quadrant was of unusually high quality, avoiding the pitfalls that plagued many such projects elsewhere. The sensitive social ramifications of urban renewal notwithstanding, several of the housing developments in Southwest DC are among the best works of large-scale urban architecture of their era.

Despite the construction of the Southwest Freeway in the early 1960s, which cut off these residential communities from the governmental and commercial areas adjacent to the Mall, the inner Southwest quadrant remained quietly stable for over a half century. The past decade has brought a new level of vitality to the area with the ongoing construction of the mixed-use District Wharf development, the new Audi Field soccer stadium, and various residential, commercial, and institutional projects on both sides of the freeway. Long overlooked by many Washingtonians, "Near Southwest" is increasingly viewed as a major entertainment destination and a dynamic place to live.

In the late 19th century, the Potomac riverfront adjacent to Washington's Southwest quadrant was an active port.

C1
Museum of the Bible

400 4th Street, SW

1923—Appleton P. Clark Jr.
1983—Conversion into design center:
Keyes Condon Florance Architects;
Associated architects: Bryant & Bryant
Architects
2017—Conversion into museum:
SmithGroupJJR

This building could be the poster child
for adaptive reuse. Built as a refrigerated
warehouse in the 1920s, it was converted
into the Washington Design Center in the
1980s and is now the Museum of the Bible.
Think of it as recycling at a grand scale.

In transforming the building into a
museum, the architects at SmithGroupJJR
(the successor to the firm that oversaw
its previous conversion into a design
center, and now known as SmithGroup)
sought to express both the industrial
history of the existing structure and the
iconography of the new museum's subject
matter—a juxtaposition that would seem
to be a recipe for disaster. Miraculously,
the design team pulled it off. The result is
a palimpsest—the architectural equivalent of a manuscript that bears traces of
multiple versions of a text superimposed
over time. The museum's main entrance,
for instance, which is framed by bronze
panels evoking the typesetting blocks
used to produce the original Gutenberg
Bible, was placed at the point where cargo
trains once entered when the building was
still a warehouse. Just inside the entrance
is the museum's main lobby: a tall, narrow
space that simultaneously re-creates the
warehouse's principal loading area while
evoking the nave of a Gothic or Renaissance church. Meanwhile, the glassy, curvilinear rooftop addition, with its prow-like

western end projecting over the entrance,
recalls the neo-industrial architecture
typical of modern train stations and air-
ports, and yet it also suggests an utterly
abstract rendition of an ancient boat—an
ark, if you will—floating above the city.

As an institution, the Museum of the
Bible has been the subject of controversy
over its collecting practices and the political views of its principal funders, but as a
building, it is a fascinating study in architectural adaptation and interpretation.

C2
DC Consolidated Forensic Laboratory

401 E Street, SW

2012—HOK

This stylishly high-tech building looks as
if it might be home to one of DC's more
illustrious nonprofit organizations or perhaps a forward-looking private company.
It's actually the DC government's central
forensic laboratory, or as the city's web-
site somewhat euphemistically describes
it, a facility providing "critical public
safety and health science infrastructure."
The building's most striking feature is
the automated glass-louvered sunscreen
that modulates daylight and heat gain in
the open offices that lie behind parts of
the fully glazed south façade. The labs
themselves were placed along the north
side, where they enjoy even light throughout the day. The building's elegance and
transparency belie the strict safety and
security protocols necessary in a facility
where evidence of crimes is analyzed.
Just hope that your DNA doesn't end up
under a microscope there anytime soon.

C3

US Department of Housing and Urban Development

(Robert C. Weaver Federal Building)

451 7th Street, SW

1968 — Marcel Breuer and Associates (Marcel Breuer and Herbert Beckhard); Architects of record: Nolen-Swinburne & Associates

1998 — Plaza landscape: Martha Schwartz

2021 — Renovation: BBGM Architects & Interiors, Inc.

The origins of the word *Brutalism* are complicated. It ostensibly derives from the French term *béton brut*, meaning "raw concrete," but one of the earliest works to be labeled Brutalist — the Hunstanton School in Norfolk, England, designed by Alison and Peter Smithson — is mostly finished in glass and steel. Some say the term is related to *Art Brut*, the "raw art" movement. Regardless, the name definitely does *not* derive from the word *brutal*.

You might have trouble convincing the movement's many detractors of that, however. Rightly or wrongly, Brutalism is widely understood to refer to monumental, often overbearing, buildings, typically with façades that include large unrelieved surfaces of concrete (or brick) and characterized by deliberately ungainly, blocky, and usually repetitive massing. A building is not necessarily Brutalist simply because it is made of concrete. Many theoreticians would argue that the movement is about "honesty" in material expression, but at its core, it is perhaps best understood as a purposeful reaction against picturesqueness.

Definitional nuances aside, Marcel Breuer's Housing and Urban Development (HUD) building certainly counts as a work of Brutalism, given its unmodulated scale, its outsized cast-in-place concrete *pilotis* (exposed ground-floor piers), and its relentless grid of precast concrete window units. The windowless ends of the wings are arguably the most Brutalist aspect of the building in their emphasis on purity of form over function, even though they are sheathed not in concrete but in dark granite. Now generally regarded as forbidding and alienating, Breuer's design initially drew critical acclaim as a departure from the boxy structures that had become standard for mid-20th-century government offices.

In plan, the HUD building is a giant stretched X, with a long spine and four bilaterally symmetrical, gently curving appendages. The spaces between the arms of the X are exterior plazas. In the 1990s, HUD commissioned Martha Schwartz to make the primary plaza more attractive as an urban space. The solution is only partially successful. While the hovering translucent doughnuts are jaunty at first glance, they are disengaged from the seating areas, rendering them almost useless as shading devices in sunny weather. The landscape architect had originally planned to introduce bright colors into the composition, but sadly that aspect of the proposal was abandoned.

L'Enfant Plaza

10th Street between Independence and Maine Avenues, SW

1968 — I. M. Pei & Partners (Araldo
Cossutta, partner in charge of design for
office buildings); Landscape architect
for Banneker Park and Circle: Dan Kiley

L'Enfant Plaza was designed during an
era in which heroically scaled, monumental buildings were in vogue, and
governmental authorities commanded
wholesale reconstruction of large urban
areas without a quiver of doubt about
the wisdom of such initiatives. The grand
intentions for this complex are evident not
only in its lofty name, honoring the city's
creator, but also in its enormous scale and
the knot of Metro lines that meet below it.
Conceived as a cultural center of a vibrant
new Southwest Washington, it is instead
a hopelessly sterile precinct (except for
the new International Spy Museum — see
following entry) and, ironically, a blatant
violation of L'Enfant's plan in its disregard
for the street pattern he so thoughtfully
devised.

The hollowness of the development is
most evident in the barren swath running
down the middle of the 10th Street spine
and leading to Banneker Circle — named
for the 18th-century Black surveyor of
the District of Columbia, Benjamin Banneker — which terminates the axis. The
circle was intended as a belvedere, but
there wasn't much to see for the first half
century after it was finished. Now, thanks
to the new Wharf development nearby
[see C6], there are some nice views from
here, and the circle is a link in the pedestrian path between L'Enfant Plaza and the
waterfront, though the design of that path
needs improvement and clarification.

For what it's worth, the individual
buildings in L'Enfant Plaza, though bombastic, are generally well composed and
constructed. The least successful from
an aesthetic standpoint is the Forrestal
Building (1970 — Curtis and Davis Architects and Planners; Fordyce & Hamby
Associates; Frank Grad and Sons), which
houses the US Department of Energy. Its
primary component is a bulky bar that
spans 10th Street, thereby creating a
grudging gateway to the complex. Every
so often, someone proposes tearing down
the whole building, or at least removing
the section that bridges the street. That
would be a step in the right direction.

International Spy Museum

700 L'Enfant Plaza, SW

2019 — Design architects: Rogers Stirk
Harbour + Partners; Architects of
record: Hickok Cole

The new home of the International Spy
Museum is anything but clandestine. The
building's sharply angled façades supported by blood-red struts, its zigzagging
glass curtain wall facing the L'Enfant
Promenade, and its super-scaled red-
and-white signage all shout for attention.

It's noisy, but L'Enfant Plaza was ready for a wake-up call.

Just behind the museum is a new entrance pavilion (2014—SmithGroupJJR) that helped to brighten L'Enfant Plaza's once-dismal underground shopping complex.

C6

District Wharf

Maine Avenue between I-395 and O Street, SW

2014-present — Master plan architects / urban designers: Perkins Eastman, Perkins Eastman DC

2016 — St. Augustine's Episcopal Church: MTFA Architecture

2017 — 1000 Maine: KPF; Architects of record: FOX Architects; The Channel: Perkins Eastman DC; The Anthem: Rockwell Group; 800 Maine Avenue: Perkins Eastman DC; Capital Yacht Club: Cunningham | Quill Architects; 525 Water Condominium: SK+I Architecture; 7th Street Park and Recreation Pier: Michael Vergason Landscape Architects

2018 — Maine Avenue Fish Market renovation and new structures: StudioMB; Landscape architects: Landscape Architecture Bureau; InterContinental Hotel: BBGM; Interior designers: BBGM and Parker Torres Design, Inc.; VIO/Incanto: Handel Architects; Architects of record and interior architects: WDG Architecture; Canopy by Hilton / Hyatt House: SmithGroup; Pier 4: StudioMB

During the late 19th century, the Potomac and Anacostia rivers teemed with tall-masted ships, many of which docked along the riverfront of the city's inner Southwest quadrant. A century later, the only remnants of that maritime past were the venerable Maine Avenue Fish Market and a few marinas for private boats. Freestanding, suburban-style restaurants and motels lined the rest of the Southwest Potomac waterfront.

That area is now being transformed by a multibillion-dollar development called the District Wharf. The first phase, which opened in 2017, has been a smashing success. Comprising rental apartments, condominiums, hotels, restaurants, shops, offices, and entertainment venues strung along a *woonerf*—a pedestrian-oriented thoroughfare also accessible by vehicles—it instantly became a regional draw. Architectural highlights of this phase include the new headquarters of the Capital Yacht Club, an essay in contrasting textures, and the 7th Street Pier, with its public swings and dramatic fire sculpture at its terminus. Just north of the Wharf project is the expanded fish market complex, which includes the restored Lunch Room and Oyster Shed dating to 1918, along with new restaurant pavilions inspired by the site's industrial heritage.

The second phase of the Wharf, currently under construction, promises to be more adventurous from an architectural standpoint, featuring some eye-catching stepped and curvilinear forms.

Riverside Baptist Church / The Banks

699 Maine Avenue, SW / 900 7th Street, SW

2018 — Church: GBR Architects; Apartment building: STUDIOS Architecture

The late 20th century was rough on urban American churches, which lost many of their congregants to the suburbs. For those that could hang on, however, the recent renaissance of American cities has presented unexpected opportunities. On top of potential new congregants moving into the neighborhood, some of these churches have benefited from sharp increases in the value of their real estate and have leapt at the chance to sell or lease parts of their property to fund new sanctuaries for themselves.

The Riverside Baptist Church struck such a deal with the developers of the District Wharf across the street, replacing the church's charming but dated A-frame sanctuary and erecting a 173-unit apartment building next door. Designed by different architecture firms, the two buildings complement each other. The church has a wall of glass facing the Wharf, affording glimpses of the river through 7th Street Park. The 7th Street façade includes a stone-covered wall segment with a vertical slit window and a narrow horizontal band of contrasting stone creating an implied cross. On the apartment building, the irregular window grid, bush-hammered precast concrete panels, and intricately patterned balcony railings add interest to the façades, while geometrical shifts in the plan reflect the building's position at the juncture between the waterfront zone and the core of the Southwest neighborhood.

Arena Stage at the Mead Center for American Theater

1101 6th Street, SW

1961 — Fichandler Stage: Harry Weese & Associates
1970 — Kreeger Theater: Harry Weese & Associates
2010 — Mead Center, including renovation of existing theaters: Bing Thom Architects

Arena Stage, according to the organization's mission statement, produces "all that is passionate, exuberant, profound, entertaining, deep and dangerous in the American spirit." It might seem surprising that a nonprofit cultural institution would court danger so brazenly, but Arena Stage has a history of taking risks. Founded in 1950, it was one of the first private nonprofit theaters in the country, and *the* first theater in Washington to be racially integrated. Its original home, a former burlesque house downtown, was notable for its innovative theater-in-the-round layout.

In 1961, Arena moved to a custom-built facility designed by Chicago architect Harry Weese in the Southwest urban renewal area. The building was monumental, abstract, and rather off-putting, but it maintained the theater-in-the-round format that had become an Arena hallmark. Weese later designed an addition, including a second auditorium with a proscenium stage, using the same architectural vocabulary.

In the late 1990s, Arena Stage hired Vancouver-based Bing Thom Architects (now Revery Architecture Inc.) to oversee an expansion. Because the complex was a locally designated historic site, key elements—namely, the two main theater spaces—had to be preserved. Thom's solution was to demolish the administrative wing of the Weese-designed complex and renovate the two existing auditoriums, encapsulating them within a larger structure lined with soaring glass walls and topped by a vast but seemingly weightless roof. Supporting the roof are canted wood-composite columns with struts that brace the sinuously curved curtain wall. Nestled between the older structures is a small new theater called the Arlene and Robert Kogod Cradle—the term *cradle* refers to both its oval shape and the fact that it is intended as an incubator for future plays. Curving stairs lead to an upper-level café and an outdoor terrace shielded by an acutely angled 90-foot cantilever pointing toward the Washington Monument in the distance.

The design of the enlarged complex is certainly idiosyncratic, and some elements, such as the tilted wood-composite columns, look like they might be more at home in Washington State than in Washington, DC, but the building is a lively and sophisticated presence in a neighborhood that sorely needed a jolt of architectural energy at the time.

C9

1000/1100 6th Street, SW, and 1001/1101 3rd Street, SW
(former Town Center Plaza)

1962—I. M. Pei & Partners
2008—Renovation of 6th Street towers: Esocoff & Associates | Architects

I. M. Pei designed four identical towers—two on 3rd Street and two on 6th Street—which were divided by the now-demolished Waterside Mall. The towers' façades exhibit a subtle balance of horizontal and vertical lines: concave grooves in the edges of the floor slabs emphasize the former, while the slender columns, split into pairs above the ground floor with operable windows between them, provide the vertical counterpoint. The concrete structure was cast in place using plastic-coated plywood and fiberglass formwork, yielding unusually smooth finishes.

C10

Tiber Island Cooperative Homes / Carrollsburg Square Condominium

4th Street between M and N Streets, SW

1965—Keyes, Lethbridge & Condon
1993—Concrete restoration: architrave, p.c., architects

The design for this complex by Keyes, Lethbridge & Condon was selected in a competition conducted by the Redevelopment Land Agency. In several respects, such as the inclusion of both towers and town houses and the incorporation of a web of small outdoor spaces, these projects are similar to Capitol Park [see C16]. These buildings have a very different character, though, especially evident in the brick-and-precast-concrete town houses, which draw more directly from the local domestic vernacular than does the relatively abstract Capitol Park.

C11
Thomas Law House
(Honeymoon House)
1252 6th Street, SW

1796—Attributed to William Lovering
ca. 1938—Addition: architect unknown
1965—Restoration: Keyes, Lethbridge &
   Condon and Chloethiel Woodard Smith
   & Associates

Soon after land speculator James
Greenleaf bought 3,000 lots from the
DC commissioners in 1793, he formed a
"syndicate" with Robert Morris, a Pennsylvania banker and US senator, and
John Nicholson, a former comptroller
general of Pennsylvania. The syndicate
built several of the oldest extant houses
in the city, including this one, which was
briefly leased to British merchant Thomas
Law and his wife, Elizabeth Parke Custis
Law, eldest granddaughter of Martha
Washington and her first husband, Daniel
Parke Custis. The Laws lived here during
their "honeymoon" while a new house
was being custom-built for them. Thomas
Law, who bought millions of square feet
of property from the syndicate, suffered
financial setbacks in later years, but he
fared better than Greenleaf, Morris, and
Nicholson, all of whom ended up in debt-
ors' prison.

The generously sized house, perched
atop a raised basement, exemplifies the
understated architecture of the Federal
period (corresponding to the first few
decades of the American republic). The
principal façade, which faces the river,
is symmetrical and almost perfectly flat,
relieved only by the shallow cornice and
stone trim, including a band that links the
inset arched windows and central doorway on the first floor. The cast iron porch
and asymmetrical staircase were likely
added in the mid-19th century. Except
for a stint as a hotel during the 1860s, the
house remained a private residence until
1965, when it became a community center
for the Tiber Island and Carrollsburg
Square apartment complexes. It was sold
in 2017 to an unknown buyer.

C12
Harbour Square / Wheat Row
**500 N Street, SW / 1313–1321 4th Street,
SW**

ca. 1794—Wheat Row: attributed to
   William Lovering
1966—Harbour Square and renovation of
   Wheat Row: Chloethiel Woodard Smith
   & Associates; Landscape architect:
   Dan Kiley

Wheat Row, named for John Wheat (who
lived at number 1315) and financed by
wheeler-dealer James Greenleaf, may be
the oldest surviving set of row houses in
the city. Saved and renovated when most
of the neighborhood was destroyed during the urban renewal era, these Federal-
style houses (along with a couple of other
historic houses around the corner of N
Street) were incorporated into the new
Harbour Square complex, the centerpiece
of which is a large reflecting pool with a
causeway-like pedestrian bridge. From
certain vantage points, passing pedestrians can see little hexagonal pavilions
atop several of the towers—these provide

access to private roof decks for upper-level apartments.

About one block down from Wheat Row, and right along the waterfront, is the sublimely beautiful Women's *Titanic* Memorial, by Gertrude Vanderbilt Whitney, which honors the men on the doomed ship who sacrificed their lives so that women and children could be saved.

C13

River Park

Between 4th Street and Delaware Avenue, and N and O Streets, SW

1963 — Charles M. Goodman Associates
2005 — Façade restorations: Ritter Norton
Architects

Quietly sitting in Southwest Washington is one of the most innovative modernist urban developments anywhere in the country — an enclave of apartment towers and town houses in which aluminum is featured as a structural and ornamental material. Most notable are the town houses, many of which are improbably and entertainingly capped with wafer-thin barrel vaults. The use of aluminum reflects the role of the developer: none other than the Reynolds Aluminum Service Corporation, eager to promote the use of its parent company's products in the many urban redevelopment projects then under way across the country.

Charles Goodman helped pioneer modernist architecture in Washington, but his national reputation was limited, probably because aspects of his work — such as those whimsical barrel vaults — did not always fit comfortably with International Style orthodoxy. His greatest work is arguably Hollin Hills, an entire neighborhood of sleek single-family houses in suburban Virginia.

C14

King Greenleaf Recreation Center

201 N Street, SW

2005 — Devrouax + Purnell Architects

The curving and angled forms of this public recreation center contrast with the rectilinearity that was typical of the mid-20th-century modern architecture in the Southwest urban renewal area. Glass walls allow views from the park into the basketball court and other interior spaces; in the evenings, the glow emanating from the building advertises its role as a gathering place for the neighborhood.

C15

The Aya

850 Delaware Avenue, SW

2019 — Studio Twenty Seven
Architecture / LEO A DALY JV

The DC government has emerged as a significant patron of innovative architecture over the past decade, commissioning dozens of widely acclaimed public libraries and schools. The Aya, which is part of Mayor Muriel Bowser's initiative to build

a short-term housing facility for homeless families in each of the city's eight
wards, reflects a similar commitment to
design excellence. It is the type of project
that could easily have been relegated to
a dispiriting institutional structure but
instead yielded an uplifting work of architecture that provides a humane environment for its users.

The east and south façades of the
Aya are visually striking thanks to their
irregular grids of windows, offset from
floor to floor, along with balconies on the
east façade that are partially shielded by
brick screen walls (which recall those
on the apartment buildings of Capitol
Park—see following entry). The building's greatest surprise, however, is the
angled and stepped west façade, whose
design derives from the triangular shape
of the site combined with floor plans that
shift as the building rises to accommodate
dwelling units of different sizes (since, of
course, resident families are of different
sizes themselves). The north façade is
almost all glass, affording views from the
adjacent communal rooms toward the
Capitol Dome in the distance.

C16

Capitol Park

Between G, I, 1st, and 4th Streets, SW

1958–63—Satterlee & Smith / Chloethiel
Woodard Smith and Associates;
Landscape architect: Dan Kiley

The first of the major modern housing
developments built in Southwest Washington, Capitol Park is a complex of
apartment towers and town houses, creating a diverse yet aesthetically cohesive
community. The apartment blocks are
distinguished by their decorative masonry
screens and shifting patterns of openings
from floor to floor, but it is the town house
clusters that make this project extraordinary, thanks to their intricate networks
of courtyards, pathways, and gardens.
Although thoroughly modern in their
materials and architectural expression,
these buildings and spaces evoke the
mysterious qualities typical of streetscapes in medieval European towns—quiet
and modestly scaled but richly layered
and full of small surprises.

This project is also noteworthy as one
of the earliest major American urban-
scale projects designed by a woman.
Chloethiel Woodard Smith was a pioneer
not just by virtue of her sex but also
because of the inventiveness and finesse
of her work.

As of this writing, another innovative
new DC Public Library branch (this one
by Perkins&Will) is nearing completion
nearby at 3rd and I Streets.

Capitol Riverfront

When the Washington Navy Yard was established in 1799, it was sited not along the Potomac River but along the Eastern Branch, later known as the Anacostia River. Its location reflected the widespread assumption that the Anacostia would become the city's principal waterway, since it was then readily navigable and ran relatively close to the Capitol at the center of L'Enfant's plan. An initial burst of industrial and commercial development along the river's northern bank never turned into a sustained boom, however, in part because the river silted up in the mid- to late 19th century. By the 20th century, it was horribly polluted and was often cited as a symbol of America's urban ills.

In 2000, the DC government launched the Anacostia Waterfront Initiative, intended to clean up the river, restore the natural ecosystem of its watershed, and spur revitalization of areas on both sides of the river. Local residents were initially quite skeptical, but within a decade, the environmental reclamation effort was showing significant progress. The completion in 2008 of a ballpark for Washington's new major league baseball team, just a block from the river along South Capitol Street, was heralded as a catalyst for future development.

Those heralds proved to be correct. Before long, private developer Forest City Washington was awarded the right to redevelop the former Navy Yard Annex, an area covering more than 40 acres between the ballpark and the Washington Navy Yard itself. Named "The Yards," this development has quickly become a thriving mixed-use neighborhood. At its heart is the Yards Park, designed by landscape architect M. Paul Friedberg, which incorporates fountains, a jaunty pedestrian bridge, and outdoor performance venues. It connects into the Anacostia Riverwalk.

The Yards is part of a larger neighborhood that has come to be known as Capitol Riverfront, which is the focus of this chapter. For now, it is a relatively small tour, with only nine entries. There is every reason to expect, however, that this neighborhood will sprout more architecturally significant sites as it continues to develop. Already in the works are two exciting infrastructure projects that will bracket the area. Nearing completion is the new Frederick Douglass Memorial Bridge, designed by AECOM, whose graceful arches will carry South Capitol Street across the river. On the horizon is the planned 11th Street Bridge Park, designed by OMA and OLIN, which will use the extant piers of a former bridge as the foundation for a linear park conceived as both a physical and a cultural link between the neighborhoods on either side of the Anacostia, which has long marked a dramatic socioeconomic divide.

City of Washington from beyond the Navy Yard, an engraving by W. J. Bennett, depicts the Anacostia waterfront in the 1830s. The two large structures on the riverbank are part of the Navy Yard, while the large flag just to the right marks the Marine Barracks nearby. The Capitol stands on the hill behind them, and the White House is faintly visible in the left background.

D1

Nationals Park

1500 South Capitol Street, SE

2008 — HOK / Populous / Devrouax +
    Purnell Architects, a Joint Venture;
    Associated architects for interiors:
    Bowie Gridley Architects

When Baltimore's Oriole Park at Camden
Yards opened in 1992, people of diverse
architectural tastes praised the ballpark—
largely for not looking like a wayward UFO
as had so many of its modernist predecessors. Its success as a catalyst for
urban redevelopment inspired a generation of historicist ballparks and stadiums
in cities across the country. By the time
Washington finally got a professional
baseball team again in 2005, however, the
retro stadium trend seemed to have run
its course.

Nationals Park is decidedly modern
in its form, materials, and environmental
profile. It was the first major professional
sports stadium to be LEED (Leadership in
Energy and Environmental Design) cer-
tified, thanks in part to a large green roof
area over concession structures, energy-
efficient field lighting, and substantial
reliance on recycled materials. To maintain the more intimate feel of some of
the retro ballparks, Nationals Park was
conceived as a series of "neighborhoods,"
each with a distinct layout and unique
sightlines. The main concourse, rather
than being raised as in many modernist
stadiums, is at roughly the same level as
the sidewalk outside, so many fans do
not have to climb ramps or stairs to get to
their seats.

Despite these thoughtful touches, some
aspects of the ballpark's design, such as

the bulky parking garages facing N Street
and the rather amorphous plaza along
Potomac Avenue, are regrettable. Fortunately, there are proposals to infill parts
of that plaza with food service pavilions
that could enhance the streetscape, and
given the burgeoning mixed-use development surrounding the ballpark, there is
reason to hope that the ground levels of
the garages might soon be filled in with
more pedestrian-friendly amenities.

D2

West Half

1201 Half Street, SE

2019 — ODA Architecture; Architects of
    record: Eric Colbert & Associates PC

The essence of urbanism is interconnect-
edness. By that measure, this new building contributes to its neighborhood in
several ways. First, of course, is its mix of
uses, including retail and restaurants on
the ground floor and apartments above.
Second, and of most interest architecturally, are the staggered, projecting window
bays and balconies, with their bright
yellow undersides, which animate the
façades and blur the boundary between
indoors and outdoors, between public and

private space. Finally, and less evident from the ground, is the building's stepped massing, which allows direct views from upper-floor apartments and common amenity spaces into the ballpark across the street. As with the famous ad hoc viewing stands built atop several build-ings next to Chicago's Wrigley Field, these private overlooks may represent lost ticket income for the stadium owners and teams, but they help to create a sense of visual and functional reciprocity that adds life and interest to urban living.

D3
DC Water Headquarters
1385 Canal Street, SE

2018 — SmithGroup; Associate architects: Leuterio Thomas, LLC; Landscape architects: OEHME, van SWEDEN | OvS

The sinuously curved new headquarters of DC Water may seem like a sculptural flight of fancy, but the building's form is actually a pragmatic response to the unique constraints of its site and the client agency's program. The curvilinear plan emerged in part as a means of protecting two existing elements of the site: a mid-20th-century pumping station that had to remain fully operational during and beyond construction, and a fragile web of tunnels and related infrastructure running underground. Having arrived at the basic plan, the architects then manipulated the building's massing and skin in order to optimize daylighting and to control solar heat gain in interior spaces. The seem-ingly random variations in the building envelope, including projecting upper floors facing the riverfront, secondary layers of glass over certain sections of the curtain wall, and modulations in the color of metal panels at the sides and rear, in fact derive from careful digital modeling of the building to simulate various envi-ronmental conditions. Happily, they also yield a visually rich building that, like its historic neighbor [see following entry], demonstrates that civic architecture and infrastructure can be beautiful.

D4
DC Water Main Pumping Station
Canal Street at N Place, SE

1907 — C. A. Didden and Son; Associate architect: Oscar Vogt
Numerous renovations and small additions

Hidden in plain sight for decades, this Beaux-Arts pumping station for the water and sewer authority suddenly finds itself in the thick of the redeveloping Capitol

Riverfront district. The design suggests the influence of the City Beautiful movement and, more directly, of the Senate Park Commission Plan of 1901–2, which sought to elevate the quality of public buildings of all types. Although the ornamental motifs tend to be simplified versions of what one would expect to see on, say, a bank or school from that era—note, for example, the plain disks embedded in the pilaster capitals at the northern end of the building—the overall effect is elegant and striking.

D5

The Lumber Shed

301 Water Street, SE

1940s—Architect unknown
2013—Renovation: Gensler

This open-air structure was used by the US Navy for drying lumber during World War II and originally included railroad tracks running down the middle to allow direct loading and unloading of material. The pavilion was enclosed in glass as part of its adaptation to retail and office use. At night, when the building is lit from within, its muscular concrete frame suddenly becomes visible like a skeleton on an X-ray.

D6

Boilermaker Shops

300 Tingey Street, SE

1919—Architect unknown
2012—Renovation and addition: Gensler

With its stepped roof, copious clerestory windows, and soaring linear interior, this former naval ship boiler factory comes off a bit like an industrial cathedral. In adapting the long-abandoned and dilapidated structure for a mix of retail and office uses, the renovation architects sought to preserve the sense of the voluminous interior, using glass partitions wherever possible and inserting a second floor that appears to float within the space. The result is reminiscent of the traditional food markets that dotted the city in the late 19th century.

D7

Washington Canal Park

200 M Street, SE

2012—STUDIOS Architecture; Landscape architects: OLIN

This linear park retraces a three-block-long section of the erstwhile Washington City Canal, which was paved over around the turn of the 20th century. The landscape design recalls the site's watery past, incorporating a system of underground cisterns and grade-level rain gardens that capture and filter storm water, recycling it for use in irrigation and in an interactive fountain on the southernmost block (which is converted into an open-air ice-skating rink in winter). The park pavilions, which accommodate food service, skate rental facilities, and storage, subtly evoke the barges that once plied the canal. At night, the translucent cubes at either end of the park are backlit to create giant lan-

terns; the acrylic panels on the larger cube at the southern end can also serve as rear-projection screens for video imagery.

D8

The Blue Castle
(former Washington and Georgetown Railroad Car House; now the National Community Church–Capitol Hill)

770 M Street, SE

1891—Walter C. Root
1902—Addition: architect unknown
2019—Renovation of theater: MTFA
  Design + Preservation
2021—Renovation of daycare: INTEC Group

Long before it was drenched in lurid blue paint, this building was one terminus of the city's first streetcar line, reflecting the importance of the Navy Yard as an employment center. Like its counterparts in Georgetown [see M30] and Capitol Hill [see E12], this car barn was designed in a Romanesque Revival style, but it is much less formal than the others, with playful little turrets sprouting from exaggerated round towers facing the street corner. The church that bought the building in 2014 has adapted the interior for ecclesiastical and performance uses and has plans for more changes down the road.

D9

Washington Navy Yard, Latrobe Gate

8th and M Streets, SE

1806—Benjamin Henry Latrobe
1881—Addition: architect unknown

Established in 1799, this is America's oldest extant naval base. It was a major shipbuilding center until the 1830s and remained Washington's most significant manufacturing facility throughout the 19th century. Early construction on the base was spotty until 1803, when Benjamin Henry Latrobe assumed supervision of its development in his new capacity as sur-veyor of public buildings. Shortly after his appointment, Latrobe designed the yard's brick entrance gate at the base of 8th Street, one of the earliest works of Greek Revival architecture in the United States. The gate was altered many times, most notably in the 1880s when a three-story Victorian structure was built around and over it. Sometime later, the entire structure was covered in stucco and painted white. If you can do so without having the guards shoo you away, take a peek through the central metal gates to see the perfectly semicircular arch at the other end of the passageway, which, unusually, springs directly from the ground.

Residential Capitol Hill

Capitol Hill is synonymous with the legislative branch of the US government, but in local parlance, the term also refers to the adjacent, mostly residential, neighborhood to the east of the Capitol. The juncture between the two faces of Capitol Hill can be strikingly abrupt, as along the unit block of 2nd Street, NE, where modest, privately owned row houses stand directly across from the seat of the highest court in the nation.

The city's founders assumed that this area would become the primary locus of nongovernmental development, since it was convenient to both the Capitol and the port facilities along the Anacostia River (then known as the Eastern Branch). Perhaps, however, they underestimated the attraction of executive authority, because over time the White House, rather than the Capitol, became the center of gravity for Washington real estate. Ultimately, the city's commercial and residential development surged in the Northwest quadrant, leaving the residential part of Capitol Hill a surprisingly quiet enclave despite its proximity to many of the nation's most important institutions.

Although the neighborhood suffered a disheartening period of high crime rates and other urban ills in the mid- to late 20th century, Capitol Hill never lost its sense of community. For decades it has been beloved by residents for its ethnic diversity. Today, despite rising housing prices and demographic homogenization, "the Hill" remains a vibrant and highly sought-after place to live.

This 1992 aerial view of Stanton Park looking toward the northwest shows the dense texture of the Capitol Hill neighborhood.

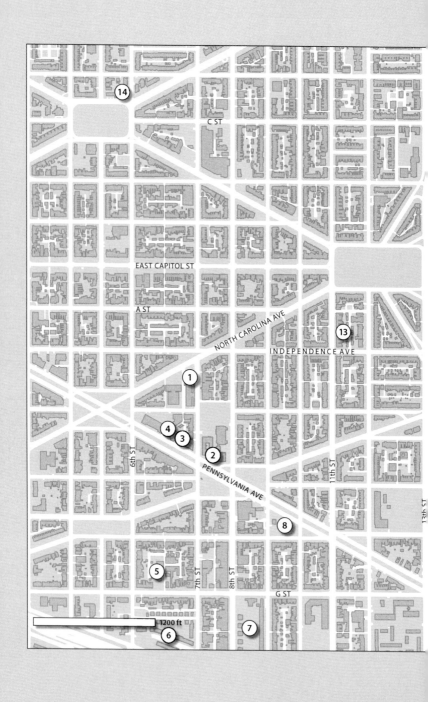

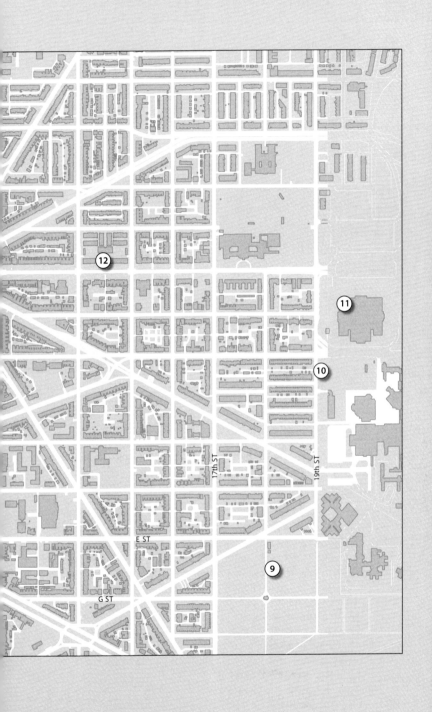

E1

Eastern Market

225 7th Street, SE

1873 — South Hall: Adolf Cluss
1908 — North Hall: Snowden Ashford
ca. 1974 — Renovation: Hans-Ullrich
  Scharnberg Architects
2009 — Rehabilitation: Quinn Evans
  Architects

Washington once boasted a number of these airy markets offering fresh produce, flowers, and other goods, including the Georgetown Market [see M28] and the O Street Market [see Q22]. Eastern Market is the only survivor still functioning as a municipal market in the traditional sense. Many Capitol Hill residents consider it to be the unofficial center of their neighborhood.

The oldest part of this building was designed by the German-born Adolf Cluss, one of Washington's most prolific mid-19th-century architects. An avid communist and close friend of Karl Marx (until they had a falling out in 1853), Cluss later was chided by his fellow travelers for becoming an "America-enthusiast," especially after he attained US citizenship in 1855 and received a substantial inheritance in 1857. He went on to hold several appointed positions with the federal and District of Columbia governments, and he designed or renovated at least 67 buildings, including schools, churches, hospitals, office buildings, and houses.

The façades of the Cluss-designed portion of the market are animated by a distinctive pattern of alternating arched and bull's-eye windows that provide light for the stalls inside. Corbelled brick brackets just below the cornice lend a faint Moorish quality to the structure while casting sharp, dramatic shadows on a bright day. The 1908 addition at the north end continues the arched-window motif, but in a more regular and subdued fashion. A cast iron shed, intended to shelter vendors, runs along the 7th Street edge of the site and visually ties the two wings together.

Eastern Market was heavily damaged by a fire in April 2007 but reopened in 2009 following an extensive rehabilitation. By virtually all accounts from vendors and patrons, the market is now more efficient, pleasant, and sustainable than ever.

E2

700 Penn / The Residences at Eastern Market

700 Pennsylvania Avenue, SE / 777 C Street, SE / 333 8th Street, SE

2017 — Weinstein Studio / Esocoff &
  Associates / Gensler; Landscape
  architects: OEHME, van SWEDEN | OvS

The renowned modernist architect Louis Kahn said, "A brick wants to be something. It aspires. Even a common, ordinary brick . . . wants to be something more than it is." Legions of aspirational bricks found fulfilling employment in this mixed-use project on the former site of a 1960s junior high school. In the residential components on the eastern and northern portions of the block, some bricks jut in and out to create three-dimensional checkerboard patterns, while others with curved profiles form implied colonettes on the section at the southeastern corner of the site. Most intriguing is the office component at the corner of 7th and Pennsylvania, which is marked by splayed brick window frames that suggest a contemporary take on early 20th-century Expressionism. The redevelopment of the site entailed reopening the 700 block of C Street, which had been closed when the now-demolished school was built, and creating a new public plaza at the northwest corner, diagonally across from Eastern Market.

E3

660 Pennsylvania Avenue, SE

1939 — Architect unknown
1943 — Addition: architect unknown
1990 — Renovation and addition:
Weinstein Associates Architects
2000 — Renovations of adjacent buildings:
Weinstein Associates Architects
2014 — Upper-level addition and infill of
alley: Weinstein Associates Architects

A one-story Art Moderne former Kresge store was the foundation for a 1991 development that involved rebuilding the old storefront and adding three stories of speculative office space above. Both the distinctive decorative panels, executed in fiber-reinforced concrete, and the pattern of glazed and unglazed bricks were inspired by textile designs of the era in which the original store was built. The office entrance lobby on 7th Street elegantly continues this decorative program and is worth a special look.

The owner of the original building later purchased the adjacent lots and, working with the same architect, renovated the existing structures there. The team then expanded those buildings vertically and infilled a narrow alley, the former location of which is now marked by the copper-clad sliver facing 7th Street. Colorful materials, including porcelain tiles on the 7th Street side and OSHA-yellow safety tiles on the Pennsylvania Avenue side, visually link the wings to the historic building at the corner.

E4

The Penn Theater Project

650 Pennsylvania Avenue, SE

1935 — John Eberson
1986 — David M. Schwarz / Architectural
Services, P.C.

The remnants of a jazzy Art Moderne–style theater served as the basis for this mixed-use development. The new structure fronting Pennsylvania Avenue employs Moderne-inspired motifs that are appropriately modest (the old theater was built during the Depression, after all, when the lavish ornament common to earlier Art Deco buildings had given way to a simpler, streamlined aesthetic). The building shares a courtyard with the red-brick apartment house at 649 C Street, which was part of the same redevelopment project but completely different in architectural expression, with façades of red brick to blend in with Eastern Market and nearby row houses.

E5

Christ Church + Washington Parish

620 G Street, SE

1807 — Robert Alexander
1824, 1849, 1874, 1891 — Additions and
renovations: architects unknown
1878 — Renovation: William H. Hoffman
1921 — Interior alterations: Delos Smith
1954 — Interior alterations: Horace W.
Peaslee
1996 — Interior renovation: Architectnique,
Edward Fleming and Berny Hintz

The myriad expansions, renovations, and reversals of previous alterations that mark the history of this Gothic Revival church — the earliest ecclesiastical structure built in the new capital city — are typical of the changes that venerable buildings tend to undergo over time. The original church was a simple brick box designed by Robert Alexander, a builder who worked with architect Benjamin Henry Latrobe on the Washington Navy Yard (Latrobe may have overseen aspects of the church's design and construction). In 1824 came a small expansion at the rear, and in 1849, the narthex and the bell tower were appended to the front. The 1870s brought an interior renovation intended to make the church more fashionably Victorian, and then in 1891, the tower was enlarged and a new entry ves-

tibule added. In the 1950s, Horace Peaslee set out to undo the fussy Victorian interiors and return the sanctuary to its more restrained origins. After all that, the little stucco building still stands serenely in its modest churchyard, looking only slightly weary from two centuries of tinkering.

E6

Townhomes on Capitol Hill
(Ellen Wilson Complex)

I Street and Ellen Wilson Place, between 6th and 7th Streets, SE

2000 — Weinstein Associates Architects

A product of the US Department of Housing and Urban Development's HOPE VI program, which was conceived to convert failed public housing projects into healthy, mixed-income communities, this complex replaced the dilapidated Ellen Wilson Dwellings. The development consists solely of row houses, each with its own direct entry from the street. Given a predictably modest budget, the architect concentrated on creating a wide range of different façades, using a kit of parts to produce varied effects (these included an inexpensive but versatile bracket of an uncertain mate-

rial that architect Amy Weinstein jokingly calls "mystery meat"). The result looks a bit like a stage set, thanks in part to the thin vertical extensions of many of the façades that are evident from certain angles, but yields a strong sense of place and communal identity.

Ellen Wilson Place, a newly created street in the middle of the block, harks back to the alleys of Capitol Hill that were once lined with working-class housing, while houses for more prosperous families were built along the main streets. The contrasting house styles and distinct spatial character of the mid-block street hint at this historical difference. Ellen Wilson, by the way, was the first wife of President Woodrow Wilson. She actively advocated improvements to the living conditions of Black Americans. When she was on her deathbed in 1914, Congress approved a bill in her honor banning substandard dwellings in alleys, but the law was later declared unconstitutional.

E7

Marine Barracks Washington and the Home of the Commandants

8th and I Streets, SE

1806 — Home of the Commandants: George Hadfield
1840, 1891, 1934 — Additions: various architects
1906 — Barracks, officers' housing, and Band Hall: Hornblower & Marshall
2004 — New dorm and band facility: BBGM

Commonly called "8th and I," after two of its four surrounding streets, Marine Barracks Washington is the oldest continuously occupied Marine Corps base in the country, and it served as the corps's administrative headquarters from 1801 to 1901. In plan the base is a simple rectangle, with a perimeter of relatively narrow buildings surrounding an expansive drill field. The 8th Street side is lined with a tidy row of duplex residences for officers, while the 9th Street edge consists mostly of a single continuous structure housing enlisted servicemembers. At the northern end of the site, on G Street, is the Home of the Commandants, which has served as the official residence of every Marine Corps chief since 1806 and has been remodeled many times, bearing witness to the shifting tastes of successive generations. It was one of the few public buildings in the city spared by British invaders during the War of 1812. Ancillary facilities form the southern edge of the complex.

E8

Hill Center at the Old Naval Hospital

921 Pennsylvania Avenue, SE

1866 — Architect unknown; Executive
   architect: attributed to Ammi B. Young
2011 — Restoration: BELL Architects

The Old Naval Hospital served as such until 1906, when a new naval medical center was built along 23rd Street, NW. After that, the old hospital was used by the navy as a training facility before being converted into a short-term dormitory for veterans visiting Washington to obtain federal benefits. Control of the building was transferred to the DC government in 1965, and since 2011 it has been home to the Hill Center, a neighborhood educational center and community gathering space.

Ostensibly designed in the Second Empire style, with a mansard roof and pronounced quoins, the building is more restrained than that label might suggest, probably because it was being planned while the Civil War was still raging. It eschewed the heavy window surrounds and other lavish ornament more typically associated with Second Empire architec-

ture, resulting in a relatively chaste structure that was nonetheless distinguished by its pleasing proportions. The iron fence that surrounds the property was almost lost when a military official proposed melting it down to make bullets during World War II — fortunately, it survived (if only barely and with some missing sections) long enough to be restored as part of the recent adaptive reuse.

E9

Congressional Cemetery

18th and E Streets, SE

Established in 1807
1816–76 — Cenotaphs: attributed to
   Benjamin Henry Latrobe
1903 — Chapel: Arthur M. Poynton
2008 — Restoration of cenotaphs: National
   Park Service

Established by a group of private citizens who later donated the property to the nearby Christ Church + Washington Parish [see E5], the Washington Parish Burial Ground earned its more common moniker — Congressional Cemetery — after becoming the semiofficial repository for members of Congress and other dignitaries whose remains could not be returned to their places of origin in the days before modern embalming techniques. Architects William Thornton, George Hadfield, and Robert Mills squeezed their way in among the politicians, as did John Philip Sousa, Push-Ma-Ta-Ha (a Choctaw chief who died while in Washington negotiating a treaty), and photographer Mathew Brady. Government officials interred here include longtime FBI director J. Edgar Hoover and Elbridge Gerry, a signer of the Declaration of Independence and vice president under James Madison, but probably best known as the inspiration for the word *gerrymander*. (In its early days, under the cemetery's articles of subscription, "infidels" were out of luck, and Black people could be buried only outside the main fence.)

Many politicians buried both here and elsewhere are commemorated in more than 160 official cenotaphs. Use of the cenotaphs, designed by Benjamin Henry Latrobe and paid for by Congress, began around 1816 but abruptly ended in 1876 (with a few 20th-century exceptions) when Representative (and future senator) George Hoar of Massachusetts remarked on the floor of the House that the ungainly structures added "a new terror to death." The sandstone cenotaphs were restored in the early 2000s under the direction of the National Park Service's Historic Preservation Training Center. The cemetery is still owned by Christ Church, but currently it is leased to a private foundation dedicated to preserving the grounds.

E10

St. Coletta of Greater Washington

1901 Independence Avenue, SE

2006 — Michael Graves & Associates

Michael Graves's best work in Washington, St. Coletta is an educational facility for children and adults with cognitive disabilities. Here, the architect's signature forms — boldly colored pavilions composed of basic geometric shapes reminiscent of children's building blocks — serve practical purposes. The distinct shapes and colors assist students in orienting themselves within the building and, taken together, create a unique visual identity and a strong sense of place. One mark of the success of the architecture is the institution's logo, which incorporates the "skyline" of the building itself.

The pavilions along Independence Avenue, covered in colorful glazed tiles, contain the entrance and common facili-

ties. Running along 19th Street is a series of gabled classroom pavilions, decorated with super-scaled masonry patterns, which are intended to relate to the row houses that are typical of the adjacent neighborhood. The classrooms are linked by the "Village Green," a wide corridor that serves as both a circulation spine and a gathering place.

E11

DC Armory

2001 East Capitol Street, SE

1941 — Nathan C. Wyeth

By the early 20th century, most every major American city had at least one armory, used by the local National Guard for training activities, munitions storage, and offices. Although these facilities were often the sites of dances, expositions, and other recreational events, their origins lay in the corporate and governmental backlash against a series of labor strikes and related unrest in the post–Civil War era. Most of the late 19th-century armories were fortress-like structures that were, in the words of historian Robert Fogelson, "designed to intimidate the 'dangerous classes.'"

Fortunately, when the DC National Guard decided to replace its old armory just before World War II, the popular image of the building type had changed dramatically. DC's talented municipal architect, Nathan C. Wyeth, designed this fashionably streamlined new facility with a soaring barrel-vaulted roof over the main space, which was intended for military drills and the like. Subtle ornamental devices, including horizontal incisions in the stone façades that continue the lines of the window muntins, help to finesse the scale of the gargantuan building.

The armory is still used by the DC National Guard but also hosts a range of concerts and other events. Since 2006, it has been home to the DC Rollergirls, the local women's roller derby league. Here you can see players with intimidating pseudonyms, such as Slamazon Prime, Megh A. Villain, and Ella Fistgerald, compete for points while whizzing around the track.

E12
East Capitol Street Car Barn
1400 East Capitol Street, NE

1896 — Waddy B. Wood
1983 — Renovation and additions: Martin and Jones

Like the former Car Barn in Georgetown [see M30], the original complex here was built as an administrative, storage, and repair facility for electric streetcars. The long, low structure facing East Capitol Street housed offices; the storage and repair sheds were located at the northern side of the block. Architect Waddy Wood's inventive use of brick corbels — brackets or horizontal bands in which each row of bricks projects beyond the one below — unifies the disparate elements of the complex. During its conversion to residential use in the 1980s, the office wing was largely preserved, while a few remnants of the other structures were kept as screen walls or incorporated into the new construction.

E13
Philadelphia Row
132–154 11th Street, SE

1867 — George Gessford
Numerous renovations and additions

According to oral tradition, George Gessford designed and built these side hall-plan row houses to assuage the homesickness of his Philadelphia-born wife. The style is clearly evocative of the Federal-period houses in that city, with

their flat, chaste brick façades, arched doors, and simple stone sills and lintels, though Victorian brackets and unusual window patterns betray the houses' anachronism.

E14
518 C Street, NE
1990 — Weinstein Associates Architects

Amy Weinstein reintroduced Washington to brick polychromy — the use of several colors of masonry forming decorative patterns — which she viewed as an economical means of lending visual texture to projects such as this small speculative office building. The primary façade, with its implied tower — the tower is not actually a discrete element in plan — has a civic, even church-like character, while the projecting bays along 6th Street clearly relate to the rhythm of row houses on that block and throughout the neighborhood.

The building faces Stanton Park, one of several squares that impart a small-town quality to the residential part of Capitol Hill. The peripheral buildings are notably diverse and include a historic school, small commercial structures, and single-family residences.

NoMa / Union Market

The area roughly between Union Station, Florida Avenue, I-395, and 4th Street, NE, has emerged as a distinct neighborhood, dubbed NoMa (derived from "North of Massachusetts"—referring to the avenue). Spanning the railroad tracks that lead to the station, the area was once one of the main industrial corridors in a city that had few of them, but it has recently seen a good deal of residential and mixed-use development. If current proposals to deck over portions of the railroad tracks to create a base for additional mixed-use projects ever see fruition, NoMa could easily become a major urban node, exploiting and reinforcing Union Station's role as a regional transportation hub.

Just to the northeast of NoMa is the burgeoning Union Market district. This longtime wholesale market complex has undergone a phenomenally rapid transformation into a precinct of hip residential buildings, restaurants, a retail market, and venues for cultural and sports events. Thanks to the revitalization of this previously little-known complex, the adjacent campus of Gallaudet University, which had felt rather isolated from the bustle of the city despite its central location, suddenly seems right in the thick of things.

Just after Union Station's completion in 1908, when intracity transportation still relied largely on streetcars and horse-drawn carriages, the adjacent plaza and surrounding streets seemed almost absurdly broad.

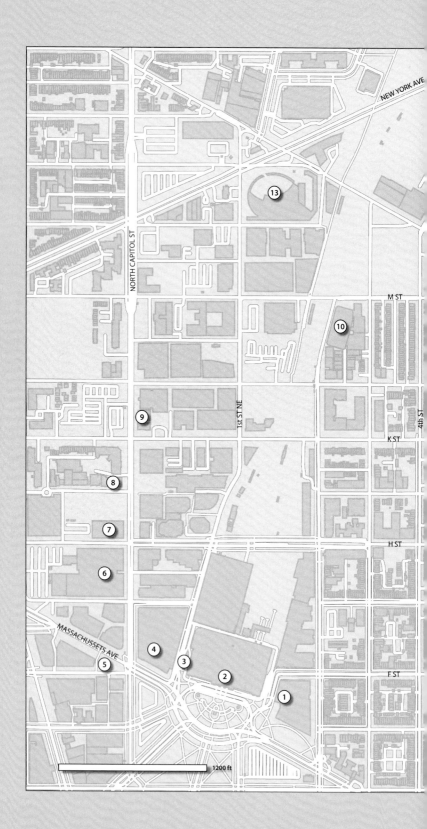

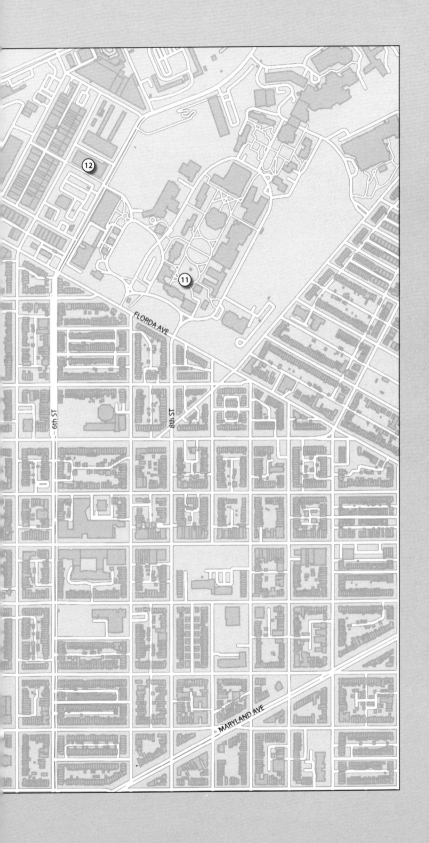

F1

Thurgood Marshall Federal Judiciary Building

1 Columbus Circle, NE

1992—Edward Larrabee Barnes Associates

Edward Larrabee Barnes's attempt to reinterpret the Beaux-Arts splendor of Union Station in a modern governmental office building next door is halfhearted and unsatisfying. The rudimentary arches and pilasters that line its primary façades exemplify the flaw in the common postmodern strategy of mimicking historic motifs in grossly simplified form: in the end, the reluctant copy just ends up making the original look that much better. The building's most successful element is its unapologetically modern atrium, which is quite inviting, particularly at night when brightly lit, although it does look more like the centerpiece of a shopping mall or entertainment center than the entry to a judicial office building.

F2

Union Station and Plaza

50 Massachusetts Avenue, NE

1908—Daniel H. Burnham; Sculptor: Louis Saint-Gaudens

1912—Columbus Fountain: Daniel H. Burnham; Sculptor: Lorado Taft; Landscape architect: Frederick Law Olmsted Jr.

1988—Renovation and new retail facilities: Harry Weese & Associates; Benjamin Thompson & Associates

2013–16—Restoration: various architects; Architects of record: Winstanley Architects & Planners

To the Senate Park Commission of 1901–2, one of the most vexing nuisances in Washington's monumental core was the train station that straddled the eastern end of the Mall, drawing smoke-belching trains directly across the primary vista from the Capitol. The commission recommended that a new station be built at the confluence of Massachusetts and Louisiana Avenues, in a style conforming to City Beautiful principles. Having settled on this location, commission member and architect Daniel Burnham went directly to Pennsylvania Railroad president A. J. Cassatt and persuaded him to re-lay the company's tracks to this site, making the grand new station possible and freeing the Mall of a sooty eyesore.

Union Station thus became the first building erected in conformance with the Senate Park Commission's recommendations. Sheathed in white Vermont granite (not marble), the station was inspired by

ancient Roman precedents. The central pavilion of the main façade, for instance, is a reinterpretation of a tripartite Roman triumphal arch. While the Roman version typically would have had one tall arch in the middle flanked by two shorter ones, here Burnham made all three arches the same height. Running along the entire length of this façade is an open-air loggia composed of a row of vaulted bays with suspended light fixtures. The view from one end of the loggia to the other is among the most beautiful in Washington.

The station's primary interior spaces create just what the Senate Park Commission had in mind: a triumphant gateway to the capital of an increasingly powerful nation. The Waiting Room, an homage to the Roman Baths of Diocletian, measures 219 feet by 120 feet and lies beneath a partly gilded, coffered, barrel-vaulted ceiling. Visitors to this space may be seen attempting to determine whether the scantily clad statues along the upper levels are anatomically correct behind their shields (answer: not really). Behind the Waiting Room is the 760-foot-long Grand Concourse, which, in its day, was among the largest uninterrupted interior public spaces in the United States.

After a period of neglect and an abortive, misguided scheme to turn the facility into a visitors' center for the city, the station underwent a comprehensive restoration and reopened in 1988. It is now a vital transportation and retail center once again. As the metropolitan area continues to grow, Union Station is expected to become an even more important regional transportation hub. Toward that end, in 2008, the Akridge development firm commissioned Shalom Baranes Associates to reimagine the station and its environs as a huge mixed-use complex called Burnham Place. The architects responded with an exciting and thoughtful master plan, but so far, work has yet to begin.

In front of the station is a D-shaped plaza organized around a fountain honoring Christopher Columbus. As an urban space, the plaza is a bit nebulous, with its curving side lacking architectural definition and its center crossed by a tangle of driveways. Setting aside the cultural sensitivities surrounding the image of Columbus, the fountain and the street furniture in the plaza are nonetheless engaging, with the Columbian theme carried through to such smaller elements as the light standards, which bear appendages designed to suggest the prows of Spanish galleons.

F3

Bikestation Washington DC

1st Street, NE, adjacent to Union Station

2009 — KGP Design Studio

This bicycle transit center is a clearly modern structure that fits comfortably among its neoclassical neighbors. The gentle arc alludes to the barrel vaults in the train station while also abstractly suggesting other imagery—a cyclist's

helmet, perhaps, or even a bicycle wheel emerging from the ground. Incorporating storage spaces for more than 100 bikes, a changing area, rental and repair services, and a small retail operation, the facility primarily serves commuters who take the train to Union Station and then switch to their bicycles to get the rest of the way to work. The louvered glass enclosure provides protection from the elements while allowing fresh air to circulate freely.

F4

Postal Square / National Postal Museum
(former City Post Office Building)

2 Massachusetts Avenue, NE

1914—Graham, Burnham & Company
1935—Addition: Graham, Anderson, Probst and White
1959—Interior alterations: Turpin, Wachter and Associates
1992—Renovation and addition: Shalom Baranes Associates; Preservation architects: Oehrlein & Associates Architects
1993—Postal Museum: Florance Eichbaum Esocoff King
2013—William R. Gross Stamp Gallery: Quinn Evans Architects

Designed by the successor to Daniel Burnham's firm, the old City Post Office, with its Ionic colonnade and projecting entrance pavilions, harmonizes with, but defers to, Burnham's Union Station across the street. The architects continued the

Ionic order inside in the former main service room, marked by opulent decorative details that were largely destroyed in a disastrous 1959 remodeling but have now been restored. The 1992 renovation entailed an almost invisible expansion of the building's floor space by 50 percent, which was achieved by filling in the courtyard, adding a mezzanine, and capturing unused space in the attic. The building now incorporates a mix of uses, including the Smithsonian's National Postal Museum, while still accommodating a working post office.

F5

Childs Restaurant Building
(SunTrust Bank)

2 Massachusetts Avenue, NW

1926—William Van Alen

Designed by William Van Alen—yes, *that* William Van Alen, architect of New York's iconic Chrysler Building—this sliver of a building was commissioned by the Childs brothers, who ran a successful chain of lunchroom-style restaurants. The entire ground floor, expensively finished in travertine, marble, and bronze, was originally devoted to dining space (the kitchen was in the basement). The building is sheathed in an unusual stone that is obviously quite soft—note the heavily weathered circular medallions between the arched windows, now barely visible. Just above the cornice on each of the two façades is the faint inscription "Capitoline," a reference to the famous Roman hill, site of the ancient temple that gave us the word *Capitol*.

At the apex of the building's acutely angled site is the poignant Holodomor Memorial to Victims of the Ukrainian Famine-Genocide of 1932–33, designed by architect Larysa Kurylas of the Kurylas Studio (with Hartman-Cox Architects as architects of record) and dedicated in 2015. A bronze bas-relief sculpture depicts a gradually disappearing field of wheat, symbolizing the mass starvation of millions of Ukrainians that was orchestrated by Soviet leader Joseph Stalin.

F6

US Government Publishing Office (GPO)

(formerly Government Printing Office)

North Capitol Street between G and H Streets, NW

1903—710 North Capitol Street: James G. Hill
1930—45 G Street: J. J. McMahon
1940—732 N. Capitol Street: Louis A. Simon (supervising architect), with Victor D. Abel and William Dewey Foster

Early Irish settlers . . . gave to this locality the picturesque, if inelegant, nickname of "Swampoodle," more on account of the swamps, however, than the poodles. . . . Perhaps Swampoodle was a corruption of "swamp-puddle." Certainly there were both swamps and puddles galore in the shadow of the GPO and the Capitol.

—*Washington, a Not Too Serious History*, George Rothwell Brown, 1930

The Government Publishing Office (GPO), formerly known as the Government Printing Office back in the analog era, first put ink to paper on March 4, 1861, the day of President Abraham Lincoln's inauguration. The agency set up shop in a group of existing low-rise buildings on the same block it occupies today, and it almost immediately began pleading with Congress for more space. It was not until 1903 that the GPO finally got a large new facility, which is now the "old" building at the corner of North Capitol and G Streets. This massive structure was clearly inspired by the muscular commercial architecture of post-fire Chicago, particularly the Auditorium Building by Louis Sullivan and the Marshall Field store by H. H. Richardson, both of which share the GPO's blocky massing and multistory, arch-topped window bays.

A small addition along G Street from 1930 closely matches the 1903 building, while the 1940 structure, at the corner of North Capitol and H Streets, is a slightly stripped-down version of the original, reflecting the Depression-era penchant for reducing historical architectural forms to their essence. Across North Capitol Street, along G Place, NE, is the GPO's warehouse, completed in 1938, designed with a dedicated rail line coming into the building for the delivery of large quantities of paper.

F7

800 North Capitol Street, NW

1991—Hartman-Cox Architects

Obviously inspired by the old GPO building down the street, this commercial office building remains one of Hartman-Cox's most faithfully historicist works. Despite

its apparent heft, it was built on a relatively modest budget using brick and cast stone, a refined concrete masonry product.

F8

St. Aloysius Catholic Church

North Capitol and I Streets, NW

1859 — Father Benedict Sestini
1887 — Rectory: architect unknown
1994 — Renovation: Duane Cahill

Bucking the mid-19th-century fashion for Gothic Revival churches, St. Aloysius was designed in the Renaissance Revival style by an Italian American Jesuit priest, Father Benedict Sestini, whose intellectual pursuits included astronomy and mathematics in addition to architecture. The exterior is a bit dour, thanks to its reliance on red brick, dark trim, and minimal ornament, but the sanctuary is bright and colorful — one of the most beautiful Renaissance-inspired spaces in the city. The painting above the main altar, depicting the first Holy Communion of St. Aloysius Gonzaga, is by Constantino Brumidi, better known for his frescos inside the dome of the US Capitol. The church merged with another parish in 2012, and the building is now maintained by the Gonzaga College High School, whose campus surrounds it.

F9

John and Jill Ker Conway Residence

1005 North Capitol Street, NE

2016 — SORG Architects

In an era in which unusual architectural forms tend to be associated with deep-pocketed clients, the John and Jill Ker Conway Residence comes as quite a surprise. This apartment building, composed of stacked and skewed blocks clad in silvery-white metal panels with glassy ends, was designed not for well-to-do professionals but for formerly homeless veterans and other low-income tenants. It contains 124 efficiency units along with communal spaces for residents.

To keep costs down, the architects worked harder than ever to minimize wasted space and specified off-the-shelf materials — including a prefabricated window wall system instead of more expensive curtain wall — wherever possible. Lead architect Suman Sorg, whose firm is now part of DLR Group, supported the project by contributing furniture, equipment, and other resources through her family's foundation. The building is named for Jill Ker Conway — the Australian American author, former president of Smith College, and cofounder of the nonprofit Community Solutions — and her husband.

F10

Uline Arena

(former Washington Coliseum)

1140 3rd Street, NE

1940 — Engineers: Roberts & Schaefer
2016 — Renovation: Antunovich Associates

Ice hockey rink, concert hall, antiwar protester detention center, and waste management warehouse are just a few of the many uses this building has served. Built for the M. J. Uline Ice Company, which had an ice plant next door, it was the first structure in DC with a thin-shell vaulted concrete roof. (The engineers of the building, Roberts & Schaefer, owned exclusive US rights to the German Zeiss-Dywidag System, which was developed by the Carl Zeiss Company, maker of planetarium projection equipment, to facilitate the construction of high-quality domes as projection surfaces).

The Uline Arena went on to host other sporting events besides hockey, and then, under the name Washington Coliseum, became a popular venue for musical performances and lectures, including a 1961 speech by Malcolm X. It was here, in 1964, that the Beatles first performed live in the United States. In the 1980s, it was known for raucous go-go music concerts. A 2016 renovation adapted the arena and adjacent buildings into a mixed-use complex, including a large store for outdoor retailer REI.

F11

Gallaudet University

Florida Avenue between West Virginia Avenue and 6th Street, NE

1866 — Master plan: Olmsted, Vaux and Co.
1866 — College Hall (east wing): E. S. Friedrich
1867–75 — President's and professors' houses: Frederick C. Withers / Vaux, Withers & Co.
1871 — Chapel Hall: Frederick C. Withers / Vaux, Withers and Co.
1877 — College Hall addition and renovation: Frederick C. Withers; Supervising architect: J. G. Meyers
1993 — College Hall restoration: Einhorn Yaffee Prescott
1995 — Kellogg Conference Center: Einhorn Yaffee Prescott
1999 — Chapel Hall restoration: Einhorn Yaffee Prescott
2008 — Sorenson Language and Communication Center: SmithGroup; Associate architects: Kuhn Riddle Architects
2010 — Denison House renovation: Ayers Saint Gross
2012 — Renovation of residence hall common spaces: Studio Twenty Seven Architecture
2016 — Renovation of STM Laboratory: Studio Twenty Seven Architecture
Numerous other buildings and renovations

Gallaudet University was founded in 1864 as the Deaf Mute College, the first institution of higher learning for the deaf in America. Later named for Thomas Hopkins Gallaudet, a pioneering educator of deaf students, the university occupies a park-like setting that is somewhat insulated from the hubbub of the city. The campus plan by Frederick Law Olmsted and Calvert Vaux is a masterpiece of informality.

While the buildings generally harmonize with each other and with the landscape, several also possess great individual character. Chapel Hall, with its asymmetrical massing, contrasting-colored stone, and striated red-and-gray slate roof, is possibly the earliest Ruskinian Gothic — a term derived from British Victorian art critic John Ruskin — college building in America. The adjacent College Hall, built of red brick with stone trim, and the cluster of houses for the president and faculty at the southwestern corner of the campus, all continue the High Victorian theme.

Several recently constructed or renovated buildings on campus were influenced by the university's DeafSpace project, which encourages design that responds to the unique practical needs and culture of deaf people.

F12

Union Market

Between Florida Avenue, 6th Street, and New York Avenue, NE

1929–39 — E. L. Bullock Jr.
1967 — Enclosed market building: architect unknown

When the last edition of this guidebook was published in 2012, most Washingtonians would have had no idea where or what Union Market was. Now, it is a booming mixed-use area that is home to some of the city's trendiest restaurants and bars, along with several bold works of architecture.

The complex owes its existence to the demolition of the Center Market, on Pennsylvania Avenue between the Capitol and the White House, to make way for the Federal Triangle project in the 1920s. A federation of wholesalers purchased this tract in 1928 and built a "model market" over the next decade, combining wholesale, retail, and farmers' markets, plus associated storage and packing facilities. An indoor market building — which has now been renovated as the centerpiece of the

burgeoning neighborhood—was added in 1967. Although many vendors decamped for the suburbs in the late 20th century, the complex has continued to operate as a market facility even as new development springs up around it.

Contemporary buildings of note in the complex include the Highline at 320 Florida Avenue, NE (2020—Eric Colbert & Associates), composed as an irregular assemblage of projecting and receding blocks; the Batley at 1270 4th Street, NE (2019—Shalom Baranes Associates; Interior architects: Hickok Cole), with its double-height façade grid; and the Signal House at 350 Morse Street, NE (2021—Gensler), notable for the huge notches at its southeast corner. Many more projects are in the works.

F13

Ariel Rios Federal Building
(Bureau of Alcohol, Tobacco, Firearms and Explosives Headquarters)

99 New York Avenue, NE

2008—Safdie Architects; Associated architects: OPX

It was a safe bet that the new headquarters of the Bureau of Dangerous Stuff was unlikely to end up looking friendly and welcoming, and indeed, it does not. The architects' fundamental goal was to adhere to the strict post-9/11 security requirements imposed upon them by the General Services Administration, which manages federal office properties, while avoiding the eerie peripheral dead zones and blank façades that are the common stigmata of high-security buildings. To achieve this, the architects placed the bulk of the secure spaces in an L-shaped structure aligning with, but set back from, N and 2nd Streets, with a separate, curvilinear office bar in front of the main block. An atrium separates the two blocks. Along N Street is a trellis that supports some welcome greenery but is ultimately just a three-dimensional fence. Along 2nd Street, a one-story retail wing serves as a physical buffer to the main building. On the other two sides of the site, the security barrier takes the form of a curving, multistory concrete pergola surrounding a planted plaza that is accessible only from within the complex. The pergola is strange and forbidding now, but if, in some happier future, the garden might be opened to the public, one could imagine some inventive uses for the curious structure.

Judiciary Square / Mount Vernon Square / Penn Quarter

Judiciary Square figured prominently in L'Enfant's plan for the city of Washington—it is one of the few spots where a specific building shape is indicated—yet strangely, he did not call it out in the key, so there is no direct explanation of its intended purpose. Evidence suggests, however, that he envisioned it as a site for judiciary functions. Early in the city's history, homeowners, innkeepers, and merchants were drawn to the neighborhood by a powerful stream that began at a spring near 5th and L Streets and raced southward to join the Tiber Creek near the Mall (sometimes, according to the *Evening Star*, the water in the canal was "deep enough for canoeing," but more often it was simply a fast-moving sewer). Italian, Jewish, and Chinese enclaves emerged at different times in the vicinity. The construction of the City Hall in 1820 established the square as a municipal hub, and that has remained the case ever since, even after the principal city government offices moved to the new District Building (now the John Wilson Building) on Pennsylvania Avenue in 1908.

The name *Judiciary Square* technically describes a multiblock area spanning from D to G Streets and from 4th to 5th Streets, NW. In the late 19th century, the full square was still easily perceptible, since it was a cohesively landscaped park containing just two discrete, though monumental, structures: the City Hall (now the DC Court of Appeals Building) and the Pension Building (now the National Building Museum). Several other structures were added in the early 20th century to house various judicial functions, and today, with E and F Streets continuing straight through the site and miscellaneous parking lots lining some of its edges, the larger historic square is illegible in person, though it is still evident on most maps.

A few blocks northwest of Judiciary Square is Mount Vernon Square, which was one of 15 public squares that L'Enfant set aside in his plan, each of which was to be "improved" by one of the 15 states of the Union at that time. Alas, that idea came to naught. In the mid-19th century, Mount Vernon Square became the site of the Northern Liberty Market, which was torn down in 1871 (the market reopened on 5th Street between K and L in 1875, but that structure was demolished in the 1980s). The square then became a park again until the turn of the 20th century, when it was selected as the site for the city's new Central Library, financed by Andrew Carnegie.

The fortunes of Mount Vernon Square mirrored those of downtown DC in the ensuing century, reaching a nadir perhaps in the 1970s and early '80s, when many surrounding blocks were vacant and the square itself was unkempt. In the early 2000s, after the DC Historical Society moved into the old Carnegie library and the new convention center opened just north of the square, the area's revitalization accelerated. This culminated with the conversion of the library building into an Apple Store—sharing space with a new DC History Center—in 2019.

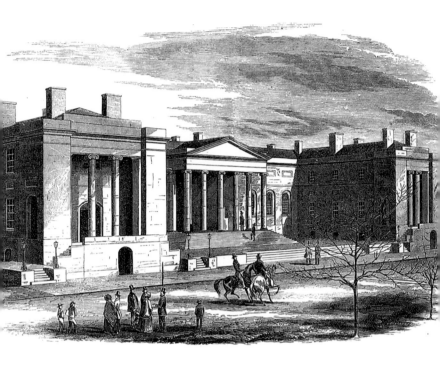

A few blocks west of Judiciary Square, the area now known as Gallery Place was called out on L'Enfant's plan as the site of a nondenominational church and shrine to national heroes. Instead, it gradually developed into a nucleus of federal offices, including the Patent Office and the Tariff Commission. The broader neighborhood, now known as Penn Quarter, declined in the mid-20th century as commercial investment became focused on the area northwest of the White House. Since the 1990s, however, substantial new commercial and residential projects have brought life to Penn Quarter—especially to the 7th Street corridor, which is now the area's central spine of restaurants, cultural institutions, and nightlife.

In the midst of these neighborhoods is Washington's current Chinatown, which has been subjected to substantial development pressures from all sides over the past few decades. Its most prominent landmark is the Friendship Arch that spans H Street just east of 7th Street. The colorful structure was designed by local architect Alfred H. Liu and completed in 1986. Liu's firm, AEPA Architects Engineers, also designed the Wah Luck House on the northwest corner of 6th and H Streets, an affordable housing development completed in 1982, which now houses a large percentage of the remaining Chinese residents of the neighborhood.

(*Above*) This 1853 engraving of Washington's City Hall (now the DC Court of Appeals) shows that the building once had a much more immediate relationship to the street and sidewalk before the street was regraded.

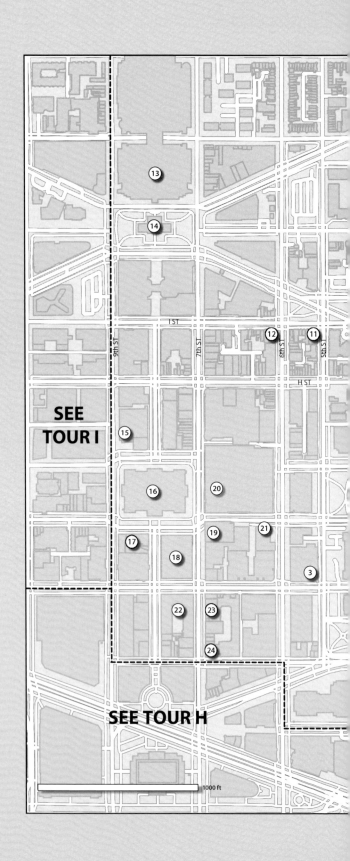

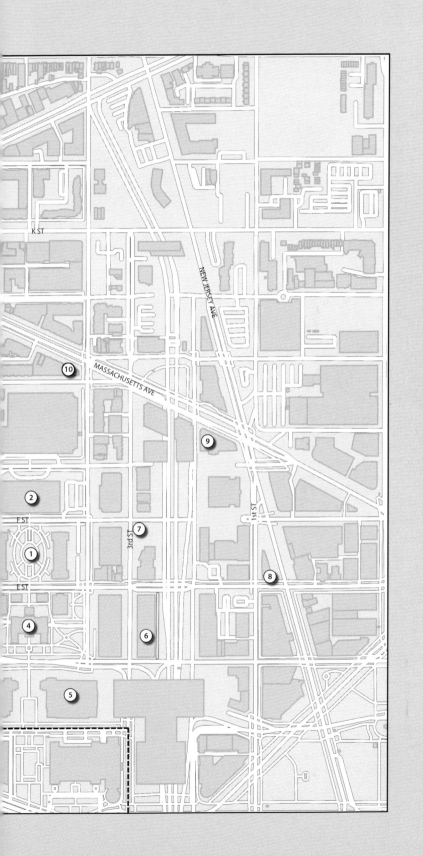

G1

National Law Enforcement Officers Memorial

Between E and F Streets, NW, across from the National Building Museum

1991 — Davis Buckley Architects and Planners; Sculptor: Ray Kaskey

The public space at the heart of Judiciary Square is now occupied by a memorial to law enforcement officers killed in the line of duty, whose names are inscribed in the low marble walls that trace broad arcs at the east and west sides of the site. The memorial is organized around an open plaza with a distinctive paving pattern inspired by that of Michelangelo's Campidoglio in Rome. The plaza has a subtle camber, with a medallion at the center marking the crown.

The site presented a design challenge in the form of two preexisting Metro elevator structures set at an angle reflecting the diagonal path of the station below. The architect cleverly restored symmetry by using the elevators as the compositional anchors for two complementary, curving pergolas. Because the pergolas stand directly over the Metro tunnel, they were constructed of aluminum to minimize their weight.

Davis Buckley Architects and Planners also designed the National Law Enforcement Museum directly across E Street from the memorial, which opened in 2018. The mostly underground museum is accessed through two glass pavilions

that flank the new entry to the DC Court of Appeals Building.

G2

National Building Museum
(former Pension Building)

401 F Street, NW

1887 — Montgomery C. Meigs
1985 — Renovation: Keyes Condon Florance Architects; Associated architect: Giorgio Cavaglieri
1991–2003 — Various alterations: Karn Charuhas Chapman & Twohey
2014 — Renovation of roof, upper façade, and chimneys: MTFA Architecture

Built, improbably enough, as a government office building, and now a museum of architecture, engineering, planning, and related disciplines, this is one of Washington's quirkiest and most beloved landmarks. Supposedly built of 15.5 million bricks, the imposing structure was designed by Montgomery C. Meigs, who had served as quartermaster general of the Union army during the Civil War. Meigs, an inventive and multitalented engineer, is credited by author David Miller as having been "second only to Grant" in his importance to the Union victory. Before and after the war, he was involved in several major Washington building projects, including the expansion of the Capitol.

This building was constructed for the federal Bureau of Pensions, which needed a large new facility to process payments to Union veterans of the Civil War and their families (at one point, nearly one-quarter of the entire federal budget was administered here). Meigs was a logical choice as architect, given his army background and substantial engineering experience, but his design was not well received at first. Many politicians derided the building as "Meigs's Old Red Barn," and William Tecumseh Sherman supposedly scoffed, "The worst of it is, it is fireproof," or words to that effect. After the Pension Bureau moved out in the early 20th century, the building was occupied by various federal agencies and even served as a courthouse. In 1980, a group of preservationists successfully lobbied Congress to save the structure, which had come to be regarded as a white elephant, and set it aside for use as a private, nonprofit museum of the building arts. Following extensive renovations, the museum opened to the public in 1985.

The exterior of the building owes a debt to the 16th-century Palazzo Farnese, designed by Antonio da Sangallo the Younger and later modified by Michelangelo, which Meigs had admired while visiting Rome. The comparison goes only so far, however—the principal façade of the museum is much longer, it is rendered in red brick rather than buff brick and stone, and it is crowned by a pedimented roof structure set back from the perimeter walls, while the Palazzo Farnese ends with a flat cornice. The window surrounds on Meigs's structure are of red brick, rather than contrasting stone, making the building appear almost as if it were carved out of a single block of clay.

The relentless "brickiness" is relieved by the building's most remarkable exterior feature: a three-foot-tall terra cotta sculptural band between the first and second floors, depicting scenes of Union military forces. Spanning the entire perimeter of the 400-by-200-foot structure, the frieze is thus nearly a quarter of a mile in total length. The sculptor, Caspar Buberl, was a Bohemian—back when that was a geographical term rather than a comment on his lifestyle—who immigrated to the United States in 1854. Buberl's other works include the sculptures over the entry to the Smithsonian's Arts and Industries Building and numerous commemorative statues of soldiers, firemen, and other heroic figures in cities across the country.

Impressive as the exterior is, it pales in comparison to the building's big surprise: the main interior space, known as the Great Hall, which is larger than a football field and soars to 159 feet at its highest point. This space—an early version of the modern atrium—was partially inspired by the courtyard of the Palazzo della Cancelleria, not far from the Palazzo Farnese in Rome. The Great Hall is divided into three courts by two rows of colossal Corinthian columns—among the tallest classical columns in the world—which are made of some 70,000 bricks each, covered in plaster, and painted to look like solid blocks of marble. Surrounding the hall is a double arcade with terra cotta columns on the

The Great Hall of the National Building Museum is one of the largest and most impressive interior spaces in Washington.

first floor and cast iron columns above. The cast-iron-trussed roof, reminiscent of a Victorian train shed, contrasts sharply with the space's predominant classicism. The hall has been the site of presidential inaugural balls going back to Grover Cleveland's in 1885 (before the building was even finished), and it now provides a place for the museum's educational programs, special events, and some exhibitions. The primary exhibition galleries are in the perimeter rooms on the first and second floors.

The building is also noteworthy for its incorporation of what would now be called "green" design strategies. Originally, small openings under each window allowed fresh air to enter the perimeter office spaces. Warmed during the winter over radiators along the exterior walls, the air then passed through the arched openings into the Great Hall. Clerestory windows at the crest of the roof vented the space, resulting in a remarkably efficient ventilation system that Meigs later claimed had dramatically reduced absenteeism among Pension Bureau employees. Now, of course, the building

is air-conditioned to museum standards and the exterior openings are sealed off, but the "Old Red Barn" survives as a testament to Meigs's ingenuity and as a handsome venue for exhibitions and educational programs about the building arts and sciences.

G3

National Academies Building
(Keck Center)

500 5th Street, NW

2003—SmithGroup; Preservation architects: Oehrlein & Associates Architects

The headquarters of the National Academies, an umbrella organization that includes the National Academy of Sciences, the National Academy of Engineering, the Institute of Medicine, and the National Research Council, was carefully inserted into a block containing some of the few remaining historic row houses in Washington's commercial downtown. Although these row houses were not landmarked at the time that the building was conceived, the architects anticipated strong objections to any proposal that involved tearing them down, and therefore devised a scheme that would save as many of the historic buildings as possible while making room for significant new construction on the site. Thus, the new, tall block is set back substantially from the street line, allowing the preserved buildings to read as discrete structures, rather than just pickled façades as seen in many similar projects from the 1980s and '90s.

G4

Old City Hall
(now the DC Court of Appeals Building)
451 Indiana Avenue, NW

1820–49 — Gèorge Hadfield
1883 — Expansion: Edward Clark
1919 — Reconstruction: Elliott Woods
2003 — Master plan: Karn Charuhas Chapman & Twohey
2009 — Rehabilitation and addition: Beyer Blinder Belle Architects & Planners; Associated architects: Gruzen Samton; Landscape architects: Rhodeside & Harwell

This was the first public building erected by and for the District's municipal government. Its original design, by George Hadfield, called for a domed Greek Revival structure with a central Ionic portico and two projecting wings facing what is now Indiana Avenue. The ends of the wings featured porches with paired columns *in antis*, meaning that they were bracketed by extensions of the side walls, with arched openings behind and steps leading to ground level.

After the seemingly obligatory funding crises (a "Grand National Lottery" was one of several unsuccessful schemes to raise cash for the building's construction), the mayor laid the cornerstone in August 1820 for "the seat of legislation and of the administration of justice for this metropolis." The central section and east wing were completed in 1826, but the west wing and the three south-facing porticos remained unfinished until 1849. Initially, the ends of the two projecting wings directly abutted the sidewalk along Indiana Avenue, but the street itself was later regraded, lowered, and realigned, resulting in a rather nebulous front yard that now slightly diminishes the building's visual impact. Hadfield's dome, which would have been located to the north of the central portico, was never realized.

During the Civil War, the federal government appropriated the building for use as a hospital and holding facility for prisoners of war. The feds then bought the building outright in 1873 to house judicial and local administrative functions. Between 1881 and 1883, Architect of the Capitol Edward Clark oversaw an addition on the north side that was largely in keeping with Hadfield's original design, minus the dome.

By the early 20th century, the building had badly deteriorated. Elliott Woods, who had succeeded Clark as architect of the Capitol, led a partial demolition and comprehensive reconstruction, completed in 1919. The work included strengthening the remnant walls with steel beams, replacing the original brick-and-stucco exterior with Indiana limestone, and removing the portico on the north side.

Ownership of the building was returned to the DC government in 1962, and it has been used for local judicial functions ever since. During the most recent renovation, a glass entrance pavilion was added at the spot where the original northern portico had been demolished. Though the contrast between old and new is striking, the new pavilion recalls its predecessor in its proportions and dignified simplicity.

G5
Municipal Building
(Henry J. Daly Building)
300 Indiana Avenue, NW

1941—Nathan C. Wyeth

One of several District government buildings in this vicinity designed by Nathan Wyeth, who served as the city's municipal architect from 1934 to 1946, this is the headquarters of the Metropolitan Police Department. The building is typical of Wyeth's spare interpretation of classicism—note the mere hint of classical pilasters inscribed into the stone on either side of each of the major window openings. Be sure to see the ceramic tile friezes that grace the building's two courtyards, illustrating *Democracy in Action* (a provocative piece by Waylande Gregory) in the west courtyard and *Health and Welfare* (by Hildreth Meière) in the east. Just tell the nice security guards you've come to police headquarters to see the art.

G6
US Tax Court Building
400 2nd Street, NW

1974—Victor A. Lundy; Associated architects: Lyles Bissett / Carlisle & Wolff

The fashion for public buildings in the late 1960s and '70s tended toward abstraction and extreme monumentality. In the case of the US Tax Court, the result was a forbidding, space-age judicial fortress. The

building does have a certain minimalist magnificence, best appreciated from the plaza over the freeway immediately to the east of the site. Along that side, an absurdly wide staircase leads visitors into an inky void obscuring the original main entrance, which has been closed for security reasons for much of the building's history. Suspended above is a huge, windowless, cantilevered slab clad in granite, which holds courtrooms and offices.

G7
Lillian and Albert Small Capital Jewish Museum
(Old Adas Israel Synagogue)
701 3rd Street, NW

1876—Architect unknown; Draftsman: Max Kleinman
1969—Moved to 3rd and G Streets, NW
2019—Moved to 3rd and F Streets, NW

The Adas Israel congregation was established in 1869 by approximately 35 conservative Jewish families who broke off from the reform-minded Washington

Hebrew Congregation (founded in 1852). The design of their new building, constructed in 1876, reflected the immigrant congregation's more orthodox bent and limited financial resources. Exterior decoration was restricted to simple wooden fans over the windows and doors, while inside, an upper-level women's gallery allowed segregation of the sexes during services.

Most, but not all, of this building originally stood at the southeast corner of 6th and G Streets, NW. Adas Israel left in 1908 for new quarters [see G12], and the structure fell into a succession of uses, including several churches, a grocery, and ironically enough, a pork barbecue carry-out. With demolition looming in the 1960s, the Jewish Historical Society of Greater Washington worked with local and federal agencies to move the building to a new location for conversion into a museum. In 1969, the upper portion of the old synagogue was sheared off and moved in one piece to the corner of 3rd and G Streets, where it was carefully placed atop newly constructed base walls.

Incredibly, the little building's journey was not yet over. When a developer obtained the rights to build the Capitol Crossing complex over the adjacent Center Leg Freeway, the master plan called for placing a new office building on the plot of land occupied by the synagogue. To make that possible, the developer agreed to fund another move of the historic building, this time to the corner of 3rd and F Streets, and to provide a contiguous site on which the Jewish Historical Society of Greater Washington could build an expanded museum. The synagogue was successfully moved in 2019, and work on the new Capital Jewish Museum, designed by SmithGroup, is under way.

G8
National Association of Realtors Building

500 New Jersey Avenue, NW

2004—Design architects: GUND Partnership; Architects of record: SMB Architects

This was the first newly constructed building in the District of Columbia to earn certification under the US Green Building

Council's Leadership in Energy and Environmental Design (LEED) rating system. The architects achieved this through such measures as high-efficiency ventilation systems, a sophisticated glass curtain wall that minimizes thermal transfer, and the copious use of recycled materials in the construction of the building. Viewed from the north, the tower at the apex reads rather like a ship's mast, with the sleek, sail-like curtain walls billowing behind it.

G9
Edward Bennett Williams Law Library, Georgetown University Law Center

Massachusetts and New Jersey Avenues, NW

1989—Hartman-Cox Architects

For two decades, Georgetown University's Law School was relegated to a dreary, if monumental, box of a building designed by Edward Durell Stone, located in what was then a rather dodgy part of town. This library was the first of several new structures that Hartman-Cox designed for the Law School, all of which now work together to create a compact but credible campus (and the once-forlorn neighborhood has seen significant redevelopment). The exterior of the library recalls the stripped classicism of the 1930s, which tended toward austerity. Here, subtle ornamental bands, deeply set windows, and delicate railings help to keep things interesting. The south façade, facing into the campus, is the most animated, with an asymmetrically placed projecting rotunda marking the main entrance and a trellis sheltering one end of the terrace.

G10

400 Massachusetts Avenue, NW

2005 — Esocoff & Associates | Architects

By the late 20th century, the stretch of Massachusetts Avenue between Union Station and Mount Vernon Square had deteriorated into a civic embarrassment, lined with weedy vacant lots and — most appallingly — the shell of one apartment building that was missing its entire front façade (infamously employed as a set in the wretched 1996 movie *Mars Attacks!*). The subsequent real estate boom brought new development to this portion of the avenue. One of the most interesting projects is the condominium at 400 Massachusetts Avenue, distinguished by its undulating façades, striated brick

patterns, and animated roofline. The project had to wrap around a historic firehouse, yielding an unusual floor plan with long, skinny apartments in the tall wing at the northwest corner of the site. The residential buildings at 401 and 425 Massachusetts, directly across the street, are by the same architecture firm — together, the three buildings form a set piece that creates a distinct sense of place in a generally nondescript part of town.

G11

Chinese Community Church

500 I Street, NW

1853 — Thomas U. Walter
2009 — Renovation: Rippeteau Architects

The saga of this humble little church building reflects the richness of Washington's ethnic history. Built as a Presbyterian church in the early 1850s, it became the Ohev Sholom synagogue in 1906 and later served a Black Baptist congregation before being bought by the Chinese Community Church (CCC) in 2006. The CCC soon embarked on a restoration, which entailed removing the Formstone — a cement-based faux stone ubiquitous in Baltimore's row house neighborhoods — which had been applied to the exterior in the 1950s, replacing missing bricks with matching masonry from a building being demolished nearby, and reconstructing the long-lost square bell tower. While conducting research for the restoration, historians discovered that the original building had been designed by Thomas U. Walter, architect of the US Capitol's dome and outermost wings.

G12

6th & I Historic Synagogue

1908—Louis Levi
1979—Addition: architect unknown
2004—Restoration: Shalom Baranes
Associates

This synagogue was built for the Adas Israel congregation after it outgrew its original home [see G7], which then stood at 6th and G Streets. With the dedication of this building in 1908, all of the city's oldest Jewish congregations were located within three blocks of each other: the Orthodox Ohev Sholom at 5th and I [see G11], the Conservative Adas Israel here, and the Reform Washington Hebrew Congregation near the corner of 8th and I Streets.

In 1951, Adas Israel moved to a still larger synagogue in Cleveland Park and sold this building to the Turner Memorial AME Church, which promptly replaced most of the Jewish symbols with Christian ones. Turner occupied the building for more than 50 years, but in 2002, it, too, moved to the suburbs. At that point, a potential buyer expressed interest in converting this structure into a nightclub. Ultimately, three Jewish developers bought the building and transformed it into a nondenominational synagogue with no fixed membership, offering cultural programming in addition to religious services.

The architecture of the building incorporates Byzantine, Moorish, and Romanesque elements. As with many Byzantine churches, it has a square plan organized around a large central dome supported by pendentives, with smaller domes at the corners (except that, in this case, there is no dome at the out-of-sight southwest corner). Balcony seating—originally reserved for women—occupies the upper level behind three of the four arches supporting the pendentives. The fourth niche is the site of the *bimah*, which serves as a platform for readings from the Torah or a stage for performances and lectures.

The interior was originally quite plain, but during the renovation, the architects and clients agreed that a more decorative approach was in order. The ceiling of the dome now bears a vibrant composition in gold leaf, red, and sky blue, with a Star of David at the center. The walls behind the arched niches are also richly colored. Stained-glass windows have been restored or re-created, as have elaborate light fixtures and other decorative details.

G13

Walter E. Washington Convention Center

801 Mount Vernon Place, NW

2003—Thompson, Ventulett, Stainback & Associates; Devrouax + Purnell Architects; Mariani Architects-Engineers

Washington's 2.3-million-square-foot convention center is a rhapsody in beige—dauntingly monochromatic, but skillfully chiseled, tucked, and squeezed to fit *relatively* unobtrusively into a low-rise residential and commercial context. To preserve as much of the existing street pattern as possible, the architects placed the primary exhibition hall underground, with various secondary halls, ballrooms, meeting rooms, and other spaces above ground, connected by wide bridges spanning L and M Streets. Although this unusual arrangement results in a rather confusing and inconvenient internal circulation pattern, the trade-off seems worthwhile.

The best features of the building are the lounge spaces cantilevered over the sidewalks along 7th and 9th Streets, near the southern end of the building, which suggest lookout platforms projecting from the bridge of a giant cruise ship. Also noteworthy are the tall pylons bracketing the main entrance on Mount Vernon Square, which incorporate stacks of flat glass strips—modern totem poles welcoming the hordes of badge-bedecked conventioneers, while also marking the corners where 8th Street originally met the square.

As of this writing, OMA and Beyer Blinder Belle are overseeing renovations intended to bring greater variety and vitality to the center's street fronts.

G14

DC History Center / Apple Store at the Carnegie Library
(former DC Central Library)

Mount Vernon Square, NW

1903—Ackerman & Ross
1980—Partial renovation: architects unknown
2003—Renovation: Devrouax + Purnell Architects, with RKK&G Museum and Cultural Facilities Consultants
2019—Renovation and adaptive reuse: Foster + Partners and Beyer Blinder Belle Architects & Planners

One of scores of library buildings across the nation built with funds donated by Andrew Carnegie, this was the District's central public library for nearly 70 years, until it was replaced by its own aesthetic

foil: the Ludwig Mies van der Rohe–designed, dark steel-and-glass Martin Luther King Jr. Memorial Library at 9th and G Streets, NW [see I13].

The exterior of this Beaux-Arts building is distinctive in several respects. The main entrance is marked by a pair of gracious curving benches leading to a lavishly ornamented central pavilion. The two flanking wings have large arched windows set into rectangular niches, with an *aedicula*—a small, shrine-like temple form—at the base of each window. The north side of the central pavilion has a dramatically different fenestration pattern, with narrow, vertical slits indicating the original location of the library stacks.

The building sat vacant from 1972 to 1977, when it was purchased by the University of the District of Columbia (UDC) in connection with a proposed new campus to be built just north of Mount Vernon Square. After that idea fell through, UDC's architecture department occupied the building until 1993. In 1999, Congress leased the building to the Historical Society of Washington, DC, which was tasked with opening and operating a museum of the city's history there. Alas, the museum venture was short-lived, though the Historical Society remained in the building until 2016, when deteriorating conditions forced the organization to move.

Later that year, Apple entered into an agreement with Events DC, the city's sports and convention authority, which

has managed the building since 2011, to open a flagship store there. Apple paid for a comprehensive rehabilitation of the building, which introduced characteristic corporate touches, such as a gleamingly white atrium space, while preserving and restoring the critical historic fabric of the structure. The project included space for what is now called the DC History Center, which comprises the Historical Society's library, offices, and exhibition spaces. Although some citizens decried the Apple lease as the privatization of an important public building, the near-bottomless pockets of a giga-corporation enabled an extraordinarily high-quality restoration of a badly deteriorated civic asset.

G15
PEPCO Headquarters
701 9th Street, NW

2001 — Devrouax + Purnell Architects

For the pedestrian or driver approaching along 9th Street from the north, the curving glass curtain wall of the headquarters for the city's electrical utility gradually reveals views of the historic Old Patent Office building [see following entry] across G Street. The bold gesture of this broad, curving wall is offset by a simple, delicate trellis that simultaneously reinforces the street edge and lends a human scale to the building's base. Amazingly, given how recently it was built, this was the first major building in downtown

Washington designed by a Black-owned architecture firm.

G16
National Portrait Gallery and Smithsonian American Art Museum / Donald W. Reynolds Center for American Art and Portraiture
(Old Patent Office Building)

Between 7th, 9th, F, and G Streets, NW

1836–42 — South Wing: Robert Mills, based on design by William P. Elliot Jr., Ithiel Town, and Alexander J. Davis
1849–55 — East Wing: Robert Mills, succeeded by Thomas U. Walter
1852–68 — West and North Wings: Thomas U. Walter and Edward Clark
1878–85 — Renovations: Cluss & Schulze
1936 — Removal of south portico steps
1968 — Renovation: Faulkner, Kingsbury & Stenhouse / Faulkner, Fryer & Faulkner; Bayard Underwood
2006 — Renovation and restoration: Hartman-Cox Architects; Preservation architects: Oehrlein & Associates Architects
2007 — Kogod Courtyard enclosure: Foster + Partners; Architects of record: SmithGroup; Landscape architect: Kathryn Gustafson

L'Enfant's plan reserved this site for a national, nonsectarian church and shrine to "heroes who fell in the cause of liberty, and for such others as may hereafter be decreed by the voice of a grateful Nation," but it was never used for that purpose. After the government's first Patent Office burned, this site was selected for its fireproof replacement. Another of Washington's innumerable design competitions ensued and was won by a young local architect, William Elliot, working in association with Ithiel Town of New York (their design was at least partly based on one by Alexander J. Davis). The construction of their design was supervised, however, by Robert Mills, whom President Andrew Jackson appointed as the official architect of federal buildings in 1836. Mills and Elliot later ended up in a highly public dispute regarding credit for specific aspects of the Patent Office's design, making a clear assessment of authorship difficult.

It was certainly Mills who designed the building's quintessential south portico, supported by eight beefy Doric columns rendered in fragile Aquia sandstone (the steps leading to the portico were removed in 1936 when F Street was widened, and the entrance was moved to the ground floor). Mills was also the lead architect for the east wing of the building, beginning in 1849, and here he switched to sturdier marble as the finish material for the new wings. Mills was ousted from the job in 1851 and replaced by Thomas U. Walter, who worked with Edward Clark to complete what Mills had begun.

When work on the north wing was finally finished, the result was the largest office building in Washington. It was a busy place—over the years clerks here issued 500,000 patents to the likes of Alexander Graham Bell, Cyrus McCormick, and Thomas Edison. During the Civil War, the building served as a hospital; one of the ministering nurses was Walt Whitman, who based his poem "The Wound Dresser" on his experiences here. Whitman returned to the building in 1865, working as a clerk for the Indian Bureau, which, like the Patent Office at the time, was a division of the US Department of the Interior. A puritanical new secretary of the interior discovered a copy of *Leaves of Grass* in Whitman's desk, however, and immediately fired him, declaring, "I will not have the author of that book in this department."

A fire in 1877 seriously damaged the west and north wings of the building, leading to a major reconstruction and subsequent renovations by Cluss & Schulze that included several of the most important interior spaces, such as the third-floor display halls for models of inventions submitted for patents. Executed in a style that author E. J. Applewhite called "Victorian Psychedelic," with encaustic tile floors, stained-glass skylights, and iron balcony railings, these fantastically ornate rooms contrast dramatically with the building's severe exterior.

By the 1950s, the elderly structure was considered thoroughly obsolete for governmental offices, and demolition loomed as a possibility. President Dwight D. Eisenhower intervened in 1955 and offered the building to the Smithsonian, which eventually assumed control and adapted it to museum use. Now known as the Donald W. Reynolds Center for American Art and Portraiture, the building houses two separate institutions: the National Portrait Gallery and the Smithsonian American Art Museum.

Recent changes to the building include a comprehensive renovation by Hartman-Cox, which freshened the gallery spaces and added art storage and conservation facilities that are visible to the public. In a separate project, the building's courtyard was enclosed and covered with an undulating glass roof by the British firm of Foster + Partners. The canopy was originally designed to be somewhat higher, but design review agencies pushed for it to be lowered, which is unfortunate, since now the roof seems a bit too constrained at the points where it meets the existing building. On a cloudy day, the space appears washed out—all beige and gray—but on sunny days, when the shadows from the roof's structure create lively patterns on the walls and floor, or at night, when dramatic lighting emphasizes the geometry of the canopy, the courtyard can be spectacular.

G17

LeDroit Block

800–818 F Street, NW / 527 9th Street, NW

1875 — 800–810 F Street (LeDroit Building): James H. McGill

1876 — 812 F Street: attributed to James H. McGill

1878 — 814–816 F Street (Adams Building): attributed to James H. McGill

1881 — 818 F Street: attributed to James H. McGill

1892 — 527 9th Street (former Warder Building / now Atlas Building): Nicholas T. Haller

2003—Renovation of existing buildings and addition: Shalom Baranes Associates

Built in the wake of the comprehensive infrastructure improvements undertaken by the DC Board of Public Works in the early 1870s, this historic row not only exemplifies the small-scale commercial architecture that was once common in downtown Washington but also illuminates the evolution of architectural technologies and tastes during the last quarter of the 19th century.

The oldest structure of the group, the LeDroit Building at the corner of 8th and F Streets, is typical of the Italianate style popular right after the Civil War. The lower two levels of the façades, with their large windows separated by slender piers, are elegant and finessed. By contrast, the projecting brick arches (known as hoods) over the windows on the top two floors are rather heavy-handed. The next two structures to the west, including the Adams Building, were built shortly after the LeDroit Building and represent slightly freer interpretations of the Italianate style. Next came the narrow building at 818 F, completed in 1881, whose façade is significantly glassier than its predecessors, presaging the curtain-wall skyscrapers that would soon revolutionize American cities. Last came the former Warder Building at the corner of 9th and F, which stands out from the rest by virtue of its then-fashionable neo-Romanesque styling as well as its greater height, made possible by one of the key inventions of the era: the safe and practical passenger elevator.

In the early 2000s, the historic block was renovated, amalgamated, and expanded to serve as the home for the International Spy Museum, which then up and moved to its new site on L'Enfant Plaza in 2019 [see C5]. As of this writing, much of the space remains available for lease.

G18

Hotel Monaco
(former General Post Office / Tariff Commission Building)

7th and 8th Streets between E and F Streets, NW

1839–44—Robert Mills
1855–66—North Wing: Thomas U. Walter, with Edward Clark; Superintendent of construction: Montgomery C. Meigs
2002—Rehabilitation: Michael Stanton Architects; Preservation architects: Oehrlein & Associates Architects
2016—Restaurant: Stanton Architecture; Design concept: Dawson Design Associates

Robert Mills worked on three extant office buildings in Washington: the Old Patent Office (now the National Portrait Gallery and Smithsonian American Art Museum) [see G16], the Treasury Building [see J2], and this former General Post Office, later the Tariff Building—the name by which it is still commonly known. If one stands at the southeast corner of 7th and F Streets and faces west, one can simultaneously see all three buildings, which employ each of the three basic Greek orders: Doric on the Patent Office, Ionic on the Treasury, and Corinthian on the Tariff Building.

Perhaps the least known of the trio, the Tariff Building occupies the former site of Blodget's (often spelled "Blodgett's") Hotel, which was built in the 1790s and ended up housing government offices until it burned to the ground in 1836. The fate of the hotel helped make fire prevention a paramount concern in the design of the new building, so Mills opted for a sturdy structure of masonry vaults and thick walls—a system also used in his sections of the Treasury Building and Patent Office. The Tariff Building is well proportioned and, though more ornate than its cousin across the street, still reflects the restrained aesthetic that Mills developed in response to budgetary limitations.

Like so many of the city's large early structures, the Tariff Building fell on hard times when the East End of downtown grew unfashionable, and its compartmentalized floor plan proved inimical to modern governmental office use. In 1997, the General Services Administration issued a request for proposals seeking the best possible use for the building. The winning idea was a hotel, which made sense because the relentless march of vaulted structural bays around the perimeter could be relatively easily converted into discrete guest rooms. The Kimpton Group, a hospitality chain known for its boutique hostelries, took a 60-year lease on the building and oversaw its conversion into a surprisingly nontraditional hotel. The former mail-sorting room, occupying a peninsular structure in the central courtyard, became part of the hotel restaurant and bar. A glass addition, which is structurally independent of the historic building, serves as a beacon when lit at night, drawing patrons through the carriageway off of 8th Street.

G19

Old Hecht Company Building
(Terrell Place)

575 7th Street, NW

1924—Jarvis Hunt
2003—Renovation and addition: Smith-
   Group; Preservation architects:
   Oehrlein & Associates Architects
2016—Interactive media displays in
   common areas: ESI Design

The former Hecht's department store at the southeast corner of 7th and F Streets was designed by a nephew of Richard Morris Hunt, architect of the Biltmore House in Asheville, North Carolina, and other opulent works of the Gilded Age. With white glazed terra cotta façades, intricate iron detailing, and an ornate clock suspended above the street corner, the building evokes the heyday of urban retail in the early 20th century.

After Hecht's moved to a new flagship store in the 1980s, the old structure sat idle for many years until it was adapted for office use during the renaissance of

the East End of downtown. Much of the exterior ornament had been removed but preserved inside the building and was put back in place during the renovation. The project also involved weaving together parts of several smaller structures on the same block of 7th Street, plus an entirely new structure immediately to the east on F Street.

G20

Capital One Arena

601 F Street, NW

1997 — Ellerbe Becket; Associate architects / exterior design: KCF-SHG Architects; Associated architects: Devrouax + Purnell Architects

Squeezing a major sports facility into a dense urban neighborhood is never an easy task, and it was especially difficult to accommodate a new basketball, hockey, and concert venue entirely within a single block of L'Enfant's plan. In fact, it proved impossible—this arena would fit only if the 600 block of G Street were obliterated. After much controversy, the developer received permission to close the street. Coincidentally, soon thereafter, the District government decided to reopen several nearby blocks, including the 900 block of G Street, which had been turned into "pedestrian plazas" in the 1970s. Restoring these failed pedestrian malls to vehicular traffic facilitated redevelopment of the city's East End, so the trade-off may have been worth it in the long run, especially since the arena itself is also widely credited with sparking the area's commercial renaissance.

Because the site was subject to the Chinatown Design Review Guidelines mandated by the DC Office of Planning, the architects also faced the unusual challenge of incorporating Chinese-inspired motifs into the design of the sports arena. To achieve this, the design team relied primarily on graphic devices and a few three-dimensional elements, such as the wavy canopy on the northwestern corner of the building, which vaguely suggest Asian architectural forms. By contrast, the main entry on F Street, with its tall columns and slanted canopy, clearly alludes to the neoclassical porticoes of the Old Patent Office next door. The rest of the façades might be described as cleanly generic. The result is a slightly haphazard building, but one that is now, for better or for worse, a fixture of its neighborhood.

G21

Sidney Harman Hall

610 F Street, NW

2007 — Office building: SmithGroup; Theater: Diamond + Schmitt Architects

Sidney Harman Hall and the Lansburgh Theatre [see following entry], which together constitute the Harman Center for the Arts, are the home bases of Washington's acclaimed Shakespeare Theatre Company. Harman Hall occupies the lower levels of a commercial office building entered from a "winter garden" to the west side. The shift of the office entrance to the side allowed the theater's public spaces to be expressed on the street front, yielding a marquee-like bay composed of frameless glass panels suspended a few feet over the sidewalk.

This projecting bay not only helps protect the box office entrance from the elements but also establishes a strong visual connection between the streetscape and the theater's interior, directly advertising the building's cultural function to passersby. A shallower projection, still mostly glass but with articulated mullions, embraces the marquee and extends another four floors above it, creating a visual transition between the theater and the office building.

At the insistence of the Shakespeare Theatre's longtime artistic director Michael Kahn, the interior of the new theater itself bears absolutely no trace of anything "Shakespearean," "Elizabethan," or even "old." It is a state-of-the-art auditorium with an easily altered layout allowing for thrust stage, proscenium, or end stage arrangements, and thus accommodating a variety of performance types from drama to chamber music. Unusual textured wall panels add visual interest to the space while helping to modulate the acoustics.

cial, retail, and residential uses, as well as the Michael R. Klein Theatre at the Lansburgh, one of two theaters used by Washington's Shakespeare Theatre Company, renowned for its resident actors and inventive reinterpretations of plays by Shakespeare and others [see previous entry]. A raised open courtyard occupies the center of the block and serves the complex's residents.

G22

The Lansburgh

420–424 7th Street, NW / 425 8th Street, NW

1890 — Busch Building (middle of block on E Street): Ed Abner
1916 — Original Lansburgh Building (corner of 8th and E): Mitburne & Heister & Co.
1924 — Addition to Lansburgh Building: Mitburne & Heister & Co.
1941 — Addition to Lansburgh Building: Clifton B. White
1918 — Kresge store (corner of 7th and E): A. B. Mullet and Company
1991 — Renovations and additions: Graham Gund Architects; Associated architects: Bryant & Bryant; Preservation architects: Oehrlein & Associates Architects

The Lansburgh complex, which gets its name from a venerable department store that once occupied part of this block, is a quilt of many patterns. Incorporating the rescued shells of several adjacent structures, including a former Kresge store (the corner of 7th and E Streets) and the Busch Building (710 E Street), the development comprises commer-

G23

District Architecture Center
(Independent Order of Odd Fellows Building)

421 7th Street, NW

1917 — Base building: W. S. Plager
2011 — District Architecture Center: Hickok Cole Architects

After operating out of a large row house in the Dupont Circle neighborhood for more than 40 years, the Washington Chapter of the American Institute of Architects

(AIA | DC) moved to the new District Architecture Center (DAC) in 2011. Occupying the first floor and basement of the Independent Order of Odd Fellows temple—no jokes about the appropriateness of that location, please—the DAC accommodates the chapter's offices, meeting space, and an exhibition gallery. The primary organizing element of the interior is the "Glass Box," a two-story volume, offset by openings in the first-floor slab, containing classrooms on both levels.

G24

Gallery Row

401–417 7th Street, NW

1877—Original buildings at 401–407: J. A. Michiels
1883—Original building at what is now 413: John G. Meyer (or possibly Meyers)
1986—New building at 409: Hartman-Cox Architects; Preservation architects: Oehrlein & Associates Architects

In the 19th century, this part of town was a vibrant mix of commercial and residential buildings. Architect Thomas U. Walter lived at 614 F Street; the *National Era* (an abolitionist newspaper that first published the serialized version of *Uncle Tom's Cabin*) was based near 7th and E Streets; the improbably named Mr. Croissant led the city's temperance drive from his Holly Tree Hotel and Dining Rooms at 518 9th Street; and Samuel F. B. Morse tinkered with his new-fangled telegraph in a since-demolished building that stood on 7th Street between E and F.

During the 1980s, the area was rediscovered—like countless other rundown urban neighborhoods with "good bones"—by artists. Hartman-Cox and Oehrlein & Associates were hired to tie together this row of buildings into an art gallery complex. The older buildings appear to have been restored in place, but in fact, they had been seriously undermined by adjacent Metro tunnel construction and had to be completely dismantled and reassembled. Hartman-Cox filled in the gap at 409 7th Street (which had been the site of a small, unexceptional structure) with a new building whose four-story rotunda acts as a lobby and a pivot for the entire project. The façade literally bends the rules of classical composition in order to mediate between the divergent floor levels of the adjacent buildings.

Pennsylvania Avenue

Pennsylvania Avenue has long been dubbed "America's Main Street." According to lore, the avenue got its official name as a sop to politicians from the Keystone State, who became disgruntled when Congress decided to build a national capital from scratch instead of bestowing that honor on Philadelphia. If true, the gesture was probably not appreciated—one early 19th-century congressman described Pennsylvania Avenue as "a deep morass covered with elder bushes," and, despite Thomas Jefferson's attempts to beautify the thoroughfare by planting flanking rows of Lombardy poplars, that description remained valid for several decades. While fretting about the street's appearance, Jefferson, perhaps unwittingly, set a precedent when he walked down the avenue after his inauguration in March 1801, leading a spontaneous parade toward the President's House. Since then, Pennsylvania Avenue has witnessed countless marches and rallies for countless organizations and causes spanning the political (and moral) spectrum.

During the Civil War, Pennsylvania Avenue, especially between 7th Street and 14th Street, became the favorite haunt of prostitutes who were drawn to Washington, in venerable tradition, by the city's hundreds of thousands of soldiers. According to one story, General Joseph Hooker tried to get the prostitutes to confine their activities to a small zone, but the women refused and started taunting him by calling themselves "Hooker's Army," later shortened to "hookers." It's a good tale, but unfortunately, the word *hooker* in that sense seems to have been in use for decades before the general came to town. At any rate, that phase of the avenue's history ended when the District outlawed brothels in 1914.

Not long thereafter, the southern side of Pennsylvania became one border of the gargantuan Federal Triangle project. By the end of the 1930s, this ambitious initiative transformed the wedge between Pennsylvania and Constitution Avenues into an impressive enclave of classically inspired government office buildings. Although the streets that cut through the area are largely lifeless, thanks to the constituent buildings' monumental scale and lack of shops or other pedestrian amenities, the project did introduce a grandeur to the two flanking avenues that is reminiscent of the famous boulevards in the great European capitals.

By the 1960s, the northern side of the ceremonial stretch of Pennsylvania Avenue, despite its historic and symbolic importance, was thoroughly decrepit. President John F. Kennedy, riding down the avenue after his inauguration, expressed shock over what appeared to be a "slum" between the nation's two most prominent public buildings. Kennedy later established the President's Council on Pennsylvania Avenue, chaired by architect Nathaniel Owings, which in 1964 released a drastic redevelopment plan that would have obliterated all of the blocks just north of the thoroughfare.

In 1972, Congress established the Pennsylvania Avenue Development Corporation (PADC), an independent federal agency given broad powers to transform the area. Over the next 24 years, until its dissolution in 1996, the corporation was extremely successful in acquiring, rehabilitating, selling, and leasing property. PADC used its design oversight authority to guide renovations and new construction, and largely as a result of the agency's work, the once-shabby avenue is now a truly magnificent, if not especially vibrant, boulevard worthy of the national landmarks that it connects.

(*Above*) In this aerial photograph from 1933 or 1934, several buildings in the huge Federal Triangle precinct are still under construction.

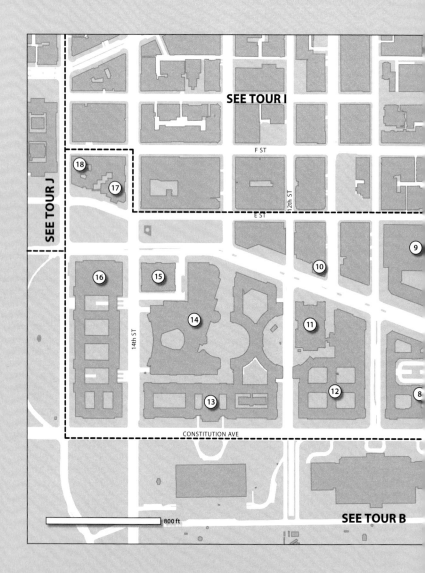

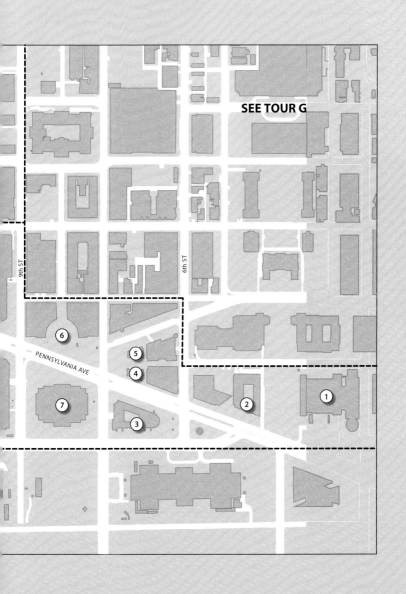

H1

E. Barrett Prettyman Courthouse

333 Constitution Avenue, NW

1952—Louis Justement
2005—Addition and renovation: Michael
  Graves Associates; Preservation
  architects: Oehrlein & Associates
  Architects; Associated architects:
  SmithGroup; Courthouse consultants:
  Ricci Architects & Planners

In the realm of stripped classicism, the original Prettyman Courthouse is the full monty—as bare as bare can be. Designed and built shortly after World War II, just as modernism was entering its heyday, the courthouse reflected official Washington's continued unwillingness to accept truly modern architecture for major public buildings. The result is a building that looks as if it is trying very hard to be nothing at all.

Meanwhile, the annex by Michael Graves seems to be trying desperately to be *something*, though what, precisely, is unclear. Oddly reminiscent of the architect's various projects for the Walt Disney Company, the addition, while undeniably monumental, somehow fails to convey the sense of gravitas one would expect in a federal court facility. Instead, it comes off as an overly coiffed tail wagging a shaved and slightly embarrassed dog.

H2

Embassy of Canada

501 Pennsylvania Avenue, NW

1989—Arthur Erickson Architects

Thanks to Washington's building height limit and stringent zoning restrictions, many of the city's commercial structures are designed to squeeze in as much square footage as possible, and often look as if they are about to burst at the seams. In contrast, the Canadian Embassy seems not quite big enough to fill its site, and in fact, that was the case. Guidelines established by the Pennsylvania Avenue Development Corporation dictated the cornice line and basic footprint for any building to go on this prominent plot, and the embassy simply did not need all of the space that the prescribed building envelope would have allowed. As a result, the building is somewhat hollow, with a profusion of architectural elements supporting little substance (though curator Nicholas Olsberg has argued that these seemingly frivolous forms were architect Arthur Erickson's way of poking fun at Washington's stuffy design constraints). On the positive side, the resulting open courtyard is publicly accessible—a rarity in an era of draconian security measures at so many diplomatic facilities.

The most prominent corner of the site, facing the Capitol, is marked by an outdoor rotunda defined by 12 columns, one for each of Canada's provinces and territories at the time the building was completed (such numerological tributes in architecture can quickly become dated—a 13th jurisdiction, Nunavut, was carved out of the Northwest Territories in 1999 and is now represented by a seal located above the entrance to the rotunda). Just inside the courtyard is a row of six huge, 80-foot-tall aluminum columns, fluted in a nod to classicism, which incongruously hold up an obviously lightweight glass canopy. The strongest exterior architectural element is the cascading planted west wall of the courtyard, which recalls similar stepped forms on several of Erickson's governmental and academic projects in Vancouver. The embassy's interior public spaces are serene and elegantly understated.

The building immediately next door to the embassy was designed as the home of the Newseum, a museum exploring the First Amendment to the US Constitution and, more specifically, freedom of the press. The Newseum faced perpetual financial struggles, ultimately closing in 2019. The building was sold to Johns Hopkins University, which is currently converting it into a facility for its Washington-based academic programs.

H3
Federal Trade Commission

Between Constitution and Pennsylvania Avenues, and 6th and 7th Streets, NW

1937—Bennett, Parsons & Frost; Sculptors: Michael Lantz et al.

The most ambitious unified architectural undertaking in the history of Washington, the Federal Triangle in many ways represents the climax of the City Beautiful movement. Conceived in the Roaring Twenties and largely executed during the Great Depression, the vast complex—stretching from 6th to 15th Streets between Pennsylvania and Constitution Avenues—is remarkable for its conceptual and visual cohesion, even though the individual buildings reflect sometimes surprisingly divergent attitudes toward ornament and architectural form. The Triangle's buildings were, in fact, designed by many different architects, but they were conceived as a single monumental composition and were guided to completion by a coordinating committee headed

by Edward Bennett, architectural advisor to Treasury Secretary Andrew Mellon.

Forming the apex of the Federal Triangle is the Federal Trade Commission, the last of the buildings completed under the original plan. Not surprisingly, given its construction late in the Depression, this is the plainest structure of the complex. The chastity of the design contrasts with the exaggerated muscularity of Michael Lantz's freestanding equine sculptures depicting, believe it or not, *Man Controlling Trade*.

H4
Apex, Gilman, and Brady Buildings
(former Sears House; now the Dorothy I. Height Building)

625–633 Pennsylvania Avenue, NW

ca. 1860—Architects unknown
1888—Apex (then Central National Bank)
   Building addition: Alfred B. Mullett
Numerous alterations: various architects
1984—Addition and restoration design
   architects: Hartman-Cox Architects;
   Architects of record: Geier Brown Renfrow Architects; Preservation architects: John Milner Associates

The westernmost structure of this group was built in the mid-1860s as a hotel in what was then a bustling—sometimes rowdy—part of town. In the 1880s, a bank bought the building and hired architect Alfred Mullett to give it a stronger presence on the avenue. He added the twin cylindrical towers. From that point, the building's fortunes mirrored those of the neighborhood, peaking perhaps in the 1920s before entering a long decline. From 1945 to 1983, it was home to the Apex Liquor Store, which derived its name from the acutely angled site and, in turn, lent its name to the whole building. In the 1960s, the store came to be symbolic of the seedy state of Pennsylvania Avenue that so distressed President John F. Kennedy during his inaugural parade. Many Washingtonians noted the irony of the busy liquor store's location within sight of Henry Cogswell's Temperance Fountain [see following entry].

The two easternmost structures of this complex date from before the Civil War. Mathew Brady, the pioneering photographer, kept his studio and office at 625 Pennsylvania between 1858 and 1881 and expanded into the upper floors of the building at 627 (long the site of Gilman's drugstore on the ground floor) in the 1860s. During a 1967 renovation of the Gilman Building, workers found original glass plates of Brady's photographs amid the debris in the long-vacant upper levels.

In the 1980s, Sears, Roebuck & Co. bought the row of buildings and converted them into offices for a division that negotiated trade agreements with foreign governments. Hartman-Cox designed a one-story addition atop the Apex Building and a narrow connector—marked by two Doric columns at the base and a pediment at the top—filling in a gap between the historic structures and creating a new entrance. The complex is now the headquarters of the National Council of Negro Women, which renamed it the Dorothy I. Height Building in honor of the activist who led the organization for some 40 years.

H5

National Bank of Washington, Washington Branch

(Argentine Naval Attaché Building)

630 Indiana Avenue, NW

1889—James G. Hill
1979—Interior renovation: P. T. Astore
1982—Renovation: Vlastimil Koubek

One of the most elegant works of Romanesque Revival architecture in the city, this former bank building is notable for its three façades of white, rough-faced marble with smooth marble window sur-

rounds, belt courses, and cornice (a large *trompe l'oeil* mural, depicting a continuation of these elements, adorns the eastern façade). The original entrance, facing 7th Street, is marked by a broad semicircular arch set into a slightly projecting rectangular bay. Above the entrance is a large dormer with finials and the year of the building's completion, 1889, carved into the stonework.

In the plaza just west of this building stands the Temperance Fountain of 1882. The fountain, which was presented to the city by temperance crusader Henry D. Cogswell, a San Francisco dentist, is now—perhaps more appropriately—dry. Dr. Cogswell picked a good site from which to launch his local anti-vice crusade, since for most of the 19th century this block marked the eastern boundary of the city's large red-light district.

H6

Market Square

Pennsylvania Avenue between 7th and 9th Streets, NW

1990—Hartman-Cox Architects; Associated architects: Morris*Architects

The team that planned the rebirth of Pennsylvania Avenue in the 1960s, during the heyday of the modern movement, could scarcely have imagined that, just a couple of decades later, this prominent site would be occupied by two buildings boasting a phalanx of five-story classical columns. Taking its name from the Center Market that once stood across the street from this site, Market Square is a mixed-use complex with residential units over offices and retail space. The late senator Daniel Patrick Moynihan, a vocal advocate for the avenue's revitalization, put his money where his mouth was and bought one of the apartments boasting spectacular views of the city's monumental core.

Nestled within the arc of Market Square is the unmemorable Navy Memorial, by the firm of Conklin & Rossant, with sculptures by Stanley Bleifeld.

H7

National Archives Building

700 Pennsylvania Avenue, NW (Exhibit Hall Entrance on Constitution Avenue)

1935 — John Russell Pope
1937 — Extension: John Russell Pope
2005 — Renovation and addition: Hartman-Cox Architects
2013 — Reconfiguration of Constitution Avenue entrance spaces: Hartman-Cox Architects

Although stylistic consistency and coherent urban design were overarching goals of the committee overseeing the Federal Triangle project, the group recognized that the National Archives Building, as the official repository of the nation's most precious documents, deserved special treatment. First, it was assigned to the most prominent site, in line with 8th Street, NW, a secondary but still important axis in L'Enfant's plan for the

city. Second, its architect, John Russell Pope, was given the freedom to break the development's otherwise consistent building setbacks from Constitution and Pennsylvania Avenues. Coupled with Pope's impressive Corinthian porticos and flanking colonnades, as well as the tall, windowless attic level over the central block, these distinctions make the National Archives Building by far the most monumental of the Federal Triangle development.

As with the design for the Scottish Rite Temple on 16th Street [see P40] by the same architect, the National Archives Building seems to have been inspired by a mausoleum—an appropriate reference, really, given its role in preserving vital artifacts. The Declaration of Independence, the Constitution, and other documents are on view in the Rotunda, which features James Bond–like security measures that protect these invaluable items from every imaginable threat. Long-term and rotating exhibitions are on view in other galleries within this building.

The plaza on the north side of the building is paved in a way that attempts to link it to the similarly paved plaza in front of the Navy Memorial across Pennsylvania Avenue, but given the six lanes of traffic slicing diagonally across the space, that relationship is more evident in aerial images than in person. More successful are the reciprocal views between the National Archives' north portico and the south portico of the Old Patent Office three blocks up 8th Street.

H8

Department of Justice
(Robert F. Kennedy Federal Building)

Between Pennsylvania and Constitution Avenues, and 9th and 10th Streets, NW

1934 — Zantzinger, Borie & Medary
2004 — Renovation: Burt Hill Kosar Rittelmann Associates; Preservation architects: Oehrlein & Associates Architects

The Department of Justice Building is a fascinating hybrid: it is fundamentally a neoclassical building but is strongly inflected by a pervasive Art Deco sensibility. On the exterior, many of the Art Deco influences are subtle—notice, for instance, the Ionic column capitals,

whose scrolls have unorthodox, bulging tops—though the sculpted doors and the flamboyant torchère light fixtures reflect the glamour and audacity associated with the style. Most of the sculptural and decorative elements are made of aluminum, then regarded as a quintessentially modern material, rather than the traditional bronze. Over the entrance portals, mosaic concrete ceiling panels by local artisan John Joseph Earley are partially visible from the sidewalk.

The building's interior, which is sadly inaccessible to average citizens with no business before the department, is a de facto museum of spectacular Art Deco murals, sculptures, and light fixtures (one percent of the construction budget was set aside for artistic works). Among the most famous sculptures are a female figure titled *Spirit of Justice* and a male figure named *Majesty of Law*, 12½-foot-tall statues by C. Paul Jennewein that flank the stage of the Great Hall. Many a televised press conference has featured a sheepish male attorney general with the bare breast of the female statue visible over his shoulder.

H9

FBI Headquarters
(J. Edgar Hoover Building)

Pennsylvania Avenue between 9th and 10th Streets, NW

1974—C. F. Murphy & Associates

The swaggering bully of the neighborhood, the FBI headquarters is ungainly, ill-mannered, and seemingly looking for

trouble. A cynic could argue that it is all too successful as a piece of architecture to the extent that the building's form so starkly reflects the clandestine work of the agency it houses: the impenetrable base, shadowy courtyard, and looming upper stories bespeak security and surveillance. As the Brutalist prototype for the Pennsylvania Avenue redevelopment plan devised in the 1960s under the direction of Nathaniel Owings, it helped to ensure that the full plan would never be realized.

In 2017, the Trump administration canceled plans that had been in the works for over a decade to move the FBI to a new, more secure facility, demolish the current, badly deteriorated building, and redevelop the site for a mix of uses. As of this writing, rumors are swirling that the Biden administration will relaunch the search.

H10

Evening Star Building

1101 Pennsylvania Avenue, NW

1899—Marsh and Peter
1990—Restoration, renovation, and addition: Skidmore, Owings & Merrill; Preservation architects: Oehrlein & Associates Architects

When this Beaux-Arts building first opened, the *Evening Star*, pleased with its new digs, ran a full-page story to announce its "architectural triumph." The article stated that the paper's publisher had decided to make the District "notable in an artistic sense" and thus chose to erect "such a building as would be harmonious with that future and an inspiration to its speedy attainments." The *Star* pursued

many crusades from this building until 1955 (then published from a different location for another generation before its demise).

The original Evening Star Building is notable as a remnant of premodern Pennsylvania Avenue, before planners in the 1960s and '70s decided to broaden the already-wide street by pushing back the building line on the north side (as evident in the adjacent blocks). Fortunately, the building survived long enough for that idea to be reconsidered, and the 1989 addition was built out to the line established by the original structure.

H11

Old Post Office Building
(now Trump International Hotel)

1100 Pennsylvania Avenue, NW

1899 — Willoughby J. Edbrooke
1983 — Adaptive reuse: Arthur Cotton Moore / Associates; Associated architects: McGaughy, Marshall & McMillan
1991 — Addition: Karn Charuhas Chapman & Twohey
2016 — Renovation and adaptive reuse: Beyer Blinder Belle Architects & Planners; Architects of record: WDG Architecture; Interior architects: Hirsch Bedner Associates

Architectural movements do not begin or end at precise moments, of course, but if one had to identify the year in which the fashion for Romanesque Revival buildings faded, 1900 would be a reasonable choice. This building, exemplary of the style and constructed as the headquarters of the US Postal Service, was completed in 1899. In

other words, it was finished just in time to be despised. The *New York Times* dismissed it as "a cross between a cathedral and a cotton mill."

Within a couple of years, the Senate Park Commission was hard at work developing its vision for a gleaming, white, politely neoclassical Washington, and structures like the rough-hewn Post Office Building (as it was then known), with its pointy roofs and its attention-grabbing, 315-foot tower, were not welcome at the architectural party. The renderings of the commission's 1902 plan were (literally) a bit fuzzy in their proposals for this specific site, but a quarter century later, Andrew Mellon's Federal Triangle initiative was clearer and specifically called for the Post Office Building to be torn down in favor of a neoclassical structure.

The vast majority of the Federal Triangle plan was realized — including the *new* headquarters for the Postal Service [see H13] — but somehow the now-*Old* Post Office Building hung on, though it faced near-constant threats of demolition. Finally, in the early 1970s, preservationists prevailed and the building was saved in a widely publicized case of adaptive reuse. Upper levels were restored for government offices, and the building's courtyard was turned into a soaring atrium, with food vendors at the base. The tower — the third tallest in the city, after the Washington

Monument and the campanile at the Basilica of the National Shrine of the Immaculate Conception — was opened to the public as an observatory. A new shopping pavilion was added next door some years later but was never a commercial success.

Indeed, the entire property was a consistent money-loser for the federal government, so in 2011, the General Services Administration issued a request for proposals seeking ideas for its adaptive re-reuse, as it were. The following year, the government selected the Trump Organization to redevelop the building as a hotel. The decision met with profound skepticism — and this was *before* Donald Trump launched his presidential campaign — from preservationists who feared that the project might compromise the building's architectural integrity. Fortunately, a team led by Beyer Blinder Belle, working closely with the US General Services Administration and the National Park Service, oversaw a meticulous renovation that protected the building's fragile fabric. Once Trump became president, the hotel was at the center of controversies over conflicts of interest and emoluments accruing to the Trump family. Trump detractors periodically projected messages of protest onto the façades of the building, turning the architecture itself into a canvas for political commentary.

H12
Internal Revenue Service (IRS) Building
1111 Constitution Avenue, NW

1930 — Louis A. Simon
1935 — North wing: Louis A. Simon
1993 — Façade completion: KCCT (Karn Charuhas Chapman & Twohey)
2005 — Renovation: Swanke Hayden Connell

The IRS Building is less elaborate than most of the other buildings in the Federal Triangle — a deliberate distinction since the agency was not a cabinet-level department, and it did not share the high profile of the Post Office and the National Archives.

The overall Federal Triangle plan included a "Great Circle" — a large, mid-block plaza — bisected by 12th Street. The eastern half of the plaza was to be formed by a semicircular arc in the IRS Building, which was obviously predicated on the planned demolition of the Old Post Office [see previous entry]. The latter structure stubbornly lingered, however, to the consternation of the neoclassical crusaders leading the Federal Triangle project, and the full circle was never realized, leaving only the partial arc on the IRS side. A raw, unfinished end at the northwest corner of the IRS Building's Pennsylvania Avenue wing was finally built out in 1993, in recognition of the fact that the Old Post Office simply was not going anywhere.

H13
William Jefferson Clinton Building / Andrew W. Mellon Auditorium
Between Constitution and Pennsylvania Avenues, from 12th to 14th Streets, NW

1934 — Auditorium and south wings: Arthur Brown Jr.
1935 — North wing: Delano & Aldrich
1998 — Façade completion: KCCT (Karn Charuhas Chapman & Twohey)
2000 — Rehabilitation: RTKL Associates

Arthur Brown Jr., best known as the architect of San Francisco's elegant City Hall, designed the southeastern and southwestern wings of this mammoth complex to house the Interstate Commerce Commission and the US Department of Labor, respectively. Sandwiched between the two office blocks is a spectacularly ornate and impeccably proportioned auditorium now named for Andrew Mellon, who, as secretary of the treasury, was instrumental in the planning of the Federal Triangle. The auditorium is a multipurpose public assembly space for important lectures, receptions, banquets, and other fancy social affairs, not to mention the occasional treaty signing. It is one of the most magnificent rooms in Washington.

The façades of the two office wings take their cues from that of the auditorium. The stone rustication on the first floor of the auditorium spans the lower two stories of the wings, while projecting pavilions with colossal, fluted Doric columns and sculpture-filled pediments recapitulate the auditorium's temple-front façade. The open passageways that run between the auditorium and the two wings are the kind of intricate urban spaces that help make many European cities so interesting but are all too rare in the United States.

The northeastern wing of the complex was originally called the Post Office Building, since it housed the headquarters of the US Postal Service after it left the "Old" Post Office across the street [see H11]. Two broad arcs, back to back in plan, lend a Baroque quality to this structure, which was conceived as the pivotal piece in the Federal Triangle master plan. Although the complementary arc of the Internal Revenue Service Building across 12th Street was never fully realized [see previous entry], the pavilions that anchor the three completed ends of the arcs extend over the sidewalks to create grand pedestrian portals, unofficially marking the transition between the Mall and the commercial downtown.

The office components of this complex, while initially considered separate build-ings, were officially combined in 2013, and the entire complex was named for former president Bill Clinton. It is now home to the Environmental Protection Agency.

H14

Ronald Reagan Building and International Trade Center

1300 Pennsylvania Avenue, NW

1998 — Pei Cobb Freed & Partners; Associated architects: Ellerbe Becket Architects and Engineers
2001 — Center for Association Leadership at the Marriott Learning Complex: VOA Associates

Conceived as the very belated completion of the Federal Triangle, the Ronald Reagan Building is a gigantic anachronism. It is ponderously and stodgily neoclassical, stripped of all but minimal ornament — the sort of building one might expect to have been built in the 1930s, like many of its neighbors, but not in the late 1990s, when modernism was resurgent. When this design was revealed as the winner of a limited competition in which all of the entries were rather conservative, there were no squeals of glee — just a general sense of resignation that the aesthetic and spatial constraints imposed by the various governmental agencies involved would have made a truly great work of architecture impossible in this case. Even

so, the building's formalism is astonishing—across the façades, it seems that clunky pilasters and expanses of solid wall often took precedence over the need for natural light on the interior.

One might assume that an unabashedly neoclassical building on this site would respect and reinforce the Federal Triangle's Beaux-Arts plan, but strangely, the east side of the Reagan building arrogantly defies its context. Toward the southern end of the east façade, there is the beginning of a curve in the plan of the new building, suggesting that the architects were thinking about creating a hemicycle to complement the one on the historic building across the plaza. Then the curve is suddenly interrupted by a long, angled wall extending almost all the way to Pennsylvania Avenue, broken only by a curious bump of a pavilion masquerading as the completion of the hemicycle. Had the architects simply pursued the obvious solution and finished the curve, most anyone—classicist or modernist alike—probably would have acknowledged the resulting oval plaza as a wonderfully grand outdoor space. Instead, visitors are left wondering why, given the enormous expense of cloaking this building in faux-classical garb, its architects worked so hard to avoid the one classical gesture everyone expected.

H15

John A. Wilson Building
(District Building)

1350 Pennsylvania Avenue, NW

1908—Cope & Stewardson; Sculptor: Adolfo De Nesti

2003—Rehabilitation and addition: Shalom Baranes Associates; Exterior preservation architects: Oehrlein & Associates Architects; Architects of record: Kendall Heaton Associates

Elegant in its way, but also a bit heavy-handed in comparison to many of its Beaux-Arts siblings, the John A. Wilson Building houses the offices of the mayor and Council of the District of Columbia. The building was begun in 1904, just a couple of years after the Senate Park Commission issued its recommendations for the city's core. In terms of both style and use, it was essentially consistent with that plan, which envisioned a municipal center in this area. Two decades later, however, the team planning the Federal Triangle had every intention of demolishing this freestanding marble structure, which did not fit in with their broader plan for a cohesive, limestone enclave, but it managed to survive.

The building was in such bad shape in the early 1990s that city officials decamped for leased space in a bland commercial structure on Judiciary Square. The District government then

entered into a complicated and rather mysterious deal with the federal government and a private developer through which this building was renovated and the U-shaped courtyard was filled in with a glassy addition. (According to the preservation architect, the exterior was so heavily caked in pigeon droppings that it took two years of restoration before the marble approximated its original color.) After lengthy negotiations with the federal government, which had planned to use the building for its own purposes, city officials were eventually able to move back in, restoring the structure's status as Washington's city hall.

Across the street from the District Building is Freedom Plaza, designed by Venturi, Rauch & Scott Brown with landscape architect George E. Patton and completed in 1980. The vast, mostly treeless plaza includes a map showing a portion of L'Enfant's plan rendered in black granite and white marble along with quotations about the capital city. The original design included tall pylons and large-scale models of the White House and Capitol (as if visitors couldn't just walk up or down the street and see the real things), but it is doubtful that these unrealized three-dimensional elements would have alleviated the desolation and cheerlessness of this widely unloved urban space.

H16

Department of Commerce
(Herbert Clark Hoover Federal Building)

Between Constitution and Pennsylvania Avenues and 14th and 15th Streets, NW

1932 — Louis Ayres / York & Sawyer
1989 — Law Library restoration: Einhorn Yaffee Prescott

A rusticated base, a parade of pedimented windows, and deeply etched masonry joints on the third through fifth levels reflect the Italian Renaissance inspirations for this 1,000-foot-long building. When new, it was the largest office building in the city, with more than 1 million square feet of floor space. (Actor and humorist Will Rogers once joked, "Take the State of Texas; put walls around it punched full of windows, and you have the Commerce Building.") The west façade, facing the Ellipse, is punctuated by four tall, shallow porticoes that mitigate the building's length. The eastern side, by contrast, has an extended central colonnade that seems to underscore the building's outsize proportions. The monumental façade of this central block was conceived as the terminus of the Federal Triangle's "Grand Plaza," a huge public space framed on the other end by the western hemicycle of the William Jefferson Clinton Building [see H13]. The plaza was never built, but the shallow arc of the Ronald Reagan Building [see H14] across the street is a reminder of the intended axial arrangement.

At the northern end of the building, on the ground floor, is the Malcolm Baldrige Great Hall, which was restored by Oehrlein & Associates Architects for use as the White House Visitor Center in 1995. The center was most recently renovated in 2014 by SmithGroupJJR. A multistage renovation of the Department of Commerce building by CallisonRTKL (originally also involving Group Goetz) is ongoing.

H17

Willard InterContinental Hotel

1401 Pennsylvania Avenue, NW

1901, 1904 (built in two phases) — Henry Hardenbergh

1926 — Addition: Walter G. Peter

1986 — Renovation and addition conceptual design: Hardy Holzman Pfeiffer Associates; Executive architect: Vlastimil Koubek

Without doubt the most fabled hostelry in town, the present Willard is the latest in a succession of hotels that have stood on this site for nearly 200 years. In 1816, John Tayloe, the original owner of the Octagon [see L6], built six houses on this lot and leased them to Joshua Tennison, who established Tennison's Hotel by 1818. Other leaseholders operated hotels under different names on the same site over the next several decades. In 1847, Tayloe's son, Benjamin Ogle Tayloe, leased the property to Henry Willard, with an option to buy it at a later date. Willard oversaw an expansion of the hotel and put his own name on it. He eventually bought the property outright, but not until after the US Supreme Court decided in 1869 that his payment in paper currency was valid (at the time the lease had been written, gold and silver were the only widely accepted forms of currency).

During the Civil War, Julia Ward Howe wrote the "Battle Hymn of the Republic" in her room at the Willard, and the building played host to so many luminaries that Nathaniel Hawthorne, covering the war for *The Atlantic Monthly*, observed, "This hotel . . . may be more justly called the center of Washington and the Union than either the Capitol, the White House, or the State Department." On a less exalted level, the Willard also supposedly gave rise to the term *lobbyist*, referring to any of the men who prowled the lobby, peering through cigar smoke and potted palms in search of political figures to accost.

The present building was the work of Henry Hardenbergh, who also designed the Plaza Hotel in New York. It exudes a sense of luxury thanks to the robust stone trim and delicate iron railings of some of the lower-level windows, the chunky projecting keystones above the mid-level windows, and above all, the soaring mansard roof, punctuated by huge, two-story dormers. At the sidewalk level, a beefy cast iron railing (which seems to cascade as it follows the slope of 14th Street) protects the areaway that brings light to the basement. Inside, the hotel's public rooms — including the main lobby, with 35 different types of marble; Peacock Alley, a block-long promenade of ritzy shops; and the Round Robin Bar, which during Carrie Nation's temperance crusade boasted a sign proclaiming "All Nations Welcome Except Carrie"—rank among the grandest such spaces in the city.

Good times and the Willard remained synonymous until after World War II, when the entire neighborhood suffered an extended, grueling decline. (One of the hotel's few bright postwar moments came in 1963, when Martin Luther King Jr. penned his "I Have a Dream" speech in a room here.) Boarded up and threatened with demolition, the Willard was finally saved through the intervention of the Pennsylvania Avenue Development Corporation and, after a lengthy restoration, reopened its opulent doors in 1986 as the Willard InterContinental Hotel. The large wing added at that time reflects a concerted effort to replicate the characteristic forms of the existing building while still deferring to it—a challenging task. The architects' solution entailed the use of multiple setbacks, diminishing the apparent scale of the new construction.

H18

Hotel Washington

515 15th Street, NW

1918—Carrère & Hastings
1987—Renovation: Mariani and Associates; Materials conservator: Ivan Valtchev
2009—Renovation: BBGM; Interior design: Dianna Wong Architecture & Interior Design
2019—Interior renovation: Studio GAIA

DC's oldest hotel in continuous use, the Hotel Washington is widely known for its rooftop restaurant and bar with a terrace that boasts some of the best views in the city. Carrère & Hastings, architects of such masterpieces as the main New York Public Library on 5th Avenue, sheathed this steel-frame structure in veneers of pale, smooth stone and brown brick. *Sgraffito* decorations (in which designs are scratched into layered plaster, revealing colors beneath the surface) adorn the window surrounds and spandrel panels on the upper levels.

As was common in the early to mid-20th century, the Hotel Washington accommodated both transient and long-term residents. Vice President John Nance Garner lived here throughout his two terms in that office (1933–41), and Congressman John W. McCormack, who became Speaker of the House in the 1960s, was a 46-year resident. According to one former hotel employee, the entire cast of the Ziegfeld Follies once stayed here and rehearsed on the roof.

Downtown — East End

The early 20th century was the heyday of the American downtown, when shoppers flocked to department stores and streetcars plied their routes amid the throngs of pedestrians. The area east of the White House and above Pennsylvania Avenue was Washington's commercial center during that period, with F Street as its principal retail strip. After World War II, however, the thriving district declined rapidly, as did so many similar areas in cities across the country, leaving dozens of grand works of architecture to decay. New office development in the postwar era shifted toward the west, particularly to thoroughfares like K Street and Connecticut Avenue.

By the 1980s, as developable sites in the West End were growing rarer, commercial interests began to reconsider the old East End. A booming real estate market, interrupted only briefly by a couple of recessions, has subsequently driven a rapid rejuvenation of this area. Although only one department store remains in the old center, some smaller retailers have moved back in, and residential development is increasingly common — a trend that will likely continue as teleworking becomes more widely accepted and traditional offices shrink.

In the early 20th century, F Street between Judiciary Square and the Treasury Building was one of the city's main retail corridors. This photograph from the late 1910s shows shoppers in front of the Woodward & Lothrop department store at 11th and F Streets, NW.

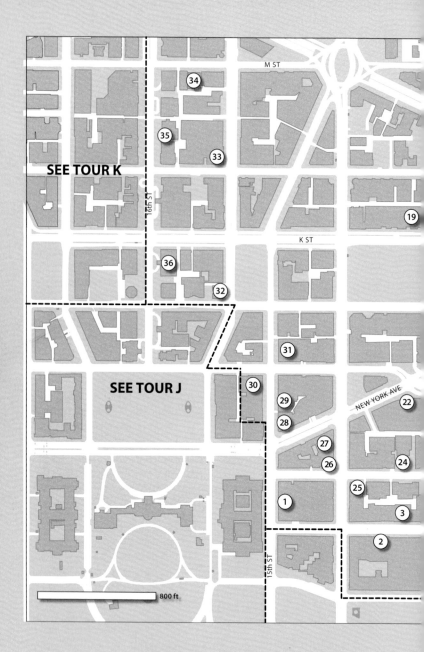

I1

Metropolitan Square

15th Street between F and G Streets, NW

1907—National Metropolitan Bank
Building façade: B. Stanley Simmons;
Gordon, Tracy and Swartout

1912—Chase's-Riggs (Keith-Albee)
Building façade: Jules Henri de Sibour

1987—Vlastimil Koubek; Consulting
architects: Skidmore, Owings & Merrill

A passerby admiring the stately façades on the east side of the 600 block of 15th Street, NW, probably wouldn't guess that this site was the subject of one of the bitterest preservation battles in DC history.

The story began with a modest, since-demolished structure at the northeast corner of 15th and F Streets, built in 1799 and long known as the Rhodes Tavern, even though it operated under that name only briefly from 1802 to 1805. In the early days of the new capital city, the tavern served as a de facto town hall, hosting numerous political and social events. Having survived the British invasion of 1814, it was bought by the optimistically named Bank of the Metropolis, whose successor, the National Metropolitan Bank, built the resplendent Beaux-Arts edifice by B. Stanley Simmons that still stands in the middle of the block at 613 15th Street.

The site next door to Simmons's building, at the corner of 15th and G, was filled in 1912 by a grand Beaux-Arts project by Jules Henri de Sibour. It included an 1,838-seat auditorium known as Chase's Polite Vaudeville Theatre (impolite vaudeville be darned!), offices for Riggs Bank, shops, and even Turkish baths. The theater was later sold to the Keith-Albee-Orpheum chain, which operated Keith's Theatre there as a major entertainment venue until the postwar suburban boom drained downtown of life.

In 1978, a developer announced plans to build a new mixed-use complex on most of this city block, requiring the demolition of the historic buildings along 15th Street. The US Commission of Fine Arts voted to allow the admittedly decrepit Rhodes Tavern to be razed on the condition that the other two buildings be saved. Concerned citizens formed a committee to oppose the project. The developer later offered to preserve the façades of the National Metropolitan Bank and Keith-Albee Building if the city would issue a demolition permit for the tavern. Ultimately, after more than six years of legal battles, the developer prevailed.

The new complex, called Metropolitan Square, includes a wing on the former tavern site that is a soulless, diluted copy of the Keith-Albee Building remnants on the opposite corner. The rest of the development is a run-of-the-mill 1980s office block. Preservation issues aside, it's a shame that downtown workers and residents can no longer enjoy a vaudeville show (whether polite or not) and a Turkish bath after a hard day.

I2

Fox / Loew's Capitol Theatre Façade

1328 F Street, NW

1927—Rapp & Rapp
1964—Demolition of theater interior
1985—Renovation of National Press
Building: HTB

Embedded in the National Press Building complex is a remnant of the Fox Theatre, later known as the Loew's Capitol Theatre. Designed by the famous theater architecture firm of Rapp & Rapp, it once boasted one of the most flamboyant interiors in DC. The auditorium was lost, but fortunately its intriguing façade, with its tall, concave, richly ornamented niche set behind a pair of four-story Corinthian columns supporting a huge entablature and shield, was preserved.

I3

The Sun Building

1317 F Street, NW

1887—Alfred B. Mullett
1904–9—Alterations and addition: B. Stanley Simmons
1927–70—Various renovations: architects unknown
1950—Demolition of steeple
1983—Restoration: Abel & Weinstein

Commissioned by the *Baltimore Sun* newspaper to house its Washington Bureau, this slender tower was widely heralded upon completion as the city's first "skyscraper." Although that term was used rather arbitrarily in those days, the Sun Building could lay a tenuous claim to the moniker, since it

was built with a steel-and-iron structural frame, incorporated passenger elevators, and initially sported a spire above the center bay that added another couple of stories to its height. The spire was removed in 1950, but the building remains interesting for its richly sculpted façade, which includes amusing references to its original owner, such as the sunburst motif on the balcony above the main entrance and carved sunflowers in the cornice.

The building was designed by Alfred B. Mullett after he left his position as supervising architect of the Treasury—the federal government's chief architect—and established his own practice. It was reportedly the most expensive private building in Washington at the time.

I4

Homer Building

601 13th Street, NW

1914—Appleton P. Clark Jr.
1990—Addition: Shalom Baranes Associates; Preservation architects: Oehrlein & Associates Architects

Appleton Clark anticipated that his original four-story, terra cotta–faced building would eventually be expanded vertically, and so he designed the structure to support the weight of additional stories (and even prepared a design for the full build-out). As it turned out, however, by the time the addition was finally commissioned many decades later, a Metro line had been constructed beneath the building, posing unanticipated engineering challenges. As a result, an entirely new structural system was required to support the upper floors, and ultimately only the façades of the original building were retained.

I5

Warner Theatre / Office Building
(former Earle Theatre and Office Building)

1299 Pennsylvania Avenue, NW

1924—C. Howard Crane and Kenneth Franzheim
1927—Addition of top floor: Zink, Atkins and Craycroft
1993—Renovation: Shalom Baranes Associates; Addition: Pei Cobb Freed & Partners Architects
2020—Interior renovations: Gensler

The original Earle Theatre and Office Building was something of a sensation when it opened just after Christmas in 1924. Designed by C. Howard Crane, architect of more than 300 theaters around the world, the project was not only hailed by the *Evening Star* as "Washington's most beautiful commercial building," but also noted for its mix of uses, incorporating a 2,500-seat vaudeville theater, a 1,000-person ballroom in the basement, a large restaurant, and commercial office

space. The summer after it opened, the Earle hosted outdoor movies and dancing on its roof, but the roof garden was soon lost when another floor of office space was added. Office tenants over the years included a variety of nonprofit organizations, among them the Federal Bar Association and the "We Want Beer" association, an anti-Prohibition group. In 1927, the theater was converted into a first-run movie house, though it continued to present live shows until 1945. With the decline of downtown in the 1960s, the theater—by then known as the Warner—was closed for a few years before reopening as a venue for rock concerts and pornographic movies (which must have been astonishing to see on the theater's huge screen). Fortunately, a comprehensive renovation subsequently returned the Warner to its former glory, and it now hosts a variety of performances.

The architecture of the building, which is actually at the corner of 13th and E Streets despite its Pennsylvania Avenue address, is exemplary of the era, with intricate terra cotta ornament and an enticing marquee over the theater entrance. The position of the auditorium within is expressed on the elevations by windowless panels carrying a decorative diamond pattern—the stage being along E Street, with one side of the auditorium along 13th Street. The interiors of the theater and other public spaces are appropriately palatial and decorated in a Renaissance Revival vein.

The large 1990s addition is articulated along E Street as if it were two buildings—the easternmost part of the façade is a modern recapitulation of the theater façade, while the central part is designed as a slightly different but compatible composition, lending a basic tripartite symmetry to the entire block.

I6

555 12th Street, NW

1995—Florance Eichbaum Esocoff King Architects
1998—Second phase: Florance Eichbaum Esocoff King Architects
2017—Renovation: SmithGroup

In the wake of the postmodern movement, many architects grappled with the

question of how to introduce ornament to modern buildings without it looking cheap or simply extraneous. In the case of 555 12th Street, the architects' efforts in that regard were quite successful. Here, all of the decorative elements—including spandrel panels, grilles, canopies, colonnettes resting on the black granite base, and even the door hardware—appear to be holistically conceived, carefully detailed, and well made. As with some roughly contemporaneous buildings by this architecture firm (previously Keyes Condon Florance, and now the Washington office of SmithGroup), the effect is reminiscent of the work of the Viennese Secession, which makes sense, as that movement produced buildings that represented a comfortably ornamented modernism.

I7
Lincoln Square
555 11th Street, NW

2001—Hartman-Cox Architects; Preservation architects: Oehrlein & Associates Architects

This project incorporated the façades of nine small commercial structures—two preserved in place and seven dismantled and re-erected on the site—into a 12-story mixed-use complex. The newly constructed sections, designed by Hartman-Cox Architects, are unassuming but well proportioned, with fenestration patterns distilled from those commonly found in the existing buildings. The choice of the pale brick for the new skin was clever—it

is, of course, compatible with all of the historic buildings' materials, but it is not quite the same color as any of them, allowing each of them to read as a distinct structure. The east façade has a surprisingly high-quality finish for the rear of a building facing the middle of a city block.

Across E Street from Lincoln Square is 1001 Pennsylvania Avenue, designed a few years earlier by the same architecture firms and exhibiting a similar incorporation of smaller historic buildings. Note the stepped forms that reflect the shift in scale from Pennsylvania Avenue, the only street in the city on which the maximum height is 160 feet (the norm in commercial districts is 130), to the lower-rise surrounding streets.

I8
Ford's Theatre
511 10th Street, NW

1863—James J. Gifford
1865—Renovation: Edwin Clarke
1894—Restoration: architect unknown
1968—Macomber & Peter; Restoration: William M. Haussmann; Charles W. Lessig
2009—Restoration: ASD

Impresario John T. Ford arrived in town in 1861, flush from a string of successes at Baltimore's Holliday Street Theatre. He set up shop in the former First Baptist Church, which he renamed Ford's Atheneum, but it burned down the next year. He began building this new theater in 1863 and seemed destined to repeat his Baltimore triumphs until April 14, 1865, when real-life tragedy struck as John Wilkes Booth shot President Abraham Lincoln in one of the theater's boxes.

After the assassination, the federal government acquired the building for use as offices, along with the Army Medical Museum on the third floor. In 1893, the structure partially collapsed, killing or injuring dozens of government clerks. At that point, the building was relegated to use as a document storage facility until being transferred to the National Park Service in 1933. It was finally restored to theater use in 1968, based in part on photographs taken by Mathew Brady in 1865. The historic site, which is now operated through a public-private partnership, includes a museum beneath the theater, as well as the Petersen House at 516 10th Street, where the wounded president was carried and soon died.

The façade of the theater today looks much as it did in 1865, with a stucco-covered ground floor and a brick wall with simple pilasters above. The block of 10th Street on which the theater stands is noteworthy as one of the most eclectic architectural ensembles remaining in downtown Washington, including, on the east side of the street, a small Second Empire commercial structure at the northern end and a sober neoclassical office building at the southern end. The west side includes examples ranging from Victorian to Art Moderne to 21st-century modern commercial architecture.

19

National Union Building
918 F Street, NW

1890 — Glenn Brown
Numerous alterations: architects unknown
2001 — Renovation: Eric Colbert & Associates PC
2012 — Renovation: Streetsense

This brawny Romanesque Revival building is an outstanding example of the small commercial structures that were common in downtown Washington in the late 19th and early 20th centuries. It was designed by Glenn Brown, longtime chief executive of the AIA, whose own architectural practice was housed here until 1905. The main façade of the six-story building is divided into three distinct but complementary two-story sections. The middle section is quirky, with corner piers composed of multiple colonnettes, a curving band at mid-level, and five small Corinthian columns in front of the bay window on each floor. An even more unusual feature of the building is the series of five-story bay windows suspended over the alley, designed to bring extra light and air to the individual offices on the upper levels. The architects for the 2001 renovation found much of the building's interior intact, including an open-cage elevator that was

still being operated by an attendant (it was replaced by a modern elevator).

A few doors down from 918 F are the remnants of the Atlantic Building at 930 F Street (1888—James G. Hill), built around the same time and in a similar style. All but the façade of that building was demolished when the new complex behind it, designed by Shalom Baranes Associates, was built. The Atlantic Building was the original home of the legendary 9:30 Club (the name of which was derived from the address), an important venue for hardcore punk and other musical performances in the 1980s and early '90s, before it moved to V Street, NW.

I10
The Ventana
912 F Street, NW

2006—Shalom Baranes Associates

A slender Miesian tower reaches out to the street line, quietly announcing the presence of this surprisingly large residential building, most of which is situated deep within the block. The project incorporates the restored façades of three small historic buildings, elements of which were salvaged and reinstalled in new structures that replicate the scale and massing of the originals. The tall narrow wing adjacent to the street contains

flats, while the bulkier mid-block core mostly consists of duplex units, which maximize access to natural light—an important consideration, since many of the apartments face an alley.

I11
Riggs National Bank Building
(Riggs Washington DC Hotel)
900 F Street, NW

1891—James G. Hill
1912—Interior renovation: architect unknown
1927—Addition: Arthur B. Heaton
1998—Renovation: Gordon & Greenberg Architects
2020—Renovation: Jacu Strauss of Lore Group; Associated architects: Perkins Eastman

The composition of this former bank building's robust granite façades, consisting of a distinct base, a four-story shaft with arch-topped bays, a two-story band above, and one final story that reads as a sort of large cornice, recalls the design of Louis Sullivan's landmark Auditorium Building in Chicago, completed just two years earlier. Notice the alternating courses of narrow and wide stones, a subtle trick that manages to lend the building a surprising degree of delicacy despite its heaviness. Along the F Street face, the vertical line between the original building and the otherwise seamless 1927 addition is quite clear thanks to a noticeable change in color. The interior public spaces are worth a look, especially the ornate banking hall that now serves as the restaurant for a boutique hotel.

I12

Old Masonic Temple

Northwest corner of 9th and F Streets, NW

1870 — Cluss and Kammerhueber
ca. 1921 — Alterations: architect unknown
1992 — Restoration: Oehrlein & Associates Architects
2000 — Renovation and new building: Martinez + Johnson; Interiors: VOA Associates
2001 — Leadership Training Hall in original building: VOA Associates

President Andrew Johnson, a Freemason, laid the cornerstone and led the parade that celebrated the start of construction of this Masonic Temple. The design is essentially Italianate, with a strong cornice and heavy pediments or arches over the windows, but it surely would be labeled Second Empire instead if the mansard roof that the architects originally planned had been executed. In its prime, the building accommodated much Gilded-Age revelry: Washingtonians fêted the Prince of Wales here in 1876, and for decades society matrons fought for the honor of having their daughters' debutante parties here. The Masons moved out in 1908, to be replaced in 1921 by Lansburgh's Furniture Store, which remained until the late 1970s. The elegant building was later abandoned for many years until it was restored in conjunction with the construction of the adjacent structure on 9th Street. The Gallup Organization now occupies both structures and uses the grand Masonic hall on the second floor of the original building for meetings and ceremonial events.

I13

Martin Luther King Jr. Memorial Library

901 G Street, NW

1972 — Office of Ludwig Mies van der Rohe
2009 — Interior alterations: BELL Architects
2020 — Renovation and addition design architects: Mecanoo Architecten; Executive architects: OTJ Architects

Washington's central public library, named in honor of Martin Luther King Jr., is the city's only work by modernist master Ludwig Mies van der Rohe, though it was executed after the architect's death. The key elements are all classically Miesian, including a rigidly geometrical structural frame of dark steel, tinted windows, and large panels of buff brick. When it opened, it was a serviceable if uninspiring flagship for the city's library system.

Over the ensuing decades, once-functional interior spaces became cluttered, maintenance was deferred, and the area around the library grew seedy. For years, the adjacent block of G Street was an unpleasant and ill-conceived pedestrian mall. The reopening of the block to vehicular traffic in 1999 coincided with a tentative renaissance in downtown's East End, which soon developed into a full-fledged boom.

In conjunction with its recent ambitious initiative to upgrade its neighborhood branches, the DC Public Library administration decided to renovate the MLK Library, as it is commonly known, preserving its essential Miesian character while bringing the facility into the 21st century both technologically and aesthetically. The competition-winning design by the Dutch firm Mecanoo, in association with DC-based OTJ Architects, generally achieves that quite well, particularly on the interior. Two new staircases — open, sculptural, and naturally lit from above — replaced Mies's gloomy and rather perfunctory stairwells. The third-floor reading room now includes a double-height space enlivened by celestial-looking artworks dangling from the ceiling. There is even a slide that leads from the children's reading room to the level below. A new fifth floor, its perimeter set well back from the edges of the building, opens onto a rooftop garden. Throughout the project, curvilinear forms and warm-toned wood surfaces distinguish the new elements from the cool, rectilinear original building fabric.

Now if only the library can find a way to animate the still-dead exterior spaces behind the ground-floor colonnades along 9th and G Streets.

l14

First Congregational United Church of Christ / 10th & G Offices

945 G Street, NW / 733 10th Street, NW

2012 — Cunningham | Quill Architects;
   Design architects for church: Tod Williams Billie Tsien Architects

The First Congregational Church, which has occupied a succession of buildings on this site since 1868, collaborated with commercial developers to build this hybrid structure containing the church's facilities and retail space on the first two floors along with leasable office space above. The two primary components are architecturally distinct but complementary. The faceted glass curtain wall of the office building, designed by Cunningham | Quill Architects, is deferential both to the church below and to the landmark Martin Luther King Jr. Memorial Library next store [see previous entry]. The angled form also distinguishes the building from the many competing structures that fill out every square inch permitted under zoning regulations.

The church, designed by Tod Williams Billie Tsien Architects of New York, is clad primarily in a dark but shimmering brick, punctuated by projecting etched-glass boxes on the second floor marking the main sanctuary on the G Street side and the chapel on the 10th Street side. The box along G Street is no mere bay window but also projects *into* the sanctuary, forming a cubic void — a volume that hovers conceptually between inside and outside. By day, it brings filtered light into the sanctuary; by night, it becomes a great lantern glowing from within.

The prominent column at the corner of 10th and G Streets is the point where the two main components of the building merge. While supporting the office block above, it is also the only piece of overt religious imagery — albeit an abstract one — on the church's exterior. The lower portion of the column, which is covered in white bronze, is augmented by simple rectilinear projections forming a creative rendition of the Christian cross.

I15

CityCenterDC

Between 9th and 11th Streets, and between H Street and New York Avenue, NW

2013—Master plan: Shalom Baranes Associates and Foster + Partners; Rental apartment buildings: Shalom Baranes Associates; Landscape architects for complex: Gustafson Guthrie Nichol with Lee and Associates

2014—Office buildings and condominium apartment buildings: Foster + Partners; Architects of record: Shalom Baranes Associates

2019—Hotel: Herzog & de Meuron Architekten; Architects of record: HKS Architects, Inc.; Interior architects: Rottet Studio

Anthony Williams, while he was mayor of DC, saw the obsolescence of the city's old convention center—a dismal, windowless megastructure completed in 1982—as an opportunity. With plans in place to build a larger, more modern convention facility at Mount Vernon Square [see G13], Williams envisioned the transformation of the old center's multiblock site into a mixed-use development incorporating relatively intimate public open spaces and, not incidentally, reopening the portions of 10th and I Streets that had been obliterated when the hulking old convention center was built.

The master plan for CityCenterDC, by London-based Foster + Partners in collaboration with DC's own Shalom Baranes Associates, is notable for the *woonerf*—a narrow thoroughfare primarily for pedestrians but accessible by vehicles—forming an east-west axis through the first phase of the complex, which extends from 9th to 11th and from H to I Streets. Flanking the *woonerf*, known as Palmer Alley, are three pairs of buildings—two each containing offices, rental apartments, and condominium apartments—with retail along the ground floors. At the juncture of the four residential buildings is a landscaped plaza with outdoor seating for restaurants. Palmer Alley and the plaza are public spaces of a scale that is uncommon in DC, famous for its wide avenues and vast parks. Despite catering to affluent residents and customers, City-Center (as locals call it for short) offers a welcome variety of urban experiences that can be enjoyed by all (the seasonal decorations that often hang above Palmer Alley have become an attraction in themselves).

The office buildings and condominium buildings, at opposite ends of the site, were designed by Foster + Partners. The office buildings to the west are sleek if bland, while the condo buildings to the east are enlivened by sliding louvered panels that introduce some variability to the façades. In between are the rental apartment buildings, designed by Shalom Baranes Associates, which are the most interesting of the bunch, with their syncopated patterns of windows, balcony openings, and solid panels clad in warm-toned terra cotta tiles. The entire complex benefits from the willingness of the site's owner—the DC government—to aim for less than the maximum square footage normally permitted on such a site, allowing the residential buildings to step down around the plaza's perimeter.

The second phase of CityCenterDC comprises the Conrad Hotel, located at the corner of 10th Street and New York Avenue. The initial design by Pritzker Prize-winning Swiss architects Herzog & de Meuron called for a scalloped glass curtain wall that promised to be quite striking. In the end, only the ground floor got the scalloped treatment, leaving the rest as a dull glass box, though the fancifully sculpted interior atrium is worth a look. The third phase of the complex, an office building at the northeastern corner of the site, is currently on hold.

I16

1100 New York Avenue
(incorporating the old Greyhound Bus Station)

1940—William S. Arrasmith / Wischmeyer, Arrasmith & Elswick
1991—Restoration: Vitetta Group; New building: Florance Eichbaum Esocoff King Architects

The dozens of terminals built by the Greyhound Bus company in the 1930s and '40s in cities across the country constituted one of the greatest collections of Art Moderne buildings in the world. Many of these stations, of which few remain, were designed by Louisville-based architect William Arrasmith. For the Washington terminal, Arrasmith adapted his Art Moderne vocabulary to the capital's then-conservative architectural culture, avoiding the striking asymmetry and bold colors that often characterized his work and using such typical Washington materials as limestone and terra cotta for the façade.

The terminal, once known as the "Ellis Island of Washington" since it had welcomed so many Black migrants from the South, was covered in cheap sheet metal in the mid-1970s, but fortunately, the original structure remained essentially undamaged beneath the crude cloak. It was restored when the large office building, whose design is inspired by the Art

Moderne terminal, was built behind it. The New York Avenue façade of the new building, like that of the terminal itself, initially appears to be symmetrical, but the eastern part of the façade curves away to follow the bend in the street. A close look reveals that the stone skin gradually gets lighter in color as the building rises.

I17
1099 New York Avenue, NW
2008 — Thomas Phifer and Partners

From a few blocks away, this looks like a fairly typical glass box. Upon approach, however, one realizes that the building's skin is no ordinary curtain wall: the glass panes overlap, like shingles or scales on a fish, clearly articulating each floor and adding a subtle three-dimensionality to the façades. The individual panes are affixed with structural silicone sealant on all four sides and supported by cast stainless steel brackets that are barely noticeable. Clear glass panes continue above the roofline, providing a parapet around the roof deck, while at the base, variations on the façade treatment call attention to the main entrance. The lobby is a minimalist space rendered vibrant by a backlit installation by artist Matthew Ritchie.

I18
Cato Institute
1000 Massachusetts Avenue, NW
1993 — Hellmuth, Obata + Kassabaum
2012 — Renovation and addition: Gensler

One of the most purely geometrical responses to the irregular intersections characteristic of L'Enfant's plan, the Cato Institute building, which houses a libertarian think tank, looks a bit like a three-dimensional puzzle. The atrium breaks away from the main body of the building to align with Massachusetts Avenue, while the masonry block containing offices is oriented to the rectilinear street grid. Subtle architectural details add interest — note the asymmetrical motifs at the intersections of the metal grid that encloses the atrium, as well as the overlapping geometries in the window patterns of the main block. The new addition is clad in white metal panels that contrast with the ruddy masonry but relate to the metal frame of the atrium.

I19
One Franklin Square
(incorporating the old Almas Temple)
1301 K Street, NW
1990 — Design architects: Hartman-Cox Architects; Architects of record: Dewberry & Davis / Habib; Preservation of Almas Temple: Oehrlein & Associates Architects

2015—Façade changes for offices of the *Washington Post*: Gensler; Renovation of public spaces and roof deck: STUDIOS Architecture

Washington's famous building height limit has always allowed certain exceptions, such as ornamental "spires, towers, domes, minarets, [or] pinnacles." One Franklin Square was among the first late 20th-century commercial buildings to take advantage of that loophole. Known colloquially as the "Twin Peaks" building, its form recalls the stepped massing of 1920s New York skyscrapers. To make room for the new building, the historic Almas Temple (1930—Allen Hussell Potts) was dismantled and reconstructed slightly to the west.

The *Washington Post* moved its headquarters to One Franklin Square in 2015. The building owner consented to a partial renovation of the K Street façade to provide floor-to-ceiling windows for the newspaper's offices on the seventh and eighth floors. The change was relatively modest in scale, yet it created a new focal point on the façade and a welcome contrast to the regularity of the window grid.

During the period of the old downtown's decrepitude, the area around Franklin Square was the city's pornography and prostitution headquarters (one

longtime porn shop in the area bore a sign that proudly identified the proprietors as "Purveyors of Fine Smut"). In the 1990s, however, commercial developers succeeded where the Metropolitan Police had consistently failed, and soon the sex workers were supplanted by lawyers and lobbyists. The square itself is now undergoing a comprehensive rehabilitation.

|20

Franklin School
(now Planet Word)

925 13th Street, NW

1869—Adolf Cluss
1992—Exterior restoration: Oehrlein & Associates Architects
2020—Renovation and adaptive reuse: Beyer Blinder Belle Architects & Planners

The notion of the District of Columbia Public Schools being touted as a paradigm for the world might have seemed farfetched in the recent past, yet that was precisely the case in 1873, when the school system received a "Medal for Progress" at the Vienna Exposition. The primary reason for the award was the design of the Franklin School, which was represented in the exposition by a high-quality scale model. It caused a sensation, inspiring educators from all

over the world to make detailed notes and sketches in the hope of emulating the school's progressive features.

Designed by German American architect Adolf Cluss, the building expanded upon innovations he had introduced in an earlier school (now demolished). In plan, the Franklin School consisted of three principal bays running the width of the structure and separated by circulation zones. On the first and second floors, each bay was divided into two back-to-back classrooms. To ensure sound isolation and cleanliness, each classroom was separated from the corridor by a cloakroom. Immediately behind the cloakroom wall was a raised platform for the teacher's desk, sitting in front of a curved niche that helped to focus sound. Boys and girls entered through separate doors and were sequestered throughout the day—each classroom in the middle bay could be assigned either to girls or to boys as necessary. The third floor included a 1,000-seat auditorium along with separate spaces for "the two grammar schools."

The exterior of the school is typical of the German *Rundbogenstil*, or "round arch style," perhaps showing some Second Empire influence in the mansard roof and even a hint of Indian architecture in the cupolas crowning the octagonal towers that originally served as ventilation shafts. The building's careful composition, high-quality materials, and fine details, both inside and out, represented a deliberate effort to demonstrate to students the value of beauty. It is a lesson that, sadly, was often forgotten in late 20th-century public buildings, though DC's recent school and library construction initiatives reflect an encouraging revival in aspirational civic architecture.

The Franklin School housed the school system's administrative headquarters for many years and served as a homeless shelter before being shuttered for an extended period. Following an extensive renovation, it is now the home of Planet Word, an innovative museum of language that features interactive displays. The most intriguing interior space in the new museum is the second-floor Library, where a mirrored ceiling makes the full-height bookshelves appear as though they soar into the upper reaches of the structure.

I21

National Museum of Women in the Arts
(former Masonic Temple)

1250 New York Avenue, NW

1908—Wood, Donn & Deming
1987—Renovation: Keyes Condon
Florance Architects; Interiors: Carol
Lascaris
1997—Addition: RTKL Associates

The Masons originally occupied a temple at 9th and F Streets [see I12], but when their growing numbers rendered that building inadequate, they hired Waddy Wood's firm to design this larger structure, which originally included an auditorium on the first floor, with offices, lodge rooms, a library, and a shrine on the upper levels. The identity of the building's original owner is evident in decorative motifs such as stone calipers on the keystones above the fourth-floor windows and other common Masonic symbols. The first-floor auditorium was leased out as a commercial vaudeville and movie theater for most of the period between 1908 and 1983 (during later years it was, like the Warner Theatre, a porno house). In 1983, the newly formed National Museum of Women in the Arts bought the building and initiated a complete renovation. The old auditorium was converted into the Great Hall, a special event space lined with faux marble panels in an attempt to achieve elegance on a limited budget.

I22

Inter-American Development Bank

1300 New York Avenue, NW

1984—Skidmore, Owings & Merrill
2004—Addition / conference center:
RTKL Associates

This project helped to define an emerging Washington "school" of architecture in the mid-1980s—neoclassical in spirit if not in literal detail. The façades indirectly evoke common classical motifs, though they are expressed abstractly and at greatly enlarged scale: recessed bays on the fourth through ninth floors are set behind paired columns that give the impression of a colossal colonnade (compare this, for example, to the façade of the Union Trust Building [see I30]); the eighth-floor windows are bracketed to suggest huge dentils; and the upper two stories are finished in a darker material and a different fenestration pattern, creating a hint of a giant cornice. An enormous arch announces the main entrance, which leads to a surprisingly large and lush atrium.

I23

Verizon Building
(former Chesapeake & Potomac Telephone Company Building)

730 12th Street, NW

1928—Voorhees, Gmelin & Walker

Anyone interested in the question of how to create a sense of depth on what is essentially a flat surface should stand next to this building and start counting the vertical lines on its façade. The four central bays on the first and second floors are framed by implied pilasters composed of myriad incisions, creases, and corruga-

24

The Church of the Epiphany

1317 G Street, NW

1844—John C. Harkness
1857—Addition: Ammi Burnham Young
1874—Renovation: Henry Dudley
1890—Addition: Edward J. Neville-Stent
1911, 1922—Additions: Frederick H. Brooke
1950, 1968—Renovations: John W. Stenhouse
2011—Renovation: Rogers Krajnak Architects, Inc.

tions and capped by bursts of intertwined tendrils. Built for the mundane purpose of housing telephone switching equipment, the building is fundamentally a plain brick box with common double-hung windows, yet thanks to its exuberantly ornamented base and crown, the entire structure seems poised to soar into the heavens.

The building was designed by Voorhees, Gmelin & Walker of New York, who effectively served as corporate architects for the Bell Telephone system at the time. The firm was renowned for its Art Deco skyscrapers, including 1 Wall Street, whose pleated limestone skin recalls the intricate folds and notches that give the DC building its jazzy character. The latter's pedimented top was somewhat unusual among Art Deco buildings, which often had stepped rooflines. Note the spread-winged eagle just below the apex of the pediment—a nod to the federal presence in DC perhaps, but also a symbol favored by many architects of the period.

Covered in an icing of white stucco, this church is interesting primarily as a reminder of the architectural scale and character that defined the center of antebellum Washington. The interior is a picturesque affair in English Gothic Revival, notable for its hammer-beam ceiling.

Historic National Bank of Washington

(former Federal-American National Bank)

699 14th Street, NW

1926—Alfred C. Bossom in association with Jules Henri de Sibour
1936, 1939—Renovations to ground floor: architects unknown

Urban banks of the 1920s often boasted grand public banking halls visible from the street. This monumental structure, built for the Federal-American National Bank, was unusual in having the banking hall on the second floor, allowing for leasable retail spaces on the ground floor. Initially, the shops had discrete show windows nestled between the bases of

the columns and pilasters lining the upper floors, but renovations in the 1930s added continuous, projecting display windows. Longtime Washingtonians will remember these windows being filled with the wares of Hahn Shoes, which operated out of this location for nearly 70 years until its closure in 1995.

The building is generally a restrained neoclassical box except for the elaborate main entry facing 14th Street. Here, the architects really went for Baroque, as it were, creating a deep portal with a curved pediment, its bottom chord broken to accommodate a shield bearing the face of a woman in an ancient Roman warrior headdress and bracketed by all manner of decorative devices (nothing says "banking" quite like cherubs). The large arched window above hints at the double-height main hall, reachable by stairs or elevators from the vestibule.

The National Bank of Washington, a successor to Federal-American, failed in 1990, and the building sat empty for decades. Following an unsuccessful campaign to turn it into a museum of the Armenian Genocide of 1914–23, developers broke ground in 2019 on a renovation and office tower addition. Rightly, the design by Shalom Baranes Associates calls for re-creating the original separate shop windows on the ground floor of the historic building, but many older locals will still miss those linear window bays filled with shoes.

126

Commercial National Bank Building
700 14th Street, NW

1917—Waddy B. Wood
1940—Interior renovation: Arthur B. Heaton
1986—Restoration and addition: Keyes Condon Florance

This austere bank building by Washington architect Waddy B. Wood was built during World War I, but it presaged the stripped classical style that became popular during the 1920s and '30s. Wood's design follows key compositional tenets of classicism, such as a clear division of the façades into a base, middle, and top, but here those elements are all greatly simplified and even suppressed. The porticos facing 14th and G Streets, while imposing, look almost as if they had been flattened with a gigantic steam iron. The seven-story shaft is entirely unornamented, without so much as a blip in the taut limestone skin. Things loosen up only a little at the cornice, where projecting lions' heads alternate with palm-like antefixes—upright flourishes at the edge of the roofline.

The client for the project, the Commercial National Bank, was placed in receivership in 1933—at one point, the value of the institution's headquarters exceeded its total assets on deposit—and was out of business by 1937.

127
Bond Building
1400 New York Avenue, NW

1901—George S. Cooper
1986—Renovation and additions: Shalom Baranes Associates

The renovation of the Bond Building was one of the harbingers of the rebirth of Washington's old downtown. It was among the first commercial projects in the area to include the construction of a new "hat"—that is, the addition of several floors on top in order to fill out the maximum volume allowable under current zoning regulations. The project also incorporated two narrow "bookend" additions whose façades were modeled after a slender building at 19 Lincoln's Inn Fields in London, which is depicted in a book that architect Shalom Baranes keeps in his library.

Other downtown buildings that were expanded vertically during the 1980s and '90s include the Army-Navy Building at the southeast corner of Farragut Square, also by Baranes, and the Colorado Building at the northeast corner of 14th and G, by KressCox Associates.

128
National Savings and Trust Company
(now SunTrust Bank)

1445 New York Avenue, NW

1888—James T. Windrim
1916, 1925, 1985—Additions: various architects
2008—Renovation of public spaces: FOX Architects

Dark red brick, a bronze-clad corner bay, ornamental terra cotta panels, and funny little roof pinnacles on the 15th Street side make this building a foil to the more staid neoclassical structures on the other three corners of this intersection. A series of additions along New York Avenue spanning many decades remained true to the original building's aesthetic, despite shifts in construction technology and performance expectations. Step inside the corner entrance to get a glimpse of the elegant banking hall.

129

Folger Building and Playhouse Theatre

(former W. B. Hibbs & Co. Building / Swartzell, Rheem & Hensey Company Building)

725–727 15th Street, NW

1907—Folger Building: Bruce Price & Jules Henri de Sibour
1908—Playhouse Theatre: Paul Pelz
1985—Addition: Mariani & Associates

Built for a brokerage firm and still occupied by its successor, the Folger Building is small but quite lavish, sheathed in gleaming white marble and crowned by an exuberant mansard roof. The building was most likely designed by Washington's own Jules Henri de Sibour, as his New York–based partner Bruce Price had died several years before it was finished. Next to it stands the former entrance to the Playhouse Theatre, originally built as offices for another brokerage firm that did not survive the Depression. It now serves as the base for a stark, modern addition that nonetheless manages to appear rather deferential to its ornate neighbor.

130

Union Trust Building

740 15th Street, NW

1907—Wood, Donn & Deming
1927—Addition: Walter G. Peter, in association with A. B. Mullett & Co.

1983—Renovation and addition: Keyes Condon Florance Architects
2014—Renovation of lobby and common spaces: STUDIOS Architecture

The "UT" crests in the pediments over the ground-floor windows are reminders of this building's original owner, the Union Trust bank. This is, in fact, a quintessential early 20th-century bank building, employing a grand neoclassical vocabulary, fine materials, and impressive massing to convey a sense of stability and integrity. Note the differing treatment of the 15th Street and H Street façades on the third through seventh levels: facing 15th, the wall is set back behind the massive Corinthian columns and finished in dark cast iron, while on H Street, the wall engages the columns and is finished in matching granite. The odd asymmetry of the ground floor along H Street is the result of the 1927 addition, which doubled the length of that façade, though on the upper levels, the original and the addition are seamlessly matched. A penthouse that was part of the 1980s addition is set back from the building edge and is visible only from a distance.

Next door to the Union Trust Building, at 734 15th Street, is the Walker Building (1937—Porter & Lockie), which is most notable for the elaborate concrete mosaics by John Joseph Earley above its first-floor windows and door.

The small office building at 1510 H Street (2009—Eric Colbert & Associates PC) is an example of an attempt to relate simultaneously to dramatically contrasting neighbors on either side. The use of limestone and the balance of horizontal and vertical elements recall the Union Trust Building, while the tautness and proportions of the curtain wall seem more compatible with the red-brick modern building to the west [see J5].

I31

Southern Building

805 15th Street, NW

1914 — Daniel Burnham and Associates
1986 — Restoration and addition: Shalom Baranes Associates; Preservation architects: Oehrlein & Associates Architects

Elaborate terra cotta ornament, including lions' heads poking out from the spandrel panels, contrasts with the plain, buff brick piers of this elegant building by Daniel Burnham. In adding another of his archetypal "hats," Shalom Baranes found justification for the scale and detailing of the addition in several little-known drawings of Burnham's showing designs for mid-rise buildings with two stories above the main cornice line.

I32

900 15th Street, NW / Camden Grand Parc Apartments

(former University Club / United Mine Workers of America Building)

1912 — George Oakley Totten Jr.
1937 — Renovation and addition: Porter & Lockie
2003 — Renovation and addition: Martinez + Johnson; Associate architects: Housing Studio

Built for the University Club, the original five floors of this building offer two distinct flavors in one big scoop of Italian Renaissance Revival architecture. Floors three through five appear to have been inspired by urban palazzi of the 15th century, with relatively small windows set into large expanses of rusticated brickwork. The lower two floors, by contrast, draw on High Renaissance and neoclassical precedents, with refined balustrades, a simple Doric porch, and vermiculated (i.e., carved with worm-like patterns) stonework on the ground floor.

The top floor is an addition by different architects hired by the United Mine Workers of America (UMW), which bought the building during the Great Depression. The more medieval-looking crown, which required the removal of the original cornice, reflected the divergent identity of the new owners, who also stripped the building of the "college boy" university seals that had adorned its fascia. For 40 years, the UMW was led by the formidable John Lewis, who exploited the building's impressive architecture and prestigious location — not far from the centers of political power — to woo allies, intimidate opponents, and elevate general perceptions of the union (Lewis himself lived in the spacious apartment on the top floor). The building was sold in 1999 and partially converted to residential use in connection with a new tower built behind it.

In 2020, the Victims of Communism Memorial Foundation announced plans to open a museum in the historic building.

I33

Midtown Center

1100 15th Street, NW

2018—SHoP Architects; Associate architects: WDG Architecture; Landscape
architects: SCAPE Studio

The stars aligned to allow this project to
break free from the traditional commercial box, incorporating a quasi-public
courtyard and myriad pedestrian paths
through the ground level of the building. In this case, those aligning "stars"
included the fact that this was the first
commercial building to go through the
permit process under new zoning laws
allowing fully occupiable penthouses
above the congressionally mandated
height limit, coupled with a client that
was open to a more civically minded
design approach.

The building's perimeter façades are
rippling tapestries of patinated copper
and glass. The projecting bays, which
were prefabricated directly from digital
design files, are offset both vertically and
horizontally, creating a wave-like pattern.
The courtyard, which is accessible via
either a wide opening along L Street or
diagonal passageways that slice between
retail spaces, consists of an irregular
pattern of crisp geometric shapes accommodating seating areas, planters, and a
cascading fountain. Soaring above the
courtyard are three "sky bridges," lined
with copper fins for solar control, which
complement the diagonal pedestrian
paths at ground level. According to the
architects, the use of copper alludes to
the prevalence of that material in many
historic Washington buildings, while the
angles of the sky bridges and ground-
level pathways recall the diagonal avenues in L'Enfant's plan for the city.

I34

Metropolitan African Methodist Episcopal Church

1518 M Street, NW

1886—Samuel Morsell (with George
Dearing)
1924—Renovation: John A. Lankford
1994, 1998—Renovations and expansion:
Baker Cooper & Associates

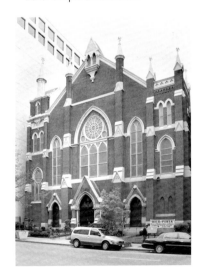

This church, known as the National Cathedral of African Methodism, is a noteworthy example of red-brick, Gothic Revival architecture. Its numerous stained-glass windows depict milestones in the growth of the African Methodist Episcopal (AME) church during the 19th century. Tracing its roots to the founding of the Union Bethel AME Church in 1838, Metropolitan played a significant role in the abolition of slavery and in the 20th-century civil rights movement. It was also the site of Frederick Douglass's funeral in 1895.

I35

Russian Embassy
(former Pullman House)

1119–1125 16th Street, NW

1910 — Nathan C. Wyeth
ca. 1915 — Addition: architect unknown
1934 — Remodeling: Eugene Schoen & Sons
1977 — Addition: architect unknown

Harriet Sanger Pullman, whose husband invented the railroad sleeping car, commissioned this mansion for her daughter and son-in-law, Illinois congressman Frank Lowden. The design of the house is ostensibly based on French Baroque models, with its simple, horizontally striated ground floor and, of course, its mansard roof, but the composition is idiosyncratic and does not correspond to any specific historical period or style. Seen today, the house is distinguished, curiously enough, by the two narrow bands of patinated copper at the top and bottom of the man-

sard — these thin, horizontal accents provide a subtle but significant counterpoint to the steepness of the roof.

Health problems kept Lowden from running for reelection in 1910, so in 1913 Mrs. Pullman sold the house to the wife of a wealthy mining engineer, who sold it to the Russian government a few months later for a tidy profit. The Russians soon added the two-story wing to the south of the main house. Following the 1917 revolution, caretakers occupied the building until the United States officially recognized the Soviet Union in 1933, at which point a modest remodeling of the building ensued. The Soviets moved most diplomatic operations to a huge new chancery complex on Wisconsin Avenue in the 1980s, retaining this as the ambassador's residence. Both properties passed to the new Russian government following the dissolution of the Soviet Union in 1991.

I36

St. Regis Hotel
(former Carlton Hotel)

923 16th Street, NW / Black Lives Matter Plaza, NW

1926 — Mihran Mesrobian
1976 — Renovation: architect unknown
1988 — Renovation: Smith, Segreti, Tepper, McMahon & Harned
2008 — Interior renovation: Sills Huniford; Restaurant and bar interiors: Rockwell Group

This elegant hotel was designed in the manner of a late Italian Renaissance palazzo, with simple massing, a rusticated base, and strongly articulated quoins at the corners. It is almost a perfectly freestanding block, save for a small commercial structure that adjoins it on the K Street side (a garden separates the hotel from the neighboring building to the south). The relative austerity of the façades is relieved by a parade of arches along the ground floor and elaborate window surrounds on the third and seventh stories. A heavy cornice line above the sixth story gives the impression that the building is shorter and more horizontal than it actually is.

Between 1934 and about 1958, the hotel's interior boasted a dazzling Art Moderne bar designed by Nat Eastman.

Highlights of the bar's design included several enamel-and-metal murals and a neon "fireplace." The star feature, however, was surely the "servidor"—a revolving bar that allowed the bartender to make and serve drinks without being seen by patrons.

Previously known as the Carlton, the hotel was designed by Mihran Mesrobian, a Turkish-born Armenian, who immigrated to the United States in 1921 and became the primary in-house architect for legendary Washington developer Harry Wardman. After Wardman declared bankruptcy in 1930, Mesrobian established his own practice, which produced a variety of residential and commercial work over the ensuing quarter century.

White House / Lafayette Square

Henry Adams, who occupied a grand house overlooking Lafayette Square from 1885 until his death in 1918, wrote that in this neighborhood's early days, "beyond the Square the country began." According to Adams, when he moved to the capital city, "No literary or scientific man, no artist, no gentleman without office or employment, had ever lived there. It was rural and its society was primitive. . . . The happy village was innocent of a club. . . . The value of real estate had not increased since 1800, and the pavements were more impassable than the mud."

Indeed, when L'Enfant selected the site for the President's House and the "President's Park" immediately to its north, the area was filled with a flourishing orchard. Construction of what came to be called the Executive Mansion began in 1792, and President John Adams and First Lady Abigail Adams (Henry's great-grandparents) moved into the semi-habitable dwelling in November 1800. Thomas Jefferson, who succeeded Adams as president in March of the following year, wrote, "we find this a very agreeable country residence . . . free from the noise, the heat . . . and the bustle of a close-built town," which makes clear how undeveloped Washington was in 1801.

L'Enfant intended that the President's Park serve as an extension of the Executive Mansion grounds, but Jefferson and others found such a large lawn uncomfortably imperial. Before long, a new stretch of Pennsylvania Avenue was laid down in front of the mansion, dividing the green space in two and creating the separate square. The square and the park at its center were named—informally at first—for the Marquis de Lafayette during his triumphant return to Washington in 1824.

Nowadays, a public square directly across from the President's House and surrounded by historic town houses would seem to be sacred, but that was not always the case. The Senate Park Commission Plan of 1901–2 envisioned a wholesale reconstruction of Lafayette Square and its adjacent blocks to create a unified enclave of enormous neoclassical government office buildings, but only two buildings were eventually erected in accordance with this plan. In the early 1960s, the character of the square was threatened again, and it was only through the personal and active intervention of First Lady Jacqueline Kennedy that the remaining town houses facing the square were saved. Sadly, security concerns following the bombing of the Oklahoma City federal building in 1995 led to the closure of Pennsylvania Avenue in front of the White House to vehicular traffic, and the once-busy thoroughfare suddenly became a rather desolate stretch disfigured by makeshift barriers. A serviceable if bland redesign of the block was finally completed in 2004.

Lafayette Park itself has figured prominently in the political and social life of the capital throughout its history. In 1829, after Andrew Jackson had defeated Henry Adams's grandfather for the presidency, he held boisterous, whiskey-fueled inauguration festivities in the square. During the Civil War, soldiers bivouacked in the park, and in the 1870s, Ulysses S. Grant started a small zoo here. By the 1920s, improbably enough, the park—virtually in the shadow of the White House—was firmly established as a safe meeting place for closeted gay men (at a time when being openly gay was to risk personal ruin, injury, or even death).

In the summer of 2020, Lafayette Square emerged as the epicenter of global anti-racism protests following the death of George Floyd at the hands of police officers in Minneapolis. Some monuments and nearby buildings were defaced and damaged during the ongoing demonstrations. Before long, federal officials erected fences and other barricades around the park, transforming what had long been a vital and symbolically important public space into an ominous void. The appalling climax came on June 1, when police and federal officers, some in unmarked uniforms, launched tear gas and flash-bangs into a group of peaceful protesters in order to clear the way for President Donald Trump to have a photo op in front of a neighboring church. Four days later, DC mayor Muriel Bowser responded with a dramatic gesture, ordering the two-block stretch of 16th Street north of the park to be emblazoned with the words "Black Lives Matter" in enormous yellow letters.

Since then, Lafayette Square and the adjacent blocks of 16th Street, now also known as Black Lives Matter Plaza, have become something of a pilgrimage site for many locals and visitors. Now that the fences have come down, and the damaged memorials and other structures are being restored, the square may look much as it did before the protests, but, like so many sites in Washington, it will surely bear traces of the ever-increasing weight of history.

(*Above*) This bird's-eye rendering shows the White House and Lafayette Square sometime before 1851, when the parks immediately surrounding the Executive Mansion were landscaped in accordance with plans by Andrew Jackson Downing. The drawing also shows idealized, symmetrical, E-shaped buildings for the War and Navy departments (*left*) and the Treasury (*right*).

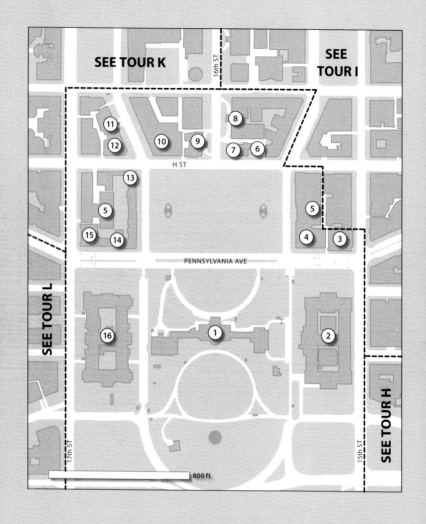

J1

The White House

1600 Pennsylvania Avenue, NW

1792–1801—James Hoban
1803–14—Renovations and colonnades/
  dependencies: Benjamin Henry Latrobe
1814–17—Reconstruction after fire: James
  Hoban
1824—South Portico: James Hoban
1830—North Portico: James Hoban
1902—Addition of West Wing and renovation of interior and East Terrace:
  Charles Follen McKim / McKim, Mead
  & White
1909—Expansion of West Wing: Nathan C.
  Wyeth
1927—Addition of third floor and new
  roof: William Adams Delano
1934—Expansion of West Wing: Eric
  Gugler
1942—Addition of East Wing: Lorenzo S.
  Winslow
1948—South Portico balcony: Lorenzo S.
  Winslow and William Adams Delano
1948–52—Reconstruction of interior:
  Lorenzo S. Winslow
1970—Renovation of West Wing and
  North Portico: architect unknown

Few buildings are as laden with symbolism as the White House. Its name is
invoked to represent the president, the
presidential administration, and even the
entire executive branch of the federal
government. It is alternately an emblem
of national pride and an object of political
scorn, which sometimes makes it difficult
to appreciate the building itself as a work
of architecture.

The White House today seems
immutable, yet it reflects more than two
centuries of nearly constant alterations
and additions. As with the Capitol, the
basic design was selected through a competition (there is evidence that Thomas
Jefferson entered and lost the competition under a gentlemanly pseudonym).
The winning proposal was submitted by
James Hoban, an Irish architect prac-
ticing in Charleston, South Carolina,
whose somewhat conservative design
was inspired by Leinster House in Dublin,
Ireland, a mid-18th-century palace that
is now home to the Irish Parliament. It
was probably not by chance that Hoban
chose the less-formal Ionic order instead
of the Corinthian used on Leinster House,
however, since his design reflected an
effort to strike a careful balance between
dignity and modesty.

Construction began in the fall of 1792,
and as with the Capitol, many of the
workers were Black—some of them

This drawing from 1792 shows James Hoban's competition-winning
design for the President's House.

enslaved and some free. Material short-ages and other impediments made for slow going, and the building was still incomplete when the government moved from Philadelphia in November 1800. The first occupants, President John Adams and First Lady Abigail Adams, were not impressed by their new accommodations. Abigail wrote to her daughter, "There is not a single apartment finished. . . . We had not the least fence, yard, or other convenience, without, and the great unfinished audience-room [the East Room] I make a drying room of, to hang up the clothes in." Jefferson displaced the grumbling Adamses in 1801, but he wasn't totally enamored of the mansion, either, supposedly grousing that it was "big enough for two emperors, one Pope, and the grand lama in the bargain" (some sources attribute the quote to an unnamed satirist instead). A diligent amateur architect, Jefferson designed low pavilions for either side of the main building, moderating the structure's grandeur. He worked in association with the omnipresent Benjamin Henry Latrobe, who humored the president even while quietly dismissing Jefferson's proposals as "a litter of pigs worthy of the great Sow it surrounds." Latrobe's own designs for the pavilions were built, and several of his other proposals inspired subsequent additions to the mansion.

Set ablaze by the British in August 1814, the Executive Mansion was saved from total destruction by a violent thunder-storm. After the fire, President James Madison and First Lady Dolley Madison rented the nearby Octagon [see L6] and brought in Hoban to oversee the man-sion's restoration. The building received a thick coat of white paint to cover char-ring from the fire, though it already had been whitewashed essentially from the beginning. It is not known who first called it the "White House," but when Theodore Roosevelt made the name official in 1902, he was merely sanctioning long-standing common usage.

In 1824, Hoban, following Latrobe's plans, added the semicircular South Por-tico, thereby creating the house's signa-ture façade, which is actually the rear of the building. He added the North Portico a few years later. The interior underwent frequent alterations, but in 1902, Theodore Roosevelt ordered an especially extensive renovation. He brought in McKim, Mead & White to remodel the original building, remove a run of Victorian conservatories, and add the West Wing. The famous Oval Office did not appear until the 1909 reno-vation by Nathan Wyeth, and even then, it was not in its current location (it was moved in 1934).

Investigations during Harry Truman's administration revealed that the aging mansion was on the verge of catastrophic structural failure. Although the exterior walls, which were, in one inspector's memorable phrase, standing "purely from habit," were salvaged, little else was — the building was gutted and its interior was reconstructed between 1948 and 1952. Steel replaced the crumbling stone and wood structure, and while the original paneling and trim were removed, repaired, and reinstalled, many historic elements were, shockingly, simply dis-carded. The rooms of the main house are thus largely replicas rather than true orig-inals, but this does not diminish the awe that these historic and venerable spaces inspire in general visitors, foreign digni-taries, and even the families afforded the temporary privilege of calling the White House home.

J2

Treasury Building

1500 Pennsylvania Avenue, NW

1836–42 — East and central wings: Robert Mills

1855 — Initial plan for completion of build-ing: Thomas U. Walter

1855–64 — South and west wings: Ammi B. Young; Isaiah Rogers

1865 — Attic floor additions: Isaiah Rogers

1866–69 — North wing: Alfred B. Mullett

1910 — Renovation and addition: York & Sawyer

1986 — East Executive Avenue redesign: Arthur Cotton Moore / Associates

1996–2005 — Exterior restoration: Quinn Evans Architects; Interior and exterior restoration: Shalom Baranes Associ-ates; Historic materials consultants: John Milner Associates

The oldest cabinet-level departmental headquarters, the Treasury Building also

represents one of the earliest serious infringements upon L'Enfant's plan. According to legend, it was President Andrew Jackson who, tired of delays in determining the exact site for the building, stood along the diagonal axis of Pennsylvania Avenue, pounded his cane into the ground and barked, "Put it here!" Actually, even if the story is true, the initial siting would not have blocked the reciprocal vista between the President's House and the Capitol, since the first wing of the new building did not extend that far south. But once the addition was built at that end, the vista—one of the most important symbolic features of L'Enfant's design of the city—was forever compromised.

The Treasury took more than three decades to build and reflects the work of several important 19th-century architects. Robert Mills was responsible for the original design, which called for an E-shaped plan with the open ends facing the White House. Like the Old Patent Office [see G16], it was a Greek Revival design, but whereas the former relied on a simple, brawny Doric portico for visual power, the Treasury Building was defined by an audacious, uninterrupted Ionic colonnade running the entire length of the east façade, a distance of 466 feet. The main entrance to the building was in the middle of that façade, behind the colonnade, and was reached by a staircase from 15th Street. The interior of Mills's original structure incorporated his signature brick-vaulted structural system,

considered the best defense against the ravages of fire.

Mills oversaw construction of the long eastern spine and the central wing between 1836 and 1842. In 1855, Thomas U. Walter, who was busy at work on the extension of the Capitol, was hired to "complete" Mills's plan. He proposed filling in the open ends of the E-shaped plan and adding shallow porticos flanking the Ionic colonnade along 15th Street, as well as deeper porticos in the centers of the new north, south, and west wings. As in the Old Patent Office, Walter abandoned Mills's masonry vault system in favor of a cast iron structure. The south and west wings were built, largely according to Walter's design, under Ammi Young, in his capacity as supervising architect of the Treasury, and his successor, Isaiah Rogers.

Construction of the north wing was delayed until after the Civil War. In completing it, architect Alfred Mullett respected the precedents set by Mills and Walter on the exterior but designed the interiors in a much more elaborate Renaissance Revival vein. The most notable of Mullett's spaces is the capacious Cash Room, which originally served as something like a commercial banking hall. It is lined with seven different types of marble, lit by enormous gilded chandeliers, and surrounded by a balcony with intricate iron railings.

Between 1908 and 1910, the building underwent a renovation that included removal of the entry staircase on 15th Street and replacement of the long row of Ionic columns, which had been built of fragile Aquia sandstone, with more durable granite replicas. In 1996, repair workers accidentally set fire to the roof, and while the building's structure held up well, there was significant water and smoke damage. The incident provided the impetus for a long-overdue restoration of the key public spaces, corridors, and offices.

J3

Historic Bank Buildings

1501–5 Pennsylvania Avenue, NW

1902 — 1503 Pennsylvania: York & Sawyer
1905 — 1501 Pennsylvania: York & Sawyer
1924 — Addition to 1503 Pennsylvania: Appleton P. Clark Jr.
1932 — Office building addition and renovation of 1501 Pennsylvania: York & Sawyer
1986 — Restoration of banking hall at 1503 Pennsylvania: John Blatteau

These two adjoining bank buildings enjoy one of the most prestigious conceivable locations for such institutions — directly across the street from the US Treasury. Built for two different clients in three phases, they were designed in such a harmonious fashion that they are often mistaken for one structure. The first building completed was the pedimented section with two Ionic columns *in antis* (bracketed by projecting walls) at 1503 Pennsylvania Avenue, which was built for the venerable Riggs National Bank. American Security

Bank then commissioned its own building at 1501 Pennsylvania. In 1924, Riggs added the narrow wing immediately to the west of its original banking hall.

American Security, which occupied the corner building for decades before being absorbed by another bank, long used the slogan "When you need a bank for your money, bank with the bank that's *on* the money." The slogan referred to the fact that, on the back of the old $10 bill, the engraving of the Treasury Building included a glimpse of the private bank's flagship facility across the street.

In 2015, billionaire Michael Milken, who pled guilty to securities and tax fraud in 1990 but was pardoned by President Donald Trump in 2020, announced plans to open the Milken Center for Advancing the American Dream, incorporating the two historic bank buildings and adjacent structures on 15th Street. Designed by Shalom Baranes Associates, the project is scheduled to be completed by 2023.

J4

Treasury Annex

701 Madison Place, NW

1919 — Cass Gilbert

The Senate Park Commission Plan of 1901–2 called for an enclave of public buildings that would have obliterated all of the row houses surrounding Lafayette Square, and in 1917, Cass Gilbert developed specific designs for the palatial marble structures the commission envisioned. Only this building and the Chamber of Commerce [see J10] were executed, however. The Treasury Annex exudes the sturdy rectitude one would expect in such a project, with impressive

Ionic colonnades lining the two exposed elevations. The lack of a portico on either side, however, is a sign of the annex's subordinate status vis-à-vis the main Treasury Building.

J5
Lafayette Square Federal Buildings
Blocks adjacent to Jackson Place and Madison Place, NW

1969 — John Carl Warnecke & Associates

Lafayette Square, the pride of 19th-century Washington, lost several of its greatest treasures to 20th-century wrecking balls, yet things could have turned out much worse. A scheme to raze nearly all of the remaining row houses on the square was under consideration again in 1961 when First Lady Jacqueline Kennedy intervened and asked architect John Carl Warnecke to devise a plan that would save what remained of the historic fabric. Warnecke's solution somehow seemed both radical and sensible at the time — the houses would be preserved, while taller "background" buildings would be built in the houses' back yards. The new buildings (the US Court of Federal Claims to the east and the New Executive Office Building to the west) were intended to relate to the historic houses by virtue of their similar materials, bay windows, and mansard roofs. Unfortunately, as con-structed, the buildings are still intrusive, with large, unrelieved red-brick walls, stingy windows, and awkwardly propor-tioned projecting bays. Still, the essential character of the square, as perceived from street level, was largely preserved — an act of deference to existing architecture that was rare at the time.

J6
St. John's Parish Building
(former Ashburton House / British Legation)

1525 H Street, NW

1837 — Architect unknown
1854 — Renovation: Thomas U. Walter
1877 — Addition and renovation: architect unknown
1955 — Renovation: Horace Peaslee
2018 — Renovation: Bowie Gridley Archi-tects

Matthew St. Clair Clarke, once and future clerk of the US House of Representatives, began building this house in 1836 but soon ran into financial trouble and was forced to sign over the property to his bankers. It was subsequently leased to a number of distin-guished people, including British diplomats Lord Ashburton and Sir Henry Bulwer (brother of Edward Bulwer-Lytton, the nov-elist responsible for the infamous opening line, "It was a dark and stormy night."). By about 1850, the house was commonly known as the British Legation — essentially an embassy. Originally finished in brick, the house was given a coat of stucco in 1854, along with new, bulky window trim and a heavy cornice. The oversized mansard roof was added in 1877. The American Federa-tion of Labor eventually bought the building and later sold it to St. John's Church [see following entry] for use as a parish hall. During the protests after the murder of George Floyd by police officers in Minneap-olis in 2020, a fire was set in the basement of the building but was extinguished before it could cause major damage.

J7

St. John's Church, Lafayette Square

16th and H Streets, NW / Black Lives Matter Plaza, NW

1816 — Benjamin Henry Latrobe
1822 — Addition: George Bomford
1842 — Renovation: architect unknown, though possibly Robert Mills
1880s — Alterations and addition: James Renwick Jr.
1920 — Renovation: McKim, Mead & White
1955 — Renovation: Horace Peaslee
2009 — Renovation: Bowie Gridley Architects

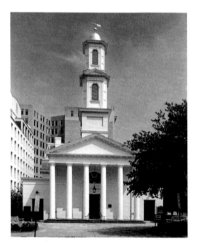

Benjamin Henry Latrobe wrote in a letter to his son that this building "has made people religious who were never before at Church." It's hard to know whether he was joking, but regardless, his initial design — a simple, dignified, well-proportioned structure with a plan in the shape of a Greek cross — was surely an impressive sight in 1816 despite its small size. His chaste little chapel did not last long, however, before it began to be altered by a succession of architects, who extended the nave toward 16th Street (creating a more typical, Latin cross plan), added both a portico and a tall steeple, and later replaced clear windows with stained glass. One can, however, sense the original plan while sitting in a pew under the central dome. Known as the "Church of the Presidents," it has hosted every chief executive since Madison. By tradition, pew 54 is reserved for the current president and first family.

Amid the protests in the wake of the death of George Floyd in 2020, the church became infamous as the backdrop for President Donald Trump's photo op with a Bible after federal law enforcement officers dispersed protesters from Lafayette Square with tear gas, smoke bombs, and stun grenades.

J8

AFL-CIO National Headquarters

815 16th Street, NW / Black Lives Matter Plaza, NW

1956 — Voorhees, Walker, Smith and Smith
1971 — Addition: Mills Petticord & Mills
2002 — Renovation: Group Goetz Architects (GGA) with Ehrenkrantz Eckstut & Kuhn Architects

An organization hoping to influence federal policy could hardly find a more auspicious site for its headquarters, virtually within shouting distance of the White House. The main body of the building is fairly typical of Washington's post–World War II commercial architecture — essentially a slightly modernized version of the stripped classicism that was so common before the war — but the top is unusual, with barrel-vaulted mechanical penthouses punctuated by perforated stone panels. A skillful 2002 renovation moved the main entrance off center, providing space for conference facilities and a welcoming lobby featuring a stunning restored mosaic, *Labor Omnia Vincit* ("Work Conquers All"), by Lumen Martin Winter. A second mosaic by Winter, titled *Labor is Life*, is in a space now used for meetings. Neither mosaic was damaged when the building was vandalized during the protests after the murder of George Floyd.

J9

Hay-Adams Hotel

800 16th Street, NW / Black Lives Matter Plaza, NW

1928 — Mihran Mesrobian
1983–94 — Renovations and addition of
   porte-cochère: LEO A DALY
2002 — Interior renovation: BBGM; Interior
   design: Thomas Pheasant
2009 — Exterior restoration: Hartman-Cox
   Architects
2011 — Rooftop addition: Hartman-Cox
   Architects; Interior design: Thomas
   Pheasant

The Hay-Adams Hotel derives its name
from two noteworthy residences that
were demolished to make way for it —
adjoining houses for John Hay and Henry
Adams designed by H. H. Richardson
and built in 1885. The houses were dark,
asymmetrical Romanesque Revival
structures typical of Richardson's work;
in contrast, the hotel, designed by Mihran
Mesrobian, is a rigorously symmetrical
composition based on neoclassical precedents and built of light-colored limestone.
While undeniably dignified, the design is
a bit ponderous compared to many other
works by the talented Mesrobian. The
shallow projecting central bays on each of
the principal façades look as though they
desperately wanted to burst out in full-
fledged three-dimensionality but couldn't
quite muster the courage. Meanwhile,
rusticated stonework — laid with deep
joints emphasizing individual blocks of
stone — lines the ground floor and climbs
up the corners of the building and of the
projecting bays, contributing to a sense
of heaviness. The recessed loggias on

the sixth and seventh floors add some
welcome depth. The hotel's principal
interior spaces, which are slathered in
dark woodwork, look like they could have
been plucked from an old-school English
"gentlemen's club."

J10

US Chamber of Commerce Building

1615 H Street, NW

1925 — Cass Gilbert
1956 — Addition: Chatelain, Gauger and
   Nolan
1980 — Addition and renovation: John S.
   Samperton
2012 — Renovations of first through third
   floors: Morgan, Gick, McBeath and
   Associates
2014 — Renovation of lower level: IA Interior Architects
2021 — Exterior restoration: Hartman-Cox
   Architects

This and the Treasury Annex [see J4]
are the only completed portions of Cass
Gilbert's plan to replace the historic row
houses surrounding Lafayette Square
with a unified cluster of neoclassical
office buildings. With a parade of three-
story-tall Corinthian columns marching
down its two principal façades — and
even a queue of matching pilasters on
the east façade, where they are barely
visible except from certain rooms in the
adjacent Hay-Adams Hotel — the building
lives up to its contemporary description
as a "temple of commerce." Interestingly,
the Chamber of Commerce Building is
conspicuously grander that Gilbert's
Treasury Annex, perhaps reflecting the
organization's belief in the supremacy of
business over government. This particular

project entailed the demolition of a brace of houses owned by several prominent historical figures, including Daniel Webster, who lived at the corner of H Street and Connecticut Avenue.

J11

816 Connecticut Avenue, NW

1987—Shalom Baranes Associates

This elegant, 28-foot-wide sliver borrows a trick from the bay-fronted row houses that characterize many of Washington's residential neighborhoods. The architect obtained permission from the District government for the projection over the sidewalk by arguing that the narrowness of the site created a unique aesthetic opportunity to accentuate the building's verticality. The advantage for the city is a slick exclamation mark that terminates the vista from up 17th Street. Vertical slits lined with glass block and lit from behind emphasize the building's proportions.

J12

800 Connecticut Avenue, NW

1993—Florance Eichbaum Esocoff King Architects

This commercial office building evokes the architecture of the Viennese Secession in its basic forms, fenestration, and ornamental details. Given its location amid the centers of political power, the building was conceived with high-powered lobbyists in mind as potential

tenants, and the architects therefore sought to provide as many "power perches" as possible, hence the profusion of corner offices and terraces. The upper levels are popular vantage points for television news cameras because of their clear views of the White House (clear, but not open—the Secret Service insisted on bullet-proof glass screens surrounding the terraces).

J13

Decatur House

748 Jackson Place, NW (Visitor entrance at 1610 H Street, NW)

1819—Benjamin Henry Latrobe
1822—Addition: architect unknown
1872—Renovation: architect unknown
1944—Restoration: Thomas T. Waterman
2004—Restoration of original kitchen: Davis Buckley Architects and Planners
2008—Restoration of entry and stair hall: Davis Buckley Architects and Planners

The Decatur House was both the first and the last building on Lafayette Square to be occupied as a private residence. Built

for Commodore Stephen Decatur, scourge of the Barbary pirates, and his wife, Susan, the original house was a textbook example of Federal-style architecture, with restrained details, a flat façade, and carefully considered proportions. A little over a year after the Decaturs moved in, however, the architect, Benjamin Henry Latrobe, was dead of yellow fever in New Orleans and the commodore himself was killed in a duel. Susan Decatur decamped for a smaller house in Georgetown and rented the Lafayette Square property to a number of prominent residents, including several British, French, and Russian diplomats. The house was the unofficial residence of Secretaries of State from 1827 to 1833, as Henry Clay, Martin Van Buren, and Edward Livingston all rented the place during their tenures in that office.

John Gadsby, proprietor of the National Hotel in DC and Gadsby's Tavern in Virginia, bought the house in 1836. Western explorer Edward Fitzgerald Beale and his wife, Mary, bought it from Gadsby's heirs in 1872. (It was Beale, then based near San Francisco, who in 1848 galloped east to announce that gold had been discovered at Sutter's Mill.) The Beales embarked on a thorough Victorianization of the chaste old Federal house and proceeded to throw lavish parties that made it a nexus of social life in the Gilded Age. They left the house to their son, Truxtun, whose widow lived there until she bequeathed it to the National Trust for Historic Preservation in 1956.

While still owned by the National Trust, the house is now managed by the White House Historical Association. Since 2010, it has been the home of the David M. Rubenstein National Center for White House History, which promotes research and conducts educational programming related to the history of the White House and Lafayette Square.

J14
Blair-Lee House

1651–1653 Pennsylvania Avenue, NW

1824 — Blair House: architect unknown
1850s — Addition of third and fourth stories and east wing: architects unknown
1859 — Lee House: architect unknown
1931 — Blair House restoration: Waldron Faulkner

1988 — Restoration and addition: Mendel Mesick Cohen Waite Hall Architects; Allan Greenberg, Architect
2014–21 — Conservation and modernization: Citadel DCA

When the US Department of the Interior placed a historical marker at Blair House in 1939, the building became, in effect, the first federally designated historic landmark in the country. In arguing for the marker, the National Park Service noted the building's construction of hand-hewn lumber with handmade nails and hardware. It's a safe bet, however, that Franklin Delano Roosevelt's desire to protect a historic house across the street from the Executive Mansion didn't hurt the nomination.

The original Blair House was built by Surgeon General Joseph Lovell; its current name came from Francis Preston Blair, who bought it in 1837. Blair was a newspaper editor from Kentucky who helped shape American politics through his influential publications *The Globe* and *The Congressional Globe*. The house was later occupied by his son, Montgomery Blair, an attorney who represented Dred Scott in the infamous Supreme Court case and who served as postmaster general under Lincoln. The adjacent house was built by the senior Blair for his daughter and her husband, Samuel P. Lee, a cousin of Robert E. Lee.

In 1942, as World War II was raging, the federal government bought Blair House to serve as guest quarters for visiting heads of state and then purchased Lee House next door for the same purpose the following year. According to a story told by Franklin D. Roosevelt Jr., his mother, Eleanor, enthusiastically supported the idea of an official guesthouse after a late-night encounter with British prime minister Winston Churchill, whom she found wandering the halls of the White House in his nightshirt, carrying a cigar, and looking for the president in order to resume a discussion from earlier in the evening. There is also evidence, however, that one reason for buying the property was to avoid potential embarrassment when foreign leaders "of non-Caucasian extraction" came to town, since such visitors might not have been accepted at racially segregated hotels.

From 1948 to 1952, President Harry Truman and his family lived here while the White House underwent major structural renovations. During this time, the Marshall Plan for the reconstruction of postwar Europe was hatched in the Lee House dining room, which served as Truman's cabinet room. In 1950, two Puerto Rican nationalists stormed Blair House in an attempt to assassinate the president. One of the would-be assassins and White House police officer Leslie Coffelt were killed in the gunfight on the front sidewalk. Truman was unharmed.

J15

Renwick Gallery of the Smithsonian American Art Museum
(former Corcoran Gallery / US Court of Claims)

1661 Pennsylvania Avenue, NW

1861 — James Renwick Jr., with Robert T. Auchmutz
1874 — Renovation: architect unknown
1972 — Exterior restoration: John Carl Warnecke & Associates; Interior res-

toration and remodeling: Hugh Newell Jacobsen
2000 — Renovation of Grand Salon: Ehren-krantz Eckstut & Kuhn Architects
2015 — Renovation: Westlake Reed Leskosky (schematic design by archi-trave, p.c., architects)

William Wilson Corcoran, cofounder of Washington's storied Riggs Bank, commissioned this building as a public gallery for his substantial art collection. Construction began in 1859, but when the Civil War broke out, the federal government appropriated the nearly completed building from Corcoran, a Southern sympathizer, and used it as a military warehouse and later as the headquarters of Quartermaster General Montgomery C. Meigs. The building was returned to Corcoran in 1869, and he finally opened his museum in 1874 following extensive renovations. The institution moved to a new facility in 1897 [see L7], and in 1899, the US Court of Claims moved in and stayed for 65 years. Along with many of the buildings surrounding Lafayette Square, this structure was saved from the threat of demolition in the 1960s thanks to the intervention of First Lady Jacqueline Kennedy. The Smithsonian took possession of the building and returned it to museum use as a branch of the Smithsonian American Art Museum focusing on crafts, which opened to the public in 1972.

The Renwick—the rare museum named for its architect, rather than its benefactor—imitated the then-popular French Second Empire style, most notably in the characteristic mansard roof. The use of red brick as the primary finish material seems to be a distinctly American touch,

however, as are the column capitals bearing ornamental motifs based on tobacco and corn (surely inspired by Benjamin Henry Latrobe's similar designs at the Capitol). Heavy, vermiculated quoins (with irregular, worm-like patterns etched into the stone) and swags bearing Corcoran's initials add to the liveliness of the façades. The interior is relatively intimate for a museum, though it does boast a grand staircase leading to an equally grand salon. Following a renovation completed in 2015, the venerable but once-fusty gallery now seems bright and thoroughly up to date.

J16

Dwight D. Eisenhower Executive Office Building
(Old Executive Office Building / former State, War & Navy Building)

1650 Pennsylvania Avenue, NW

1871–88 —Alfred B. Mullett, with William Potter, Orville Babcock, and Thomas Lincoln Casey; Interior engineering and design: Richard von Ezdorf
1997–2001 —Various interior restoration projects: Kemnitzer, Reid & Haffler Architects; Quinn Evans Architects; Einhorn Yaffee Prescott; SmithGroup
2004–14 —Modernization design architects: SmithGroup; Architects of record: AECOM

The transitory taste for French neoclassicism, fostered by the École des Beaux-Arts in Paris, has few more striking expressions.
— *The WPA Guide to Washington, D.C.*, 1942

Washington's largest Second Empire–style building took 17 years to build, and when finally finished, it was widely reviled as a symbol of Gilded-Age excess. Its ornate style had fallen out of fashion, and the building's great cost —more than $10 million (equivalent to about a quarter of a billion dollars in 2020) —was considered scandalous. Henry Adams acerbically dubbed it an "architectural infant asylum." Alfred Mullett, who designed the building while serving as supervising architect of the Treasury, resigned his position in 1874 and later took his own life after unsuccessfully suing the federal government for additional compensation.

The building was repeatedly threatened with radical revisions that seemed almost punitive in spirit. In 1917, the US Commission of Fine Arts asked John Russell Pope to cloak the hulking structure in more orthodox classical garb to match that of the Treasury Building, and in 1929, after President Herbert Hoover groaned about the "architectural orgy" that loomed over the White House, Waddy Wood was given a similar assignment. Neither Pope's nor Wood's drastic proposal came to pass thanks to a lack of money, but in 1957, a presidential commission recommended total demolition, and it was not until the 1960s that general opinions of the building began to soften.

Built of dense, purplish-gray granite, the structure is lined with some 900 columns, accented with dramatically projecting bays, and topped with a steep mansard roof and tall chimneys. Immense and undeniably eccentric, the building managed to survive decades of ignominy and is now, at long last, widely beloved as a welcome exception to the sedate architecture more typical of governmental buildings.

Downtown — West End

S trategically located between the White House and the elegant neigh-borhoods of Georgetown and Dupont Circle, the West End was the primary focus of Washington's commercial development during the major post–World War II economic booms. Although development in the old, eastern part of downtown took off again beginning in the 1980s, the area west of 16th Street and north of Pennsylvania Avenue continues to be a prestigious precinct of nonprofit organizations and corporate offices. The area also contains the most consequential stretch of K Street, a thoroughfare once synonymous with high-powered law firms and lobbyists, though many such firms have since dispersed to other parts of the city center. While this neighborhood suffers from a certain blandness, it does contain a number of architecturally noteworthy individual buildings.

In the early 20th century, the area around Farragut Square, now lined with commercial offices, was predominantly residential. Pictured here are the Stoneleigh Court Apartments (*left*) and an elegant trio of town houses called Shepherd's Row at the northeast corner of Connecticut Avenue and K Street. Alexander Robey "Boss" Shepherd lived in the corner house, and architect Adolf Cluss, who designed the row, lived next door.

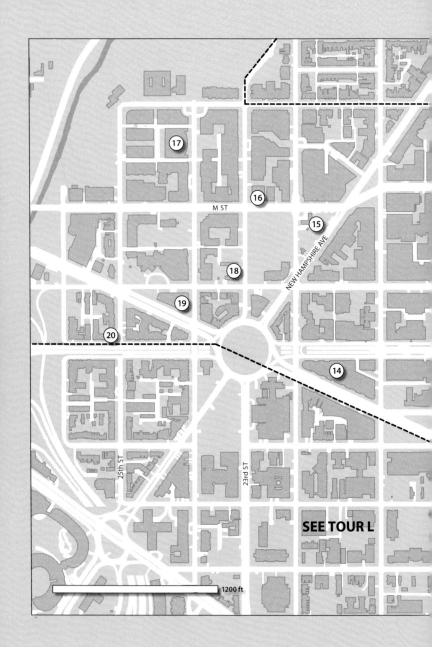

SEE TOUR L

1200 ft

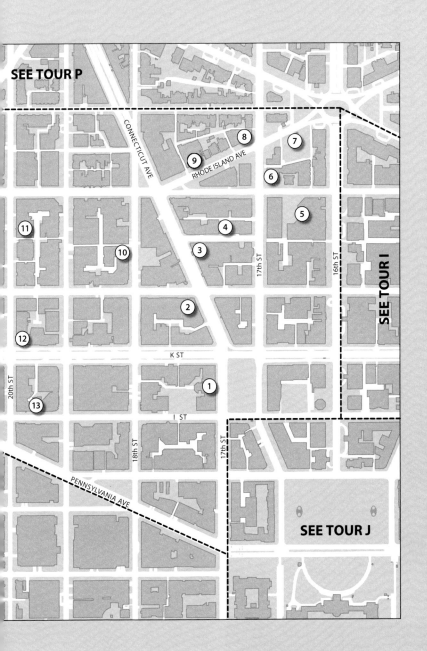

SEE TOUR P

CONNECTICUT AVE

RHODE ISLAND AVE

SEE TOUR I

SEE TOUR J

PENNSYLVANIA AVE

K ST

I ST

20th ST

18th ST

17th ST

16th ST

①
②
③
④
⑤
⑥
⑦
⑧
⑨
⑩
⑪
⑫
⑬

K1

Barr Building

910 17th Street, NW

1926—B. Stanley Simmons

Rich ornament in the English Gothic Revival style lends an ecclesiastical character to this office building—indeed, the vacant niches on its façade look as if they were destined to accommodate saintly statuary. E. J. Applewhite declared the Barr Building to be "a rebuke to the boring borax banality of the computer-designed structures which adjoin it at either side." Although the adjacent structure to the south was built before the digital age, and the one to the north is new since Applewhite's time, his remark remains apt.

K2

Washington Square

1050 Connecticut Avenue, NW

1982—Chloethiel Woodard Smith & Associates

The intersection of Connecticut Avenue and L Street is sometimes called "Chloethiel's Corner" because Chloethiel Woodard Smith designed three of its four buildings (all but the one on the northeast corner). Of these, Washington Square is by far the most stylish, thanks to its serrated façades composed of shallow bay windows, its mezzanine-level outdoor terrace, and its pair of glassy, towering atria, all of which make it look more like a glitzy convention hotel than a typical downtown office building.

K3

Mayflower Hotel

1127 Connecticut Avenue, NW

1925—Warren & Wetmore; Associated architect: Robert S. Beresford

1941—Partial interior renovation: Dorothy Draper Inc.

1947—Restoration: architect unknown

1958—Apartment wing converted to hotel rooms: architect unknown

1984—Renovation and addition: Vlastimil Koubek; Interior designer: Louis Cataffo

2019—Interior renovation: Studio GAIA

Best known as the architects of New York's Grand Central Terminal, Warren & Wetmore also designed dozens of luxurious hotels, mansions, and office buildings that epitomized gentility and urbanity in early 20th-century America. The Mayflower Hotel is emblematic of the era in its subdued elegance. The main body of the building is rather plain, with simple windows set into unadorned brick walls, but the hotel achieves quiet dignity thanks to its tastefully ornamented limestone base, the bold terra cotta quoins climbing the corners of each wing, the subtle curves of the two wings facing Connecticut Avenue, and the parade of loosely spaced urns running along the edge of the roof. (The southernmost two bays of the Connecticut Avenue façade are technically an "annex," though finished in the same year as the rest of the hotel, which explains the seemingly superfluous tiers of quoins and the clump of four urns at the top of that section.)

Significant interior spaces include the 212-foot-long "Promenade" connecting the Connecticut Avenue and 17th Street entrances, and the Grand Ballroom, site of numerous presidential inaugural festivities since Calvin Coolidge's day. The political figure most closely associated with the Mayflower, however, was longtime FBI director J. Edgar Hoover, who ate lunch in the hotel's restaurant with his colleague and companion Clyde Tolson virtually every working day for two decades.

K4
ABC News Washington Bureau
1717 DeSales Street, NW

1981 — Kohn Pedersen Fox Associates

Now a global mega-firm, Kohn Pedersen Fox started out in 1976 as an office with only the three partners. ABC was the client that gave the young architects their big break, and the firm went on to design a number of facilities for the network, including the Washington News Bureau, one of the firm's earliest completed proj-

ects. The taut, convex curve of the façade distinguishes the mid-block building from its neighbors without unduly disrupting the streetscape.

K5
National Geographic Society Headquarters
M Street between 16th and 17th Streets, NW

1903 — Hubbard Memorial Library: Hornblower & Marshall
1904 — Interior of Hubbard Memorial Library: Allen & Collins
1913/1931 — Administration building (facing 16th Street): Arthur B. Heaton
1964 — 17th Street building: Edward Durell Stone
1984 — M Street building and renovation of Hubbard Memorial Hall: Skidmore, Owings & Merrill; Landscape architect: James Urban
2016 — Interior renovation (4th floor): STUDIOS Architecture
2019 — Interior renovation (remaining offices and other spaces): Hickok Cole

The National Geographic Society complex is a small, tightly packed campus, consisting of several quite disparate buildings. At the corner of 16th and M Streets stands the original building, now known as the Hubbard Memorial Library, named after Gardiner Greene Hubbard, the society's first president. It was Hubbard's son-in-law, inventor Alexander Graham Bell, who succeeded him and laid the groundwork for the organization's transformation into the famously popular enterprise that it is today. Bell's wife, Mabel, had a strong interest in architecture and was the de facto client for the Hubbard building.

Local architects Hornblower & Marshall won a limited competition for the project, but Mrs. Bell was never fully pleased with their work, which she considered "showy." She constantly pushed for a simpler, more "functional" design, and although the architects tried to accommodate her wishes, Mrs. Bell remained dissatisfied and ultimately fired them, bringing in another firm to complete the interior.

Adjacent to the library on 16th Street is an administrative building executed in a complementary Renaissance Revival style in two phases ending in 1913 and 1931. The initial phase included the five northernmost bays visible today plus the "hyphen" connecting it to the Hubbard building. Arthur Heaton's preliminary designs for the second phase included a tall homage to an Italian campanile, but this was eliminated in favor of a wing matching the earlier expansion and linked to it by a pedimented portico.

At the 17th Street corner is Edward Durell Stone's 1960s tower, which is strangely reminiscent of an unbuilt Frank Lloyd Wright project from 1913 for the *San Francisco Call* newspaper, with slender, tightly spaced columns and a boldly cantilevered, perforated "cornice." Unlike Stone's widely reviled Kennedy Center [see L19], which languishes by the Potomac like a blocky beached whale, this building is welcoming and comfortable in its urban setting. It also houses the society's museum.

At the center of the block lies the newest element of the complex, a modern rendition of a ziggurat, with an L-shaped plan creating a courtyard as a focal point for the motley campus. The new building's insistent horizontality contrasts with the equal verticality of Stone's structure, while mediating between the modern tower and the older neoclassical buildings to the east. A new entrance plaza and event pavilion by Hickok Cole are expected to begin construction in 2022.

Sumner School and Sumner Square

1201 17th Street, NW

1872 — Sumner School: Adolf Cluss
1887 — Magruder School: architect unknown

1985 — New structures: Hartman-Cox; Associated architects: Navy, Marshall, Gordon; Preservation architects: The Ehrenkrantz Group, RTKL, and Oehrlein & Associates Architects

A symmetrical clock tower and array of polychrome arches are the hallmarks of the Sumner School building, designed by Adolf Cluss. Named for abolitionist Charles Sumner, it was a well-regarded school for Black students during the era of legal segregation. Ironically, with integration came neglect, and the Sumner School sat, largely ignored and rapidly decaying, until the District's Board of Education finally decided to restore it and the Magruder School next door while incorporating them into a new commercial development.

The Sumner School was retained by the Board of Education for its own use while the Magruder School was converted to office use (the underground component of the project required that the Magruder building be dismantled and reconstructed on a new foundation). The bulk of the new structure is unobtrusively rendered in a gray curtain wall, making it a true background building that avoids visual competition with the schools. The one wing of the new building that comes out to the street line, however, is covered in buff brick, which deftly relates to the existing buildings on either side — the basic material, brick, is the same as that of the Magruder School, while the beige color blends with the stone façades of the Jefferson Hotel (1923 — Jules Henri de Sibour) at the corner of M and 16th Streets.

K7
Center for Strategic and International Studies
1616 Rhode Island Avenue, NW

2013—Hickok Cole

The Center for Strategic and International Studies (CSIS) is a bipartisan think tank whose headquarters includes offices for resident experts and staff along with extensive conference facilities. Because the site was hemmed in on three sides by other buildings or alleys, the architects had the luxury of concentrating their design efforts—and their construction budget—on the principal façade. Drawing inspiration from the organization's description of itself as a "window on the world," they conceived that façade as a single, abstracted, large-scale window asymmetrically framed by bands of pink-ish Tennessee marble. The base of the frame defines the entry and the main conference spaces. To the west is a wide pier marking the circulation and service zone, while to the east is a slender pier that is angled to allow views out toward Scott Circle. At the top is an outdoor terrace just off the boardroom, which is sheltered by a thin horizontal band that completes the frame.

K8
1701 Rhode Island Avenue, NW
2019—Hickok Cole

The athletic facilities of the YMCA that occupied this site for nearly a half century are missed by many area residents, but the building itself—a lump of hermetic, nearly blank brick walls—is not. The old Y was demolished except for a portion of its structural skeleton, which was incorporated into this new building, currently leased to a flexible workspace firm. The building turns heads thanks to the projecting frames on its two principal façades, which are covered in custom-made copper shingles. The shingles' unusual shape and cascading installation pattern—reminiscent of scales on some fantastical amphibian—were inspired by the façades of a roughly contemporary library in Seinäjoki, Finland. The warm color of the shingles, which were chemically treated to retard oxidation, and the two-story modules of the projecting frames relate nicely to the similar terra cotta frames of the building across the avenue at 1200 17th Street (2014—ZGF Architects).

K9

Cathedral of St. Matthew the Apostle

1725 Rhode Island Avenue, NW

1893–1913 — C. Grant La Farge (Heins and La Farge)
1910 — Rectory: C. Grant La Farge
1940 — St. Francis Chapel: architect unknown
1968 — Baptistery: Johnson & Boutin
2003 — Restoration: Oehrlein & Associates Architects

The 190-foot-tall copper dome of St. Matthew's, the seat of Washington's Catholic Archdiocese, was a prominent landmark for half a century before it was gradually surrounded by mid-rise office buildings. The cathedral's main façade recalls the sober architecture of early Christian churches (the one bit of relative exuberance, the mosaic over the main door, was added in 1970). The spartan exterior, however, belies the opulence of the interior, which teems with rich marble and colorful mosaics bearing a debt to Byzantine architecture. Heins and La Farge, both of whom apprenticed in the office of H. H. Richardson, were also the original architects of the gigantic and perpetually unfinished Cathedral of St. John the Divine in New York.

K10

1150 18th Street, NW

1991 — Don M. Hisaka & Associates
2010 — Renovation: Group Goetz Architects (GGA)

In designing this small office building, Don Hisaka was eager to avoid not only the "granite or marble cliché" of traditional federal architecture but also the banal glass curtain walls so common in the city's more recent commercial buildings. Nonetheless, the architect wanted the project to fit comfortably into the DC cityscape. His solution was to create an elaborate, sunscreen-like façade of white-painted steel. In its color, depth, and interplay of light and shadow, the façade alludes abstractly to the city's classical landmarks, while its extruded steel components and industrial detailing firmly establish its modernity. By organizing the interior around a bright atrium and cantilevering the upper floors over an adjacent alley, Hisaka was able to maximize both square footage and access to natural light on a very constricted site.

K11

Brewood Office Building

1147 20th Street, NW

1974 — Wilkes & Faulkner

A small surprise among the generic behemoths so common in this part of town,

the Brewood Building is unusual not only because of its scale but also by virtue of its delicately expressive architectural form. The façade details suggest the patterns, scale, and connection methods of old-fashioned wood construction. As a result, the small building has an almost handcrafted quality that is rare in modern commercial architecture.

K12

1999 K Street, NW

2009—Murphy/Jahn

Among the many recent glass-box buildings in downtown Washington, this one stands out for three reasons. First, of course, is the Big Gesture: the angled, glass screen wall on the K Street side that is anchored at the sidewalk, soars above the roofline,

and then extends around to the eastern end of the upper floors. Vertically cantilevered from the outermost curtain wall, this huge fin serves no functional purpose, but it lends a sense of depth to the façade while helping to solve the compositional challenge posed by the setback of the top few floors from the building next door (which makes room for a three-story outdoor terrace, barely visible behind the curtain wall at the upper right). The screen wall also draws the eyes of passersby upward, encouraging them to notice the building's second distinguishing feature: the array of smaller glass fins set into the curtain wall, which are as subtle as the big fin is bold but add a surprising amount of visual interest, especially as light conditions change throughout the day and night. Finally, there is the luminous lobby, whose backlit panels dematerialize the space and constitute a room-size piece of minimalist art that also can be appreciated from the street.

K13

1915 I Street, NW

1917—Frank Russell White
1982—Addition: Kerns Group Architects

While the addition to this structure echoes the form of the original building's Dutch gable, its animated, multiple setbacks change what was previously an inconspicuous structure into a minor landmark. The stepped façades unabashedly reveal their false historicism at their edges, where they are offset from the side walls by glazed notches.

K14

International Finance Corporation Headquarters

2121 Pennsylvania Avenue, NW

1997 — Michael Graves & Associates; Associated architect: Vlastimil Koubek (Koubek Architects)
2005 — Store: Michael Graves & Associates
2019 — Addition: Shalom Baranes Associates

A division of the World Bank Group (which is almost big enough to warrant its own world), the International Finance Corporation (IFC) occupies this mammoth building comprising more than 1 million square feet of office space. Designed by Michael Graves in a classicized neo-Rationalist style reminiscent of the later work of Italian architect Aldo Rossi, the IFC Building is daunting in its no-nonsense massing, its ominously tall four-story "base," and its dizzying array of perfectly cylindrical columns (especially on the K Street façade). It is interesting that, by the time an expansion was needed, the IFC opted for a much more mainstream modernist glass curtain-wall building at the northeastern corner of the block.

K15

22 West Condominium

1177 22nd Street, NW

2008 — Shalom Baranes Associates

Occupying a narrow triangular block conveniently located between downtown and Georgetown, this site seemed ideal for a high-end residential development,

except for one snag: a gas station at the northwest corner with an unbreakable long-term lease. The architects' solution was to close the gas station temporarily, modernize its facilities, and then cover as much of it as possible with a green roof. The result is effective from the condominium's perspective — the elevator lobby on each floor has a view over the station, and from that vantage point, the roof comes off as a simple garden — one is hardly aware of the gas pumps and related equipment beneath it.

The condominium building itself sports two distinct façade treatments. The New Hampshire Avenue façade is layered, incorporating broad expanses of glass and substantial balconies, taking advantage of an eight-foot projection into public space. The west façade, which is subject to problematic heat gain on warm, sunny afternoons, is covered in an irregular pattern of tall, narrow windows and zinc panels offset from floor to floor. Although apparently random, the placement of the windows is quite pragmatic, reflecting the varied arrangements of the apartments within — living areas have more glass, for instance, while bedrooms have less. The contrasting façade patterns meet along the short north and south ends of the building, creating interesting juxtapositions and emphasizing the narrowness of the structure's plan.

Square 37 / Squash on Fire Building

2233 M Street, NW

2017—TEN Arquitectos; Executive
architects: WDG Architecture;
Consulting architects for fire station:
LeMay Erickson Willcox Architects

When people hear the term *mixed-use
development*, the combination that comes
to mind is probably not "fire station, squash
club, and affordable housing," yet those
are exactly the three major components of
this building, and each is clearly expressed
in the architecture. The fire station, which
spans most of the first two floors, is partially cloaked in perforated metal doors
(aptly painted fire-engine red) that invite
passersby to peek in for a glimpse of the
equipment. Above that is the squash club,
cheekily named Squash on Fire, which is
expressed as a rectangular metal tube with
a wall of glass facing M Street. Hovering
above the sports facility is a white metal-
paneled box, partially cantilevered over
a setback transition floor, which contains
the affordable dwelling units. Staggered

windows on the apartment block add
variety to the minimalist façades. The
assemblage of distinct forms makes for an
interesting composition when viewed from
M Street, though the utilitarian treatment
of the lower levels facing 23rd Street is less
successful.

This building and the Westlight [see K18]
were built as a pair by a private developer
on DC government–owned land.

1250 24th Street, NW
(former B and W Garage)

1925—Designer-builder: Peter Reinsen
1988—New building incorporating
existing façade: Hisaka & Associates
Architects

This office building, like the garage that
originally occupied the site, is simultaneously industrial and classical in spirit.
The front façade of the two-story garage
was preserved (though the deteriorating
brick had to be painted) and now serves
primarily as a screen defining small
courts in front of the new building, which

K18

Westlight / West End Neighborhood Library

1111 24th Street, NW / 2301 L Street, NW

2018 — TEN Arquitectos; Executive architects: WDG Architecture; West End Neighborhood Library: CORE architecture + design

Suggestive of a game of Jenga in progress, the Westlight condominium is a three-dimensional puzzle of cantilevers and setbacks. In contrast to typical apartment buildings, in which separate living units are often indistinguishable, the Westlight's design imparts a sense of individuality and diversity (even though the discrete blocks do not exactly conform to internal divisions between apartments). Designed by Mexico-based TEN Arquitectos, it exemplifies founder Enrique Norten's fondness for bold and sometimes surprising geometries.

features a curving curtain wall bracketed by two painted brick towers that replicate the architectural vocabulary of the old garage. The bowed façade imparts a sense of grandeur without overwhelming the low wall of the original structure.

The ground floor on the L Street side is occupied by the West End branch of the DC Public Library, which was designed separately by local firm CORE architecture + design. The library boasts a dramatic main reading room punctuated by tree-like clumps of angled structural columns. WDG Architecture served as architect of record for the entire project, ensuring that the public and private components work together seamlessly.

K19

2401 Pennsylvania Avenue, NW

1991—Keyes Condon Florance

This mixed-use building employs a whimsical assortment of materials and decorative motifs. Many of the details are subtly amusing, such as the donkey- and elephant-head brackets holding the cables that support the ground-floor canopies, while others are downright kitschy, such as the cast stone flags on either side of the curved bay at the southeast corner. The sweeping curve of the Pennsylvania Avenue façade prefigures the sculptural forms in more recent projects by Phil Eso-coff [see G10 and P25], who was the lead architect for this building before establishing his own firm.

K20

Barclay House

2501 K Street, NW

1980—Martin and Jones

In Washington, the term *postmodern architecture* is popularly associated with rather straightforward historicism. Actually, the city has relatively few *truly* postmodern buildings—those that expressly and provocatively challenged modernist orthodoxies. The Barclay House is an example of this more mischievous vein of the movement. Dozens of conventions are broken here—expected hierarchies are subverted, grids and planes dissolve and reappear seemingly at random, and projecting bays seem to hang illogically from columns.

Foggy Bottom

There are various stories about the origins of this neighborhood's moniker, which suggests a dismal fen to be avoided at all costs. Some say the name commemorates the noxious fumes emanating from several now-defunct industries—the Heurich brewery, the city gas plant, and a glass factory—while others believe that it was simply an apt description of a low-lying, marshy area that was often shrouded in fog rolling off the Potomac. Then again, the name may have been a euphemistic reference to the fetid Tiber Canal, which emptied into the river near the neighborhood's southeast corner. By the time the Civil War broke out, the canal had degenerated into an open sewer, swarming with flies and mosquitoes.

Before the establishment of the District of Columbia, part of what is now Foggy Bottom was an inchoate town called Hamburgh, also known as Funkstown, conceived as a kind of suburb to the bustling port of Georgetown. Hamburgh never developed on its own, and its modest street grid was wiped out when L'Enfant's plan was imposed upon the landscape. Currently, Foggy Bottom is known primarily as the home of the US Department of State and of the George Washington University, a growing institution whose facility-related requirements often lead to conflicts with neighbors fearful that what remains of the area's residential character is endangered.

TOUR L

The Christian Heurich Brewing Company operated out of this facility at 26th and D Streets, NW, along the Potomac River, from 1895 to 1956. The building was demolished in 1961 to make way for the John F. Kennedy Center for the Performing Arts.

SEE TOUR K

PENNSYLVANIA AVE

SEE TOUR J

SEE TOUR B

CONSTITUTION AVE

NEW YORK AVE

F ST

C ST

21st ST

19th ST

17th ST

1a
1b
1c
2
3
4
5
6
7
8
9
10
11
12
13

L1
The George Washington University

The George Washington University (GW), previously known as Columbian College, moved to Foggy Bottom from what is now Columbia heights in 1912. The most urban of Washington's major collegiate institutions, GW does not enjoy a cohesive campus and, partially as a result, lacks a clear architectural identity. Nonetheless, the school includes several notable individual buildings.

L1a
University Student Center
800 21st Street, NW

1970 — Mills, Petticord & Mills
2002 — Renovation and addition: Smith-
    Group; Associate architect: Kevin Hom

Built in an era when many academic buildings were concrete fortresses, the original section of GW's student center was never architecturally exciting, but it was relatively hospitable. The 21st Street façade has generous banks of windows bracketed by two solid towers clad in light-colored brick. A deep balcony on the second floor provides some outdoor space while also enhancing the building's sense of depth. The main thing that the center lacked was a welcoming entrance, which was solved by a glassy addition in the early 2000s.

Previously known as the Cloyd Heck Marvin Center, after a past GW president

who fought to keep the university segregated, the facility was officially renamed the University Student Center in 2021 following protests over its namesake's racist views.

L1b
Lisner Auditorium
730 21st Street, NW

1943 — Faulkner & Kingsbury

An enigmatic, perfectly rectilinear block relieved only by a vestigial portico on the front, emergency exits and walkways on the sides, a stage door at the rear, and a smattering of perforated stone panels embedded in all four façades, Lisner Auditorium is a magnificently minimalist work of architecture. Its beauty derives from its impeccable proportions, the inherent quality of its limestone skin, and the alternation between wide and narrow

courses in the stonework, creating a subtle horizontal emphasis. The interior is equally stark, though curves in the ceiling and seating introduce a gracefulness that contrasts with the severity of the exterior. With nearly 1,500 seats, Lisner Auditorium was one of the primary performance venues in Washington before the opening of the Kennedy Center, and it continues to offer a variety of programming for students and the public.

L1c
Law School
20th and H Streets, NW

1892 — President's Office (Theodore A. Harding House): George S. Cooper / Victor Mindeleff

1925 — Stockton Hall: Albert Harris and Arthur Heaton

1967 — Jacob Burns Law Library: Mills, Petticord & Mills

1984 — Lerner Hall and renovation of existing buildings: Keyes Condon Florance Architects

1996 — Renovation of Stuart Hall: Einhorn Yaffee Prescott

1999–2002 — Renovations (including President's House) and addition: KressCox Associates

2004 — Renovation of Burns Library and Stockton Hall: cox graae + spack architects

The GW Law School is interesting as a mélange of quite different structures that have grown together over time. Initially, the school occupied the unprepossessing mid-block Stockton Hall. The library to the south of the original building was added in the 1960s, then came postmodern additions in the 1980s. Eventually the school gobbled up the entire west side of the 700 block of 20th Street, including the older building at the southern end that had been built for the university's president in 1892.

L2
World Bank
1818 H Street, NW

1997 — Kohn Pedersen Fox Associates; Associate architects: Nägele Hofmann Tiedemann und Partner and KressCox Associates

Kohn Pedersen Fox became famous in the 1980s for designing corporate office buildings that had one foot in the steady stream of the modern movement and the other in the turbid waters of postmodernism. The World Bank Headquarters was one of a series of buildings the firm designed in the 1990s that reflected a kind of retro-modernist approach, in this case evoking both the International Style and the Futurist movement of the 1910s and '20s.

The complex takes up an entire city block, incorporating remnants of two preexisting buildings (one by Skidmore, Owings & Merrill, the other by Clas & Riggs / Vincent Kling) along G Street. The cheerless gray concrete wall that ties the old and new structures together at ground level is unfortunate, but above that, things get much livelier, especially along the side facing Pennsylvania Avenue, which is dynamically canted outward and accentuated by emphatically horizontal muntins and projecting metal rails. In a few special places, distinct volumes break from the main building envelope, providing visual relief from the insistent geometry and marking important interior spaces, such as the boardroom high up on the northeast corner of the building, which is capped by a swooping upturned roof.

L3
Consumer Financial Protection Bureau / Liberty Plaza
1700 G Street, NW

1977 — Max O. Urbahn Associates;
   Courtyard: Sasaki Associates
2018 — Renovation: CallisonRTKL

The present-day architecture buff, weary of the terrorism-inspired paranoia that has rendered many "public" buildings nearly inaccessible, may long for the halcyon days of 1976. In that year, Congress passed the Public Buildings Cooperative Use Act, which directed the head of the General Services Administration to "encourage the location of commercial, cultural, educational, and recreational facilities and activities within public buildings." This call for the integration of mixed uses into governmental structures was part of a broader initiative intended to break down barriers between federal

agencies and the citizens they serve, and to encourage true urban vitality around such facilities.

The building that now houses the Consumer Financial Protection Bureau was among the first federal projects to reflect this new spirit of openness, accommodating shops and restaurants beneath government office space while also meeting increasingly strict energy conservation standards. Architecturally, it is remarkable in its use of a standard 1970s vocabulary — cylindrical concrete columns, thin concrete slabs, and dark-tinted glass — to create façades of unusual depth and character, yielding one of the most successful Brutalist buildings in the city. This spare vocabulary also alludes, in a highly abstract way, to the multicolumned façades of the Eisenhower Executive Office Building [see J16] across the street. Perhaps reflecting a lesson learned from the nearby AIA headquarters [see L5] and its relationship to the Octagon [see L6], the new building wraps around, and defers to, the historic Winder Building [see following entry].

L4
Winder Building
600 17th Street, NW

1848 — Richard A. Gilpin
1930–48 — Various renovations: architects unknown
1975 — Restoration: Max O. Urbahn Associates
1990 — Exterior restoration: architrave, p.c., architects

It may not look like it now, but when new, the Winder Building was one of the most

innovative structures in the city. The first to employ a central heating system and cast iron beams throughout, it was also the tallest (75 feet) and largest (130 rooms) office building in the capital. The building was among the earliest examples of a now-ubiquitous Washington type—speculative office space developed in order to be sold or leased to the federal government. Indeed, the builder, William H. Winder, sold it to the government in 1854, and for much of its history, it was used by the Navy, War, and Treasury departments. It now houses the headquarters of the US Trade Representative.

L5

American Institute of Architects Headquarters

1735 New York Avenue, NW

1973—The Architects Collaborative
1989—Interior renovation: Malesardi + Steiner / Architects
1993—Library expansion: The Architects Collaborative; Malesardi + Steiner / Architects

In the 1960s, the AIA sponsored a competition for the design of a new headquarters building to be set behind the historic Octagon, its long-term home. First place went to the entry by Mitchell/Giurgola Architects, which featured an expansive concave glass curtain wall stretching almost all the way across its primary façade. A revised version of this design, bolder and more complex, was rejected by the US Commission of Fine Arts, which feared that it would overwhelm the historic house at the corner. Ultimately,

Mitchell/Giurgola withdrew from the project, and the institute hired The Architects Collaborative (TAC), whose simpler solution won approval from the commission.

TAC's design, with its largely unrelieved ribbons of concrete and dark glass, might be overlooked among the many other buildings of that era based on a similar architectural language. The AIA building, however, is more elegant and interesting than most of its contemporaries, thanks to the boomerang shape of its plan, which provided a deferential backdrop to the historic house at the corner, accented by the bold, projecting volume off the New York Avenue wing, which houses the boardroom. Originally, the area beneath this projection was a dark, disused corner of the otherwise pleasant courtyard between the new structure and the Octagon, but during the 1993 renovation, this space was enclosed as part of the expansion of the library (it is now used for offices). This change was a great improvement, alleviating the ominousness of the broad overhang and helping to direct visitors to the main entrance just to the left of the new space.

L6

The Octagon

1799 New York Avenue, NW

1802 — William Thornton
1817 — Alterations: George Hadfield
1898 — Interior restoration: Glenn Brown
1911–70 — Numerous restoration projects:
 various architects
1989–95 — Restoration: Mesick Cohen
 Waite Architects

The Octagon isn't. In plan, it is actually more like a "pregnant hexagon," in the words of Sherry Birk, former director of the Octagon Museum and Collections, thanks to the semicircular bay protruding from its main façade. The origins of the misnomer are unclear, but regardless, the building's unusual geometry was an inventive response to the acutely angled site, yielding one of the most distinctive houses of the Federal period in Washington. The plan also created a number of atypical spaces inside the house, including a copious circular entry hall and an oval stair hall that affords surprisingly vertiginous views between floors. Several doorways in the house are shaped to fit seamlessly within curved walls.

The house was designed by William Thornton, original architect of the Capitol, for Colonel John Tayloe III, a scion of one of Virginia's most prominent and wealthiest families. During the British invasion of 1814, Tayloe's wife, Ann, who had been at the Octagon alone as the city began to burn, convinced the diplomatic minister of France to occupy the house and fly his country's flag from its roof, most likely saving the structure from the torch. From 1814 to early 1815, President James Madison and First Lady Dolley Madison lived here while workers repaired the

charred Executive Mansion. In 1815, in the Octagon's second-floor parlor, President Madison signed the Treaty of Ghent, formally ending hostilities with Great Britain, following its ratification by the Senate.

In the mid- to late 19th century, the building had a succession of occupants, including a girls' technical school, and gradually fell into disrepair. The AIA leased the house as its headquarters beginning in 1898 and soon purchased it outright. Having overseen various renovations of the historic structure, the AIA eventually moved into a larger commercial building next door, which was torn down when the present headquarters was built [see previous entry]. In 1968, the AIA Foundation — later known as the American Architectural Foundation (AAF) — assumed control of the Octagon and converted it into a historic house museum. Since 2010, the property has been owned and managed by a distinct organization now known as the Architects Foundation (the AAF ceased operations in 2019).

L7

Corcoran School of the Arts & Design
(former Corcoran Gallery of Art /
Corcoran College of Art + Design)

500 17th Street, NW

1897 — Ernest Flagg
1915 — Renovation: Waddy B. Wood
1928 — Addition: Charles Adams Platt
2019 — Renovation: LEO A DALY; Historic
 preservation architects: Davis Buckley
 Architects and Planners

Officially established in 1869, the Corcoran Gallery of Art was the first art museum in Washington and one of the first in the nation. It initially occupied what is now the Renwick Gallery [see J15] but moved to this building, designed by Ernest Flagg, after outgrowing the original facility. The institution thrived for a century until a series of administrative and financial mishaps led to its demise as an independent entity. To the great distress of local art lovers, the institution was formally dissolved in 2014. Most of the museum's collection went to the National Gallery of Art, while both the school and the building itself were transferred to the George Washington University.

Flagg's building makes a powerful impression thanks to its closeness to the street, its rusticated base, and its strong horizontal banding, not to mention the pair of lounging lions imperturbably guarding its entrance. The simplicity of the inscription above the doorway—"Dedicated to Art"—enhances the building's aura of nobility. But the most commanding aspect of the exterior is the broad, blank stone panel between the main floor and the row of attic-level windows (which are actually vents) along the 17th Street façade. The masterful proportions of this panel in relation to the rest of the façade, coupled with the sheer audacity of incorporating such a vast unadorned surface into an otherwise richly ornamented composition, make the Corcoran one of the most elegant and self-assured buildings in the city.

A skylit atrium, surrounded by a parade of simple, fluted Doric columns on the main floor and Ionic columns on the balcony, is the building's primary interior space. Glass panels in the floor, originally intended to bring natural light to art studios in the lower level, add a surprisingly modern touch. A grand staircase, flanked by stepped pedestals intended for the display of sculpture, connects to upper-level gallery spaces.

The northeast corner of the building was originally a two-story curved room known as the Hemicycle, which served as a sort of knuckle connecting the museum to the New York Avenue wing housing the art school. This space was split into two separate levels in 1915, with the lower floor becoming an amphitheater for lectures and the upper floor becoming additional gallery space. The wing along E Street was added in the 1920s to accommodate a substantial bequest from Montana senator William A. Clark that included paintings, sculptures, tapestries, and an entire room known as the Salon Doré. Originally part of an 18th-century private residence in Paris, this heavily gilded chamber previously had been dismantled and reinstalled in Clark's mansion in New York.

In 1999, the Corcoran conducted a competition for the design of another addition to be built adjacent to the school wing. The winning design, by Frank Gehry, featured the architect's characteristic billowy, metal-clad forms, in striking contrast to the formality of the existing building. The cancelation of the planned addition seems, in retrospect, to have marked the beginning of the end for the institution. The trustees eventually received court approval to break William Corcoran's original deed of trust and distribute the organization's assets. After assuming control of the school, the George Washington University embarked on an extensive renovation of the Flagg Building, as it is now formally known, which once again hosts exhibitions and programs, though at a more modest scale than in its previous incarnation.

L8

American National Red Cross

430 17th Street, NW

1917—A. Breck Trowbridge and Goodhue Livingston
1929, 1931—North and west buildings: Trowbridge and Livingston
2005—Renovation: Shalom Baranes Associates; Preservation consultants: John Milner Associates

2013 — Restoration of Library lay light (Memorial Continental Hall): Quinn Evans Architects

2018 — Renovation of Museum Gallery (Administration Building): Quinn Evans Architects

2021 — Restoration of Constitution Hall: Quinn Evans Architects

President Woodrow Wilson laid the cornerstone in 1915 for the main building in this complex, which was conceived as a memorial to "the heroic women of the Civil War, both North and South." It is a straightforward but stately neoclassical building, with a Corinthian portico and a recessed third story, partially obscured by a balustrade (the lowest level is technically a raised basement). The highlight of the interior is the Board of Governors Hall, featuring a trio of Tiffany windows depicting evocative figures such as Santa Filomena, which was Henry Wadsworth Longfellow's name for Florence Nightingale, and Una, the future wife of the Redcrosse Knight (appropriately enough) from Edmund Spenser's *The Faerie Queene*. Two other buildings on the block, designed by the same architects in a complementary fashion, were completed in 1930 and 1932.

L9

National Society Daughters of the American Revolution (DAR) Headquarters

1776 D Street, NW

1910 — Memorial Continental Hall: Edward Pearce Casey

1923 — Administration Building: Marsh and Peter

1929 — Constitution Hall: John Russell Pope

1950 — Addition to Administration Building: Eggers and Higgins

1994–97 — Renovations of Constitution Hall: Blackburn and Associates; KressCox Associates

2012 — Exterior restoration of Administration Building: Quinn Evans Architects

The national headquarters of the Daughters of the American Revolution is reputed to be the largest complex of buildings in the world owned exclusively by women. Facing 17th Street is Memorial Continental Hall, an imposing structure boasting heavy quoins, a dense balustrade at the roof level, and an abundance of gleaming marble. The main entrance is marked by an unusual *porte-cochère*, with columns set on tall pedestals and steps rising between them. On the south façade is a semicircular porch with 13 columns representing the original colonies.

At the center of this building is a magnificent skylit space that originally served as the DAR's main auditorium. This was the venue for the annual "Continental Congress," drawing thousands of members from across the country. It is now the library and is worth a visit even if you have no interest in conducting research there. Surrounding the library are more than 30 distinct rooms, each of which was sponsored by a DAR state chapter. Some of these rooms served as offices until the administrative wing was added to the west of the main building, at which point they were restored as period salons. Visitors may tour all of these spaces, as well as the museum in the central wing.

The Continental Congress soon outgrew the original building, necessitating the addition of a large auditorium dubbed

Constitution Hall. John Russell Pope's preliminary designs for the addition were extremely grand, but budgetary constraints forced him to tame his ambitions. The completed structure is staid in comparison to the main building, with large expanses of blank wall relieved only by subtle recesses and belt courses. Two long, copper canopies—one on C Street and the other on D—add welcome jaunty touches.

Constitution Hall became one of the most prominent performance venues in 20th-century Washington and the primary home of the National Symphony Orchestra for more than four decades. But this site is most famous for the concert that did *not* take place here in 1939, when Black singer Marian Anderson was denied the opportunity to perform because of her race, prompting First Lady Eleanor Roosevelt to resign her DAR membership and arrange an outdoor concert by Anderson at the Lincoln Memorial. Anderson subsequently performed here on several occasions, and fortunately, everyone is now welcome at the DAR.

L10

Organization of American States
(former Pan-American Union)

200 17th Street, NW

1910—Albert Kelsey and Paul P. Cret
1912—Annex: Kelsey and Cret
2005—Renovation: John Milner
   Associates

Funded in part by a $750,000 gift from Andrew Carnegie, the "House of the Americas" was built as the headquarters of the Pan-American Union (now the Organization of American States, or OAS)

and intended to symbolize the peaceful relations among the countries of North, South, and Central America. It occupies the former site of the Van Ness mansion, designed by Benjamin Henry Latrobe, which was built around 1816 and thought to be the most expensive residence in the United States in its day. A former stable from that estate, also by Latrobe, still stands at 18th and C Streets, though its stucco finish is not original.

The OAS building was the first major commission for the French-born Paul Philippe Cret, who had collaborated with Philadelphia-based architect Albert Kelsey on the winning entry in the design competition conducted in 1907. The exterior of Kelsey and Cret's building is in keeping with Beaux-Arts traditions but is inflected with allusions to the Spanish Colonial architecture of Latin America, such as the red tile roof and bronze gates. The sculptures flanking the entrance represent North America (to the right, by Gutzon Borglum, best known for his work on Mount Rushmore) and South America (to the left, by Isidore Konti). The bas-relief panels above the large sculptures depict the "great liberators" of the Americas: George Washington in the northern panel and Simón Bolívar and José de San Martín in the southern panel.

Inside, classical formality yields to tropical exoticism, as the building is organized around a lushly planted patio that was originally covered with a sliding glass roof, though modern air-conditioning now precludes the use of this feature. The centerpiece of the garden is Gertrude Vanderbilt Whitney's fountain incorporating references to Mayan, Aztec, and Zapotecan art. The building also contains elegant event and conference rooms, most notably the 100-foot-long, barrel-vaulted Hall of the Americas on the second floor.

Behind the main building is the Annex, also by Kelsey and Cret, which now houses the Art Museum of the Americas. The highlight of this structure is the interior loggia, which is a riot of colorful glazed tile. Between the two buildings lies the Blue Aztec Garden, featuring a small reflecting pool. Presiding over the garden is a statue of Xochipilli, the Aztec god of flowers, art, and music, not to mention hallucinogenic drugs.

L11

Stewart Lee Udall Department of the Interior Building

1849 C Street, NW

1936—Waddy B. Wood
1994–2017—Rehabilitation and
   modernization: Shalom Baranes
   Associates

The first DC building to be designed and completed under the New Deal, the US Department of the Interior's headquarters is enormous and aesthetically severe. Behind those forbidding façades, however, there are some real surprises. Most noteworthy are the dozens of spectacular New Deal murals and sculptures, including *The Negro's Contribution in the Social and Cultural Development of America* and works addressing Indigenous American themes. There is also a small museum on the first floor, as well as the Indian Craft Shop (sadly, the Federal Duck Stamp Office, a longtime Interior Department oddity, has migrated to Arlington). The building's floor plan is unusual for its era:

instead of the more typical courtyards to bring light to office spaces within a huge block, architect Waddy Wood organized the plan around a central north-south spine, with six pairs of narrow wings projecting east and west.

L12

Federal Reserve Building
(Marriner S. Eccles Building)

2051 Constitution Avenue, NW

1937—Paul Philippe Cret
1977—Renovation: Wilkes & Faulkner

E. J. Applewhite called the Federal Reserve the "very Valhalla of the dollar," and Paul Cret won an invited design competition to create an appropriately monumental temple for America's warriors of economic policy. The exterior design may be the apotheosis of "starved classicism" in Washington, and with the eagle sculpture over its main doorway starkly lit at night, the building is perhaps uncomfortably reminiscent of the roughly contemporary work of Hitler's architect, Albert Speer (suggesting that stylistic trends often outweigh ideology in architecture). The eagle motif is carried throughout the building, even appearing as an outline in the glass ceiling of the atrium, an elegant space lined with buttery travertine and intricate railings by notable Philadelphia ironworker Samuel Yellin. Surprisingly, as a sideline to its stewardship of the nation's financial system, the Federal Reserve maintains a significant art collection, parts of which are displayed throughout the building, which is open for public tours by reservation only.

L13

National Academy of Sciences

**2101 Constitution Avenue, NW
(2100 C Street, NW)**

1924 — Bertram Grosvenor Goodhue;
  Sculptor: Lee Lawrie
1962, 1965, 1970 — Additions: Harrison
  & Abramowitz
1979 — Landscape design for Einstein
  statue: Oehme, van Sweden &
  Associates; Sculptor: Robert Berks
2013 — Renovation and additions: Quinn
  Evans Architects

Bertram Goodhue supposedly tried to convince the National Academy of Sciences (NAS) — chartered by Congress in 1863 to advise the government on science and technology policy — to hire another architect for its headquarters because he felt uncomfortable designing a building so near the Lincoln Memorial and other major landmarks. He finally relented and went on to create a subdued structure — a boiled-down Beaux-Arts palace with hints of the Egyptian, Byzantine, and Spanish Colonial Revival styles that Goodhue favored at various stages of his career. Goodhue himself dubbed the style of the building "God-knows-what-kind-of-Classic."

The exterior walls appear at first glance to be perfectly flat planes of stone, but in fact each course is set back slightly from the one below, creating subtly battered — or inwardly sloping — façades. Famed sculptor Lee Lawrie created all of the three-dimensional artistic works, including the enormous bronze entry doors and spandrel panels depicting major figures and events in scientific history. The bronze crest lining the cornice includes alternating figures of lynxes and owls, symbols of observation and wisdom, respectively.

The NAS building contains not one, but two of DC's most spectacular interior spaces. The Great Hall, the academy's original assembly hall and now a reception and circulation space, is topped by a 60-foot-high dome built using the Guastavino tile vaulting system. The mosaics on the dome, depicting various scientific themes, were created by Hildreth Meière, who also collaborated with Goodhue on his masterpiece, the Nebraska State Capitol. The academy's second extraordinary room is the new auditorium added in 1970 by Wallace K. Harrison, who had worked in Goodhue's office in his younger days. This astonishingly futuristic space, now named for physicist and philanthropist Fred Kavli, is encased in a wildly faceted shell.

In 1979, the endearingly frumpy Albert Einstein Memorial, by Robert Berks, was dedicated in the academy's front yard. The map at the base of the monument has more than 2,700 metal studs representing planets, stars, and other heavenly bodies in their relative positions as of the dedication date.

L14

American Pharmacists Association
(former American Institute of Pharmacy / American Pharmaceutical Association)

2215 Constitution Avenue, NW

1933 — John Russell Pope
1962 — Addition: Eggers & Higgins
2009 — Renovation and addition:
  Hartman-Cox Architects

The tourist coming upon this complex for the first time would be excused for guessing that the small marble-faced structure in front is a shrine of some kind — a war memorial, perhaps, or a dignified little museum dedicated to some archaic, vaguely remembered civic cause. In fact, it is the headquarters of the American Pharmacists Association, and for nearly seven decades, it was the only private building on Constitution Avenue, NW (the new private office building at 101 Constitution [see A12] now anchors the other end of this important thoroughfare). The building was financed entirely by the organization's members, but because of its sensitive location, federal design review authorities dictated its siting, the treatment of the surrounding landscape, and the choice of white marble as the finish material.

The shrine-like character of John Russell Pope's design may derive from its basis in an earlier project. He originally developed it in 1907–8 for the Lincoln Birthplace Museum in Kentucky, where it would have served as a shell for Lincoln's natal log cabin, but the design proved too expensive—not to mention oddly urbane for its rustic setting—so Pope prepared a revised scheme for that site that was simpler and more robust (and which was executed). Some 20 years later, he conjured up the initial Lincoln Birthplace design and, with a few modifications, turned it into the pharmaceutical building.

The architects of the recent addition to the rear, which contains more than 20 times the floor space of the Pope building, deliberately chose a contrasting stone and set the new wing back as far as possible to allow the original structure to continue to read as a freestanding form.

L15

US Institute of Peace

2301 Constitution Avenue, NW

2011—Safdie Architects

The location and scale of the US Institute of Peace make it one of Washington's most prominent new buildings in decades (the site, ironically enough, used to be part of the military complex immediately to the north). The building consists of three rather stolid blocks sheathed in acid-etched precast concrete with punched windows, separated by two atria that fan out from the entrance at the northeast corner. The atria are covered by milky white translucent panels that appear opaque from the outside by day but glow from within when artificially lit at night. The latter quality caused some consternation among federal design review authorities, who insisted on thorough study of the lighting scheme to ensure that it would not visually overwhelm the nearby Lincoln Memorial.

Knowing the building's purpose, one cannot help but interpret the billowing

white roofs of the atria as abstractions of a dove's wings, yet curiously, the architects contend that these forms were intended only to suggest the idea of peace in some more general way. Regardless, they are graceful additions to Washington's skyline, even if the contrast between the curving translucent forms and the uninspired rectilinear blocks is too stark.

L16

Pan American Health Organization

525 23rd Street, NW

1965 — Design architect: Román Fresnedo Siri; Architects of record: Justement, Elam, Callmer & Kidd
2001 — Renovation: Ai
2012 — Renovation of Knowledge Center: KCCT

Like many Latin American architects of the mid-20th century, Román Fresnedo Siri, of Uruguay, was enthralled by Corbusian modernism. His competition-winning design for the Pan American Health Organization (PAHO) headquarters reflects Le Corbusier's influence in the visual interplay between the cylindrical structure (containing the Council Chamber and related spaces) and the gently curved "Secretariat" tower, as well as in the *brise-soleil* that shades the cylinder's glass curtain wall from the sun and the *pilotis* that lift the main office block off the ground. In contrast to the hulking ground-floor columns of the Department of Housing and Urban Development [see C3], the *pilotis* here seem to do their job effortlessly — pedestrians can pass beneath the building without feeling as though the mass overhead is poised to crush them.

Upon completion, PAHO's headquarters drew widespread praise as a symbol of international cooperation and the prospects for improving the quality of life throughout the hemisphere. "Health is akin to beauty," said John W. Gardner, secretary of health, education, and welfare at the time. "It is fitting that a building dedicated to the ideal of better health for the people of the Americas should express that beauty in its form and design."

L17

St. Mary's Church, Foggy Bottom
(St. Mary's Episcopal Church)

730 23rd Street, NW

1881 — Parish Hall: architect unknown
1887 — Church: Renwick, Aspinwall and Russell
1909 — Parish House: architect unknown
1913 — Rectory: architect unknown
2005 — Restoration: Fetterman Associates

St. Mary's is the oldest Black Episcopal congregation in Washington. It held its first service on this site in 1867 in a reconstructed wooden chapel formerly attached to a decommissioned Civil War hospital in Kalorama. The congregation prospered and grew, necessitating the new church by James Renwick Jr., which replaced the original chapel a couple of decades later. The main entry to the building is through an open gateway beneath a tower than is decorated with large terra cotta panels depicting griffins, swirling vines, and shields bearing fleurs-de-lis. Inside, above the altar, are leaded glass windows made in France and depicting saints of African descent, including St. Cyprian, a Carthaginian who became a Christian bishop and martyr.

L18

The Watergate

2500–2700 Virginia Avenue, NW / 600–700 New Hampshire Avenue, NW

1963–71 — Luigi Moretti with Mario di Valmarana; Associated architects: Corning, Moore, Elmore & Fischer; Landscape architect: Boris Timchenko
1994 — Renovation of office building public spaces: Bass Architects and Nora Fischer Designs
2000 — Renovation of hotel: RJShirley & Associates Architects; Interiors: Hughes Design Associates
2016 — Renovation of hotel: BBGM; Interiors: Ron Arad Architects and BBGM
2017 — Renovation of Watergate 600 lobby and elevator cabs: LSM
2018 — Renovation of Watergate 600 ground floor: IA Interior Architects

2019 — Renovation of Watergate East
   lobbies: McInturff Architects
2020 — Renovation of Watergate 600
   rooftop event spaces: OTJ Architects

Setting aside its tawdry fame as the site of a bungled, politically motivated burglary, the Watergate complex — which includes residences, offices, and a hotel — likely would have made occasional headlines on its own because so many people of power and influence have lived, worked, or stayed here. Monica Lewinsky and Bob and Elizabeth Dole, for instance, were briefly improbable next-door neighbors. Other famous residents included Elizabeth Taylor and Plácido Domingo. The complex is also notable, however, as one of the most inventive and ambitious works of modernist architecture in DC.

The announcement of the planned project in 1960 drew howls from various quarters. Some local architects and design review agencies were concerned that the proposed complex was too tall and would compete visually with the city's major landmarks. An organization then known as Protestants and Other Americans United for Separation of Church and State objected that the project may have received zoning or building code waivers because the Italian developer, SGI, was partially owned by the Vatican. Curiously, the fact that the lead designer, Luigi Moretti, had been one of Benito Mussolini's favorite architects and never fully recanted his fascist sympathies didn't seem to raise many eyebrows.

Political leanings aside, Moretti was a talented architect whose works included the exquisite Academy of Fencing at the Foro Mussolini (now Foro Italico) in Rome. For the Watergate complex, he consciously produced a design that departed from what he saw as the rigid formality and rectilinearity of official Washington architecture. From certain vantage points, the Watergate buildings are suggestive of ocean liners, with gentle curves and prow-like balconies. Lozenge-shaped penthouses animate the rooftops of the residential and hotel buildings, while the freeform landscape (including multiple, curvilinear swimming pools) creates a resort-like atmosphere. Admit-

tedly, some of the architectural detailing is awkward — the chunky balcony railings, for example, look as if they might have been excavated from Fred Flintstone's yard — but Moretti's colleagues recalled that, while working on the project, he was listening obsessively to Igor Stravinsky's *The Firebird*, and Moretti's own sketches of the balcony designs look remarkably like musical staffs with notes.

The complex's curious name, by the way, derives from the nearby Watergate Steps, an arc of stairs providing access to the Potomac riverfront. Completed in 1932, the steps were originally intended as a ceremonial entrance to the city for dignitaries arriving by water, and as a docking point for recreational boats. As it turned out, not a lot of 20th-century dignitaries actually arrived by water, but from 1935 until the 1970s, the steps served as an amphitheater for musical performances, the stage for which was a barge anchored at their base.

L19

John F. Kennedy Center for the Performing Arts

2700 F Street, NW

1971 — Edward Durell Stone Associates;
   Landscape architect: Edward Durell
   Stone Jr.
1979 — Terrace Theater: Philip C. Johnson
1997 — Renovation of Concert Hall: Quinn
   Evans Architects; Design architects:
   Hartman-Cox Architects
2003 — Renovation of Opera House: Quinn
   Evans Architects; Renovation of public
   spaces: Tobey Davis with Polshek
   Partnership
2005 — Family Theater: Richter
   Cornbrooks Gribble
2008 — Renovation of Eisenhower
   Theater: Quinn Evans Architects
2012 — Renovation of Theater Lab: Richter
   Cornbrooks Gribble; Theater designers:
   Theatre Projects Consultants;
   Renovation of North and South
   Millennium Stages: Grimm + Parker
2015 — Renovations of lounges: Richter
   Cornbrooks Gribble
2017 — Renovation of Terrace Theater:
   Quinn Evans Architects; Theater
   designers: Schuler Shook

If a Las Vegas developer were to open a casino under the theme of "Palace of the Soviets"—and unlikelier things happen hourly in Vegas—the result might look something like the Kennedy Center. Cut off from the adjacent Foggy Bottom neighborhood by a tangle of freeways, and from the Potomac riverfront by an enormous cantilevered balcony, the building is a gaudy concoction of vast marble planes, spindly bronze columns, overwrought chandeliers, and acres of bordello-red carpet. It brings to mind the work of Morris Lapidus, but without the sensuous curves (though architect Edward Durell Stone produced an earlier scheme with a curvilinear plan) and with, instead, a hefty dose of Stalinist bombast. Critic Ada Louise Huxtable decried the

center as "a cross between a concrete candy box and a marble sarcophagus in which the art of architecture lies buried."

Some government officials had been calling for a major performing arts facility in central Washington since the 1930s, but the effort did not get under way in earnest until the Eisenhower administration. After Kennedy's assassination, the project was rechristened in his name as a "living memorial." It opened in 1971 with a requiem mass in honor of the slain president. Since then, various renovations of the theaters and other spaces have mitigated the architectural shortcomings of the complex, which has become a successful hub for music and theater.

L19a

The REACH

Immediately south of the original Kennedy Center building

2019—Design architects: Steven Holl Architects; Architects of record: BNIM

The REACH was so named to express the Kennedy Center's goal of engaging new audiences through additional performance and rehearsal spaces. Designed by Steven Holl, it consists of three above-ground pavilions that evoke icebergs both in their form and in the fact that they

are the relatively small visible portions of a much larger complex that is mostly underground. The pavilions, whose exteriors incorporate sweeping concave curves, are crafted of board-formed concrete that appears seamless from afar but reveals its texture up close. Ground-level windows provide glimpses of activity within, while large panels of laminated glass, composed of translucent white film sandwiched between etched-glass panes, glow from within at night. Inside, "crinkle concrete" surfaces on the walls of rehearsal and performance spaces introduce a surprising visual texture, highlighted by raking light, while modulating the spaces' acoustics.

Although the 72,000-square-foot REACH may meet the Kennedy Center's immediate programmatic needs, it does not fully solve its architectural and urban design problems. Holl's decision to break up the aboveground elements of the addition in order to avoid competing with the original building is understandable, but a more aggressive aesthetic stance might have been welcome in this case. The landscaped areas between the irregularly sited pavilions read as leftover voids rather that purposefully designed spaces, making the addition appear rather weak in comparison to the monumental mother ship. Finally, while the REACH does incorporate a new connection to the riverfront, it consists of a narrow bridge and ramp, foregoing a bold architectural gesture that might have lent a fresh new character to the entire complex (Holl's original proposal to have one of the pavilions floating in the river was sadly quashed). Despite these disappointments, the REACH does offer some delightful experiences for visitors, whether attending a program or merely wandering among the bold sculptural forms.

Georgetown

Founded in 1751 in what was then the Maryland colony, Georgetown was named not for America's first president, as many people suppose, but most likely for King George II of England (or possibly for George Gordon and George Beall, the two men who owned most of the land on which the town was established). The initial community covered about 60 acres between the Potomac and a line south of N Street (then known as Gay Street), bounded on the east by what is now 30th (then Washington) Street, and on the west by the land now occupied by Georgetown University. Even after it was absorbed into the newly established District of Columbia in 1791, Georgetown remained legally a separate jurisdiction until formal annexation by "Washington City" 80 years later.

While Georgetown is now virtually synonymous with gentility, much of its history is rather gritty. In its early days, Georgetown was a bustling port, thanks to its strategic location near the falls of the Potomac and its proximity to vast tobacco plantations that provided the primary commodity to be shipped. Like most ports of that era, it was a scrappy town, home to workaday wharves and rowdy taverns, populated by notoriously crude sailors and probably more than a few merchants with fungible business ethics. Abigail Adams dismissed the place as "a dirty little hole."

Busy ports may be seedy, but they also generate wealth for those positioned to reap the profits of commerce. Georgetown quickly grew a substantial class of prosperous entrepreneurs, many of whom were quite cultured, and who built houses that still reign as some of the most elegant in the District. In fact, Georgetown's elite regarded the nascent—and, at the time, absolutely distinct—capital city to the east with some skepticism, suspicious as they were of the questionable enterprises (i.e., politics and government) practiced there. As late as 1826, one observer noticed that "the people of Georgetown . . . form a striking contrast to their neighbors in Washington, their minds being generally more cultivated. It is hardly possible to conceive how towns so near . . . should differ so widely."

As the 19th century progressed, however, Georgetown did not fare so well. The river silted up, and the C&O Canal, dug to lure the rich Midwest trade to the Potomac, proved no match for the B&O Railroad. Trade soon bypassed Georgetown's once-flourishing port in favor of Baltimore. The Civil War brought significant social rifts, since Georgetown, though situated in the capital of the Union, was home to a number of prominent Confederate sympathizers. In the war's wake, the town absorbed an influx of freed slaves, most of whom were, of course, quite poor, and whose presence displeased some affluent Georgetowners, who chose to move elsewhere. The community grew increasingly shabby, and eventually even officially lost its name when, upon annexation in 1871, it became legally known as "West Washington."

Georgetown then entered a period of quiescence that lasted until the New Deal, when the growth of the federal government—and the consequent rise in Washington's population—brought about the rediscovery of "West Washington" as a choice place to live, with convenient access to the office buildings of Foggy Bottom and downtown. The pace of this rediscovery quickened after World War

ll until it began to look as if Georgetown might be spoiled by its success. The Old Georgetown Act, passed by Congress in 1950, officially made Georgetown a historic district and gave the US Commission of Fine Arts the authority to appoint an advisory panel—the Old Georgetown Board—to review proposals for additions and alterations to both public and private structures throughout the neighborhood, reinforcing its rapid gentrification.

Tourists are often surprised to learn that a substantial percentage of the "historic" houses in present-day Georgetown were actually built in the aftermath of the 1950 legislation. Many of these Eisenhower-era structures fit stealthily into the historic fabric, thanks to their modesty and reliance on red brick as the primary finish material. Even so, they are often readily distinguishable by their less-grand proportions, smaller windows, shallower façades, and brick patterns that were uncommon in the 19th century.

Today, Georgetown may be appreciated as a microcosm of American urbanism, miraculously encapsulated within a small precinct of one metropolis. Starting at the waterfront and walking northward, one passes the remnants of the town's industrial origins, moves through a thriving commercial and entertainment zone, and then traverses dense residential blocks. Continuing, one discovers streets lined with larger, detached houses, followed by an area of palatial "country" estates, and finally, the edge of Rock Creek Park—a swath of wilderness (well, almost) in the heart of the city.

(*Above*) This lithograph view of Georgetown, published by E. Sachse & Co. in 1855, reveals that parts of the town retained a pastoral quality well into the 19th century.

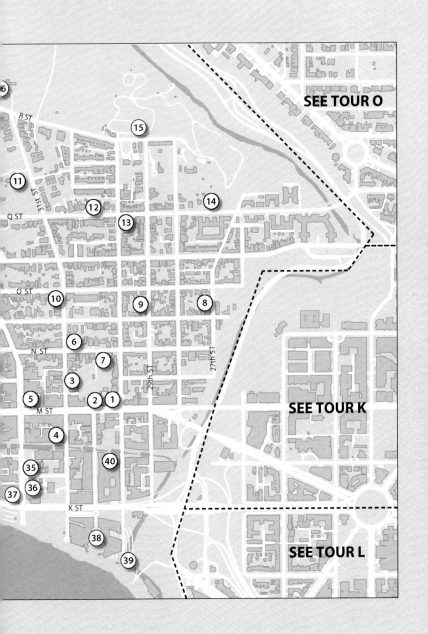

SEE TOUR O

SEE TOUR K

SEE TOUR L

M1

Thomas Sim Lee Corner

3001–3011 M Street, NW / 1206–1210 30th Street, NW

ca. 1794 — 3001–3003 M Street: Thomas Sim Lee, owner-builder

ca. 1812 — 3005–3011 M Street / 1206–1210 30th Street: Andrew Ross & Robert Getty, builders

ca. 1955 — Reconstruction: William Dewey Foster of Howe, Foster and Snyder

Numerous alterations and additions: various architects

Thomas Sim Lee was a delegate to the Continental Congress and served two terms as governor of Maryland. Like many prominent local politicians of the day, he also dabbled in Washington real estate. One of his ventures was the construction of 3001–3003 M Street, which was originally a single, six-bay town house. He later sold the adjacent properties on M Street and 30th Street to Andrew Ross and Robert Getty, who built houses in a similar Federal style.

By the 1950s, the Lee houses had been neglected for decades and faced demolition. A group of private citizens, led by Dorothea de Schweinitz and the nascent Historic Georgetown, Inc., eventually bought the properties and restored them. The successful project spurred similar renovation projects and may have been the single most important factor in bringing Georgetown's commercial district back to life.

M2

Old Stone House

3051 M Street, NW

1765 — Christopher and Rachael Layman, owner-builders

1767, 1775, 1790 — Additions: architects unknown

1959 — Restoration: National Park Service

The original cottage at Rosedale [see S10] is now believed to be the oldest extant structure in DC, but it has been heavily altered and incorporated into a larger house. The Lindens in Kalorama [see O17] dates from 1754, but it was built elsewhere and moved to DC. That leaves the aptly, if unimaginatively, named Old Stone House as the city's oldest existing structure that is both essentially intact and in its original location.

Supported by thick walls of blue granite and fieldstone, the house probably survived only because generations of locals were told either that George Washington was headquartered here while surveying the area or that L'Enfant used it while drawing up plans for the new capital city. These and other traditional stories have been debunked, and it now seems that this was just a simple house and shop begun by a Pennsylvania-born cabinetmaker and completed by his widow. Purchased by the National Park Service and restored in the late 1950s, the house is open to the public, as is the narrow garden to the rear of the property.

M3

Georgetown Customhouse and Post Office

1215 31st Street, NW

1858—Ammi B. Young
Numerous alterations: architects
  unknown
1997—Restoration: Sorg and Associates
2014—Renovation and addition: CORE
  architecture + design

This small but imposing granite structure
was built as a combined post office and
customhouse—the latter a reminder that
Georgetown remained a prominent port
well into the 19th century. The architect,
Ammi B. Young of New Hampshire, had
already designed the Greek Revival Vermont State House (1833–38) and Boston
Custom House (1837–47) when, in 1852, he
was appointed supervising architect of the
Treasury—effectively, the chief architect
for the federal government. In that capacity, Young designed a number of custom-
houses across the country, often drawing
inspiration from the dignified urban palazzi
of the Italian Renaissance. During Young's
tenure, the Treasury Department sometimes reused specific building designs: a
duplicate of the Georgetown building, but
made of limestone instead of granite, was
erected at the same time in Galena, Illinois.
This historic building still houses a post
office branch, now accompanied by offices
of a technology firm.

M4

Canal Square

1054 31st Street, NW

ca. 1850—Architect unknown
1970—Arthur Cotton Moore / Associates

This seminal project, best appreciated
from the courtyard at its center, was
among the earliest successful examples
of the adaptation of antique industrial
facilities to contemporary commercial
purposes. From the street, the new
portion of the complex appears to be a
mere pastiche of the existing warehouse
that was renovated as part of the project.
Seen from the courtyard, however, the
new wing is unmistakably modern, with
horizontal ribbon windows and balconies
anchored by soaring, windowless elevator
and stair towers.

It was in the original warehouse here
that Herman Hollerith perfected his pioneering punch-card tabulating machines.
In 1890, the Census Bureau used Hollerith's new gadget to process that year's
survey data in a fraction of the time it had
taken previously. In 1911, Hollerith's firm
merged with several others to form a
company now known by its initials: IBM.

M5

Farmers and Mechanics Branch
(now PNC Bank)

1201 Wisconsin Avenue, NW

1922—Marsh & Peter
1985—Renovation: architect unknown

This historic bank building, widely
recognized for its corner clock, gilded
dome, and cupola, presides over the
intersection of Wisconsin Avenue and M
Street—the heart of Georgetown. Built
for the Farmers and Mechanics National
Bank, which was founded in 1814 and
initially headquartered a block away, it
became a "branch" after that institution

was acquired by Riggs National Bank in 1928. The masterful exterior design emphasizes verticality, with window bays on the principal façades set back behind two-story pilasters and the recessed corner entrance framed by full columns of the same height. Open balustrades in the parapet continue the lines of the window bays above the cornice. The streamlined Corinthian ornament on the pilaster and column capitals further enhances the sense of vertical thrust.

M6

Wheatley Houses

3041–3043 N Street, NW

1859 — Francis Wheatley, builder
Numerous alterations: architects
  unknown

This almost mirror-image pair combines the flat façades more typical of Federal-era row houses with details that reveal the houses' true Victorian character: tall, narrow parlor windows, pronounced cast iron window hoods (sporting huge medallions on the lower floors), and strongly rhythmic decoration on the cornices. By placing the first floor well above street level, builder Francis Wheatley could drop the windows on that level to the floor and still preserve privacy for the rooms inside. Note the service entrance, suitable for hobbits, between the two houses.

M7

Laird-Dunlop House

3014 N Street, NW

ca. 1798–99 — Original (central) section:
  attributed to William Lovering
Various alterations and additions:
  architects unknown

The design of the earliest portion of this house is attributed to William Lovering, a self-trained amateur architect who is also believed to have designed the Law House [see C11] and Wheat Row [see C12] in Southwest Washington. Additions to the east and west are stylistically consistent with the original block, though their ever-so-slight setbacks and reduced height help to disguise the true bulk of the mansion today. The modest main porch was likely added in the 1930s.

John Laird, a wealthy tobacco merchant, was the original owner. The house eventually passed to his daughter, Barbara, and son-in-law, James Dunlop, a judge whose Confederate sympathies led to his ouster by President Abraham Lincoln. Coincidentally, a subsequent resident was none other than Robert Todd Lincoln, Honest Abe's only surviving son. The late *Washington Post* editor Ben Bradlee and his wife, author Sally Quinn, were more recent longtime owners.

M8
Trentman House

1350 27th Street, NW

1968 — Hugh Newell Jacobsen

Hugh Newell Jacobsen, one of the most prominent residential architects in the country for half a century, was best known for his abstract, freestanding houses — assemblages of white pavilions whose simple, iconic shapes remind some people of Monopoly houses. In historic settings, however, Jacobsen tended to pursue a more contextualist path. Acknowledging, but not quite replicating, the scale, color, and certain compositional elements of classic Federal row houses, the Trentman House is clearly modern, with sleek bay windows popping out from frames of highly unusual curved bricks.

M9
Mount Zion United Methodist Church

1334 29th Street, NW

1884 — Architect unknown
1904 — Alterations and addition: architect unknown

The area of Georgetown east of 29th Street and below P was once a predominantly Black neighborhood known as Herring Hill. Mount Zion United Methodist Church, believed to have been the first organized Black congregation in the District of Columbia, was a major fixture of the community. The original church, built around 1816, stood on 27th Street and served as a station on the Underground Railroad. This larger brick structure, built

after the old church was destroyed by fire, bears a sober brick façade, though the sanctuary contains a rather elaborate stamped iron ceiling.

M10
Christ Church, Georgetown

Southwest corner of 31st and O Streets, NW

1887 — Cassell & Laws / Henry Laws
1923 — Addition: architect unknown
1968 — Chapel of St. Jude: Philip Ives
2003 — Interior restoration: STUDIOS Architecture

With its acutely angled gables and almost skeletal tower, this church suggests a Gothic cathedral rendered in miniature and in dark red pressed brick rather than stone. Note the sharp right triangle implied by the overall composition of forms along the O Street side. Inside, the ceiling is supported by exposed scissor trusses.

M11

Tudor Place

1644 31st Street, NW

1795 — East and west wings: architect
unknown
1805–16 — Central section and connecting
structures: William Thornton
1876 — Kitchen addition: architect
unknown
1914 — Renovation: Walter Gibson Peter

Tudor Place — William Thornton's masterpiece — marks a significant break from the
more sedate Federal-style architecture
popular in early 19th-century Georgetown,
as represented by the Bowie-Sevier House
directly across Q Street. Like the Capitol,
for which Thornton was the original architect, Tudor Place began ingloriously as a
pair of wings with no connecting body.
Then, in 1805, these stubs and the eight-
and-a-half-acre property on which they
stood were bought by Thomas Peter and
Martha Custis Peter, granddaughter of
Martha Washington, using $8,000 left to
Mrs. Peter by her step-grandfather,
George. The Peters hired Thornton to
remodel the wings and design the central
connecting piece. The house is linear in
plan, with the public rooms marching along
the south side of the ground floor and private and service spaces lining the north
side. At the center of the south façade is a
domed circular porch, half of which is
embedded into the adjacent room, known
as the "Saloon" — a curious space given the
convex arc of the porch projecting into it.
Huge windows in the arc can be raised into
a hidden pocket above, allowing people to
pass through the opening.

Incredibly, Tudor Place was continuously occupied by six generations of
the Peter family over the course of 178
years. It is now a museum boasting
extensive collections of art objects and
household items, as well as meticu-
lously maintained gardens. The estate
provides unparalleled insights into the
evolution of domestic life — including the
role of slavery — in early Washington.

M12

Cooke's Row

3007–3029 Q Street, NW

1868 — Starkweather and Plowman
2009 — Renovation of 3007 Q Street:
Christian Zapatka Architect
Numerous other alterations: architects
unknown

This parade of picturesque duplexes hints
at the stylistic promiscuity of the Victorian era, while dramatically refuting the
perception of Georgetown as solely an
enclave of Federal-style architecture. The
row's two end units are quintessentially
Second Empire, while the middle two
are equally classically Italianate. All four
pairs of houses sport some of the more
ebullient roof brackets in the city, but the

ones supporting the porches at 3007 and 3009 deserve particular note.

M13
Francis Dodge House

Southeast corner of 30th and Q Streets, NW

1853 — Andrew Jackson Downing and Calvert Vaux
Numerous alterations: various architects

One of a pair of houses built for the Dodge brothers, Francis and Robert, who made their fortunes in shipping, this grand residence is quite literally a textbook example of Victorian Italianate design. Calvert Vaux described both dwellings at length in his book *Villas and Cottages* (1857), though he lumped them together as "Design No. 17 — Suburban Villa." He noted accurately that "although these two houses have their principal features

in common, neither is a servile imitation of the other."

As designed, each house was an asymmetrical but balanced composition, intended to accommodate the informality of daily domestic life while yielding a pleasing "painter-like effect." The architects did not supervise the construction of either house directly. When Vaux wrote to Francis Dodge seeking a report on the progress of the work, Dodge replied, "We find the cost of our houses to be much beyond what Mr. Downing led us to expect — say about $15,000 each; yet we have fine houses, and very comfortable and satisfactory in every respect."

Robert Dodge's house still stands at 1534 28th Street, at the corner of Q Street, but was substantially altered during the 20th century.

M14
Dumbarton House
(The National Society of the Colonial Dames of America)

2715 Q Street, NW

1799 — Samuel Jackson, owner-builder
1804, 1900 — Alterations: architects unknown
1915 — Move to present site and reconstruction of wings: architect unknown
1932 — Restoration: Horace W. Peaslee; Consulting architect: Fiske Kimball
1991 — Renovation: Martin Rosenblum

One of the oldest of Georgetown's large houses, Dumbarton was formerly known as Bellevue, because of its spectacular site just beyond where Q Street once dead-ended on the east side of Rock Creek. The builder, Samuel Jackson, went bankrupt, and the house was unoccupied until Joseph Nourse, who had worked with Alexander Hamilton to organize the financial system of the fledgling United States, bought it in 1804. The two semicircular bays at the rear of the house appear to be additions, based on their divergent brick patterns, and probably date to around the time that Nourse moved in.

Demolition of Dumbarton House seemed imminent in 1915 when the District government unveiled plans to extend Q Street into Georgetown across the new Buffalo Bridge. Preservationists managed

to save the building and move it about 100 feet to its present location. The National Society of the Colonial Dames of America, an organization dedicated to historic preservation and education, bought the house in 1928 to serve as its headquarters. The society soon undertook a restoration to remove pseudo-Georgian appliqués, such as stone quoins at the corners of the house, which had been added in the early 20th century.

M15

Oak Hill Cemetery

30th and R Streets, NW

1833—Van Ness Mausoleum: George Hadfield
1850—Chapel: James Renwick Jr.
1853—Gatehouse: George de la Roche
1867—Additions to Gatehouse: architect unknown
1872—Van Ness Mausoleum moved from original site on H Street, NW

Oak Hill Cemetery was laid out in a fashionably romantic manner over naturally terraced land donated by banker and philanthropist William Corcoran in 1849. Local luminaries interred here include architect Adolf Cluss, politico James G. Blaine, and Corcoran himself.

The Italianate gatehouse was designed by George de la Roche, who was also responsible for the overall cemetery plan (though there is evidence that Andrew Jackson Downing played a role in the landscape design). Inside the grounds, but visible from the street, is James Renwick's impeccable Gothic Revival chapel—a giant paperweight made of gray Potomac gneiss stone and contrasting red sandstone. The large rose window over the entrance beckons visitors from across the adjacent lawn. At the eastern end of the cemetery is the Van Ness family mausoleum, designed by George Hadfield and inspired by the ancient Temple of Vesta in Rome. Although it seems perfectly at home here, the structure was actually built for the family's private burial grounds, in what is now downtown Washington, and was later moved to this site.

M16

Dumbarton Oaks

Museum entrance: 1703 32nd Street, NW
Garden entrance: R Street at 31st Street, NW

ca. 1801—William Hammond Dorsey, owner-builder
ca. 1805–12—Orangery: architect unknown
ca. 1860s—Alterations: Edward Linthicum, owner
1922–59—Landscape architect: Beatrix Farrand
1923—Alterations: Frederick H. Brooke
1926—Service Court buildings: Lawrence White / McKim, Mead & White
1929—Music Room: Lawrence White / McKim, Mead & White
1938–46—Byzantine wing and other additions: Thomas T. Waterman
1964—Rare Book Gallery and Reading Room: Frederic Rhinelander King / Wyeth and King
1989—Courtyard Gallery: Hartman-Cox Architects

1996—Pool renovation: Richard Williams Architect

2001–5—Library, Gardeners' Court, and rehabilitation of existing structures: Venturi, Scott Brown and Associates; Preservation architects: Oehrlein & Associates Architects

2011—Renovation and addition to Orangery: cox graae + spack architects

2016—Pool house and pool renovation: cox graae + spack architects

Dumbarton Oaks is the most impressive of the large estates along the northern edge of Georgetown, built when this was still a pastoral area near to, but decidedly apart from, the young capital city. The main structure is characteristic of the Federal period, with planar brick walls, evenly spaced windows, and a modest cornice. Some slight scroll work above the main entry and a series of subtle inset panels between the first- and second-floor windows are among the few decorative flourishes—if that's even the right word—on the primary façade of this grand but understated building.

Robert and Mildred Bliss (stepbrother and -sister, who were unrelated by blood, raised together, and later married) acquired the house and 53 acres in 1920 and began to modify the estate to accommodate their exceptional collections of Byzantine and pre-Columbian art. Beatrix Farrand's evolving design for the grounds, with their numerous terraces and "garden rooms," is a masterpiece of American landscape architecture. Her Dumbarton work captures her romantic spirit: she once wrote to the Blisses about a patch of woods near the music room, urging them "to keep it as poetic as possible . . .

the sort of place in which thrushes sing and . . . dreams are dreamt."

The Blisses, whose wealth derived from their family's ownership of the patent for Fletcher's Castoria, a children's medicine, moved to California in 1940. After donating 27 acres north of the house to the city as a public park and selling 10 acres to the government of Denmark for its embassy on Whitehaven Street, they gave the rest of the estate to Harvard University for use as a study center and museum. Farrand's maintenance guidelines for the grounds urged the university to respect the dual nature of the property—on the one hand it offers "a pleasant sense of withdrawal from the nearby streets," while on the other it allows "an intimate connection with all that a great city can offer."

Between August and October 1944, the estate was the site of a series of meetings collectively known as the Dumbarton Oaks Conference, in which senior representatives of the United States, Great Britain, Russia, and China laid the organizational groundwork for the United Nations.

M16a

Pre-Columbian Collection Pavilion
Dumbarton Oaks grounds

1963—Philip Johnson

2007—Restoration: Venturi, Scott Brown and Associates; Preservation architects: Oehrlein & Associates Architects

In a long but erratic career, which on the one hand produced the sublime Glass House in New Canaan, Connecticut, but also yielded several fatuous postmodern skyscrapers, Philip Johnson produced a few masterpieces. The Dumbarton Oaks

Pre-Columbian Collection Pavilion is among them.

It was the 1960s, and the idea of appending an abstract molecule of little cylindrical structures made of marble, teak, bronze, and glass to a historic brick Georgetown mansion was less surprising than it might be now. For the visitor who can set aside any preconceptions about such a juxtaposition, this gem of a museum is a wondrous building to experience. It consists of eight circular, domed exhibition pods surrounding a central open court with a fountain. Each pod is itself defined by a constellation of robust round columns, subtly recapitulating the larger organization of the structure, while curved glass walls blur the boundary between inside and out.

M17
Scott-Grant House
3238 R Street, NW

ca. 1856 — Architect unknown
1907, 1930 — Alterations: architects unknown
1984 — Renovation: David M. Schwarz / Architectural Services, P.C.

Representative of the gracious freestanding estates that give the northern end of Georgetown its genteel suburban character, this highly formal, symmetrical house is loosened up by relatively florid decorative elements. The property was purchased around 1857 by Alfred Vernon Scott of Alabama, who died in 1860 and whose widow not surprisingly fled southward with the onset of the Civil War. The house is more closely associated, however, with General Ulysses S. Grant, who lived there off and on for a few months after the war and is widely believed to

have used the mansion as a summer White House while he was president (though documentation of that is lacking). Grant had been invited to stay there by fellow general Henry Walker Halleck, who rented the place during the war. Halleck drew the ire of his neighbors by quartering soldiers in the house, turning what is now R Street into a drill field and supposedly having the company bugler sound reveille and taps at dawn and dusk each day.

M18
Duke Ellington School of the Arts
(former Western High School)
3500 R Street, NW

1898 — Harry B. Davis
1910 — Addition: Snowden Ashford
1915 — Renovation and addition: Snowden Ashford
1925 — Addition: Albert L. Harris
2017 — Renovation and addition: cox graae + spack architects and Lance Bailey & Associates Inc., Joint Venture

According to a brochure for Western High School published in 1940, its lunchroom featured "spotless linen, bright silver, china of graceful shape and beautiful decoration," all of which contributed to an atmosphere of "universal courtesy and quiet." Alas, such lavish amenities were long gone by 1974, when the school began sharing its facilities with the newly established Duke Ellington School of the Arts. Offering academic concentrations in both performing and visual arts, the Ellington school eventually became the building's sole occupant.

Perched on high ground, slathered in white paint, and sporting a deep central portico, the school is a neighborhood landmark (as is the colossal green Adirondack chair parked on the school's front lawn, originally built for an art installation on the National Mall in 1996). Grand though it is, the building perpetually looked a bit dowdy until a comprehensive renovation and expansion, completed in 2017, which yielded state-of-the-"arts" performance and rehearsal spaces, ceramics and visual art studios, and a media center. On the exterior, the expansion is evident in the gently bowed additions on the side elevations (which Christoffer Graae, of cox graae + spack architects, jokingly calls "saddle bags")

and another at the rear. The project's pièce de résistance, however, is on the inside: a massive egg-shaped form, suspended above the floor of the central atrium, containing an 850-seat theater.

M19
Volta Bureau

1537 35th Street, NW (3417 Volta Place, NW)

1894—Peabody and Stearns
1949—Russell O. Kluge
2000—Renovation architects of record: Horsey & Thorpe; Interior: RTKL Associates

In 1880, after the French government awarded Alexander Graham Bell the Volta Prize of 50,000 francs (about $10,000 in 1880s dollars) in recognition of his invention of the telephone, Bell invested the money in further research that led to the graphophone, an improved version of the phonograph. The profits from this device helped him to establish the Volta Bureau, dedicated to "the increase and diffusion of knowledge relating to the Deaf," a subject near to Bell's heart because both his mother, Eliza Grace Bell, and his wife, Mabel Hubbard Bell, were deaf. Bell's prodigy, Helen Keller, broke ground for its construction. The temple-like building, which still houses successor organizations to the Volta Bureau, seems to be mined from the same architectural vein as the small but impeccably detailed classical bank buildings that once stood on Main Streets in countless American towns. The entrance is marked by a pair of intricately decorated columns *in antis*, meaning that they are bracketed by the side walls of the building. Note the contrasting east façade, which is composed of a row of vertical slit windows.

M20
Georgetown Visitation Preparatory School / Monastery of the Visitation

1524 35th Street, NW

1821—Chapel: Joseph Picot de Clorivière
1832—Monastery: architect unknown
1857—Additions/alterations to monastery and chapel: Richard Pettit
1874—Founders' Hall (Academy Building): Norris G. Starkweather

1995 — Restoration of Founders' Hall:
KressCox Associates
1996 — Renovation of Chapel: KressCox
Associates
1998 — Athletic and Performing Arts
centers: KressCox Associates
2002–19 — Various new structures
and renovations: cox graae + spack
architects

Founded in 1799 by three "Pious Ladies" —
French nuns who had fled the revolution — under the auspices of Georgetown
College's president, this is one of the oldest Catholic girls' schools in America. The
campus is a catalogue of period architecture, from the austere Federal-style monastery building (at the corner of 35th and
P), to the neo-Gothic stuccoed chapel, to
the ornate Victorian Founders' Hall, with
its mansard roof and elaborate brickwork. The last of these was the victim of
a spectacular fire in 1993, after which the
nuns not only oversaw a meticulous restoration of the damaged structure but also
embarked on a broader building and renovation campaign, adding new ancillary
facilities designed in a low-key historicist
mode. From around the corner, in the 3500
block of P Street, one can catch glimpses
of the long wooden porches that line the
rear of the monastery.

M21
Georgetown University
Main entrance at 37th and O Streets, NW

The nation's oldest Catholic institution
of higher learning, initially known as
Georgetown College, was formally established in 1789 by Father John Carroll, the
first American Catholic bishop. Carroll

considered placing the new school on
what is now Capitol Hill but dismissed
the site as being "too far in the country."
Instead, he opted for a high spot just
upriver from the bustling port, enjoying a
commanding view. The present campus
is organized around two primary centers,
with most of the historic academic buildings and residential clusters toward the
southern end and a sprawling medical
school and hospital complex at the northern edge along Reservoir Road.

M21a
Healy Hall

1879 — Smithmeyer & Pelz
1901 — Gaston Hall: Smithmeyer & Pelz
1971 — Renovation and master plan: LEO
A DALY
1982 — Restoration of Riggs Library:
Environmental Planning & Research
1988 — Renovation: Cannon Faulkner
1995 — Upgrades: Einhorn Yaffee Prescott

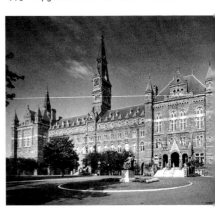

The centerpiece of the Georgetown campus is named for Father Patrick Healy,
the university's dynamic president from
1873 to 1882. The son of an Irish American
father and a mixed-race mother who had
been enslaved, Healy was the first person of acknowledged African American
descent to earn a PhD and the first to head
a predominantly white university.

Designed by the stylistically ambidex-
trous architects of the original Library of
Congress building, Healy Hall has exterior
walls of dark gray Potomac gneiss and is
capped by a 200-foot clock tower, making
it one of low-rise Washington's most
widely visible landmarks. Glimpsed from
the Potomac River, the imposing structure
could almost be mistaken for a baronial

fortress overlooking the Rhine. Healy Hall's exterior was largely completed by 1879, but interior construction carried on for decades. The building's most notable space is the Riggs Library, distinguished by four levels of delicate cast iron stacks. Also impressive is Gaston Hall, an opulent 743-seat auditorium framed by myriad murals, cartouches, brackets, and arches beneath a coffered wooden ceiling.

M21b
Old North Hall

1795 — Attributed to Leonard Harbaugh
1809 — Addition of towers: architect unknown
1926 — Renovation: Marsh and Peter
1983 — Restoration: Mariani & Associates
2013 — Renovation: FOX Architects

The oldest extant academic building at Georgetown, Old North is typical of the simple but dignified Georgian and Federal structures found on a number of the country's most venerable campuses, though the two octagonal towers on the north façade, added in the early 1800s, are unusual. As with Healy Hall, its interior construction continued for years after the exterior was finished. Old North now houses the university's McCourt School of Public Policy. As of 2020, 14 US presidents, from George Washington to Barack Obama, had visited Old North while in office, many of them to deliver speeches from the porch facing the quadrangle to the south.

M21c
Joseph Mark Lauinger Memorial Library

1970 — John Carl Warnecke & Associates
1990, 1993 — Renovations: Einhorn Yaffee Prescott
2014 — Renovation (Special Collections Suite): Bowie Gridley Architects

The Brutalist exposed-aggregate concrete surfaces and angular forms of the Lauinger Library are not widely favored today, but when it opened, the structure was praised — if rather faintly — for being deferential to its historic neighbors. *Washington Post* critic Wolf Von Eckardt declared that the architects of the library "managed to blend it into the cityscape, if not unobtrusively, successfully." Indeed, the new building's low physical profile preserves views to and from the older structures, while its incorporation of dark gray aggregate in the concrete and its abstract asymmetrical towers are clear allusions to Healy Hall.

M22
Holy Trinity Catholic Church
3513 N Street, NW / 1301 36th Street, NW

1794 — Original church (now Chapel of St. Ignatius Loyola): Leonard Harbaugh
1851 — Present church: architect unknown
1870 — Rectory: Francis Staunton (moved to current location in 1916–17)
1877 — Expansion of original church: "Architect Duffy" (first name unknown)
1918 — Upper and Lower schools: F. Pierson

1979 — Renovation of main church: Giuliani Associates Architects

2000 — Renovation of chapel and parish facilities: Kerns Group Architects

2015 — Renovations of Upper and Lower Schools: cox graae + spack architects

1900–38 — Numerous alterations and additions: Albert Adsit Clemons

1942–66 — Various renovations: architects unknown

1978–95 — Renovations and additions: John Dreyfuss; Stavropoulos Associates; Landscape architect: James Urban

2017 — Renovation: Rill Architects; Interior designers: Jodi Macklin Interior Design; Landscape architects: Graham Landscape Design

The various structures in this complex reflect several different eras in religious history. The original brick church on N Street was the first building in DC erected for public Catholic services, and its small-scale and modest character testify to the still-tenuous state of Catholicism in late 18th-century America. By the mid-19th century, that tiny church had become inadequate for the growing congregation, and it was superseded by the dignified Greco-Roman Revival structure on 36th Street, whose larger size and more refined architectural expression suggest American Catholicism's improved condition. Finally, the more elaborate, mansard-roofed rectory, around the corner on O Street, as well as the self-assured neoclassical school buildings at the corners of N and O Streets, attest to the financial stability that came with the arrival of millions of industrial-era immigrants from Ireland, Italy, and elsewhere, swelling the ranks of the Roman Catholic Church in the United States.

M23
Halcyon House
(former Benjamin Stoddert House)

3400 Prospect Street, NW

ca. 1787 — Benjamin Stoddert, owner-builder

The bizarre history of this large urban estate, one of Washington's quirkiest buildings, could warrant a book in its own right. The short version begins with Benjamin Stoddert, merchant, landowner, and America's first secretary of the navy, who built Halcyon House "after the manner of some of the elegant houses I have seen in Philadelphia," which then reigned as the American model of urban sophistication. The south façade remains largely intact, but the north is another matter.

Albert Adsit Clemons acquired the mansion around 1900 and soon began to tinker with it. Supposedly convinced that he would die if he stopped working on the house, Clemons spent nearly four decades obscuring Stoddert's chaste structure in a labyrinth of rooms, hallways, and stairs, most of which no one ever used. The peculiar results of his obsession are still visible on the north façade — note, just for starters, the mix of irregularly shaped stone and brick, the partially hollowed-out bases under the skinny half-columns, and the chamfered windows in the pediment. According to the *Washington Times-Herald*, Clemons subsisted on money "provided by his wife on condition that he stay away from her."

Georgetown University bought the house in 1961 and used it as a dormitory. In 1978, sculptor John Dreyfuss moved into the mansion, which his father, architect Edmund Dreyfuss, had bought in 1966 with the hope of developing the property. During the 1980s and '90s, the younger Dreyfuss and his then-wife, photographer Mary Noble Ours, removed many of Clemons' greater excesses. They also commissioned a cavernous new studio space, under a revamped rear garden, which is illuminated by large skylights made of translucent, composite panels.

The house was sold in 2011 to Japanese pharmaceutical executives Sachiko Kuno and Ryuji Ueno, whose S&R Foundation operates it as an incubator for talented individuals in science, art, and social entrepreneurship.

M24
Cox's Row
3327–3339 N Street, NW

ca. 1818 — John Cox, owner-builder
Numerous alterations: various architects

Built by Colonel John Cox, these five Federal-style houses are notable for their setbacks from the street, allowing for small but attractive front yards. Cox engineered the gerrymandering of city boundaries so he could run for mayor of Georgetown; he won, entering office in 1823 and holding the post for a record 22 years. When the Marquis de Lafayette returned to town in 1824, he accepted Cox's offer to reside at 3337 N Street for his entire visit.

M25
Smith Row
3255–3267 N Street, NW

ca. 1815 — Walter and Clement Smith, owner-builders
Numerous alterations: various architects

Along with Cox's Row one block down N Street [see previous entry], these five houses are classic examples of domestic architecture of the Federal period, with flat fronts and muted ornament. While the houses in the neighboring row enjoy small front yards, Smith Row, completed shortly after the War of 1812, boasts raised parlor floors reached by elegant entrance steps.

M26
St. John's Episcopal Church, Georgetown
3240 O Street, NW

1804 — Based on a design by William Thornton
1849 — Bell tower: George de la Roche
1875 — Rectory: Norris G. Starkweather
1961 — Renovation of nave: Milton Grigg
1995 — Renovation and addition: Egbert & Houston
2012 — Renovation: Hartman-Cox Architects

William Thornton, the original architect of the Capitol, as well as of Tudor Place [see M11] and the Octagon [see L6], provided drawings for this church, but most likely did not supervise its construction. Early members of the congregation, which was founded in 1796, included Secretary of

Hyde-Addison Elementary School

3219 O Street, NW

1885 — Addison School: architect
  unknown
1907 — Anthony Hyde School: Arthur B.
  Heaton
2009 — Renovation of Addison School:
  Lance Bailey & Associates
2019 — Renovation and addition:
  Shinberg.Levinas

The DC Public Schools system is in the midst of an ambitious modernization program that is transforming perceptions of public education in the city. The recent renovation of, and addition to, the Hyde-Addison Elementary School exemplifies the system's renewed commitment to good design. The addition, which links the two once-separate schools (located within the same city block but facing different streets), boasts eye-catching façades lined with terra cotta "baguettes"—thin, loaf-like ceramic panels—which are normally installed in horizontal patterns but are applied vertically here. The baguettes help to shade the glass walls behind while creating a sense of depth and texture. The addition includes the new main entrance to the complex along with classrooms and an art center. The new gymnasium was placed underground, making room for a courtyard that is open to neighborhood families after school hours.

The architecture firm for the renovation and addition, Shinberg.Levinas, has also designed a number of interesting public charter schools throughout the city.

the Navy Benjamin Stoddert and Francis Scott Key, and President Thomas Jefferson contributed $50 to the building fund. Despite auspicious beginnings, the church was bankrupt by 1829. A few years later, the building was sold to William Corcoran in order to pay back taxes, but Corcoran, who had attended the church as a child, soon donated the building back to the congregation. The structure has been modified greatly over the years, but the foundations and most of the exterior walls seem original. A modern atrium connecting the church and the parish hall is crowned by a row of skylights between timber trusses.

M28
Georgetown Market

3276 M Street, NW

1865 — Architect unknown
1992 — Renovation: Jack Ceglic, designer;
   Associated architects: Core Group

Public markets have been located on this site since 1795, and in 1802, the ground was formally deeded to the town "for the use of the market aforesaid, forever, and for no other use, interest or purpose whatsoever." The current structure, reminiscent of a small Victorian train station, dates to the Civil War. Generations of hucksters enjoyed a brisk business in the market until chain stores rendered the independent vendors obsolete. After a period of neglect, the old building, with its round-arched windows, bracketed cornices, and central parapet, was carefully restored to house a branch of the high-end Dean & DeLuca specialty grocery. Alas, the chain's finances went stale in 2019, leading to the closure of most of its stores, including this one. Georgetowners now eagerly await the next incarnation of this venerable community fixture.

M29
Cady's Alley

Between 33rd and 34th Streets, NW, and between M Street and the C&O Canal

2004 — Master plan and bridge: Shalom
   Baranes Associates; Individual
   buildings and stores: Sorg and
   Associates, Frank Schlesinger
   Associates, McInturff Architects,
   Martinez + Johnson, and Shalom
   Baranes Associates with Leopold
   Boeckl; Landscape architects: The
   Fitch Studio

Cady's Alley runs between 33rd and 34th Streets just north of the C&O Canal, but the name is also used loosely to refer to a group of adjacent buildings containing stores selling high-style furniture and housewares. This publicly accessible design center is all the more interesting because a number of different architects had a hand in the various buildings, some of which are relatively edgy looking for Georgetown. Note in particular the corrugated metal façade of 3335 Cady's Alley, the bridge spanning the alley at 3330, and the addition on top of 1028 33rd Street at the eastern end of the alley.

M30
Capitol Traction Company Union Station
(former Georgetown Car Barn)

3600 M Street, NW / 3520 Prospect Street, NW

1897 — Waddy B. Wood
1911 — Expansion and alterations: architect
   unknown
1960 — Renovation: architect unknown
1986 — Renovation: Arthur Cotton
   Moore / Associates
1999 — Renovation: RTKL Associates

Engaging the precipitous bluff at the western end of the Georgetown waterfront, this former streetcar storage facility towers over M Street but appears from Prospect Street to be merely a series of modestly scaled pavilions and sunny terraces. In its original form, this was a highly complex building incorporating

multiple levels of streetcar tracks, passenger stations, and offices. It is now used by Georgetown University for classrooms and office space. The steep staircase immediately to the west of the Car Barn is the one made famous in the movie *The Exorcist*—happily, it is now more commonly populated by ambitious joggers than by plunging priests.

M31

Washington Canoe Club

3700 Water Street, NW

1905—Georges P. Hales
1910—Addition: George P. Hales
ca. 1922—Addition: architect unknown

A classic example of early 20th-century recreational architecture, this shingle-style boathouse conjures up images of the days of full-body bathing suits and Teddy Roosevelt's vigorous outdoorsy antics. Designed by avid canoeist and early club member George P. Hales, the building was supposedly built by the club's members using wood salvaged from derelict barns. The structure features a large ballroom with a massive brick fireplace and a grill room on the first floor decorated by a cartoon frieze, executed by *Evening Star*

cartoonist Felix Mahony, showing early members of the club. Floods, ice, and time have wreaked havoc with the building, and the original structure is currently unoccupied for safety reasons. The club, which was instrumental in the establishment of flatwater canoe racing as an Olympic sport, is raising money for a restoration.

M32

3303 Water Street

2004—Frank Schlesinger Architects in association with Gary Edward Handel + Associates

Inspired by the 19th-century industrial architecture of the Georgetown waterfront, this condominium apartment building achieves elegance through the interplay of plain brick surfaces and a glass curtain wall divided into relatively small units with dark metal frames. The curtain wall appears in several different forms. On the north and south façades, the main block of the building is divided into regular bays in which the outermost plane of the curtain wall is flush with the brick piers but is notched back at both corners, creating spaces for small balconies. On the east and west ends of the building, the curtain wall begins to break out from the brick armature, creating several fully glazed corners. On the south façade of the wing extending toward the river, a three-story section of curtain wall is cantilevered out from the brick structure to become the dominant compositional element. The butterfly-wing panel immediately adjacent to the freeway was conceived as being convertible to a glass curtain wall should the elevated road ever be torn down.

M33

The Flour Mill
(former Bomford's Mill)

1000 Potomac Street, NW

1845 — George Bomford, owner-builder
1883, 1932 — Alterations: architects
   unknown
1980 — Addition and renovation: Peter
   Vercelli

Mills for cotton and flour were once fairly common near the Georgetown waterfront, yet of the many such buildings erected hereabouts, this is the sole survivor. It was built as a cotton mill by Colonel George Bomford, converted into a flour mill by subsequent owners in 1866, and expanded by still later owners in 1883 and 1932. It continued to produce flour well into the 20th century.

Architect Peter Vercelli used the historic structure, which runs along Potomac Street, as the core of a large office and residential condominium complex. The serrated balconies of the new residential building, which is set at an angle to 33rd Street, contrast dramatically with the planar façades of the original structure. This was one of a number of late 20th-century projects in Georgetown reflecting an almost fetishistic reliance on red brick as a medium for creating clearly modern buildings that still seemed sympathetic to their historic contexts. While those large brick expanses can be a little overwhelming, the new buildings do fit quite comfortably among their much older cousins. The vaguely threatening bollards at the corner of the plaza to the northeast of the site are inexplicable, however.

M34

Chesapeake & Ohio Canal Warehouses
(Canal House / Georgetown Park Apartments)

Along the C&O Canal between Wisconsin Avenue and Potomac Street, NW

ca. 1828 and after — Architects unknown
1977–82 — Adaptive reuse: Chloethiel
   Woodard Smith / Lockman Associates
   et al.
2019 — Renovation of Grace Street
   warehouse: HOK

The C&O Canal, which runs roughly 185 miles from Cumberland, Maryland, to Washington, DC, never enjoyed the commercial success its backers had anticipated. The canal, obsolete even when new, could not compete with its archrival, the Baltimore & Ohio Railroad, which easily garnered most of the lucrative Ohio Valley trade. Closed to commerce since 1923, the canal was purchased by the federal government to be used for recreational purposes. It is now the subject of a master plan orchestrated by the firm of James Corner Field Operations, in collaboration with the National Park Service and Georgetown Heritage, which seeks to enhance the canal's accessibility, among other goals.

Back in the early to mid-19th century, the canal carried enough traffic to warrant several large warehouses, which, more than a century later, caught the eye of developers eager to address the growing interest in loft spaces for both residential and commercial purposes. These dour, burly buildings — rare in a city nearly bereft of industrial heritage — proved readily adaptable for modern living, retail, and office use. Old and new elements, while distinguishable by virtue of their differing materials and details, are nonetheless seamlessly integrated into a coherent whole.

M35
Grace Episcopal Church
1041 Wisconsin Avenue, NW

1867 — Thomas Plowman
1895 — Rectory: architect unknown
1898 — Parish Hall: Waddy Wood
1923 — Renovation: architect unknown
1970s — Renovations: architects unknown

Set back on a raised and tree-shaded courtyard, this humble Gothic Revival church, built as a mission for the families of neighborhood laborers and craftsmen, seems oblivious to the passage of time and the substantial development that has occurred around it. The original structure is built of granite with sandstone window and door surrounds. The entry façade is distinguished by a porch that mimics the shape of the larger building, shallow buttresses at the corners, and a bellcote — a diminutive turret containing a bell — at the peak of the gabled roof.

M36
Ritz-Carlton Georgetown
3100 South Street, NW

1932 — Incinerator: Metcalf and Eddy
2002 — Renovation and additions: Gary Edward Handel + Associates and Shalom Baranes Associates; Hotel interiors / architects of record: Gary Edward Handel + Associates; Theater interiors: Rockwell Group; Preservation architects: Brawer & Hauptman, Architects

Talk about adaptive reuse. This swanky mixed-use complex occupies the site — and remnants — of a Depression-era garbage incinerator. The project posed substantial technical challenges, not the least of which was the need to blast out an enormous volume of rock in order to make room for a parking garage, theaters, and other lower-level components. Meanwhile, a clump of little historic houses, standing just to the west of the hotel entrance on South Street, had to be carefully picked up, moved to a temporary site, and later moved back to their original locations to ensure that they didn't go sliding down the hill during all that blasting. And of course, the 130-foot smokestack and the incinerator building, an attractive work of industrial Art Deco, were contributing structures in the Georgetown Historic District and had to be preserved.

The architects broke up the massing of the complex into relatively small blocks and organized them to secure views to and from the various components. Not surprisingly, they chose red brick as the principal material for the new structures, matching the incinerator building and smokestack. The architects also picked up on the dark window frames of the incinerator, using a matte black metal both in the frames for individual punched windows and as cladding for larger sections of the new structures. Battered stone walls at the base of the building along K Street define a separate zone, creating a distinct identity for the entrance to the movie theaters while alluding to the tons of rock that had to be removed in order for the theaters to exist.

The incinerator building itself has been incorporated into the hotel, accommodating the lobby, lounge, and restaurant spaces. The highlight of the complex, however, is surely the Chimney Stack Room—a space accommodating a single dining/meeting table at the base of the old smokestack, which is now protected by a glass roof and highlighted with appropriately dramatic lighting. Patrons inclined toward vertigo are advised to go easy on the martinis before gazing upward.

M37
Waterfront Center
(former Dodge Center)

1010 Wisconsin Avenue, NW

1813–24—Original warehouses: architects unknown
1975—Hartman-Cox Architects

Its angled profile mimicking the natural bluff that rises steeply from K Street (formerly known as Water Street), this office building offers a modern take on the industrial character of the old Georgetown waterfront. The finish brick replicates the texture of that used in surrounding historic structures, including the onetime warehouse of Francis Dodge, at the corner of Wisconsin and K, which was incorporated into the new complex. The building's open-air atrium has a Piranesian quality—its overall shape not fully intelligible, its concrete frame soaring into the mysterious upper reaches of the space. It also recalls the raw visual power of the area's old mills and warehouses, while affording intriguing views between the various offices and circulation spaces throughout the building.

M38
Washington Harbour

3000–3020 K Street, NW

1986—Arthur Cotton Moore / Associates
2012—Lobby renovations: HOK;
    Fountain / ice rink / exterior
    renovations: Gensler

Dubbed "Xanadu on the Potomac" by the late J. Carter Brown, longtime chair of the US Commission of Fine Arts, Washington Harbour is a curious concoction of archi-

tectural motifs, which, according to architect Arthur Cotton Moore, refer to such
diverse antecedents as the "exuberant
three-dimensional vocabulary of Victorian Georgetown," the "classic, rhythmic,
columnar quality" of Washington's monumental architecture, and even what he
calls "Jeffersonian domes." Add to this the
cartoonish metallic ornamentation that
exemplifies Moore's "Industrial Baroque"
style, and the result is visually staggering.

The mixed-use complex is, however,
unquestionably successful in creating a
place, predictably aswarm with diners,
drinkers, boaters, and strollers on any
pleasant day. The slightly skewed, cross-
shaped plan incorporates an implied continuation of Virginia Avenue (which actually dead-ends on the other side of Rock
Creek), intersected by a pedestrianized
extension of Thomas Jefferson Street,
culminating in an oval plaza with a fountain and an extremely idiosyncratic tower.
The relative narrowness of the complex's
"streets" provides a respite from the
famous—and, sometimes, seemingly
relentless—broad avenues of Washington. The freestanding columns that dot
the perimeter of the development provide
support for floodwalls that can be raised
from below ground when the Potomac has
one of its destructive mood swings.

M39

House of Sweden

2900 K Street, NW

2006—Gert Wingårdh and Tomas Hansen;
   Architects of record: VOA Associates

Leave it to the Swedes to rethink the very
concept of an embassy. This building
houses not only the Swedish chancery
but also exhibition and event spaces, as
well as corporate apartments and, in a
gesture of international cooperation, the
Embassy of Iceland. These days, "diplomatic" facilities are often fortresses set
back far from surrounding streets, but the
House of Sweden is transparent, open,
and accessible.

Glass—the primary exterior material—
is used in several different ways. On the
lowest level, large windows allow passersby to get clear views into the building.
On the next level, glass panels are suspended in front of the exterior wall, lending a slightly mysterious sense of depth to
that part of the façades. One level above
that, the building is girdled with ribbons
of laminated glass containing a layer of
film imprinted with wood-grain patterns.
The architects originally intended to use
actual thinly sliced sheets of wood to
achieve this effect but determined that
Washington's infamous humidity would

wreak wrinkly havoc on them. The alternative was risky—a reliance on fake, computer-generated wood grain might seem like a recipe for kitsch—but thanks to the exaggerated scale of the grain, coupled with the semi-regularity of the pattern embedded in each pane of glass, the effect is intriguingly abstract.

With its simple but rich material palette, its organizational clarity, and even the slight frivolity of its translucent, faux wood-grain glass panels, the House of Sweden perfectly captures the aesthetic spirit of its home country. In the words of one former staff member, "This building speaks Swedish."

M40
The Foundry
1055 Thomas Jefferson Street, NW

1856—Architect unknown
1977—Renovation and new construction:
    Arthur Cotton Moore / Associates;
    Architect of record: Vlastimil Koubek;
    Landscape architects: Sasaki
    Associates

William Duvall's 1856 machine shop at 1050 30th Street, which was once used as a veterinary hospital for the mules that worked the C&O Canal, inspired the design and name of this complex. The modern building may not look like much from the side streets, but from the canal side, it can be appreciated for its simple lines, expansive windows, and sensitive massing. This development has struggled to retain retail and entertainment-oriented tenants— its movie theaters closed years ago, for instance—perhaps because it is somewhat removed from the bustle of Georgetown's primary commercial corridors.

Foxhall

The thoroughly suburban—at some points almost pastoral—character of the Foxhall area belies its proximity to Georgetown and central Washington. Indeed, less than a century ago much of the property along Foxhall Road was open farm country. In the 1920s and '30s, cows from the nearby Palisades Dairy Farm grazed the land now occupied by the Mount Vernon Campus of the George Washington University.

The neighborhood takes its name from Henry Foxall (without the *h*), whose family farm, Spring Hill, was near where Foxhall Road and P Street now intersect. Foxall was a close friend of Thomas Jefferson—the two occasionally met for violin duets—and a major cannon manufacturer. His foundry, located in what is now Glover Archbold Park, was an obvious target during the War of 1812; when a timely thunderstorm prevented British troops from attacking the facility, Foxall credited divine providence and, in gratitude, established the Foundry Methodist Church, which initially stood at 14th and G Streets and later moved to its current location on 16th Street, NW.

Agricultural enterprises became increasingly impractical within the District of Columbia during the late 19th century, and the Foxall farm was sold in 1910. By 1927, construction was under way on the neo-Tudor Foxhall Village (with the *h*—according to legend, a careless sign-maker bears responsibility for the misspelling) just below Reservoir Road, and station wagons, cocktail parties, and bridge games soon supplanted plows, cattle, and chicken coops.

The Wetzell-Archbold Farmstead, built in 1843, is the earliest known log dwelling in Washington. It still stands along Reservoir Road in the Foxhall area.

Embassy of Germany Chancery

4645 Reservoir Road, NW

1964 — Egon Eiermann
2014 — Renovation: HPP Architekten
    GmbH; Architects of record: GBR
    Architects

The two major buildings in the German Embassy complex, the chancery and the ambassador's residence [see following entry], both reflect the Teutonic penchant for precision and orderliness, but with strikingly different results. The sleek and finely detailed chancery, one of the most underappreciated buildings in Washington, demonstrates that rationalist, hard-edged modernism can also be visually rich and inviting. Architect Egon Eiermann skillfully obscured the bulk of the building by nestling it into the sloping terrain and stepping down its mass at both ends. The intricate façade, composed of layered grids in wood, metal, and glass, further dematerializes the structure. An influential architect in post–World War II Germany, Eiermann was perhaps best known for his hauntingly beautiful additions to the ruins of the Kaiser Wilhelm Memorial Church in Berlin.

German Ambassador's Residence

1800 Foxhall Road, NW

1994 — O. M. Ungers

In contrast to the delicate chancery [see previous entry], the German ambassador's residence is monumental, bordering on sepulchral. Severe though it may be, the building does offer some visual treats for the design aficionado. Many of the forms and patterns that appear in the residence's façades, flooring, and furnishings — most notably the repeated grids of open squares — recall the starkly elegant motifs of Josef Hoffmann and other designers associated with the *fin-de-siècle* Viennese Secession movement. The residence's architect, O. M. Ungers, who studied under chancery architect Egon Eiermann, was notoriously obsessive: his contract for this project empowered him to dictate the exact and unalterable placement of all furniture in the building's public spaces.

Florence Hollis Hand Chapel

**The George Washington University,
Mount Vernon Campus
2100 Foxhall Road, NW**

1970 — Hartman-Cox Architects

Conceived as part of a master plan for the Mount Vernon Seminary and College, this chapel was finished after the last seminary class graduated in 1969. The institution continued as an independent women's college until it was absorbed into the George Washington University in 1999. The chapel is now used primarily for performances and special events.

The design was inspired by the work of Finnish modernist Alvar Aalto, as well as by the restrained architecture of American colonial churches. The experience of the building is exceptionally well choreographed. On approach, the chapel appears to be a relatively plain brick structure, but a series of shed roofs hints at the interior spatial sequence, which is itself a response to the dramati-

Belgian Ambassador's Residence
(former Anna Thomson Dodge House)

2300 Foxhall Road, NW

1931 — Horace Trumbauer
2007 — Modernization: Quinn Evans
    Architects

Mansions are almost commonplace in parts of Northwest Washington, but few can compete with this one for sheer Gatsbyesque opulence. It was commissioned by Anna Thomson Dodge, the widow of car manufacturer Horace E. Dodge, as a wedding gift for her daughter. The house's stately façade was inspired by that of the early 18th-century Hôtel de Rothelin-Charolais in Paris. The architect, Horace Trumbauer, whose prolific Philadelphia-based firm designed palatial houses for many of America's wealthiest families,

cally sloping site. Once inside, the visitor descends a staircase that offers glimpses of the main sanctuary below. That space is capped by a stepped roof with clerestory windows at each tier admitting ethereal light. Windows at the sanctuary level afford views to the wooded site and a trickling stream.

was also involved in the design of the imposing Philadelphia Museum of Art and the campus plan for Duke University. Like many projects by Trumbauer's firm, however, this one is now believed to have been the work of his chief designer, Julian Abele, one of the most prolific Black architects of the early 20th century.

N5
Spanish Ambassador's Residence
2350 Foxhall Road, NW

2003—José Rafael Moneo and Moneo Brock Studio

Pritzker Prize winner José Rafael Moneo tends to rely on the inherent beauty of high-quality materials to lend character to his buildings, and such is the case with the unadorned walls of narrow Roman brick that define this large but unassuming residence. Several interior spaces stand out, including the barrel-vaulted reception hall whose bold, simple dormers are visible from the street, and the skylit *orangerie* adjacent to the baronial formal dining room. Without resorting to literal historical quotation, Moneo imbued the residence with a distinctly Spanish feel through such devices as the use of Moorish-inspired tiles, reflecting the influence of seven centuries of Muslim presence on the Iberian Peninsula during the Middle Ages.

N6
Kreeger Museum
2401 Foxhall Road, NW

1967—Philip Johnson and Richard Foster

When insurance executive David Lloyd Kreeger and his wife, Carmen, commissioned Philip Johnson to design a house that could accommodate their burgeoning art collection, they were already planning for its eventual conversion into a museum. Johnson's design strongly evokes ancient Mediterranean villas, with travertine walls, outdoor sculpture terraces, and groin-vaulted interior spaces reminiscent of the great Roman baths. Inside, the unusual choice of cotton carpet as a wall covering serves two practical purposes: it enhances the acoustics for musical performances and facilitates the quick rearrangement of paintings.

Sheridan-Kalorama / Massachusetts Avenue Heights

Kalorama is an artificial word derived from the Greek for "good view." It is the fitting name that poet, liberal activist, and diplomat Joel Barlow gave to the estate he bought in 1807 near the present-day intersection of 23rd and S Streets, overlooking the nascent federal city and Georgetown. Barlow, one of Thomas Jefferson's most trusted friends, embraced whatever was new and advanced in any field — politics, literature, science — as long as he thought it would improve the condition of humankind. For him, that included improving the condition of the new United States: "My object is altogether of a moral and political nature," he wrote. "I wish to encourage and strengthen in the rising generation, the sense of the importance of republican institutions."

Barlow's house burned during the Civil War, was rebuilt, and then was demolished in the 1880s. Soon thereafter, Kalorama Woods, as realtors originally called the neighborhood, began to attract rich, famous, and powerful families, who raced in to build their mansions and gardens. The area's architectural purity and unimpeachably tasteful landscaping prompted Russell Baker to quip, "Kalorama has the quiet, slightly sinister atmosphere of the aristocratic quarter of a Ruritanian capital."

Baker might have extended his criticism to cover most of Massachusetts Avenue, the city's longest and grandest boulevard, a stretch of which skirts the western edge of Kalorama. "Mass Ave," as it is colloquially known, was perhaps the most sought-after address for the many robber barons and aristocrats who moved to Washington in droves during the late 19th and early 20th centuries. Life along the avenue changed perforce, however, during the Great Depression, as suddenly impoverished moguls, dowagers, and debutantes slipped out the back door and diplomats from around the world strode in the front, and a new Embassy Row was born.

The house that Anthony Holmead built in 1795 on what is now Mitchell Park in Kalorama was appropriated by the US government for use as a hospital during the Civil War. It is shown here in ruins (*left*) after a fire in 1865. The house was later rebuilt and was twice owned by the German government, which demolished it in the 1920s.

SEE TOU

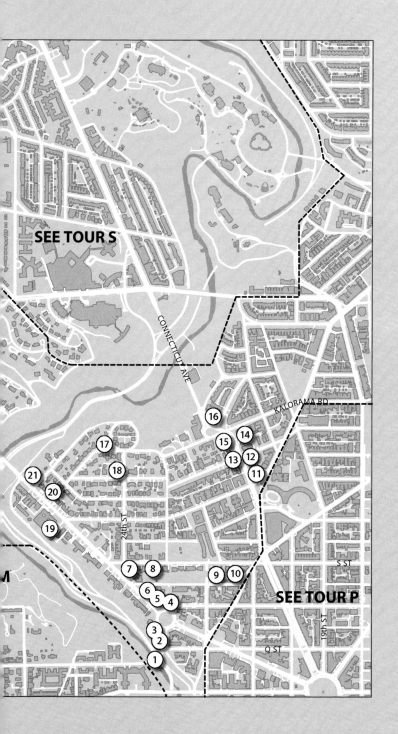

01

Buffalo Bridge
(Dumbarton Bridge)

Q Street, NW, at Rock Creek Park

1914 — Glenn Brown and Bedford Brown IV;
    Sculptors: A. Phimister Proctor (buffalo)
    and John Joseph Earley (heads)

Brown *père* and *fils* designed this amazing
bridge to connect Georgetown with the
then-developing Dupont/Kalorama area.
Curving in plan, supported on large semicircular arches, and crowned by a cantilevered row of smaller bracketed arches
(visible from Rock Creek Parkway below),
the powerful structure evokes ancient
Roman aqueducts and medieval European fortifications. In contrast to such
"Old World" precedents, the decorative
scheme is pure Americana, from the giant
buffalo sculptures that give the bridge
its unofficial name to the series of heads
(also visible from below) sculpted from a
life mask of the Sioux chief Kicking Bear.

The lower part of Rock Creek is tra-
versed by several other noteworthy
bridges, including the majestic William
Howard Taft Bridge of 1906, which car-
ries Connecticut Avenue over the creek
(George Morison, architect; Roland Hin-
ton Perry, sculptor), the 1931 Connecticut
Avenue bridge over Klingle Valley (Paul
Cret, architect), and the Duke Ellington
Bridge at Calvert Street [see S1].

02

Turkish Ambassador's Residence
(former Everett House)

1606 23rd Street, NW

1915 — George Oakley Totten Jr.
2006 — Renovation and restoration:
    Archetype

The prolific George Oakley Totten Jr., like
many architects of his day, was stylistically promiscuous — compare his Venetian Gothic "Pink Palace" on Meridian Hill
[see R6] or his Beaux-Arts Moran House
[see O6] to this restless Renaissance
Revival mansion. The gently bowed front
portico brings to mind the south façade of
the White House before the addition of the
Truman Balcony, but the two buildings differ greatly in almost every other respect.
This mansion's south wing, containing a
conservatory and a trellised rooftop terrace, breaks the symmetry of the façade,
for instance, while the tripartite windows
on the third floor of the main block add
an unexpected and rather awkward horizontal component. The best-resolved
elevation is the short one facing Sheridan
Circle, which exhibits a better balance
between the primary architectural forms
and the delicate ornamentation of the
frieze and window surrounds.

Edward Hamlin Everett, who commissioned the mansion and moved here from
his native Cleveland, was one of scores of
industrialists who flocked to Washington
in the Gilded Age. Everett derived some of
his wealth from the usual sources, such
as mining, oil, and gas, but he was also a
pioneer in the automated manufacture of
glass containers, and for a time supposedly controlled some 80 percent of the
country's bottle-making business.

Although built for Everett, the house
may have been destined to serve as the
Turkish Embassy. Totten had visited Turkey in 1908 and designed the American
Chancery there, as well as a residence for
the prime minister. Sultan Abdul-Hamid

was so impressed with these buildings that he offered Totten a position as his "personal and private architect." Totten accepted, but the sultan was deposed the following year, and the architect returned to the United States to resume his career.

03
Alice Pike Barney Studio House
(now Embassy of Latvia)

2306 Massachusetts Avenue, NW (on Sheridan Circle)

1903 — Waddy B. Wood
1979 — Renovation: architect unknown
2005 — Renovation: Balodemas Architects

In the early 1900s, this eccentric house was a nexus of cultural life in Washington, buzzing with activity under the direction of artist, patron, and social activist Alice Pike Barney. Designed by Waddy Wood with substantial input from Barney herself, it was the site of concerts, theatrical performances, exhibitions, and parties where artists and socialites mixed liberally. Barney once complained of the still-young city, "What is capital life after all? Small talk and lots to eat, an infinite series of teas and dinners. Art? There is none." Doing her part to change this situation, she painted, wrote plays, and hosted salons, one of which in 1916 was attended by a frail, elderly Sarah Bernhardt, who arrived in a litter carried by four liveried footmen. Also a well-regarded musician, Barney was commissioned by no less than Anna Pavlova to score a ballet for the

great Russian dancer on her triumphant 1914–15 tour of America.

The exterior of the Studio House is in the Mission Revival style, inspired by the early Spanish Colonial architecture in what is now the American Southwest. Distinctive features include the two second-floor windows whose shape is derived from the superimposition of two ovals and a rectangle, as well as the arched opening in the curved gable—a remnant of the planar bell towers on Spanish missions. The interior is an essay in Arts-and-Crafts woodwork. Barney threw her first party in the house soon after its completion and invited everyone who had been involved in its creation, from the architect to manual laborers.

Barney died in 1931, and several decades later her daughters donated the house to the Smithsonian Institution, which never quite figured out what to do with it. It was opened to the public in 1979 for tours, exhibitions, and programs. The Smithsonian finally sold the building in 1999, and it now serves as the Latvian Embassy.

The Barney Studio House faces Sheridan Circle, named after General Philip H. Sheridan, who built his reputation on the scorched-earth Valley Campaign in Virginia during the Civil War and subsequently on the slaughter of countless Indigenous people out west. The equestrian statue of the general is the work of Gutzon Borglum, who later showed what he could do at a larger scale when he created Mount Rushmore.

04
Egyptian Ambassador's Residence
(former Joseph Beale House)

2301 Massachusetts Avenue, NW

1909 — Glenn Brown
2002 — Renovation and restoration: Archetype

Commissioned by Joseph Beale and now the Egyptian ambassador's residence, this neo-Renaissance palazzo is an exceptionally skillful composition. The central Palladian arch, marking a recessed loggia, creates a void that plays off against the subtle convex curvature of the façade. Note how the bulging horizontal stone band just below the first-floor windows turns to form the backs of the projecting benches, which culminate in armrests sculpted as griffins.

05

Embassy of Haiti
(former Fahnestock House)

2311 Massachusetts Avenue, NW

1910—Nathan C. Wyeth

Haiti is one of several underdeveloped countries whose Washington embassies occupy incongruously opulent mansions. This soaring Beaux-Arts town house, commissioned by financier Gibson Fahnestock, harmoniously blends with the rows of similar structures that line the blocks around Sheridan Circle. In contrast with the Moran House next door [see following entry], however, this is a rather restrained and tightly controlled composition. Because of the tautness of the façade and shallowness of the pilasters, the Corinthian capitals seem to explode like fireworks from the wall plane.

06

Moran House

2315 Massachusetts Avenue, NW

1909—George Oakley Totten Jr.
2013—Rehabilitation and renovation:
　Stephen duPont Jr.

This building and the Fahnestock House next door [see previous entry] were commissioned by different plutocrats, and designed by different architects, but together form a single cohesive composition, sharing similar materials, shallow pilasters, aligned cornices, and mansard roofs. Even so, the effects are not the same: the Moran House is much more idiosyncratic, with unusual figural sculptural motifs and surprisingly large windowless expanses on what would seem to be the primary floor. The bold tower is an architectural exclamation point terminating one of the city's most elegant blocks. Long serving as the Pakistani Chancery, the house became vacant when a new facility was built in the International Chancery Center. As of this writing, the building is for lease.

07

Embassy of the Republic of Cameroon
(former Hauge House)

2349 Massachusetts Avenue, NW

1907—George Oakley Totten Jr.
1934—Addition: Smith Bowman Jr.
1972—Renovation: architect unknown
2019—Renovation: Quinn Evans

This romantic limestone mansion marks the western end of Massachusetts Avenue's grand turn-of-the-century Beaux-Arts residences. As with many of the buildings along this stretch of the avenue, the design of the Hague House was derived from French sources, but in this case, the inspiration lay in the châteaux of the early French Renaissance, which melded Gothic motifs with classically derived compositions. Christian Hauge, a Norwegian diplomat, commissioned the

mansion shortly after he was appointed his nation's first minister to the United States in 1905 (the year Norway gained its independence from Sweden). Hauge died in 1907 while snowshoeing back home, but his Kentucky-born widow stayed in the house, which became, according to *The Mayflower's Log* magazine, "the scene of much of Washington's most brilliant entertaining" until Mrs. Hauge's death in 1927.

08
The President Woodrow Wilson House
2340 S Street, NW

1916—Waddy B. Wood
1921—Remodeling: Waddy B. Wood
2005—Exterior restoration: Archetype

As President Woodrow Wilson's second term was coming to an end, his wife, Edith Bolling Wilson, came across this Georgian Revival house for sale and decided it

would be their perfect retirement home. They lived here together until Woodrow's death in 1924, and Edith stayed in the house until she died in 1961. She bequeathed the property to the National Trust for Historic Preservation.

The front façade of the house is noteworthy for the trio of Palladian windows on the second floor with pleated "fan" arches above. The first-floor porch is small but intriguing, with concave sides that negotiate the transition from the relatively narrow entry portal, defined by a pair of columns, to the slightly wider stone frame with four pilasters set into the brick wall. The rear façade has a single Palladian arch, with an open loggia behind it on the second floor, and a semicircular bay on the first floor containing the door to the terraced back yard.

The house was designed by Waddy Wood for Henry Fairbanks of Massachusetts, who came to Washington to serve on a government commission. Wood was from a prominent Virginia family and became one of upper-class Washington's favored architects in the early 20th century, earning commissions for more than 30 mansions in the Kalorama area alone. Woodrow Wilson shared his deep Old Dominion roots and chose Wood to design the viewing stands for both of his inaugurations. Wood's professional (and social) views were quite conservative—in an unpublished essay, he decried originality for its own sake, which he termed "Architectural Bolshevism."

09
Codman-Davis House
(now Thai Ambassador's Residence)
2145 Decatur Place, NW

1907—Ogden Codman Jr.

The entry courtyard of this mansion would be at home in Paris, but the house itself, designed by Ogden Codman Jr. for his cousin Martha, is more in the English Georgian style. The building's prim aspect is hardly surprising, since Mr. Codman was Edith Wharton's collaborator on that classic book of architectural do's and don'ts, *The Decoration of Houses* (1897), in which the authors purse their lips and take a firm stand against such modern horrors as electric lighting, with its "harsh

white glare, which no expedients have as yet overcome" (they encouraged their readers to rely on wax candles instead). The house was later owned by Dwight F. Davis, a "gentleman politician" and tennis player for whom the Davis Cup is named. It now serves as the residence of the Thai ambassador, who probably uses electric lights without a trace of shame.

The stairway just west of the house, connecting 22nd Street to S Street and nicknamed "the Spanish Steps," is one of Washington's hidden treats.

O10

Friends Meeting of Washington

2111 Florida Avenue, NW

1930 — Walter F. Price; Landscape architect: Rose Greely
1950 — Addition: Leon Chatelain II
2019 — Renovation and additions: Gauthier, Alvarado & Associates with Lippincott Architects

The election of Herbert Hoover, the first US president to be a member of the Religious Society of Friends, better known as Quakers, was the immediate impetus for the construction of this Meeting House. First Lady Lou Henry Hoover was actively involved in its planning and design. The north wing, which contains the meeting room — the principal space — on the upper level, follows Quaker architectural conventions in its simple gabled form, stone walls, and dual entrances (traditionally one each for men and women). One of the ground-floor rooms includes ceiling beams that had been installed in the White House when it was repaired after the British invasion in 1814 but were removed during a subsequent renovation. Rose Greely designed and planted the informal, tranquil grounds to resemble a small private park.

In 1970, the Friends Meeting bought the neighboring house at 2121 Decatur Place, NW (1923 — Frederick H. Brooke) and its carriage house (1930 — George N. Ray). A recent renovation and addition wove all of the buildings together and created a new rear terrace for special events.

O11

Lothrop Mansion
(Russian Trade Representation)

2001 Connecticut Avenue, NW

1909 — Hornblower & Marshall
1970s — Interior renovations: architects unknown

Alvin M. Lothrop and Samuel W. Woodward founded the business that eventually became the prominent local department store chain Woodward & Lothrop, which sadly was subsumed into a national retail company in the 1990s. Lothrop commissioned this 40-room urban villa for one of the most spectacular residential sites in the city, commanding the view down Connecticut Avenue. The main façade is actually the rear of the house, designed purely for its public impression, with a raised terrace surrounded by a low balustrade and with curving stairs leading up to the porch. The entrance is on the opposite side, facing a small courtyard. For years the building has housed the offices of the Russian (previously Soviet) Trade Representation [*sic*], a branch of that country's embassy.

012

2029 Connecticut Avenue, NW

1916 — Hunter and Bell

What Gilded-Age mansions are to Massachusetts Avenue, elegant apartment houses are to Connecticut Avenue, but none can surpass 2029 Connecticut for glamour. The base and top of the building are sheathed in glazed terra cotta, as are the two projecting porticoes, whose decorative sculptures include salamanders and fleurs-de-lis, which, as historian James Goode noted, were favorite symbols of a 16th-century French king, Francis I. With just three huge apartments on each of the main floors, the building has long been a favorite of Washington's elite, from former president William Howard Taft to entertainer Lena Horne. The velvet-voiced Horne occupied one of the units facing the avenue, running the entire width of the building and featuring a 43-foot-long foyer, a 33-foot-long living room, and five bedrooms.

013

2100 Connecticut Apartments

1940 — Berla & Abel

Drawing on International Style precepts in its unornamented façades and ribbon windows, but retaining hints of Art Moderne

streamlining in its curving bays of glass block, 2100 Connecticut Avenue marked a startling departure from the elegant but old-school apartment buildings and town houses typical of this neighborhood. Interestingly, one of the architects of this boldly forward-looking structure, Joseph Abel, was also the lead designer of 2101 Connecticut [see next entry], built just over a decade earlier and relying entirely on historical precedents.

014

2101 Connecticut Avenue, NW

1928 — Joseph Abel and George T. Santmyers

1977 — Renovation: architect unknown

In case there was any doubt that this colossal apartment house with only 64 apartments was aiming for well-heeled tenants when it opened in 1928, the initial leasing brochure made it clear: "The elimination of small apartments carries with it assurance of a permanent, quiet, and socially attractive atmosphere." Originally, every unit had either three or four bedrooms, one or two servants' rooms, a heated porch (!), and, thanks to the building's eight-winged plan, fully three exposures.

The exterior design is a mélange of styles including Renaissance Revival (as in the graceful arched entrance portico) and Gothic Revival (as in the pointed-arch decorative brackets just below many of the eighth-floor windows). Some of the details are charmingly odd. Note, for example, the parrot-shaped gargoyles in between the arches at the main entrance and the smattering of ominous figures along the roof parapet, poised to hurl orbs down on unannounced guests.

The Dresden

2126 Connecticut Avenue, NW

1909—Albert H. Beers
1974—Renovation: Peter Voghi
1996—Restoration: Oehrlein & Associates
    Architects

While serving as the chief architect for developer Harry Wardman (a position later held by Mihran Mesrobian), Albert Beers designed a large number of apartment buildings all over Washington. The Dresden is distinct because of its curving neo-Georgian façade, holding the street line of the avenue. One of the side effects of the curve is that the apartments running along that façade contain rooms that are slightly tapered in plan.

Woodward Condominium

2311 Connecticut Avenue, NW

1909—Harding and Upman
1970—Renovation: architect unknown

Not long after Alvin M. Lothrop built his mansion at the corner of Connecticut

and Columbia [see O11], his partner, Samuel W. Woodward, developed this apartment house. The design is a rather tame Spanish Colonial affair, but with one big splash of ornament: the polychrome terra cotta frame surrounding the main entrance, which adds a touch of Baroque exuberance. Crowning the narrow tower at the oblique corner of the building is a little open-air pavilion for residents' use. The Woodward, which was converted into a condominium in 1973, was notable as one of the earliest apartment buildings in Washington to contain duplex (two-story) units, though there are just a few of them facing Connecticut Avenue.

The Lindens

2401 Kalorama Road, NW

1754—Robert "King" Hooper, owner-
    builder
1934—Moved to Washington
1937—Restoration: Walter Macomber
1985—Renovation: Sharon Washburn
    Architect and Walter Macomber

This wood-frame Georgian house can claim a superlative, but with a couple of qualifiers: it is the oldest fundamentally *intact* building *in* DC, though it was not *built* here, and it is not quite as old as one *heavily modified* portion of the Rosedale farmhouse [see S10]. Its complex history begins with Robert "King" Hooper, a prosperous New England merchant who erected the house in Danvers, Massachusetts. More than a century and three-quarters later, George and Miriam Morris,

who were avid collectors of Colonial furniture and art, bought the building, dismantled it, moved it in sections, and reconstructed it on a sloping Kalorama lot, where it immediately seemed at home among its eclectic neighbors.

The house's entrance bay, carried up three stories to the pedimented attic and partially defined by the flanking Corinthian columns, adds a strong vertical accent to the otherwise foursquare dwelling. The main façade is made of wood blocks that have been notched and coated with sand-infused paint to resemble more expensive rusticated stone.

O18
Devore-Chase House
(now Ambassador's Residence, Embassy of the Sultanate of Oman)
2000 24th Street, NW
1931—William Lawrence Bottomley
1965—Addition: Douglas Stenhouse

William Bottomley, a specialist in creating "new-old" houses, is perhaps best known for the neo-Georgian brick villas he built in and around Richmond, Virginia, in the 1920s and '30s. The Devore-Chase House,

covered in textured limestone, is more in the 18th-century French mode, however, with heavy quoins at the corners and pronounced dentils under the cornice. Ornament is largely reserved for the lavish sculpture in the pediments. The Chase family offered the mansion to the federal government as an official residence for the chief justice of the United States, but nothing came of that, and it now serves as the Omani ambassador's residence.

O19
Japanese Embassy
2516 Massachusetts Avenue, NW
1931—Delano & Aldrich
1960—Teahouse: Nahiko Emori

The main building of this complex, which was, unlike most of its contemporaries, designed expressly as an embassy, has a simple pedimented Georgian Revival façade that makes the structure seem modest by comparison with the architectural stage sets that dominate this stretch of Massachusetts Avenue. Note the "swept eaves," which curve up slightly as if lifted by a breeze, and the unusual radial arch above the main door. The rear gardens contain an authentic teahouse that was built in Japan, taken apart, shipped to America, and reassembled on this site; the little structure marks the 100th anniversary of diplomatic relations between the two nations.

O20
Turkish Chancery
2525 Massachusetts Avenue, NW
1999—Shalom Baranes Associates

The Turks must like the neighborhood, since they built this new chancery just down the street from their ambassador's residence on Sheridan Circle. Eschewing

the usual hierarchical grandeur associated with diplomatic architecture, the chancery seems almost domestic in scale, with two distinct wings linked by a low-rise connector. The building's design evokes vernacular Turkish architecture in several ways, including the massing of the wings, with their shallow-pitched roofs and deep eaves, and the abstract geometrical patterns in the façades that suggest the intricacies of traditional Mediterranean and Islamic decorative motifs. The building cuts into the steeply sloping site, resulting in massive retaining walls visible at the sides.

021

Islamic Center

2551 Massachusetts Avenue, NW

1957 — Egyptian Ministry of Works with Mario Rossi; Associated architects: Irwin Porter and Sons

Officially serving as the religious center for all American Muslims, this steel-framed mosque was built through a joint initiative of the ambassadors of the leading Islamic countries. While the main façade of the building follows the line of Massachusetts Avenue, the mosque proper, in the center, is canted so that the *mihrab*, or altar-like niche, is oriented toward Mecca. Persian carpets cover the floors, stained glass sparkles in the clerestory, and verses from the Koran are rendered in mosaics around the entrance, throughout the front courtyard, and atop the 160-foot minaret. The designers did make a few concessions to the building's physical context, particularly in deciding to face the mosque in limestone, the favorite material of Massachusetts Ave-

nue's château builders. Visitors of any or no faith are welcome except during prayer times, provided that they observe customs of dress, which guides can explain to those not in the know.

022

Embassy of Italy Chancery

3000 Whitehaven Street, NW

2000 — Sartogo Architetti Associati; Associated architects: LEO A DALY

This is an example of a chancery designed to relate to its physical context while evoking the architectural culture of the country it represents. The building is essentially a diamond in plan, split down the middle to create two right triangles separated by an atrium, and oriented so that one side is parallel to Massachusetts Avenue. The points of the diamond thus align with the cardinal points on a map. In other words, the chancery's plan is an abstraction of the original map of the District of Columbia — before Arlington and Alexandria were retroceded to Virginia — which was a perfect diamond with the Potomac River slicing lengthwise through it. Most visitors are unlikely to make this connection on their own, but it does help to explain what would otherwise seem to be an illogical plan resulting in multiple acute corners within the building.

Meanwhile, in its massing and façade composition, the chancery is an abstract rendition of a Tuscan palazzo, with pinkish stone walls, relatively small windows, and a projecting patinated copper roof. A couple of larger openings along the Massachusetts Avenue façade, one of which features panels of copper to match the roof, help to break up the vast, solid plane

of stone. The result is rather forbidding, though it has become less so over time as the surrounding trees have enveloped the building.

023

Danish Embassy

3200 Whitehaven Street, NW

1960 — Vilhelm Lauritzen; Associated architects: The Architects Collaborative
2006 — Renovation design architects: Vilhelm Lauritzen; Architects of record: VOA Associates

In the mid-20th century, when the most important foreign missions in Washington typically occupied grand Gilded-Age mansions, then-Danish ambassador Henrik Kauffmann proposed a break from tradition. He envisioned a new embassy that would exemplify Denmark's culture, its values, and its decidedly progressive architectural tastes. The result was the first modernist embassy in the United States.

The Danish Embassy combines chancery functions and the ambassador's residence in a single building. The distinction between the two is subtly evident in their differing façades: those of the chancery wing are taut, with ribbon windows at the outermost plane, while those of the residence are layered, with windows set back behind rows of columns, creating spaces for balconies. Both sections are built of reinforced concrete partially covered in white marble from Greenland (an autonomous territory of Denmark).

While visiting the newly finished embassy, architect Vilhelm Lauritzen wrote in a letter home, "An American colleague [Benjamin Thompson from The Architects Collaborative] was here yesterday and said that it was the only building in Washington worth looking at." Lauritzen added, "I would like to show the servants' wing to the Americans. They say that we are socialists and perhaps we are; here they can see how it works."

Unfortunately, the parking lot at the entrance compromises the initial impression of an otherwise masterfully refined work of architecture.

024

McCormick House
(now Brazilian Ambassador's Residence)

3000 Massachusetts Avenue, NW

1912 — John Russell Pope

John Russell Pope designed this mansion as the Washington lair of retired diplomat Robert S. McCormick, whose uncle invented the mechanized reaper,

and Katherine Medill McCormick, whose father founded the *Chicago Tribune*. Pope likely referred to the detailed drawings in Paul Letarouilly's landmark work, *Édifices de Rome moderne*, first published in 1840, for potential models for this project. Ultimately, he drew heavily from several High Renaissance works by Baldassare Peruzzi, most notably the Palazzo Massimo alle Colonne, in Rome, which directly inspired the recessed entry portico. Since 1934, this has been the residence of the Brazilian ambassador.

025

Brazilian Chancery

3006 Massachusetts Avenue, NW

1971 — Olavo Redig de Campos; Associated architects: Ricardo de Abreu & Hans-Ulrich Scharnberg

The Brazilian Chancery is an apt foil to the ambassador's residence next door [see previous entry]. Each is a near-perfect rectilinear box, but while the residence is a solid block firmly rooted to the ground, the space-age chancery is a glassy volume that appears from the street to

hover effortlessly off the ground, thanks in part to the use of clear glass around the first-floor lobby (which also allows glimpses of the swooping spiral reception desk inside). The architect, Olavo Redig de Campos, was born in Rio de Janeiro but studied in Rome, where he may have developed an appreciation for the same buildings that inspired John Russell Pope's design 60 years earlier.

026

British Embassy

3100 Massachusetts Avenue, NW

1928 — Sir Edwin Lutyens; Associated architect: Frederick H. Brooke

With its broad entry court and tall, narrow wings reaching out to the avenue, the British Embassy is imposing yet welcoming. The plan is actually quite unusual and reflects the building's dual purpose as chancery and residence (the much larger modern chancery next door, of course, came later). On the ground floor, the two functions are separated by a *porte-cochère* deep within the complex, behind the U-shaped office building, but on the upper level, the ambassador's study, which spans the driveway, serves as both a literal and a figurative bridge between the public offices and the private residence. The central axis of the chancery flows into the residence where, in the main foyer, it is reoriented 90 degrees to face the elegant gardens.

Sir Edwin Lutyens, who called architecture "the great game," rather mischievously incorporated colonial American references in the new embassy (which, after all, represented the country that had done the colonizing way back when). The Massachusetts Avenue façade is a pastiche of Colonial Williamsburg — the reconstruction of which was in the news at the time—while the garden façade of the residence, dominated by a giant Ionic portico, suggests vintage movies about the Old South.

027

Embassy of Finland

3301 Massachusetts Avenue, NW

1994—Heikkinen-Komonen Architects; Associate architects: Angelos Demetriou & Associates

The Finnish Embassy is simultaneously sensational and subtle, confident and modest, coolly rational and arrestingly picturesque. Its opening in 1994 caused quite a stir in both architectural and diplomatic circles. Here was a chancery that not only eschewed the typical grandeur of official Washington but also subverted common assumptions about the visibility, accessibility, and security of foreign missions. Plus, it had a sauna.

The building is organized as a series of linear zones running parallel to the main façade. First comes the porch-like layer defined by an ivy-covered copper trellis. Just inside is a zone of security and reception spaces, followed by the main circulation spine. A graceful but dramatic curving staircase breaks the rectilinear geometry, connecting the lobby to the main public event space one level below. A glazed rear porch, which can be opened up to the main space or closed off depending on the weather, runs the length of the rear façade. The backyard surprise is a pier-like walkway, partially sheltered by tensile fabric awnings, that juts into the woods, affording visitors a view back to the building, which is particularly beautiful when lit at night.

In its simplicity, its energy-efficient design, and its deference to the natural setting, the embassy seems quintessentially Finnish, and yet it also incorporates a number of allusions to the landscape and culture of its host country. The narrow linear atrium, for example, was inspired by the Grand Canyon, which the architects considered to be America's most glorious natural feature. And that curving staircase was partially inspired by the glamorous sets in classic Hollywood musicals.

A former press counselor for the embassy once remarked, "I had no idea a building could be such an important diplomatic tool." The Finns take full advantage of that tool, graciously hosting exhibitions, receptions, lectures, and other events for Washingtonians who enjoy spending time in such a serenely elegant building.

028

St. Albans School, Marriott Hall

Massachusetts Avenue at Garfield Street, NW

2009—Skidmore, Owings & Merrill

Like the National Cathedral School for girls [see 030], the St. Albans School for boys is administered by the Protestant Episcopal Cathedral Foundation, though its earliest building predates the cathedral itself. The school gradually grew and added various buildings without benefit of a master plan, and by the dawn of the 21st century, the campus was scenic but disjointed. The new Marriott Hall does a remarkably good job of tying the campus together without upstaging the historic structures that it connects. Through a system of terraces, staircases, and passageways, the addition deftly negotiates its sloping site while creating a sensible circulation pattern linking four existing buildings. Although the new building is much glassier than its Gothic Revival neighbors, it blends in by virtue of its copious use of bluestone (which closely matches the Potomac gneiss in the older buildings), its landscaped terraces, and its green roof.

029

Washington National Cathedral
(Cathedral Church of St. Peter and St. Paul)

3101 Wisconsin Avenue, NW

1907—George Frederick Bodley: Supervising architect: Henry Vaughan
1907–17—Henry Vaughan; Superintending architect: Arthur B. Heaton
1907–28—Landscape architects: Olmsted Brothers
1921–44—Frohman, Robb & Little; Consulting architects (1921–29): Cram and Ferguson
1944–71—Philip Hubert Frohman
1971–73—Superintending architects: Godwin & Beckett
1973–81—Superintending architect: Howard B. Trevillian Jr.
1981–90—Superintending architects: Smith Segreti Tepper Architects and Planners; Landscape architects for West Front: EDAW Inc.

2007—Visitor Gateway project: SmithGroup; Landscape architects: Michael Vergason Landscape Architects

The notion was preposterous, really: to build from scratch a "true" Gothic cathedral, icon of feudal Europe, in the capital of the world's first modern democracy and the epicenter of the classically inclined City Beautiful movement. Having overcome this improbable genesis and the infamously protracted construction process that ensued, the Washington National Cathedral today stands majestically atop Mount St. Albans, one of the highest points in the District of Columbia.

The idea for a nondenominational cathedral in Washington dates back to L'Enfant, who envisioned a "great church for national purpose . . . equally open to all" on the present-day site of the Old Patent Office. There was no sustained effort to create such a church, however, until 1893, when Congress chartered the Protestant Episcopal Cathedral Foundation as a private nonprofit organization. Then came a years-long search for the right site, followed by design competitions, or rather, a series of what the longtime clerk of the works, Richard Feller, called "wranglings." Church officials initially approved a design by Ernest Flagg for a domed, Renaissance-style cathedral, but Bishop Henry Yates

Satterlee traveled to England to persuade the aged architect George Frederick Bodley to develop a Gothic-inspired alternative, which was ultimately adopted. Finally, in 1907, President Theodore Roosevelt tapped the cornerstone into place and cried, "God speed the work!" But the work was anything but speedy: construction continued in spurts for 83 years until the building was finally officially finished in 1990.

Bodley's design, not surprisingly, was primarily derived from English Gothic precedents, with a Latin cross plan, a tall square tower at the intersection of the two axes, and twin towers flanking the west façade. Construction began at the eastern end and proceeded westward. The walls were built using traditional masonry techniques similar to those used in actual Gothic churches, though reinforcing steel rods were added for greater stability, and the roof is partially supported by steel trusses. As successive architects took charge of the project, they tweaked the design of subsequent sections while generally remaining true to Bodley's intentions. Many aspects of the cathedral's lengthy construction period are legible in the architecture. One subtle surprise, for instance, is the slight kink in the plan of the nave, best witnessed from the choir area behind the altar—curiously, this minor discrepancy goes a long way toward making the cathedral seem genuinely Gothic.

The National Cathedral is replete with fascinating integral artworks. The strangely erotic sculptures by Frederick Hart in the tympanums (the areas within the arches over the main doors) are among the numerous artistic elements that seem strikingly modern in comparison to the structure they adorn. On the north side of the building is a colonnade in which the column capitals are decorated with unusual motifs reflecting aspects of American culture and geography, from animals to igloos. One of the gargoyles on the northwest tower depicts *Star Wars* villain Darth Vader (the idea was proposed by one entrant in a national design-a-carving competition for children). Inside the sanc-tuary, there is a famous stained-glass window with an embedded Moon rock.

The earthquake that struck the mid-Atlantic region in 2011 did significant damage to the cathedral. Various buttresses, turrets, and carvings were dislocated and some were precariously close to collapse. A 350-pound pinnacle did fall from the top of one of the towers to the ground, only to be stolen in the middle of the night. As of this writing, repairs are ongoing.

030
National Cathedral School, Hearst Hall
3101 Wisconsin Avenue, NW (at Woodley Road)

1900 — Robert W. Gibson; Superintendent of construction: Adolf Cluss
ca. 1987 — Renovation: Notter Finegold + Alexander

The main building of what is now the National Cathedral School was completed years before the church itself was even begun. Today it stands out as a regal Renaissance Revival work amid the predominantly Gothic Revival cathedral compound. The hall was named after Phoebe Hearst, the mother of William Randolph Hearst, who donated $200,000 to build a girls' school under the auspices of the National Cathedral Foundation. The bas-relief sculptures between the arches on the Wisconsin Avenue façade, by Louis Amateis, depict "Qualities of Womanhood," to wit: *Purity*, *Truth*, *Love*, *Woman as Mother*, and *Woman as Nurse*. Seen from the rear, the steeply pitched roof appears almost as tall as the building's base walls.

Dupont / Logan

During much of its first century, Washington was generally a scruffy and inconsistently developed town with a few monumental buildings that stood out like ermine-clad royalty among the mud-soaked peasants. That began to change in the 1870s with Board of Public Works commissioner Alexander Robey "Boss" Shepherd's highly successful (but fiscally disastrous) civic improvement campaign. The city soon showed more signs of architectural maturity and sophistication, and by the 1890s, to the astonishment of the upper classes everywhere, Washington was becoming a fashionable place for the wealthy—especially the newly wealthy—to hobnob, throw fabulous parties, and build immense mansions.

Around the turn of the 20th century, more than 100 grand residences sprang up in the area near Dupont Circle, making this once-quiet section of the city suddenly the rival of New York's 5th Avenue as *the* place in the nation to live. Perhaps Henry Adams was thinking of this trend when he wrote in 1904: "The American wasted money more recklessly than any one did before; he spent more to less purpose than any extravagant court aristocracy; he had no sense of relative values, and knew not what to do with his money when he got it, except to use it to make more, or throw it away."

The evolution of the park in the circle itself reflects the broader trends in the neighborhood during that period. In 1882, Congress decided to commemorate Admiral Samuel Francis du Pont, a Civil War naval hero, by naming this new circle for him (the area had been known as "The Slashes") and by placing a small bronze statue of him in the center. That wasn't enough for the admiral's family, who, in good Gilded-Age style, decided to circumvent the federal government by directly hiring the team that gave the city the Lincoln Memorial—architect Henry Bacon and sculptor Daniel Chester French—to create the present, far grander, monument. At some point, the spelling of the admiral's last name was modified to yield the one-word version applied to the circle today.

The establishment of a federal income tax in 1913, coupled with the Great Depression of the 1930s, obliterated much of the wealth that had made all of this possible, and when World War II came, many of the grand mansions were lent, sold, or donated to governmental and other agencies to aid the war effort. By the 1950s, a number of the buildings here had been converted to boarding houses. Not coincidentally, the circle itself and some nearby buildings were becoming popular with hippies, artists, and other alternative types that the decade produced in abundance. Soon the area was recognized as a historic district, and repeating a pattern common to analogous areas in so many American cities, gay men and lesbians began to move here in large numbers, leading a wave of renovation. Over the past generation, the Dupont Circle neighborhood has blossomed once again, becoming one of the most vibrant residential areas in the city.

Just to the east of the Dupont Circle area is the Logan Circle neighborhood, centered on the 14th Street commercial spine, which had its heyday in the 1920s when it was Washington's "automobile row." Elegant but architecturally restrained car dealerships, typically sporting huge windows to show off their merchandise to good effect, lined the street. Peripheral businesses, such as auto repair shops, were also common along 14th and on the adjacent blocks of several cross streets.

The corridor was devastated during the 1968 riots following the assassination of Martin Luther King Jr., and for decades, it was a vexing symbol of urban disinvestment and decay. In the 1990s and early 2000s, however, a gradual surge of gentrification soon turned into a tidal wave, transforming the long-decrepit 14th Street corridor into one of the city's hottest spots for restaurants and shops. The surrounding residential blocks, many of which were nearly abandoned just a couple of decades ago, now contain some of the city's priciest real estate.

(*Above*) This aerial view of Dupont Circle from 1924 shows several of the mansions that defined the neighborhood, including the Boardman House at lower left, the Patterson House next door, and the Leiter Mansion (since demolished) at right, with its large portico.

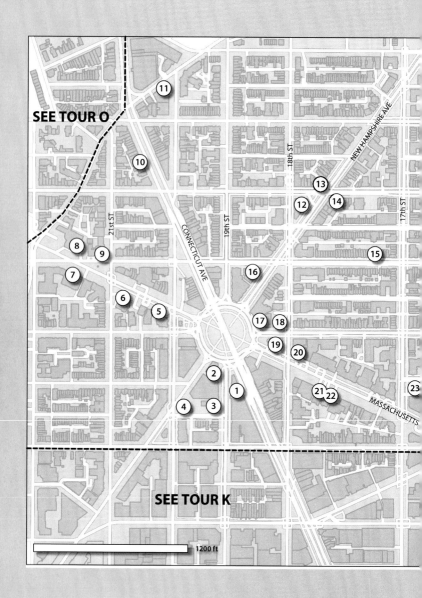

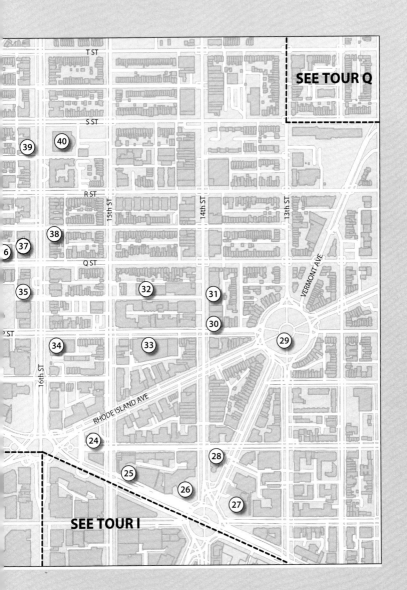

P1

Dupont Circle Building

1350 Connecticut Avenue, NW

1931 — Mihran Mesrobian
1942 — Conversion from apartments to
       offices: architect unknown
1987 — Renovation: Oldham and Seltz

The genius of this wedge-shaped structure lies in its masterful bas-relief ornament, which lends visual depth and rhythm to the main façades but keeps the profile of the building taut and planar so as not to distract from its apparent geometrical purity when viewed on end. In this regard, it outdoes New York's famous Flatiron Building, which has a heavily sculpted skin that competes with the acutely angled form for attention. Another notable element of the Dupont Circle Building is its stepped mechanical penthouse — a technical necessity that Mesrobian turned into an architectural asset.

P2

21 Dupont Circle, NW
(former Euram Building)

1971 — Hartman-Cox Architects
1992 — Renovation: Oldham & Seltz

All too often, a project that begins as an elegantly simple architectural diagram, when finally realized in three dimensions, lacks the purity and clarity of the initial concept. This modestly scaled building is a brilliant exception. Structurally, 21 Dupont Circle is composed of a series

of post-tensioned concrete bridges spanning between unadorned, brick-clad piers at the corners of the site and surrounding an open courtyard. The resulting office spaces are narrow and column-free, affording all tenants access to views outside and plenty of natural light. The principal façades neatly express the essential structural scheme, thanks in large part to the bands of floor-to-ceiling, mullion-less windows, which allow the bridge-like concrete beams to be read clearly.

P3

Sunderland Building

1320 19th Street, NW

1969 — Keyes, Lethbridge & Condon,
       Architects
2005 — Renovation and lobby addition:
       Envision Design

This relatively small office building is an intriguing geometrical exercise. The

façades of the rectilinear structure are animated by several asymmetrical design gestures: first, the exterior columns (some of which house ventilation ducts, rather than structural supports) are flared on just one side of each vertical slit window; second, the regular grid of these slit windows on the second through seventh floors is interrupted by a large blank panel to the right; and third, on the top floor, the pattern of solid and void is switched, with a large expanse of glass to the right and a smaller blank panel to the left. Taken together, the four virtually identical façades thus create a dynamic composition suggesting rotational movement.

P4

Heurich House Museum
(The Brewmaster's Castle)

1307 New Hampshire Avenue, NW

1894 — John Granville Myers; Interiors: Charles H. and Hugo F. Huber
1914 — Addition: Appleton P. Clark
1987 — Interior restoration and elevator addition: Geier Brown Renfrow

Knotty and lugubrious, the Heurich House is an example of what historian Richard Howland dubbed "beer-barrel baronial"

grandeur. Its New Hampshire Avenue façade, made of dark, rough sandstone, is punctuated by a chunky *porte-cochère* bristling with gargoyles. Around the corner on Sunderland Place, a less intimidating brick, terra cotta, and sandstone façade ends with a copper-and-glass conservatory, the delicacy and bright green patina of which contrast sharply with the main body of the house. Supporting all of the robust masonry is a structure that was innovative in its day — the first significant use of reinforced concrete in a residential building in the United States.

The shadowy interiors, intact and original, attest to the extravagant taste of the house's builder, Christian Heurich, a German immigrant who became a highly successful brewer and, at one time, the second largest landowner in DC after the federal government. Heurich, whose company's slogan was "Beer recommended for family use by Physicians in General," made no bones about acknowledging the source of his wealth. The walls of the breakfast room in the basement are covered with murals depicting the virtues of beer-drinking interspersed with aphorisms such as "Raum ist in der kleinsten Kammer für den grossten Katzenjammer" ("There is room in the smallest chamber for the biggest hangover"). Clearly, Heurich, who actively managed the business until his death at the age of 102, was a man who loved his work.

Heurich's widow donated the house to the organization now known as the DC History Center. When the organization moved to its new headquarters at Mount Vernon Square in 2003, two of Heurich's grandchildren bought the house back and formed a foundation to preserve it as a museum.

P5

Blaine Mansion

2000 Massachusetts Avenue, NW

1882 — John Fraser
1921 — Renovation and additions: George N. Ray
1949 — Conversion to office use: Maurice S. May
2009 — Renovation and addition: Van Dusen Architects

This brooding pile of bricks is the last of several stern Victorian-era mansions that once loomed near Dupont Circle. The house was built for James G. Blaine, a man known to his friends as "the Plumed Knight" of American politics, and to his enemies as "Slippery Jim." One of the founders of the Republican Party, Blaine held a number of important posts, including Speaker of the House and secretary of state, and thrice ran unsuccessfully for the presidency. Soon after this house was finished, Blaine decided that it was too expensive to maintain and leased it to some of his more cash-laden contemporaries, such as Levi Leiter, an early partner of retailer Marshall Field, and George Westinghouse, whose surname speaks for itself. Westinghouse bought the place outright in 1901 and lived here until his death in 1914.

John Fraser, a former partner of the great Philadelphia architect Frank Furness, originally designed the house for a different site, which helps explain its rather incidental relationship to the surrounding streets. There are subtle but significant variations in the treatment of the façades—note, for instance, how some of the chimneys are flush with the walls below the cornice line, while others bulge from the wall plane at the second floor. The one-story retail strip along P Street was added in 1921 and was updated during a recent renovation, which also involved the addition of a major new wing to the west. The contrasting materials, colors, and forms of this addition allow the original structure to continue to be perceived as a freestanding block. In fact, on the Massachusetts Avenue side, the new wing angles away from the mansion so dramatically that it almost looks as if it were an addition to the building next door. The complex now contains a mix of uses, including restaurants along P Street, office space, and apartments on the upper levels.

P6

Embassy of the Republic of Indonesia
(former Walsh-McLean House)
2020 Massachusetts Avenue, NW

1903—Henry Andersen
1952—Renovation: architect unknown
1982—Addition: The Architects
   Collaborative

In 1869, an Irish teenager named Thomas Walsh came to the United States to seek his fortune, and he soon found it during the Black Hills Gold Rush. He then struck it richer, as it were, when he bought the Camp Bird Mine, which contained one of the thickest veins of gold in the world. Walsh later sold the mine for the then-remarkable sum of $3 million plus a percentage of future yields. Obscenely rich, he moved his family to Washington in 1897 with the goal of joining "society."

Walsh quickly realized that one of the most important instruments of social status was an impressive mansion, so he commissioned Henry Andersen to design this 60-room extravaganza. The house is organized around a three-story, galleried Art Nouveau stairwell that was inspired by one in Walsh's favorite White Star ocean liner. The exterior, with its undulating walls, rounded corners, and even curving chimneys, defies stylistic nomenclature, but it could be described generically and with some understate-

ment as "neo-Baroque." "Baroque" also describes Walsh's lifestyle: "At one New Year's Eve party," reported the *New York Times*, "325 guests consumed 480 quarts of champagne, 288 fifths of scotch, 48 quarts of cocktails, 40 gallons of beer and 35 bottles of miscellaneous liquors."

Walsh later grew reclusive, and in 1910 he died in virtual isolation. His daughter, Evalyn, inherited the house but refused to move into it, stating that "it was cold, but its deepest chill lodged in my breast." She married publishing heir Edward Beale McLean (his family owned the *Washington Post*), and the pair lived lavishly at their estate on Wisconsin Avenue. According to James Goode's *Capital Losses*, the couple "managed to dissipate almost all of the vast McLean and Walsh fortunes, amounting to 100 million dollars." (Evalyn "dissipated" a portion of the money when she bought the Hope Diamond.) The Indonesian gov-

ernment purchased the Massachusetts Avenue mansion in 1951 for $335,000—less than half of its original cost—and later added a wing with a curving façade echoing the fluid form, but not the quirky character, of the exuberant main house.

P7

The Society of the Cincinnati
(former Anderson House)

2118 Massachusetts Avenue, NW

1905—Little and Browne
1968—Restoration and renovation: Clas, Riggs, Owens & Ramos
1998—Restoration and interior alterations: Archetype

Career diplomat Larz Anderson III and his wife, Isabel Weld Perkins, an author who had inherited a large fortune, commissioned this neo-English Baroque mansion as their winter residence to take advantage of Washington's "social season." And social they were, hosting prominent industrialists, members of Congress, at least two US presidents, numerous ambassadors, and foreign heads of state—the king and queen of Siam were among those visitors who surely found the 50-room house appropriately palatial.

After Mr. Anderson's death in 1937, his widow, in accordance with the couple's long-standing intentions, donated the mansion to the Society of the Cincinnati, a hereditary organization of which Mr. Anderson was a member. The society was founded by a group of Revolutionary War

officers and took its name from Lucius Quinctius Cincinnatus, a Roman "civilian general" who humbly returned to his farm after each of two victorious military campaigns. He was therefore seen as a parallel to America's own nonprofessional military hero, George Washington. Washington somewhat reluctantly agreed to become the organization's first "president general" despite the objections of contemporary politicians who feared that it represented the beginnings of an American aristocracy.

The house's arched gateways and stately forecourt are unusual in Washington, and they suggest the presumption that all visitors would arrive by carriage rather than on foot. Huge lanterns, suspended from curved iron armatures, hang just inside the archways. The mansion's cavernous interior, which is open to the public as a museum, is eclectically decorated, to say the least. Notable items on display include a set of Flemish tapestries commissioned by King Louis XIII of France and later owned by Cardinal Francesco Barberini, papal representative to the French court. The premier space is the ballroom on the first floor, which boasts an astonishing cantilevered staircase leading to a musicians' balcony supported by spiral red Verona marble columns. The building also houses a library notable for its 18th-century military history collections.

P8

Cosmos Club
(former Townsend House)

2121 Massachusetts Avenue, NW

1900 — Carrère & Hastings; Interior design: Allard & Sons
1904 — Addition: Carrère & Hastings
1909 — 2164 Florida Avenue: Speiden & Speiden Architects
1952 — Alterations and addition: Horace W. Peaslee
1962 — Addition and renovation: Frank W. Cole
1989 — Addition: Keyes Condon Florance
1997 — Renovation of 2164 Florida Avenue (Hillyer House): O'Neil & Manion Architects
2012 — Ballroom restoration: JMA Preservation

Railroad money lay behind this entry in the unspoken contest to build the grandest house in turn-of-the-20th-century Washington. The clients were Mary Scott Townsend, a coal and railroad heir, and her husband, Richard H. Townsend, who had run a railroad company himself. Mr. Townsend died shortly after the house was completed.

Mrs. Townsend supposedly insisted that their mansion be built around an existing house on the site, which dated to 1873, because a "gypsy" had once predicted that she was destined to die "under a new roof." Apparently, Mrs. Townsend was hoping to fool Fate on a technicality, because by the time the new mansion was done, few traces of the underlying structure remained.

Designed by the New York firm of John Carrère and Thomas Hastings, both of whom had studied at the École des Beaux-Arts in Paris, the Townsend House is a majestically symmetrical and hierarchical composition. The four-story central block has a strong vertical emphasis thanks to its two-story-tall pilasters and the trio of arched dormer windows set into the mansard roof. A delicate cast iron and frosted-glass canopy shields the main entrance. The grandest interior spaces — the ballroom and the library — are on the second floor of the north and south wings, respectively, and each is marked on the front façade by a single window bracketed by two blank but elaborately framed panels. Lest the effect of all this be insufficiently regal, the architects added a quartet of ring-chomping lions' heads to the frieze above the first floor of the central pavilion.

The Townsends' daughter, Mathilde, inherited the house after her mother's death in 1931. She was married to B. Sumner Welles, a diplomat who played several crucial roles in Franklin Delano Roosevelt's administration. The prestigious Cosmos Club acquired the property in 1950. In adapting the building for its new function as a private club, Horace Peaslee had to take away much of the original landscaping but was able to maintain surprisingly substantial portions of the interiors. Still largely intact, the core of the mansion thus serves as a veritable museum of railroad-financed Gilded-Age grandeur.

P9
Phillips Collection
1600 21st Street, NW

1897 — Hornblower & Marshall
1907 — Music Room: Hornblower & Marshall
1920 — Second-floor addition: McKim, Mead & White
1923 — Fourth floor: Frederick H. Brooke
1960 — Original annex: Wyeth & King
1989 — Renovations and addition: Arthur Cotton Moore / Associates
2006 — Addition and renovation: cox graae + spack architects
2018 — Renovation of original building: Bowie Gridley Architects

The first museum of modern art in the United States, the Phillips Collection was born in 1921 when Duncan Phillips and his mother opened two rooms of their own residence as a public gallery in memory of Duncan's recently deceased father and brother. Today, despite a succession of additions and renovations, portions of the museum retain the intimate domestic character of its original incarnation. Even when the museum is crowded with art lovers, a visitor almost expects a member of the Phillips family to pop in and invite everyone to sit down for tea.

The Phillips Collection, which is best known for its Impressionist and Post-Impressionist paintings, was conceived as a museum of "modern art and its sources," reflecting Duncan's interest in both contemporary art and past works that he considered to be important antecedents. An heir to the Jones and Laughlin steel fortune, Duncan developed his avocation early on — while still an undergraduate, he wrote an article titled "The Need of Art at Yale," and he called his first book, published when he was 28, *The Enchantment of Art*. His wife, Marjorie, was a well-regarded painter.

The original mansion is a subdued, mildly eclectic affair, combining Georgian and Federal elements, and even a hint of Art Nouveau in the decoration on the columns and frieze of the entrance bay. The house was modestly expanded several times in the early 20th century, and the mansard-roofed fourth floor was added to provide more living space after the initial rooms were opened to the public. By 1930, the collection had grown so large that the family had to move out entirely.

The original annex, as completed in 1960, was a necessary but uninspired addition, lending a more institutional tone to the complex. In 1989, the annex was thoroughly revamped to make it more compatible with the older structures and a more commodious setting for art in its own right. Yet another renovation of the complex, including the incorporation of an existing apartment building to the north, was completed in 2006, and the original building was renovated in 2018.

P10
1718 Connecticut Avenue, NW

1982 — David M. Schwarz / Architectural Services, P.C.

An architectural Jekyll and Hyde — which side is which depends on the viewer's own stylistic proclivities — this retail and office building is fancifully neo-Romanesque in front and no-nonsense International Style in back. A bold diagonal line, best observed from a vantage point a few blocks up Connecticut Avenue, strikingly cleaves the two halves of the building.

Although obviously more deliberate in this case, the dichotomy evokes that of many historic Washington row houses and commercial structures, which were often built with relatively ornate fronts and quite plain rear façades.

P11

American Geophysical Union Headquarters

2000 Florida Avenue, NW

1994—Shalom Baranes Associates
2020—Renovation: Hickok Cole

The metal-and-glass prow of the headquarters of the American Geophysical Union (AGU) seems to break through a more typically Washingtonian structure of masonry walls and punched windows, suggesting the slow but inexorable tectonic processes by which our planet

forges new landscapes—appropriate symbolism for an organization dedicated to Earth and space sciences. The horizontal bands of precast concrete and brick on the façades are meant to evoke the layers beneath the Earth's surface. Note the decorative elements in the sidewalks adjacent to the building, in which the orbits of the planets in our solar system are depicted to scale.

When the building was due for a renovation, the AGU board, acutely aware of the threat of climate change, decided that it should meet net-zero-energy goals. The most striking feature of the renovated building is the new rooftop solar array, which is supported by tree-like columns sprouting from the top of the existing walls (the rooftop structure was inspired by a similar addition to 360 Newbury Street in Boston, designed by Frank Gehry in the 1980s). The addition reads as an abstract cornice that enhances the building's presence. Additional sustainable design features include an energy-efficient radiant cooling system and a direct-current electrical grid to power critical equipment without having to convert electricity from the city-supplied alternating-current system.

P12

International Headquarters, Order of the Eastern Star
(former Perry Belmont House)

1618 New Hampshire Avenue, NW

1909—Paul-Ernest Eugène Sanson with Horace Trumbauer

The Belmont House is symbolic of the era when many of the nation's wealthiest families routinely "wintered" in Washington to take advantage of the capital's then-fashionable social scene. In effect, this enormous slice of limestone pie with all the trimmings was built as a party house.

Diplomat Perry Belmont, a grandson of Commodore Matthew Perry, hired Paul-Ernest Sanson, a popular French architect, to design the house. Horace Trumbauer, who had a substantial portfolio of estates for American plutocrats, oversaw the construction. The mansion, estimated to have cost between $500,000 and $1.5 million in early 1900s dollars, was laid out in the preferred French manner of

the time, with bedrooms on the first floor and the primary public rooms elevated to a *piano nobile*—the principal floor, raised above ground level. Its ornate interior is decorated with Italian marble, German woodwork, and metalwork from France.

Belmont sold the house during the Great Depression to the General Grand Chapter of the Order of the Eastern Star, an organization accepting both women and men as members, but widely known as the distaff counterpart to the Masons. The price tag of just $100,000 came with the stipulation that the order's "Right Worthy Grand Secretary" must live in the house. Thus, despite the building's institutional use, it is now actually a year-round residence—an awful lot of house for one family, no matter how right, worthy, or grand.

Thomas Nelson Page House

1759 R Street, NW

1896—McKim, Mead & White (Stanford White)
1903—Alterations: Stanford White
1906—Alterations: architect unknown (possibly Stanford White)
2019—Renovation: ISTUDIO Architects

New York architect Stanford White designed this house for Virginia-born lawyer and writer Thomas Nelson Page, infamous for his racist and revisionist "plantation tradition" novels. The Georgian Revival mansion makes a clean break from the faux châteaux then so popular with Washington's architects and their clients. The R Street façade, which presaged

McKim, Mead & White's later design for the Percy Rivington Pyne House on New York's Park Avenue, is extremely reserved and projects a somewhat institutional character. The loggias on the second and third floors of the asymmetrical New Hampshire Avenue façade were originally open but were glassed in during renovations in the early 1900s. The house is now owned by a foundation dedicated to conservation, among other causes.

German Marshall Fund of the United States

(former Butler Mansion)

1744 R Street, NW

1914—Clarke Waggaman of Waggaman & Ray
2006—Renovation: OPX

One suspects that architect Clarke Waggaman might have been sober when he began designing this residence but finished some of the window details after a few glasses of wine. The façades of the Italian Renaissance–inspired mansion are, for the most part, splendidly serious, with a rusticated base, stern-looking faces carved into the keystones over the first-floor arches, a row of square attic-style windows lining the third floor, and a tidy cornice and roof parapet. But then there are the end windows of the main façade (along with the one around the corner facing New Hampshire Avenue), which are swaddled in carvings of luxuriantly spiraling grapevines dangling from the tops of the pediments, where pairs of *putti* are holding

shields. The effect is the visual equivalent of muffled giggles at an otherwise formal event—a welcome lighthearted note.

The mansion was designed for Oklahoma oilman Alban B. Butler and his wife, Luvean Jones Butler. It housed the Federal Republic of Germany's diplomatic mission (elevated to embassy status in 1956) from 1952 to 1964 and is now the headquarters of the German Marshall Fund, a transatlantic think tank and grant-making organization.

P15
Schneider Row Houses
1700 block of Q Street, NW

1889–92—Thomas Franklin Schneider
Numerous alterations: various architects

Designed and built by T. F. Schneider of Cairo Hotel fame, these three-story brown- and greenstone row houses form a parade of turrets, projecting bays, tiled mansard roofs, and Richardsonian Romanesque decorative detailing. Called a "young Napoleon" by one of his contemporaries, Schneider paid $175,000 for the long row of lots on the north side of Q Street and audaciously developed the whole tract in one fell swoop.

P16
Woman's National Democratic Club
(former Whittemore House)

1526 New Hampshire Avenue, NW

1894—Harvey L. Page
1967—Addition: Nicholas Satterlee

A great cape of a roof—punctuated by an occasional raised-eyelid window—drapes languidly over this spectacularly idiosyncratic mansion. Sarah Adams Whittemore, an opera singer and descendant of President John Adams, commissioned the house, whose modest entrance is partially sheltered by an overhanging copper-and-leaded-glass bay window. Subtle patterns in the orange-brown Roman brick add interest to the façades, while a procession of rather simple and serviceable brackets remarkably turns the roof gutter into a substantial architectural element. Now the headquarters of the Woman's National Democratic Club, the building contains a

P17
Patterson House / Oakwood Suites & Studios

15 Dupont Circle, NW

1903 — McKim, Mead and White (Stanford White)

1951–56 — Alterations: architects unknown

1985 — Restoration: Oehrlein & Associates Architects

2016 — Renovation and addition: Hartman-Cox Architects; Interior designers: Darryl Carter Inc.; Rockwell Group; Maurice Walters Architect, Inc.

small museum mostly devoted to political memorabilia, including items pertaining to Eleanor Roosevelt, a club member who, when she became First Lady, used the organization as a vehicle to advance her social agenda. A starkly contrasting rough concrete addition at the rear contains event spaces and peripheral functions.

Now on display in the house's garden along Q Street are several works by local sculptor John Cavanaugh, whose studio was once nearby. Other works by Cavanaugh are sprinkled around the neighborhood, including pieces incorporated into the façades of 1614, 1736, and 1742 Corcoran Street, as well as 1801–3 Swann Street, NW, among others.

Designed by Stanford White for Robert Wilson Patterson Jr., editor-in-chief of the *Chicago Tribune* and president of its parent company, this palazzo appears extremely grand from Dupont Circle but assumes a surprising intimacy up close, thanks to its tiny forecourt defined by the two wings and the angled entry connecting them. Lavishly iced with swags, fruit, and other sundries, the façades of glazed terra cotta and starkly white marble are further decorated with flat panels of variegated marble, abstractly suggesting framed paintings. This same variegated

marble appears on the columns of the central porch, which became famous in 1927 when Charles Lindbergh, freshly returned from his solo flight across the Atlantic, was photographed there waving to crowds. (Lindbergh was visiting President Calvin Coolidge and First Lady Grace Coolidge, who were living at the Patterson mansion temporarily while the White House was undergoing renovation.)

The most famous Patterson to live in the house was not Robert but his redoubtable and scandal-prone daughter, "Cissy," who worked her way up through the family publishing business and ultimately purchased two newspapers that she combined to create the *Washington Times-Herald*. Briefly a countess by marriage, Cissy was a vociferous opponent of Franklin D. Roosevelt, and she used the medium at her disposal to disseminate a blizzard of highly sensational "news" that made her the *bête noire* of official Washington. "The trouble with me," she once said, "is that I am a vindictive old shanty-Irish bitch." Cissy's death in 1948 marked the end of a feverish era in the capital's social life. She left the building to the Red Cross, which sold it to the Washington Club in 1951.

Facing an aging membership, the Washington Club put the building up for sale in 2014. It was bought by a team led by B. F. Saul III, scion of the local real estate dynasty, who converted it into a sort of hybrid property: part rental apartment building, part hotel, and part social club. The entertaining rooms in the mansion were renovated to serve as communal spaces for residents, while the former bedrooms and servants' rooms on upper levels became studio apartments. Additional apartments are located in the glassy addition to the east of the mansion, which deftly relates to the historic building in its proportions and milky white tones. Particularly clever touches include glass panels that were photographically imprinted with marble-like patterns, recalling the mansion's variegated marble panels, and a band of greenish glass at the very top of the addition that subtly alludes to the copper gutters on the historic building.

P18

Chancery of Iraq
(former Boardman House)

1801 P Street, NW

1893—Hornblower & Marshall
Numerous alterations: architects unknown

Tricks with bricks—such as the splayed jack arches over the windows and the eccentric zigzag frieze between the first and second floors—help to animate this otherwise staid quasi-Romanesque block. Also noteworthy are the balustrades along the top of the bay window and on the small balcony above, comprising rows of tiny Ionic columns. Curiously, the house's most elaborate decorative element, a beautiful mosaic, is tucked under the entry arch, where, on a sunny day, it is sometimes almost invisible in the shadows.

Mabel Boardman, the house's most notable occupant, was well known for her work with the Red Cross. Boardman also cofounded the Sulgrave Club, whose members met here until 1932, when they were able to buy and remodel their present building across the street [see following entry]. Now, after more than a decade of disuse between the two Persian Gulf wars, this house serves once again as the Iraqi chancery.

P19

Sulgrave Club
(former Wadsworth House)

1801 Massachusetts Avenue, NW

1902—George Cary
1932—Remodeling: Frederick H. Brooke
1952—Alterations: architect unknown

Designed as the winter residence of Herbert Wadsworth, an engineer who also

During World War I, the Wadsworths turned the entire house over to the Red Cross. In 1932, it was sold to a small group of women led by neighbor Mabel Boardman [see previous entry], who formed a private club named for George Washington's ancestral home in England, Sulgrave Manor. Architect Frederick Brooke, hired to convert the house to club use, also worked as the local consulting architect for Sir Edwin Lutyens's British Embassy on Massachusetts Avenue [see O26].

P20

McCormick Apartments
(now American Enterprise Institute)

1785 Massachusetts Avenue, NW

1917 — Jules Henri de Sibour
1941–50 — Interior alterations: architect unknown
1979 — Restoration/renovation: Yerkes, Pappas and Parker
2016 — Renovation and addition: Hartman-Cox Architects; Interiors: CORE architecture + design; Brayton Hughes Design Studio

owned vast farms in western New York, and his wife, musician and artist Martha Blow Wadsworth, this mansion makes the most of its triangular site. Rounded bays soften the acute angles of the west and southeast corners while creating gracious rooms on all three main levels. The house originally had a drive-through carriageway running from what is currently the main entrance on Massachusetts Avenue all the way to P Street. It also boasted an "automobile room" — that is, an internal garage (with a car turntable no less) — right across from what was then the main door.

The most assured and sophisticated of the numerous Beaux-Arts buildings in Dupont Circle, this one would be perfectly at home in any of the finest *arrondissements* of

Paris. Incredibly, the elegant structure was commissioned as a rental apartment building, albeit one with only six units. Full-floor apartments, each measuring a total of 11,000 square feet spread over 25 rooms, occupied the second through fifth floors.

The building was designed by the mellifluously named Jules Henri de Sibour, who claimed descent from King Louis IX of France (that's *Saint* Louis to you). His client for this building was ostensibly Stanley McCormick, son of Cyrus and heir to the International Harvester fortune. Stanley wanted to build "the most luxurious apartment house in Washington" but soon became incapacitated by mental illness, leaving his wife, Katharine Dexter McCormick, to oversee the completion of the project. (Katharine became famous herself as a suffragist and philanthropist who personally funded the vast majority of research that led to the development of the birth control pill.)

The McCormick Apartments quickly became some of the most sought-after residences in the city, attracting such tenants as Pearl Mesta (later known as the "Hostess with the Mostest"), Lord Joseph Duveen, and Andrew Mellon. Duveen, an international art dealer, never actually lived in his apartment—he rented it as a private gallery for the express purpose of selling a large collection of paintings and sculptures to Mr. Mellon. The strategy worked. After padding downstairs—perhaps in his robe and slippers—almost daily for three months, Mellon finally bought the entire lot in one fell swoop for a record-shattering sum. He later donated these and other artworks to the nation as the basis for the National Gallery of Art.

The armies of servants who looked after these nabobs lived in tiny rooms crowded onto eight mezzanine levels facing a narrow light well. Fortunately, the building offered several amenities to make work easier for the housekeeping staff, including a central vacuum system, centrally refrigerated tap water, and laundry chutes to individual washing machines in the basement. The building was later converted to office use, serving as the headquarters of the National Trust for Historic Preservation for a number of years, and was recently renovated and expanded by its current owner, the American Enterprise Institute.

P21

Peterson Institute for International Economics

1750 Massachusetts Avenue, NW

2001—Kohn Pedersen Fox Associates

A modern jewel set among the grand old buildings of Massachusetts Avenue, the Peterson Institute for International Economics demonstrates that sensitive historic contexts can readily accommodate contrasting architecture when it is thoughtfully designed and appropriately scaled. The new building's roofline suggests a gable that has been split and reassembled in an unexpected way, creating a dynamic composition without relying on fussy details or decoration. The specialty glass wall to the left of the entrance filters light and lends an ethereal quality to a conference area within. At night, when the interior lights are on, the curtain wall on the upper levels almost disappears, and the tidy individual offices read as rooms in a dollhouse. The only unfortunate note is the long blank party wall along the east side of the property, next to the Embassy of Uzbekistan—if only it could have been executed in metal or stone rather than cheap artificial stucco.

P22

Embassy of the Republic of Uzbekistan

(former Clarence Moore House / Canadian Embassy)

1746 Massachusetts Avenue, NW

1909—Jules Henri de Sibour (of Price & de Sibour)
1917—Addition: Jules Henri de Sibour
Various alterations: architects unknown

and mansard roof, this house contrasts with the much more subdued Wilkins House (now the Peruvian Chancery) down the street at 1700 Massachusetts, which the same architect designed a few years later. The Canadian government acquired the Moore property in 1927 and maintained it as a chancery until 1988, when embassy staff moved to their new quarters on Pennsylvania Avenue [see H2]. It now serves as the Embassy of Uzbekistan.

P23

The Drake

1355 17th Street, NW

2014 — Eric Colbert & Associates PC

An excellent example of contextual modernism, the Drake takes design cues from several surrounding buildings while remaining distinctly of its own era. The buff brick and bronze-colored metal trim pick up on the similarly colored brick and stone panels on the Art Moderne Bay State apartments across 17th Street, while the precast concrete band above the second floor echoes the line over the open colonnade of the Air Line Pilots Association building next door and the equivalent band on the Richmond condominium across O Street. The Drake also complements the First Baptist Church, facing

Clarence Moore, a West Virginia coal tycoon, and his wife, Mabelle Swift Moore, commissioned this Louis XV-style *palais*, but Clarence was able to enjoy it for only a few years before he had the misfortune to book passage on the maiden voyage of the *Titanic* in 1912 (the "50 pairs of English foxhounds" he had bought for hunting purposes did not accompany him on the ill-fated trip). With its light-colored Roman brick, elaborate stone and iron ornament,

16th Street, to which it is technically an addition (the church was able to benefit from soaring land values by leasing a portion of its property to a developer, who built the apartment building). The Drake is notable as the first completed building in DC to consist primarily of "micro-unit" apartments, ranging from 390 to 450 square feet each. The units were carefully designed to make the most of the limited space—the developer even built a full-scale mock-up of a typical unit, allowing the design team to tweak critical dimensions to maximize efficiency and comfort. A second phase, occupying the space between the church and the apartment building, is currently on the boards.

P24

Embassy of Hungary
(former Brodhead-Bell-Morton Mansion)

1500 Rhode Island Avenue, NW

1879—John Fraser
1889—Addition: John Fraser
1912—Renovation: John Russell Pope
2021—Renovation: Krisztina Boleracz and KCCT; Renovation of historic interiors: GDG (Georgetown Design Group, Inc.)

Sometimes buildings are tweaked over the years to reflect changing architectural tastes. In this case, a house built in the 1870s in a rambling, romantic red-brick Victorian style was completely transformed into a prim, stone-clad Beaux-Arts mansion in the 1910s. Drawings by John Russell Pope, the architect for the wholesale renovation, illustrate his purposeful efforts to wrestle the original house's turrets and hip roofs into a taut neoclassical composition.

The house's initial owners, John and Jessie Brodhead, soon sold it to Gardiner Greene Hubbard, founder of the National Geographic Society, and his wife, Gertrude. The Hubbards' daughter, Mabel, and son-in-law, inventor Alexander Graham Bell, then lived there for several years. In 1889, the Hubbards sold the house to Levi P. Morton shortly before he was inaugurated as vice president under President Benjamin Harrison. Morton later rented the house out to a series of other prominent political figures but returned in 1912, at which point he com-

missioned Pope to revamp it. The mansion was later owned for more than 85 years by what is now the American Coatings Association, which sold it to the government of Hungary in 2016.

P25

Post Massachusetts Apartments
1499 Massachusetts Avenue, NW

2002—Esocoff & Associates | Architects

The exterior design of this large apartment building is clever in several respects. Its scalloped façades and vibrant blue projecting bays establish a strong rhythm of vertical elements that diminish the building's apparent bulk, while also yielding a sculptural quality that is rare in the bottom-line world of developer-driven construction. This design strategy was no mere caprice, however. It emerged logically from two factors: first, the prevalence of flat-plate concrete construction in Washington—commonly used because it often allows architects to squeeze an extra floor in commercial buildings governed by the city's height restrictions—and second, the District's public space regulations, which allow parts of residential buildings to project beyond the property line within certain guidelines. In flat-plate construction, it is relatively easy to create unusual shapes at the edges of the concrete floor slabs, so the scalloped façade design took advantage of local building traditions to make curved forms efficiently and economically. Meanwhile, under District law, the projections into public space—in this case, over the sidewalks—do not count against the maximum floor area permitted by zoning regulations, so the developer can build a larger building, gaining extra rentable space on a given piece of land.

Architect Phil Esocoff cites the work of Antoni Gaudí as one source of inspiration, and indeed, this building would fit well in Barcelona or many other European cities. It is one of a series of structures by Esocoff employing similar façade design strategies, including 400 Massachusetts Avenue, NW [see G10], and Quincy Park at 1001 L Street, NW.

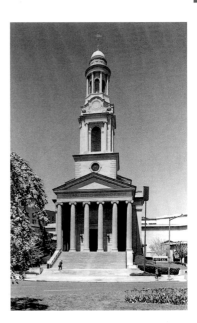

P26

National City Christian Church

5 Thomas Circle, NW

1930—John Russell Pope
1954—Addition: Leon Chatelain Jr.
1962—Wilfley Memorial Prayer Chapel:
    Clair S. Buchart
1980–86—Renovation and addition: Carl T.
    Cooper Jr.

This huge structure—its immense size becomes apparent only as the viewer approaches—was inspired by the early 18th-century church of St. Martin-in-the-Fields, on Trafalgar Square in London, designed by James Gibbs. National City is thus in good company, as Gibbs's iconic composition of pedimented front and stepped tower has served as the inspiration for countless Protestant churches throughout the United States. John Russell

Pope took some liberties, however, most notably by placing the structure atop a substantial mound, thereby necessitating the intimidating staircase leading to the portico, and by terminating the tower in a small dome rather than a pointy conical spire. Inside, the sanctuary is a bright rendition of the English Baroque, with a stunning coffered ceiling and a semicircular apse covered by a hemispherical dome.

The curious little hexagonal structure on the church's east lawn, surrounded by a stone gazebo, is a replica of the study used by Alexander Campbell, one of the founders of the movement that gave rise to the Christian Church (Disciples of Christ), the denomination that built this complex. In 2017, the church sold its west wing, which is now being renovated by Nelson Architects for use as commercial office space.

P27

Washington Plaza Hotel
(former International Inn)

10 Thomas Circle, NW

1962—Morris Lapidus
1981—Demolition of pool dome

One could easily walk or drive by the Washington Plaza Hotel and barely notice it, but it becomes much more interesting when one discovers that it was designed by Morris Lapidus, the architect of glitzy Miami Beach hotels such as the Fontainebleau and the Eden Roc, whose motto was

"Too much is never enough." Admittedly, this hotel would have been easier to recognize as a Lapidus work in its early years, when the principal façade was still clad in its original alternating black and white panels, and the swimming pool just off Thomas Circle was covered by a retractable glass dome that was probably described as "groovy" back in the day. The dome was dismantled in 1981, and the horizontal concrete bands on the façade have long been painted a uniform white, but one can still appreciate the Lapidus touch in the building's curving plan and some remaining elements of the lobby.

Lapidus designed several buildings in Washington, including the Capitol Skyline Hotel on I Street at South Capitol Street.

Built as a gesture of thanksgiving for the end of the Civil War, this red sandstone Gothic Revival church contrasts sharply with the neoclassical National City Christian Church across the street [see P26]. The beefy octagonal main tower, which bursts into a crown-like ring of gables and pinnacles just below the spire, anchors the corner of the triangular site. Behind the main tower is the sanctuary, which is ovoid in plan, as evident from the bowed side façades along 14th Street and Vermont Avenue. The somewhat spartan interior gains visual interest from the unusual wooden trusses that support the roof. A curving corridor separates the sanctuary from a rectilinear office wing, which is angled in plan to align with N Street.

P28
Luther Place Memorial Church

1226 Vermont Avenue, NW (at Thomas Circle)

1873—John C. Harkness and Henry S. Davis, based on original design by Judson York (towers completed ca. 1884)
1905—Restoration: Frank H. Jackson
ca. 1939—Renovation: L. M. Leisenring
1951—Parish House: L. M. Leisenring
1970—Renovations: Neer and Graef
1990—Parish House addition and renovation: Weihe Partnership
2006—Renovation of sanctuary: Kerns Group Architects

P29
Logan Circle

1875-present—Various architects

The houses surrounding Logan Circle, along with those lining adjacent streets (note, for example, the beautiful rows along the 1300 block of Rhode Island Avenue), form Washington's finest enclave of carefully restored Victorian town houses. Most were built during a 25-year period from about 1875 to 1900 to house the District's powerful and wealthy. Originally called Iowa Circle, the roundabout was renamed in 1930 for John A. Logan, a prominent Civil War general and senator from Illinois, who had lived in a house on the circle for a short time. (This honor was bestowed despite Logan's efforts to have the national capital moved to St. Louis, though perhaps as vengeance, city officials later allowed another house in which he lived to be destroyed to make way for a parking lot.) In the early 20th century, Washington's fickle society folk abandoned the neighborhood for Dupont Circle, and Logan Circle entered a deep sleep. Having miraculously survived an excruciating period as one of the city's more notorious drug and prostitution centers, the neighborhood is now once again one of the most desirable residential areas in the city.

P30
The Studio Theatre
1501 14th Street, NW

1919 — 1501 14th Street: Murphy & Olmsted
1920 — 1507 14th Street: architect unknown
1922 — 1509 14th Street: John Mahon Donn

1987 — Renovation: Devrouax + Purnell Architects; Theater designer: Russell Metheny
1997 — Renovation: Russell Metheny and O'Marah & Benulis
2004 — Renovation and addition: Bonstra Architects; Theater designer: Russell Metheny

One of the harbingers of the urban revitalization to come, the Studio Theatre, founded in 1978, moved to a former automobile showroom at 14th and P Streets in 1987. The original renovation preserved the essential character of the existing building, while adding striking graphic elements—a giant sign, rendered in dressing-room-style lights, cleverly set within the windows along P Street, and large, high-contrast black-and-white photographic images of faces, filling in the window areas to create the enclosure necessary for the theater spaces.

The well-regarded theater company embarked on a major expansion in 2002, buying the two buildings along 14th Street immediately to the north of the original facility. The separate structures were combined and visually unified by a glassy atrium atop the middle building, where the entrance to the complex is now located. Inserting a new theater in the northernmost building, long occupied by the Ace Electric Company, required the removal of the second-floor slab and the transfer of structural forces to

a series of three-foot-deep steel beams spanning the width of the building. The latest renovation also updated the large photographic faces, adding backlighting to create a glowing band of images.

As of this writing, another renovation of the theater by Hickok Cole is under construction.

P31

1525 14th Street, NW

2014 — Eric Colbert & Associates PC

This project comprises a historic former car showroom plus an addition built next to and above the existing building. In an era in which many new commercial buildings are sheathed in bland, flat glass curtain walls, the main façade of this addition, with its irregular grid of gray zinc-clad panels, recessed windows, and inset glass louvers, is refreshingly animated and three-dimensional. Where the façade abuts the historic building — both vertically and horizontally — the skin shifts to a simpler composition with white metal panels and uninterrupted bands of windows, allowing the older structure to read as a distinct block.

P32

Rainbow Lofts

1445 Church Street, NW

1926 — Howard Etchison
2004 — Renovation and addition: Eric Colbert & Associates PC

A façade-wide sign of individual letters declares the original purpose of this former auto body repair garage and explains the derivation of the condominium project's otherwise corny-sounding name. The interiors of the apartments in the existing three-story, brick-faced structure retain a raw industrial character, with exposed masonry walls and pivoting steel-frame windows. The addition, running up the west wide and across the top, is a dramatic contrast, sheathed in white metal panels (each composed of a polyethylene core sandwiched between two aluminum sheets) and large expanses of glass. Sunscreens partially shield the windows of the addition, while minimalist glass railings line the edges of the roof deck and upper-level terraces.

P33

Whole Foods Market

1440 P Street, NW

2000 — Mushinsky Voelzke Associates / MV+A
2010 — Renovation: Mushinsky Voelzke Associates / MV+A

When the parent company of what was then called Fresh Fields announced an interest in opening one of its markets on an urban site in Washington, a group of Logan Circle residents launched a concerted effort to bring the natural food store to their neighborhood. The campaign was successful, and all parties are apparently thrilled with the results. Not only is the store, now a Whole Foods Market, an excellent performer for the chain, it also served as a major catalyst for additional commercial and residential development in the area. Built on the site of a former service garage, the new building includes both underground and rooftop parking. Conceptually, the main façade is a stretched and folded store-front inspired loosely by the industrial architecture of the neighborhood, though it also bears hints of Art Deco, Amsterdam School modernism, and 1950s commercial architecture. Note the subtle green and blue colors in the small panes of glass at the top of the serrated windows.

P34

Carnegie Institution of Washington
(commonly known as the Carnegie Institution for Science)

1530 P Street at 16th Street, NW

1909 — Carrère & Hastings
1938 — Delano & Aldrich; Auditorium murals: J. Monroe Hewlett
1998 — Rehabilitation: Florance Eichbaum Esocoff King; Preservation architects: Oehrlein & Associates Architects
2017 — Interior renovation: Rippeteau Architects

Beginning in 1902, industrialist and philanthropist Andrew Carnegie gave funds to endow an institution "to encour-

age, in the broadest and most liberal manner, investigation, research, and discovery and the application of knowledge to the improvement of mankind." The institution's headquarters building by Carrère & Hastings soon followed. The design is undeniably impressive, if a little quirky in several respects. The huge portico facing 16th Street, for instance, with its paired Ionic columns and heavy balustrade, appears as though it aspired to introduce a much larger structure — in fact, the architects diminished the building's scale several times during the design process in response to Carnegie's directive to avoid excessive grandeur. The scale of the portico seems particularly grand now that it no longer serves as the primary entrance — the main door is actually around the corner on the P Street side, under a relatively modest canopy, at the point where the original building meets the addition by Delano & Aldrich. The exterior of the addition is a slightly simplified version of the original, while the interior boasts a sleek Art Moderne auditorium lined with spectacular murals.

In the spring of 2021, the Carnegie Institution announced plans to sell its historic headquarters building to the government of Qatar for use as its embassy. Many Carnegie scientists, students, and staff members were outraged by the decision, citing both disapproval of the Qatari government's notoriously poor human rights record and concerns about trends toward corporatization of academic institutions.

P35

Church Place Condominium
1520 16th Street, NW

1964 — Architect unknown
2000 — Renovation: Eric Colbert & Associates PC

The original, exceedingly banal, apartment building had degenerated into a crowded tenement when an electrical fire and flood led to its condemnation. Architect Eric Colbert's colorful metal appliqués, suggestive of a de Stijl painting, give life to the once-drab façades. The architect worked to maximize window area in the new apartments to compensate for their low ceiling heights.

Next door is the Hightowers, a classic late–Art Deco apartment building by Alvin E. Aubinoe Sr. and Harry L. Edwards, completed in 1938.

P36

The Cairo

1615 Q Street, NW

1894 — Thomas Franklin Schneider
1904 — Addition: Thomas Franklin
    Schneider
1976 — Renovation: Arthur Cotton
    Moore / Associates
2000 — Lobby renovation: James
    Cummings AIA: A Collaborative Design
    Group

The Cairo is a very large curio. Some might equate the building with one of those rare objects occasionally encountered that appear so ugly or ungainly as to attract rather than repel.

— *Sixteenth Street Architecture, Volume 2,*
    The Commission of Fine Arts, 1988

Contrary to popular belief, the structure that engendered the District of Columbia's first building height limitation was neither the Capitol nor the Washington Monument but rather this bizarre "Moorish" pile of bricks and limestone. At a height of more than 160 feet, the 12-story tower — the upper floors of which were beyond the reach of fire ladders available at the time — so alarmed its neighbors that they successfully lobbied the District's Board of Commissioners to enact restrictive zoning regulations in July 1894, before the building was even finished (the first federal *legislative* height restriction was enacted by Congress in 1899; the current law was passed in 1910). In truth, the Cairo's opponents probably represented a strange alliance of architectural sophisticates appalled by its ungainly design, and Luddites who feared that it was only a matter of time before such a "skyscraper" would topple from sheer weight and hubris.

The architect was the enterprising T. F. Schneider, who had visited the 1893 Columbian Exhibition in Chicago, marveled at the fair's literally spectacular architecture, and apparently, learned little. The Cairo is ill-proportioned and capped by a ridiculously boxy cornice, and its fancy front façade stops abruptly after turning the corners, leaving bare brick walls on the sides and back. Nonetheless, the building certainly has its charms — note, for instance, the attenuated elephant heads that bracket the sills of the two outermost windows on the first floor, and of course, the great entry arch, with its wispy lettering.

One of the first residential towers in America to employ steel-frame construction, the Cairo was built in less than 10 months. An effusive promotional brochure touted it as "the most thoroughly equipped establishment of this nature south of New York," and it even promised pleasant summer living thanks to "cooling zephyrs" from Rock Creek Park, despite the fact that the park is at least a half-mile away. The flyer also acclaimed the establishment's bakery, two billiard rooms, and rooftop garden complete with tropical plants and electrically powered fountains "bubbling here and bursting forth there." The building originally had a dining room on the top floor, marked by a change in window pattern that is still visible on the east façade.

The Cairo was converted into a hotel in the 1920s, beginning a slow but dramatic decline. By the 1960s, it was visited more frequently by police than by tourists, and rats outnumbered both. Finally, in 1976, a HUD-sponsored renovation, accomplished on the cheap, returned the building to apartment use. It became a condominium in 1979, and now, for all its quirks, the awkward tower reigns as one of Washington's guilty architectural pleasures.

P37
The Tapies Apartments
1612 16th Street, NW
2005 — Bonstra Architects

Squeezed onto a 21-foot-wide site previously occupied by a much-abused little wood-frame house, this svelte apartment building was conceived as a stretched,

abstracted version of a typical row house with an asymmetrical bay. It accommodates just five apartments, four of them duplexes with living rooms almost as tall as the building is wide. A ladder-like trellis on the front façade, intended to serve as an armature for greenery, provides a series of small, horizontal counterpoints to the building's overall verticality. The landscaping of the front yard creates a surprisingly dense grove shading the sidewalk that zigzags toward the entrance.

P38
Church of the Holy City
(National Swedenborgian Church)
1611 16th Street, NW

1895 — Herbert Langford Warren;
   Associated architects: Pelz and Carlisle
1912 — Parish House: Warren & Smith;
   Associated architect: Paul Pelz

This rugged neo-Gothic structure was designed by Herbert Langford Warren, a Swedenborgian who later served as the first dean of Harvard University's Faculty of Architecture. Construction was overseen by Paul Pelz, architect of the main Library of Congress building. A brawny bell tower, which anchors the corner of the modestly scaled building, adds a boldly asymmetrical note. The sanctuary interior is notable for its hammer-beam trusses with slim iron tie rods spanning between the ends of the beams, and its intricate apse lined with narrow Gothic-arched windows. The south wing, added in 1912, contains a glorious cantilevered spiral staircase that begins just inside the arched doorway. As of this writing, ongoing renovations of the church by Marc Fetterman are under way.

P39

Toutorsky Mansion

(now Embassy of the Republic of the Congo)

1720 16th Street, NW

1894—William Henry Miller

1943—Interior alterations: architects unknown

1992—Renovations: various architects and designers

This 12,000-square-foot mansion was built for Supreme Court justice Henry Brown, who wrote the majority opinion in the infamous 1896 case of *Plessy v. Ferguson* legitimizing racial segregation. It later housed the Persian Legation and the Zionist Organization of America (no, not at the same time). In the minds of longtime neighborhood residents, however, the house is indelibly associated with the Russian musician Basil Toutorsky and his English Mexican wife, opera singer María Ignacia Howard Toutorsky, who ran a music school here for four decades beginning in 1947. The Toutorskys bequeathed the house to the Peabody Conservatory of Music in Baltimore, which sold it to a private buyer who turned it back into a residence. It is now the embassy of the Republic of the Congo.

With its stepped and scroll-edged gables, insistent rows of windows, dark red brick, and strong horizontal stone courses, the Toutorsky Mansion is a rare iteration of Flemish Renaissance architecture in a city whose architectural ancestry is overwhelmingly English, French, and Italian. The façades are intriguing assemblages of symmetrical and asymmetrical components, making the building appear simultaneously balanced and dynamic. The interior is replete with dark wood and over-the-top, ornate fireplaces.

P40

Scottish Rite Temple
(House of the Temple)

1733 16th Street, NW

1915 — John Russell Pope; Consulting
architect: Elliott Woods
2015 — Renovation: Hartman-Cox
Architects

"Supreme Council," answers the reception-ist at the headquarters of the Ancient and Accepted Scottish Rite of Freemasonry, Southern Jurisdiction, USA. It goes without saying that subtlety is not a hallmark of the Masons, who are known for their pomp and secretive rituals. Inspired by all that pageantry, John Russell Pope had a field day in designing the organization's headquarters. Basing his building on the Mausoleum at Halicarnassus, one of the Seven Wonders of the Ancient World, Pope erected an awe-inspiring temple in the midst of a relatively quiet enclave of houses and apartment buildings.

As one would expect, the temple is replete with symbolism — some of it obvious, some requiring a good deal of esoteric knowledge on the part of the viewer. The colonnade surrounding the building, for instance, consists of 33 columns, an allusion to the 33rd Degree (sometimes abbreviated as 33°), an honorary designation

bestowed upon Masons for outstanding service to the fraternity. The front steps rise in flights of 3, 5, 7, and 9 (four of the "sacred numbers" of Freemasonry, all of which are odd). The steps are guarded by a pair of monumental sphinxes, representing *Power* on the left and *Wisdom* on the right. Inside the great bronze doors is the "Atrium," which is actually only a one-story space but is resplendent in Greek and Egyptian decorative motifs and rich in Masonic associations. The chairs, for example, are modeled after the seats in the Theater of Dionysus, and a pair of statues in ancient Egyptian style — three-dimensional representations of the hieroglyph that precedes the name of a god or of a sacred place — flanks the grand staircase.

Upstairs awaits the Temple Chamber, soaring some 88 feet (the original height of Jenkins Hill, where the Capitol now stands — why does this seem significant?) to the inside of the stepped pyramidal roof. Visit the space on a bright day, if possible, to witness the spectacle of sunlight streaming in through the giant windows. The room is dripping with sumptuous materials, including marble, granite, and bronze. Back downstairs are other intriguing spaces and displays, including a handsome library with stacks radiating along a gentle curve.

Shaw / U Street

Although solidly within the original boundaries of L'Enfant's plan for Washington, the neighborhood to the east of Logan Circle, roughly between Mount Vernon Square and Florida Avenue, was still sparsely populated by the mid-19th century. That began to change in the aftermath of the Civil War, when several camps for freed slaves were built here. As those camps were replaced by permanent residential and commercial development, the area grew into a center of Black cultural and social life. It was not until the 1960s that the neighborhood began to be called Shaw, after the Shaw Junior High School—named for Robert Gould Shaw, the white Union army officer who led an otherwise all-Black regiment in the Civil War—which was a cornerstone of the community.

In the 1920s and '30s, the adjacent U Street corridor was a vibrant entertainment hub for Black Washingtonians, rivaling and often exceeding the glamour of even the most exclusive "white" establishments in the heavily segregated city. Arguably the cultural capital of Black America, rivaling Harlem in New York, U Street was synonymous with jazz, attracting many of the world's greatest musicians to its theaters and dance halls. Ironically, it was desegregation that ended all of this in the post–World War II era, as Black patrons quickly took advantage of their new freedom to visit clubs and theaters that were previously inaccessible to them, leaving U Street businesses with fewer and fewer customers.

Like the nearby 14th Street corridor in the Logan Circle neighborhood, Shaw and U Street were also devastated by the 1968 uprisings in the wake of the assassination of Martin Luther King Jr. The physical and psychological scars of that tragic period are still evident in many corners of these neighborhoods despite a phenomenal wave of gentrification that began in the 1990s and continues to this day. For now, the area maintains a degree of racial and cultural diversity, as people of all ethnicities flock to its restaurants and clubs, but rising property values have inevitably led to substantial displacement of families whose roots in the neighborhood went back generations.

The Republic Theatre on U Street, seen here in 1945 or early 1946, was one of the many popular entertainment venues for Black Washingtonians during the segregation era. It closed in 1976 and was later demolished in preparation for construction of the Metro Green Line.

Q1

Lincoln Theatre

1215 U Street, NW

1922 — Reginald Geare
1994 — Restoration architects of record:
LEO A DALY; Preservation architects:
Oehrlein & Associates Architects; Sorg
and Associates

At the height of the jazz era, U Street reigned, in the words of native Washingtonian singer Pearl Bailey, as the "Black Broadway." Its grand theaters and lively nightclubs, which regularly featured the most talented musicians of the period, provided elegant entertainment venues for Black Washingtonians in the still-segregated city. The Lincoln Theatre was a popular first-run movie and vaudeville house, which the *Washington Afro-American* declared to be "perhaps the largest and finest for colored people exclusively anywhere in the United States." Immediately behind the theater once stood the Lincoln Colonnade, a dance hall that was a prestigious site for proms and other celebratory events and was frequented by jazz greats such as Duke Ellington, who was also a native of Washington.

The theater's front façade is far from fancy compared to its contemporaries built for white audiences, but it achieves beauty and dignity through a few key design gestures. Foremost is the large yet delicate marquee suspended from rods attached to two small anchors on the façade. The main window on the second floor is capped by an arch with a recessed, pressed-metal sculptural panel bearing a fan motif. Two round medallions on the central bay and rectangular panels with swags to the sides add a bit of flair near the top. Behind the unassuming façade is a somewhat more ornate interior, with a lobby that evokes the era of silent films and an auditorium surrounded by curved balconies and an elaborate proscenium stage bracketed by large Palladian arches.

The Colonnade was demolished in the 1960s, and the Lincoln Theatre itself closed its doors the following decade. As the U Street corridor began its slow resurgence in the early 1990s, the District of Columbia government assumed ownership of the theater and sponsored its restoration. The theater now hosts live performances, film festivals, and a variety of special events.

Q2

True Reformer Building

1200 U Street, NW

1903 — John A. Lankford
1937 — Renovation: John A. Lankford
1947 — Renovation: architect unknown
1949 — Renovation: Leon Chatelain
2001 — Renovation: Sorg & Associates

Commissioned by the Grand Fountain of the United Order of True Reformers, a Black benevolent society that provided insurance and financial services to its members, the True Reformer Building was the first major commercial structure in the nation designed, financed, and built solely by Black people. John Lankford, believed to have been the first Black registered architect in the District of Columbia, produced a building of restrained elegance, with tall floors, subtle pilasters that match the wall surface behind them, and a contrasting frieze of swags just below the cornice. The building housed shops, offices, meeting rooms, and an auditorium, in which Duke Ellington—who grew up nearby—gave his first paid performance (the cover charge was five cents). A mural by G. Byron Peck on the west-facing party wall commemorates that musical milestone and contributes to the building's status as a U Street landmark. Today, the building is owned by the Public Welfare Foundation.

This memorial to the United States Colored Troops (USCT)—including Black and other nonwhite troops who fought for the Union during the Civil War—is centered around a compact bronze sculpture depicting three soldiers and a sailor on the convex front side, and a military family on the concave rear. Surrounding the sculpture are curving walls bearing the names of more than 200,000 USCT members. The outer wall angles off at a tangent toward the northeast, thus helping to define the edge of the plaza. A related museum is located nearby.

Q3
Industrial Bank of Washington
2000 11th Street, NW

1917—Isaiah T. Hatton
2019—Renovation: DEL Studio

The Industrial Savings Bank, the only Black-owned bank in DC when it opened in 1913, commissioned this building as its headquarters in 1917. The bank failed during the Great Depression but reopened under its current name in 1934 and has been in operation ever since. Although the 11th Street façade of this building, which is now one of the bank's branches, appears similar in scale to nearby row houses, the long U Street front, with its extended bay window, reveals its commercial purpose. The blue-and-white sign and clock over the angled corner entrance are fixtures of the neighborhood.

Q4
African American Civil War Memorial
Southwest corner of U Street and Vermont Avenue, NW

1998—Devrouax + Purnell Architects and Edward D. Dunson Jr.; Sculpture: Ed Hamilton

Q5
Thurgood Marshall Center for Service and Heritage
(former Anthony Bowen Young Men's Christian Association Building)

1816 12th Street, NW

1912—William Sidney Pittman
2000—Renovation: Shalom Baranes Associates

Designed by local Black architect William Sidney Pittman, who had studied at the Tuskegee Institute and later married Booker T. Washington's daughter, Portia, this was originally the "Colored Men's Branch" of the YMCA. The facility was well appointed, including 54 guest rooms, ample reception and meeting rooms, a heated swimming pool, and a gymnasium with two tiers of metal running tracks suspended above the floor. Just as important, its understated yet handsome Renaissance Revival exterior was on a par with contemporary buildings for similar white organizations. The completed building was touted as a model for similar facilities across the country.

The building now houses a social services organization named in honor of the first Black Supreme Court justice, Thurgood Marshall.

Whitelaw Hotel

1839 13th Street, NW

1919 — Isaiah T. Hatton
1992 — Restoration: R. McGhee & Associates

Financed by the Whitelaw Apartment House Corporation, all of whose shareholders were Black, the Whitelaw Hotel was *the* place to stay for Black travelers visiting Washington during U Street's heyday as an entertainment hub. The building is handsome but by no means ostentatious on the exterior, where the only flourish is a Palladian arch over the main entrance. Inside, however, the hotel was known for its ornate lobby and ballroom, which featured a large, intricately patterned glass skylight. Severely damaged by fire in 1981, the building was later restored and reopened as apartments under the auspices of Manna, Inc., a local affordable housing developer.

Union Row

2125 14th Street, NW

2007 — SK&I Architectural Design Group

This condominium and retail development consists of two separate components. The "Flats" occupy the new nine-story structure running along 14th Street, which is divided into three distinct segments to break up the long façade. Midway along the block is a one-story open-air passage that leads to the second component — the "Warehouses," which is where things get interesting. A linear courtyard, running perpendicular to the main building, is flanked by two historic structures that have been renovated and expanded vertically, creating a sort of industrial mews. Black metal canopies modulate the scale of the complex while calling attention to the individual unit entries. Simple light fixtures suspended from cables spanning the courtyard add visual rhythm and evoke the streetlight systems found in many European cities.

Manhattan Laundry Main Building

1328 Florida Avenue, NW

1937 — Bedford Brown IV
1986 — Renovation: KressCox Associates
2014 — Façade restoration and building rehabilitation: BLDG Architects

This surprisingly festive Depression-era building once housed the offices of a commercial laundry operation. The façade cleverly uses flat materials — mostly porcelain-enamel panels and glass block — to create a cartoon of the three-dimensional ornament typically found on fancier historic buildings. On the

first floor, for instance, the narrow green bands alternate with wider white bands to suggest rusticated stone. A colorful Greek key design, framed in turn by an egg-and-dart pattern, surrounds the entrance. At the top of the façade is a "cornice" made of alternating bands of green and white metal tiles, punctuated by red diamonds.

The architects of the renovation in the 1980s initially wondered where they might find a manufacturer capable of producing porcelain-enamel panels to match the originals. They ultimately found a company that, as it turned out, had been making the panels for some time for a steady client: the White Castle hamburger chain.

Q9

The Lacey

2250 11th Street, NW

2008 — Division1 Architects

It's a safe bet that when Lacey C. Wilson Sr. and his wife, Bertha, opened a soul food restaurant in an almost exclusively Black neighborhood in 1944, they could never have imagined that someday apartments in the building next door would be selling for nearly a million dollars. But when their son, Lacey Jr., sold the venerable Florida Avenue Grill and the adjacent parking lot to a New York lawyer in 2005, it was a sign of imminent change. While the new owner had no intention of messing with the success of the grill, he had an ambitious vision for the adjacent site.

He hired Division1 to design a condominium building that stands out from the typical low-rise brick architecture of the neighborhood. The curtain wall on the street façade is an intricate, three-dimensional composition, with an irregular pattern of clear and etched glass in various shades of blue and glass-railed balconies set behind the primary plane. At ground level are four units with direct entrances from the street, establishing a rhythm that mimics that of nearby row houses. On the south façade, a relatively solid wall clad in cement-bonded particle board is interrupted by an open, partially screened staircase that appears poised to leap from the body of the building. That stair aligns with a spacious atrium running longitudinally through the building, intended to facilitate chance meetings of residents and foster a sense of community.

Q10

W Street Residence

1024 W Street, NW

2007 — Division1 Architects

As of 2021, there were 75 officially designated DC Historic Districts, which include much of the territory originally laid out by L'Enfant. This is particularly true of the inner residential areas in the Northwest quadrant. Just north of U Street, NW, however, there is a little pocket of L'Enfant's plan, bounded roughly by 12th Street, V Street, and Florida Avenue, which remains outside of any Historic District. This compact neighborhood has become known as the site of some adventurous architecture, since projects here are not subject to the approval of design review authorities.

The W Street Residence is a striking example. The composition is abstract — the architects acknowledged that they made no effort whatsoever to allude to specific forms or motifs common among nearby row houses — and yet in its scale, its proportions, and the layering of its façades, the house seems to fit comfortably within the neighborhood (which, admittedly, was already something of an architectural hodgepodge). Surprisingly for a single-family house, the W Street Residence has a structure of steel rather than wood. The architects, who developed this speculative project themselves, worked hard to come up with a composition they liked and wanted to discourage future owners from modifying it willy-nilly. A steel structure, they reasoned, would make casual changes difficult and was therefore worth the added cost.

Rounded bricks at the apex of the acute triangle lend the house a vaguely nautical character. On the east side, a few feet behind the apex, is the projecting bay that makes it all work, accommodating the main living area on the second floor and the primary bedroom on the top floor — both of them perfectly rectangular. On the opposite side, balconies project from the brick façade at an angle similar to that of the enclosed bay, providing slivers of private outdoor space and ensuring that the house appears balanced when viewed from the acute corner.

Q11

Speck House

990 Florida Avenue, NW

2008 — Designer: Jeff Speck; Architect of record: Brie Husted

In designing this house for his own family, urban planner Jeff Speck had to figure out how to fit a square peg in a triangular hole — or at least, on an acute triangular site. Speck had long been fascinated by the many small "flatiron"-shaped plots within L'Enfant's plan and was eager to demonstrate that such a site, despite its apparent constraints, could accommodate a comfortable house by means of a few clever geometric tricks. His design for this 500-square-foot property took advantage of allowable projections over public space (like the bay windows in many 19th- and 20th-century Washington row houses) to build a surprisingly roomy house totaling some 2,200 square feet. Still, he ultimately needed three distinct zoning variances in order to maximize the structure's habitable area.

Q12

The Floridian

919–929 Florida Avenue, NW

2008 — Eric Colbert & Associates PC

The Floridian condominium consists of a pair of fraternal twin towers designed by the same firm at the same time, though that was not the original intention. The architects were initially hired to design what is now the south building and were well into the construction documents phase when the project's developer purchased the lot immediately to the north and decided to build on that parcel simultaneously. Having studied the prospects for reworking the existing design to create a larger building, the architects determined that maintaining two separate cores

would actually yield more sellable square feet. So, they proceeded with plans for the first tower while developing a complementary design for the second one.

The façade treatments of the two sections are both lively, but in different ways. The north tower is primarily an exercise in patterns and colors, while the south tower relies on layers and textures in various shades of gray. On the southernmost wing, set back from the street, notice the perforated metal panels, which filter sunlight entering the rooms within. Both towers are crowned by simple metal canopies that are lit from below at night and serve as open-air pavilions where residents can gather on the shared roof deck. The notched plan of the buildings helps to maximize views, especially from apartments in the western wings, many of which have clear lines of sight to the Washington Monument.

Q13
Atlantic Plumbing Apartments
2112 8th Street, NW

2015 — Design architects: Morris Adjmi Architects; Architects of record: Eric Colbert & Associates PC

In a city where most large buildings are built of concrete (chiefly because a thin-slab concrete structure allows the maximum number of floors to be squeezed in under the height limit), one way to make your building stand out is to give it a heroically scaled steel exoskeleton. This rental apartment building, which sits on a parcel of land previously occupied by the Atlantic Plumbing Supply Company, could easily have been built using more conventional methods, but the design architect, Morris Adjmi, drew inspiration from the industrial landscapes visible on the train ride between New York and DC. The building's weathered COR-TEN steel frame projects beyond the glass façades, allowing room for balconies on the south elevation and planters along the west side (as the plants grow, they will likely intertwine with the steel structure, evoking the greenery that has engulfed many of the industrial structures that Adjmi saw along the train tracks). The two-story

painted brick base, which seems to bear little relationship to the structure above, alludes to the warehouses that were once common in the neighborhood. The big expressionistic structural gesture certainly increased the building's budget—although the use of external X-bracing did allow the elimination of internal shear walls, which would normally be needed to resist lateral forces—but the result is a new landmark that almost invariably causes passersby to stop and gawk.

Across V Street (at 2030 8th Street) is a much smaller condominium apartment building by the same design team, with an exposed steel frame that mimics the offset pattern of a typical running bond brick wall. The final parcel of the former Atlantic Plumbing site, around the corner at 945 Florida Avenue, NW, is marked by a giant A-shaped portal supporting a bridge that connects its north and south towers.

Q14

Howard University

Howard University is a private historically Black college/university (HBCU) that was chartered by the federal government in 1867. Its primary campus is just north of Florida Avenue on relatively high ground, affording excellent views over the city from several spots. The architecture of the university is predominantly Georgian

or Colonial Revival, which might seem ironic, given the often-painful associations of colonialism for Black Americans, but the result is a cohesive, dignified core campus reminiscent of numerous prestigious northeastern colleges, which may have been a more important association for Howard's architects. The campus also contains a number of startlingly functionalist buildings from the mid-20th century, which manage to blend in with the earlier structures remarkably well due to their shared materials and similar scale.

Q14a

Interdisciplinary Research Building
2201 Georgia Avenue, NW
2015—HDR Architecture, Inc.; Associated architects: Lance Bailey & Associates

Town meets Gown in Howard's new Interdisciplinary Research Building, which contains academic offices and laboratories along with ground-floor retail accessible to the general public. Laboratories and support spaces occupy the tall main block of the building, perpendicular to W Street, and the smaller wing at the northwest corner of the site that steps down toward Georgia Avenue. At the corner of Georgia and W is circular café space with a nearly cubic block of offices above, pivoted from the primary building grid to match the angle of the avenue.

Earth-toned terra cotta panels evoke the campus's red-brick past, while the glass curtain walls with narrow vertical fins look fresh and sophisticated.

Q14b
Lewis K. Downing Hall
2300 6th Street, NW

1952 — Hilyard Robinson and Paul R. Williams
2011 — Renovation: Bryant Mitchell Architects

Paul Revere Williams was the first Black member of the American Institute of Architects, its first Black Fellow, and the first Black architect to win the institute's Gold Medal (albeit posthumously). Based in Los Angeles, he broke numerous professional barriers and built a portfolio that included houses for members of Hollywood's white elite, such as Frank Sinatra and Lucille Ball. His work was featured in an exhibition at Howard University in 1931, and he was subsequently hired to design nine buildings on the campus in collaboration with local architect Hilyard Robinson. The Robinson/Williams works, including the Russell A. Dixon College of Dentistry Building (1954), Charles R. Drew Hall (1956), Ernest Everett Just Hall (1956), Cramton Auditorium (1961), and the Ira Aldridge Theater (1961), turned the campus into a hotbed of academic International Style architecture.

Downing Hall, which houses the College of Engineering and Architecture, is a case in point, with its simple massing, horizontal ribbon windows, and largely unadorned façades. In fact, the decorative elements visible today—the clock, the horizontal and vertical bars at one corner

of the tower, and the bas-relief sculpture on the south wing—were all added later. The numerous little vents between the bands of windows were also added, and while they serve practical purposes, they also do distract somewhat from the building's starkly minimalist aesthetic.

Q14c
Howard Hall
(General Oliver Otis Howard House)
607 Howard Place, NW

1867 — Architect unknown
1996 — Restoration: Oehrlein & Associates Architects

Howard Hall, a tall Second Empire mansion, is the oldest extant building on the campus. Built of hollow white bricks and later painted a succession of colors, it was the home of General Oliver O. Howard, a founder (and later president) of the university and a commissioner of the Freedmen's Bureau. The university purchased the house in 1909, and after years of neglect, it has now been fully restored.

Q14d
Andrew Rankin Memorial Chapel
6th Street and Howard Place, NW

1895 — Architect unknown

The exterior of the Gothic Revival Rankin Memorial Chapel is mostly understated, except for a bold corner tower whose spire is bracketed with dormers that have their own spiky roofs. The adjacent entryway is marked by a broad, pointed arch, with the initials "A.E.R.," for Andrew E. Rankin, and the words "Memo-

cated to liberty, there was no more appropriate design for Howard University's major building to emulate."

rial Chapel" carved into the stones. The interior, which somehow seems larger than expected, has a dark wood ceiling supported by arches resting on dramatically projecting brackets.

Q14e

Founders Library

500 Howard Place, NW

1939—Albert I. Cassell; Principal
  designer: Louis E. Fry Sr.

Founders Library is the most prominent building on campus by virtue of its location at one end of the main quadrangle and its 165-foot-tall clock tower. The building was modeled after Philadelphia's Independence Hall, and in this case, the principal designer of Founders Hall shed some light on the source of inspiration, saying that "since the Library was dedi-

Q15

Bryant Street Pumping Station

301 Bryant Street, NW

1904—Henry F. Brauns

The McMillan Reservoir supplies water to a large portion of DC. While areas downhill of the reservoir are fed by gravity, this facility was built to pump water uphill. It was designed in the Romanesque Revival style, which is often associated with somber structures of red brick or dark stone, but here, gray brick (with a subtle pinkish cast) and marble trim give the building a lighter countenance. On the main façade, the broad arched windows flanking the main entrance further lessen the building's apparent weight, while a row of porthole-like windows adds an almost whimsical touch. When the facility opened, the *Washington Post* proclaimed it "not only one of the largest and most

efficient, but also one of the handsomest buildings for such a purpose to be found in the United States."

Q16
LeDroit Park

Between Florida and Rhode Island Avenues, and 2nd and 7th Streets, NW

1873–77 — James McGill
2001 — Multiple renovations and new houses: Sorg and Associates
Numerous newer buildings by various architects

Although it was originally built as an exclusively white neighborhood, LeDroit Park has long played a key role in the cultural and social life of historically Black Howard University. The neighborhood was developed by Amzi L. Barber, one of the university's founders, who was white. In 1888, a group of Black neighbors, frustrated by having to walk around what was, in effect, a gated community, tore down part of the fence that surrounded it, and within a few years, the remaining fences and walls were dismantled and the area was integrated. It became a center of Black cultural life in the early 20th century, with residents including the poet Paul Laurence Dunbar, teacher and civil rights activist Mary Church Terrell, and the first elected mayor of DC, Walter E. Washington.

James McGill designed many of LeDroit Park's houses in the highly popular romantic styles of the period: Gothic Revival, Italianate, and Second Empire. The area remains largely intact, with some 50 of the original 64 dwellings still standing. The neighborhood was once marked by pastoral street names — Elm, Maple, and so on — that were later officially changed to fit the District's rational system of letters and numbers.

Q17
Howard Theatre

620 T Street, NW

1910 — J. Edward Storck
2012 — Renovation concept planning, design, and architects of record: Martinez + Johnson; Interior architects: Marshall Moya Design

The first major theater and music hall built primarily for Black Americans (predating New York's Apollo Theater by several years), the Howard helped make U Street a cultural mecca in the 1910s and '20s. It also played an important role in fostering emerging talent. Ella Fitzgerald, for one, got her start by winning an amateur night here in the 1930s.

Despite its initial success, the theater suffered multiple setbacks throughout the 20th century, closing briefly during the Great Depression and operating in fits and starts after desegregation. It closed indefinitely in the 1980s, and the building deteriorated badly over the ensuing decades. Miraculously, it reopened in 2013 following a comprehensive renovation, which included reconstructing exterior ornament and details that had been stripped away in the 1940s.

With its shallow front façade that extends above the roofline and slightly beyond the side walls of the plain brick structure behind it, the Howard is reminiscent of the "false front" commercial buildings of the Old West. Architectural excitement is largely limited to the central bay of the main façade, with two Corinthian columns supporting a round arch surmounted by twin light standards, which bracket a window with a shallower arch. Above that is a short attic window set into a break in the entablature, with an exaggerated keystone capping the parapet. On either side of the main arch are what appear to be two window frames in search of windows—a curious motif, but one that is consistent with the original design. Sadly, the historic interior of the theater was almost entirely lost; the renovation preserved the basic layout of the space but reinterpreted the original design in a more modern vein.

Progression Place

(United Negro College Fund Building / 7th Flats Apartments)

1805/1825 7th Street, NW

2012—Office section: Eric Colbert & Associates PC; Design concept: Devrouax + Purnell Architects
2013—Residential section: Eric Colbert & Associates PC

The Progression Place development introduced greater density and a mix of uses to a site immediately adjacent to a Metro station. The 205-unit residential component, with its main entrance at 1825 7th Street, is largely set back from the street front in order to preserve the character of a row of historic two-story commercial buildings, which were renovated as part of the project. The apartment building's buff brick and dark gray metal panels complement the historic masonry structures. The office component, at the southern end of the site, is sheathed in floor-to-ceiling glass and silvery metal panels, and its principal façades are canted outward to form an unusually dynamic composition (the two façades stop just short of meeting, creating a tapered bay at the corner). An acutely angled pavilion projects into the Metro station plaza, framing the space and providing a spot for signage announcing the building's principal occupant, the United Negro College Fund.

Just across the alley from the office building, at 641 S Street, is the former Wonder Bread Bakery, an excellent example of early 20th-century industrial architecture. The building was built in two phases—the two-story part in 1915 (by Simmons & Cooper) and the three-story addition in 1922 (by A. B. Mullett & Co.)—for Dorsch's White Cross Bakery, which explains the white-cross motifs at the tops of the columns and in the roof parapets.

Watha T. Daniel / Shaw Library

1630 7th Street, NW

2010—Davis Brody Bond

The previous branch library on this site was a rough and rude concrete bunker, built in an era in which "urban" architecture often meant "defensive" architecture. The new building is everything its predecessor was not: open, light-filled, inviting, and environmentally sustainable to boot. Its most prominent feature is a perforated, corrugated aluminum screen suspended in front of the south façade, which reduces solar heat gain and helps to protect the library's holdings from the fading effects of direct sunlight. At night, it filters the artificial light emanating from inside, turning the building into a kind of civic lantern. Much of the rest of the building is covered in translucent Kalwall panels, which achieve similar but complementary effects. The library's sustainable credentials include a substantial reliance on recycled materials and a green roof.

Q20

Asbury Dwellings
(former William McKinley Manual Training School / Shaw Junior High School)

Southeast corner of 7th Street and Rhode Island Avenue, NW

1900–11 — Henry Ives Cobb
1982 — Renovation and addition: Wanchul Lee Associates

At the turn of the 20th century, the DC school system embarked on an initiative to improve the quality of its facilities. To that end, it hired Chicago architect Henry Ives Cobb, whose impressive portfolio included several buildings for the University of Chicago, to design the new William McKinley Manual Training School, a vocational school for white students (Black vocational students attended the separate and inherently unequal Armstrong Manual Training School). Cobb's design, built in stages over a decade, is distinctive for the rather frenetic rhythm of its façades — especially the spirited row of interlocking semicircular arches running along the top floor. Ornamental flourishes, most notably the column capitals, are simplified versions of traditional motifs. The ornamentation

around the original main door at the corner of 7th Street and Rhode Island Avenue is reminiscent of work by Cobb's Chicago contemporary Louis Sullivan. Cobb moved his office to DC for a few years while working on this project as well as the campus plan for American University and the original Woodward & Lothrop department store on G Street downtown (he later moved permanently to New York).

After the McKinley school moved in 1928, this became Shaw Junior High School (which lent its name to the neighborhood). That school in turn moved to a new location in 1977. In the early 1980s, the DC government collaborated with the Asbury Methodist Church to convert the building into senior housing.

Q21

Bread for the City

1525 7th Street, NW

1906 — Arthur M. Poynton
1994 — Renovation and addition: Wiebenson & Dorman Architects
2011 — Addition: Wiebenson & Dorman Architects

The original building in this complex was built as a warehouse for the George M. Barker Company, which supplied lumber to Washington contractors in the early 20th century. The second-floor window with the Juliet balcony in the middle of the main façade was once a loading door serviced by a block-and-tackle pulley system. Bread for the City, a nonprofit food bank and social services agency, bought and renovated the building in the 1990s. An addition to the south of the historic building, dedicated in 2011, doubled the size of the facility. The addition was financed in large part by a grant from the DC government, using funds from the Tobacco Master Settlement Agreement of 1998, under which American tobacco manufacturers compensated state governments for medical costs associated with smoking-related illnesses. The new wing, which contains a medical clinic and related facilities, is marked by a perforated metal billboard proclaiming the organization's identity. A glass-lined atrium separates the old and new wings, allowing them to read as distinct elements and reducing the apparent scale of the complex.

Q22

City Market at O

Between O, P, 7th, and 9th Streets, NW

1881 — Original market: Jesse B. Wilson
2014–17 — New residential buildings and renovation of market: Shalom Baranes Associates
2014 — Hotel: Perkins Eastman

The historic market building that anchors this mixed-use complex is one of the last three such structures still standing in DC, though only the exterior walls are original — the roof of the then-abandoned structure collapsed under the weight of snow in 2003. The shell managed to remain standing long enough for the market to be resurrected (in the form of a modern grocery store) as part of a comprehensive redevelopment spanning two city blocks. All of the new buildings except the hotel at the southwest corner were designed by the same firm but are varied in their architectural expression. Most striking is the building immediately to the west of the market, with its chartreuse panels and cantilevered volumes. The project also reestablished a one-

block stretch of 8th Street that had been removed during a previous redevelopment in the mid-20th century.

Q23

Metropolitan Community Church of Washington DC

474 Ridge Street, NW

1992 — Suzane Reatig Architecture

One of the first entirely new structures in the country built expressly for an LGBTQ religious congregation, the Metropolitan Community Church of Washington DC was a harbinger of gentrification in this neighborhood. The church's auxiliary functions are housed in an L-shaped band along the two street façades, sheathed in split-face concrete block that relates to the texture of nearby masonry row houses. These wings embrace a bright and airy sanctuary of steel and glass, which is covered with a shallow barrel vault supported by delicate bowstring trusses. From the inside, at certain times of day, the sanctuary appears to be twice as long as it really is thanks to the use of reflective glass.

Q24

Ridge Place Co-Living

446–452 Ridge Street, NW

2018 — Suzane Reatig Architecture

Filling four previously vacant lots, this eight-unit residential complex is both a modern reinterpretation of historic DC row house typologies and a creative response to the site's zoning and historic preservation restrictions. The composition of the street façade reflects the rhythm of surrounding row houses, while the wood siding — rare in the city's innermost neighborhoods since building codes were changed in the 1870s to require masonry structures — is aptly con-

textual on this block, which includes several pre-1870 wood-clad houses. Vividly colored doors, suspended entrance canopies, and carefully positioned downspouts provide visual accents.

This is one of several staunchly modern, small-scale multifamily residential projects that architect Suzane Reatig has designed in the Shaw neighborhood, a number of them developed by the United House of Prayer for All People. Others include the row at 413–419 Ridge Street, just down from this site; 442–444 N Street, NW; and a larger apartment house at 625 Rhode Island Avenue, NW.

Q25

Paul Laurence Dunbar High School

101 N Street, NW

2013 — Perkins Eastman; Associate architects: Moody Nolan

Dunbar High School is the successor to the Preparatory High School for Colored Youth, founded in 1870 as the nation's first public high school for Black students. In 1916, after having been renamed for the poet Paul Laurence Dunbar, the school moved into a new Tudor Revival building at 1st and N Streets, NW, which the NAACP declared "The Greatest Negro High School in the World." Throughout the early to mid-1900s, Dunbar was noted for its academic excellence, high graduation rates, and prominent alumni.

The much-loved but decrepit 1916 building was razed in 1977 after the school moved into a new Brutalist building on a different corner of the site. The 1977 building was initially hailed as breath of fresh air but came to be described by countless students and teachers as prison-like, and while the issue of cause and effect can be complicated, there is no doubt that Dunbar's reputation plummeted in the following decades.

The current building was built on the site of the original Dunbar school and is everything its Brutalist predecessor was not. It is open and welcoming, with a broad forecourt leading to a glassy entrance framed by a modern portico. Its material palette of buff brick, cast stone, and dark metal-composite panels fits comfortably amid the mostly residential neighborhood while projecting an academic aura. It is too early to tell how the new facility will affect student achievement, but anecdotal evidence indicates that it has engendered a resurgence in school pride and satisfaction.

Meridian Hill

I n the late 1880s, former Missouri senator John Brooks Henderson, who had drafted the constitutional amendment abolishing slavery, built a gruff stone "castle" at the corner of 16th Street and what is now Florida Avenue, just beyond the "boundary" of L'Enfant's plan. His wife, Mary Foote Henderson, seemingly alarmed to find herself suddenly living in quasi-rural suburbia, soon began an audacious—and ultimately quite successful—campaign to turn the pastures around her house into a fashionable residential enclave. Mrs. Henderson thus became, in effect, one of the country's earliest female real estate developers, and however selfish her motivations, and despite numerous setbacks, her efforts yielded an extraordinary park and a collection of grand buildings that brought new glamour to the capital.

One of Mrs. Henderson's earliest ideas for improving her neighborhood was to try to convince Congress to declare the area Washington's official Embassy Row. She failed, but a few brave—or possibly intimidated—governments did establish outposts here. She later sought to have 16th Street rechristened the "Avenue of the Presidents"—she succeeded briefly in 1913, before Congress changed its collective mind and restored the numerical designation. Other ambitious schemes included commissioning Paul Pelz to design an imperially scaled new Executive Mansion for "her" hill and lobbying Congress to place the proposed new Lincoln Memorial there. Even though all of these initiatives came to naught, Mrs. Henderson nonetheless was highly successful in her broader goal of acquiring socially desirable neighbors. Meridian House, perhaps the most elegant private house in town, bears witness to her labors.

As for "Henderson Castle" itself, the main structure was demolished in 1949, leaving only the dark red stone retaining walls running along 16th Street and Florida Avenue. The site of the house is now occupied by the regrettably mundane Beekman Place condominiums.

The "Castle" of Senator John Henderson and Mary Foote Henderson once loomed over 16th Street at the base of Meridian Hill, just beyond the boundary of L'Enfant's original plan. All that remains of the estate today are the craggy walls along the public sidewalk.

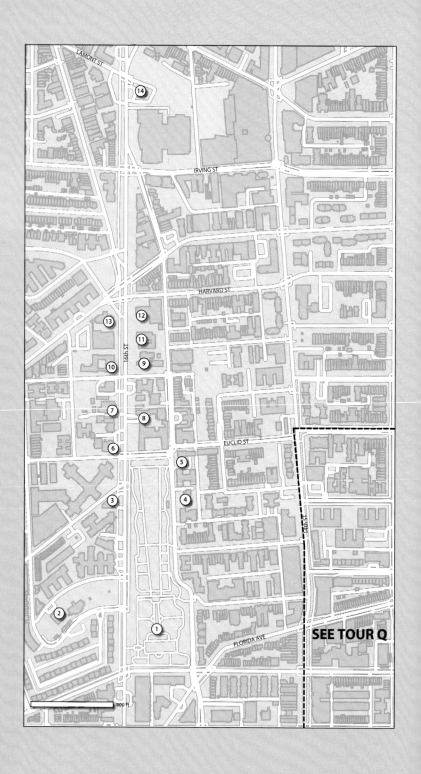

SEE TOUR Q

Meridian Hill Park

Between Florida Avenue and Euclid Street, and 15th and 16th Streets, NW

1912–36 — Horace W. Peaslee; Concrete designer: John Joseph Earley; Landscape architects: Vitale, Brinckerhoff & Geiffert; based on design by George Burnap
2006 — Various restorations: architrave, p.c., architects
2015 — Reconstruction of lodge: architrave, p.c., architects

Meridian Hill gets its name from one of the unofficial prime meridians — lines of longitude used as reference points for surveying or navigation — that run through DC, in this case, through the center line of the White House and thus 16th Street, NW. The "hill" is actually the edge of the fall line, a steep bluff that served as a natural boundary to L'Enfant's original plan for the city. The top of this bluff affords outstanding views of the capital's monumental core.

The Senate Park Commission Plan of 1901–2 proposed placing a park here, but it was ultimately the enterprising Mary Foote Henderson, whose own mansion was across the street, who succeeded in convincing Congress to buy the land in 1910. Construction of the park spanned two decades. Architect Horace Peaslee wrote that he based the park's lower level, with its axial plan, 13 stepped pools, and cascading falls, on "the Pincian Hill in Rome," though the Villa d'Este in Tivoli, Italy, also provided inspiration. The upper terrace is clearly French in spirit — flat for some 900 feet from the edge of the hill, it is centered on a broad grass mall with promenades and hedges culminating in a bronze statue of Joan of Arc.

The park is extraordinary for its reliance on rough exposed-aggregate concrete, rather than stone or brick, in its massive retaining walls, walks, and basins. The concrete elements were the work of John Joseph Earley, an inventive DC-based designer renowned for his concrete mosaics at the Franciscan Monastery [see T24] and elsewhere. As the city's chief engineer observed in 1926, "Meridian Hill Park is neither wholly architecture nor yet is it landscape design. There is nothing like it in this country." Miraculously, the park has survived more or less as Mrs. Henderson and Peaslee envisioned it, despite a period in the 1970s and '80s when it was a notorious haven for drug dealers and a symbol of racial and economic inequality. The real estate boom of the 1990s, abetted by a nationwide drop

in drug-related crime, led to rapid gentrification of the surrounding neighborhood and, in turn, to the park's rejuvenation. Today, despite those demographic shifts, diverse users enjoy the park for picnics, soccer games, yoga, and even some curious gymnastic activities.

Restoration work under the direction of Mills + Schnoering Architects is ongoing.

R2

Meridian House
(part of Meridian International Center)

1630 Crescent Place, NW

1923—John Russell Pope
1960—Alterations: Faulkner, Kingsbury & Stenhouse
1976—Alterations: Faulkner, Fryer & Vanderpool
1994—Renovation: Archetype

John Russell Pope designed Meridian House for Irwin Boyle Laughlin, heir to one of the country's greatest steel fortunes. Laughlin, a career diplomat, purchased the hilltop site in 1912 but postings abroad kept him from building anything until 1920. A recognized scholar of 18th-century French art, Laughlin worked closely with Pope on the project. A 1929 article on the building in *Architectural Record* commented, "Because of [Laughlin's] detailed knowledge of the art and

architecture of that period and because of his indefatigable interest in every detail, Meridian was immediately recognized as one of the finest examples of architecture in the French style in America." Laughlin continued the French themes out into the terraced garden, where pollarded linden trees and raked gravel strongly evoke the quietly elegant landscapes of Parisian palaces.

Laughlin maintained his interest in art and architecture throughout his life. He helped his friend Andrew Mellon organize the new National Gallery of Art and, according to David Finley, the gallery's first director, the steel heir influenced everything about the original building — also designed by Pope — including the choice of fountains for the garden courtyards and paint colors for the galleries. Laughlin died in 1941, just missing the National Gallery's opening.

Next door to the Meridian House is the White-Meyer House (1912), yet another Pope design. It was for many years the home of Eugene Meyer, owner of the *Washington Post*, and his wife, Agnes (their daughter, Katherine Graham, later became the newspaper's publisher). Both the Meridian House and the White-Meyer House are now parts of the Meridian International Center, an organization that promotes international understanding through cultural exchange and other programs.

R3

Old French Embassy
(now Council for Professional Recognition)

2460 16th Street, NW

1908—George Oakley Totten Jr.
1962—Renovation: Milton Scheimgarten

"Let me build an embassy for you." This was Mary Foote Henderson's simple offer to French ambassador Jean Jules Jusserand, who had been complaining about his country's current diplomatic quarters sometime around 1907. Monsieur Jusserand accepted, and Mrs. Henderson—thrilled to have landed such a prestigious tenant for her budding embassy row—called on George Oakley Totten Jr.

a prominent diplomatic mission, was converted into a run-of-the-mill rooming house. It was later the Embassy of Ghana and is now the headquarters of a nonprofit organization.

R4

Josephine Butler Parks Center

2437 15th Street, NW

1927 — George Oakley Totten Jr.

to design an appropriately French château for her future neighbors.

Totten responded with an opulent Beaux-Arts mansion in limestone with terra cotta trim. The design exploits the shape of the site — essentially a right triangle, with the hypotenuse facing the side street — to create a distinctive, vertically accentuated composition. A domed cylindrical tower anchors the right angle at the southeast corner, rather than the acutely angled northeast corner as one might expect. The short sides of the triangle (facing south and east) contain the principal rooms, while the hypotenuse is lined with circulation and service spaces. This arrangement seems odd now, but when the building was finished, there were no structures immediately to the south, so the rooms on that side had open views toward the city. Still, the long façade on the side street and the two short gabled ends facing north and west appear almost unfinished in contrast to the building's main elevations.

In 1936, the embassy moved to what is now the French ambassador's residence in Kalorama. Incredibly, within a few months, the Totten building, which had served for nearly three decades as

George Oakley Totten Jr., working on Mary Foote Henderson's dime, ended up designing nearly a dozen residences in the Meridian Hill area as part of his sponsor's grand plan to make the neighborhood a center of international society. Mrs. Henderson supposedly had this one constructed so as to block the city's plans to extend Clifton Street westward, potentially lopping off the northern portion of the adjacent Meridian Hill Park. Formerly the embassy of Hungary and later of Brazil, the building is now the headquarters of Washington Parks & People, as well as a venue for weddings and other events. It is named in honor of Josephine Butler, a community activist, a founder of the District of Columbia statehood movement, and an influential advocate of urban park revitalization, including the one across the street. The building's arched *porte-cochère*, yellow stucco walls, generous windows, and metal balcony railings lend it a decidedly Mediterranean air.

Stoiber + Associates is currently developing plans for a transformation of the building into a museum of the "greening" movement that Washington Parks & People envisions as the "Embassy of the Earth."

R5

Embassy of Ecuador

2535 15th Street, NW

1927—George Oakley Totten Jr.

Another of the speculative mansions developed by Mary Foote Henderson, the Embassy of Ecuador suggests that Totten was looking toward the 17th-century French architect François Mansart for inspiration here, at least for the elements above the cornice line (most notably, the tall mansard roof—a term derived from Mansart's name, after all). The rest of the façade is more modest, though Totten managed to create a good deal of interest in the main body of the building using only simple pilasters, a few vertical reveals, and barely articulated panels beneath the third-floor windows.

R6

Inter-American Defense Board
(Pink Palace)

2600 16th Street, NW

1906—George Oakley Totten Jr.
1912, 1920–27—Addition and alterations:
  George Oakley Totten Jr.
1923–86—Numerous alterations: various
  architects
1988—Addition: Frank Koppel

This neo-Venetian Gothic mansion, which acquired the nickname "Pink Palace" when its stucco walls were painted that color in the past, was the first building completed as part of Mary Foote Henderson's efforts to make Meridian Hill the center of Washington's social life. Notable residents included Secretary of the Treasury Franklin MacVeagh (before he moved down the street to 2829 16th Street) and Delia Spencer Caton Field, the extremely wealthy widow of Chicago retail mogul

Marshall Field. The building has been altered significantly, including the removal of several balconies on the principal façades and the enclosure of the formerly open-air galleries along the south face. Since 1949, it has been occupied by an international organization dealing with defense-related issues throughout the Americas.

R7

Cuban Embassy

2630 16th Street, NW

1918—Macneil & Macneil

The architectural origins of the Cuban Embassy offer a brief lesson in the arbitrariness of style. When Mary Foote Henderson sold this site to the Cuban government, she offered to throw in predeveloped plans for a five-story Elizabethan-style building designed by George Oakley Totten Jr. The Cubans declined the offer and hired the firm of

Macneil & Macneil instead. The architects apparently suggested something in a Spanish style, thinking it appropriate given the two countries' historic connections, but having only recently gained independence from the "mother country," the Cubans informed the architects that that was the last thing they wanted.

So that's how a Caribbean island nation with Spanish and African roots ended up with an embassy that looks like it could have been built for King Louis XVI of France. Two semi-octagonal bays frame the front façade, whose upper levels are lined with elegantly proportioned windows and lithe, tapering Corinthian pilasters. Sculptural panels above the second-floor windows and niches are models of tasteful ornament. While some elements, such as the *porte-cochère* and the open loggia on the south façade, suggest other European influences, the overall effect remains confidently French.

Between the world wars, the Cuban Embassy was a center of cultural and artistic life, including "moonlit garden parties" that attracted Washington's elite. After Fidel Castro came to power and the United States broke diplomatic relations with Cuba, the building was maintained by the Czechoslovakian government and then became the Cuban

Interests Section—sort of an unofficial embassy—under the auspices of the Swiss government. It was restored to full embassy status with the resumption of (strained) diplomatic relations in 2015.

Flanking the Cuban Embassy are the embassies of Lithuania (to the south, at 2622 16th Street) and Poland (to the north, at 2640 16th), both of which were designed by George Oakley Totten Jr. for Mary Foote Henderson. A portion of the Lithuanian Embassy was demolished in the 1960s and replaced by the current apartment building.

R8

Warder-Totten Mansion

2633 16th Street, NW

1888—Warder Residence: H. H. Richardson
1916—Totten Residence: George Oakley Totten Jr.
1925—Reconstruction of Warder Residence: George Oakley Totten Jr.
2002—Renovation/restoration: Sadler & Whitehead Architects / Commonwealth Architects

Benjamin Warder commissioned Henry Hobson Richardson's firm to design a house for him, but Richardson himself seems to have had a rather limited role in the project, which began construction just

two months before his death. The house originally stood on K Street between 15th and 16th Streets, NW. When George Oakley Totten Jr., himself a pupil of Richardson's, learned that the house was being demolished, he bought as many pieces of the original structure as possible from the wrecker, hauled them across town, and reassembled them in a slightly different configuration on this site, adjacent to his own quirky residence, which now stands at the center of the property. After years of neglect and abandonment, the building was renovated in 2002 and converted into a 38-unit corporate apartment complex, though as of this writing it looks as though the building still could use some TLC.

R9

Former Residence of the Ambassadors of Spain
(now Spain-USA Foundation)

2801 16th Street, NW

1923 — George Oakley Totten Jr.
1927 — Chancery addition: Jules Henri de Sibour
1949–65 — Renovations: architects unknown
2009 — Renovation: KCCT

Standing on the 16th Street sidewalk and staring at the former Spanish ambassador's residence, one is tempted to blink repeatedly, hoping that the building's massing, composition, and ornamental details will somehow begin to make sense. Alas, that will prove futile.

This was yet another project developed on a speculative basis by Mary Foote Henderson and designed by George Oakley Totten Jr. Squat and disjointed, the building appears as if Totten wasn't quite sure how many stories it should be. The third floor, for example, is set back from the front of the main block, weakening what could have been a commanding form, while the ballroom wing at the northwestern corner seems to be of a scale entirely unrelated to the rest of the structure. Stranger still are some of the ornamental details, such as the hat-shaped blank arch set into the third-floor parapet. Speaking of that parapet, it is punctuated by open railings with geometric designs whose origins — Islamic? Chinese? — remain a mystery. After this visual onslaught, the sedate chancery addition at the rear, by Jules Henri de Sibour, is a welcome relief.

Since 2009, the building has been occupied by the Spain-USA Foundation, which organizes exhibitions and cultural programs.

R10

Old Italian Embassy
(Modera Sedici)

2700 16th Street, NW

1925 — Warren & Wetmore, with Ambassador Gelasio Caetani

ca. 1930 — Addition to chancery wing: architect unknown
ca. late 1950s — Renovations: architects unknown
2018 — Renovation and addition: DCS Design

The Italian government bought the land for its new embassy from Mary Foote Henderson in 1923 — in the early days of Benito Mussolini's fascist regime — but did not choose her preferred architect to design the building. The commission instead went to the New York firm of Warren & Wetmore, though contemporary newspaper accounts suggested that then-ambassador Gelasio Caetani, who was an architect and engineer himself, played an active role in the project. The result, which was based, predictably enough, on Italian Renaissance precedents, is the most conventionally beautiful of all of the embassy buildings on the 16th Street row.

The building originally housed both the ambassador's residence, facing 16th Street, and the chancery, which was entered from Fuller Street. The chancery wing was later extended, and the connector between the two, initially an open loggia, was eventually filled in. The historic building was recently renovated and is now part of an apartment complex that includes a new mid-rise building at the rear.

R11

Mexican Cultural Institute
(former MacVeagh House / Mexican Embassy)

2829 16th Street, NW

1911 — Nathan C. Wyeth
1922 — Additions: Clarence L. Harding
1942 — Addition: Marcus Hallett

Commissioned by Emily MacVeagh as a surprise gift for her husband, Franklin, who was secretary of the treasury under William Howard Taft, this mansion is marked by a high ratio of wall to window area and rather oddly stretched proportions. After his wife died, MacVeagh made the building available to the federal government as a guesthouse for visiting dignitaries. In 1921, the Mexican govern-

ment purchased it for use as its embassy, and shortly thereafter added the boxy Italianate portico and a new office wing.

Mexico produced a number of great muralists, and the three-story stairwell of this building features colorful and richly layered murals by Roberto Cueva del Rio depicting the history of the country. The building now houses the embassy's cultural arm, which sponsors a variety of programs and events.

R12

All Souls Church, Unitarian

1500 Harvard Street, NW, at 16th Street

1924—Coolidge & Shattuck / Coolidge, Shepley, Bulfinch and Abbott
1936—Expansion: Ernest D. Stevens
1970—Alterations and addition: Grigg, Wood, and Browne
2015—Renovation: Kerns Group Architects

The architecture of All Souls Church, Unitarian is derived from the Baroque church of St. Martin-in-the-Fields on London's Trafalgar Square. The tall spires of All Souls, the Unification church across the street [see following entry], and the National Baptist Memorial Church (1924—Egerton Swartout) a block to the north make this stretch of 16th Street one of the most architecturally dramatic nongovernmental enclaves in the city. Originally established in 1821 as the First Unitarian Church of Washington, the All

Souls congregation has a long history of social activism, particularly in its early advocacy of the abolition of slavery and, more recently, in support for the civil rights movement and LGBTQ rights. The church's bell, which was moved from an earlier structure downtown, was cast by Paul Revere's son, Joseph, in 1822–23.

R13

Family Federation for World Peace and Unification—Family Church National Cathedral
(former Church of Jesus Christ of Latter-day Saints)

2810 16th Street, NW

1933—Don Carlos Young Jr. and Ramm Hansen
1977—Restoration: architect unknown

Severe and insistently vertical, this former Church of Jesus Christ of Latter-day Saints is reminiscent of the multispired Mormon Temple (no, not the Tabernacle—that's different) in Salt Lake City, but it also reflects the influence of Art Deco and the stripped classicism so prevalent in the 1930s. One of the architects, Don Young, was a grandson of Brigham Young, the influential successor to church founder Joseph Smith. The bird's-eye marble that covers the church was quarried in Utah. Rather surprisingly, the underlying structure is steel frame. The building is now owned by the controversial Unification Church of Sun Myung Moon.

R14

3149 16th Street, NW

1930 — George Oakley Totten Jr.

This faux château was the last of the embassy buildings commissioned by Mary Foote Henderson, and its timing was inauspicious. It was completed after the onset of the Great Depression and just a year before Mrs. Henderson's death. Long known generically as "Embassy Building No. 10," it never found a buyer or tenant for that purpose. It was used as a boarding house during the Depression and occupied by what is now the DC Department of Parks & Recreation (DPR) from 1943 to 2012.

In plan the building is V-shaped, with the two wings meeting at the round turret and a grand staircase filling most of the notch between the wings. The conical roof of the turret is truncated to match the height of the adjacent gables. The delicate metal finials running along the crest of the roof are among the building's many elegant details, while the grotesques— carved faces in this case—at the endpoints of the rectilinear hoods over the second-floor windows add humorous notes.

In 2020, DPR announced that it would lease the building to Junior Achievement of Greater Washington. Plans for a renovation and addition by Gensler have been approved by the Historic Preservation Review Board, but the project was delayed by the COVID-19 pandemic.

Woodley Park / Cleveland Park / Van Ness

I n the 19th century, many people believed that low-lying urban areas harbored "miasmic vapors"—mysterious gases that somehow caused illness, especially during hot, humid weather. An easy solution for Washingtonians who had the wherewithal was to seek weekend or summer refuge in the nearby sylvan highlands. Though now considered quite close to downtown, Cleveland Park and Woodley Park were, in those days, unquestionably "in the country," and they were popular sites for second houses of wealthy city dwellers. Named after a prominent summer visitor (Grover Cleveland, who often stayed at Red Top, now demolished) and a specific estate (Woodley, built by Philip Barton Key), these areas gradually developed into bucolic, close-in suburbs replete with commodious, detached houses. Today they are among the most storied neighborhoods in the city, popularly—and not inaccurately—associated with well-to-do professionals with a penchant for driving European cars and listening to National Public Radio. Meanwhile, the Woodley Park and Cleveland Park commercial strips along Connecticut Avenue attract patrons from throughout the city, while the National Zoo and Rock Creek Park, which rambles nearby, are major recreational attractions for the entire region.

Just up from Cleveland Park is the Van Ness neighborhood. In the early 20th century, this was a pastoral area that included the campus of the National Bureau of Standards (NBS). Commercial development along the Connecticut Avenue corridor picked up after World War II, and when the NBS moved to suburban Maryland in the 1960s, a portion of its former campus soon became the home of the Washington Technical Institute (later incorporated into the University of the District of Columbia). The remainder of the campus was given to the State Department, which developed it into an enclave of foreign embassies.

TOURS

Easter Monday was a popular day for a stroll at the National Zoo in the early 1900s.

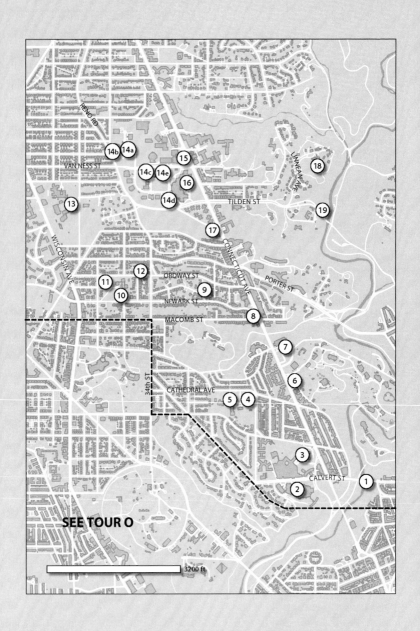

SEE TOUR O

3200 ft

S1

Duke Ellington Bridge
(Calvert Street Bridge)

Calvert Street over Rock Creek, NW

1935 — Paul Philippe Cret

One of several notable bridges in the area, this handsome structure, with wide sidewalks and graceful stone-covered concrete arches, carries motorists and pedestrians over Rock Creek, which gurgles along more than 100 feet below. The pedestals at the ends of the bridge are decorated with stylized sculptures symbolizing travel by air, rail, water, and highway. Unfortunately, the bridge, which was named in Duke Ellington's honor following his death in 1974, became a platform for suicides, leading to the addition of spiky metal railings, which, though reasonably well integrated, greatly diminish the pleasure of crossing.

S2

Omni Shoreham Hotel

2500 Calvert Street, NW

1930 — Joseph Abel
1935 — Addition: Joseph Abel / Dillon and Abel
1946–64 — Numerous alterations and additions: various architects
1997–2000 — Renovation: BBGM; Interiors: Hughes Design Associates
2008 — Renovation of ballroom and guestrooms: BBGM
2014 — Renovation of lobby and function spaces: Champalimaud Design
2019 — Renovation of guestrooms: Van Dresser Company

The exterior of the Shoreham is a somewhat timid rendition of jazz-age architecture, bearing hints of Art Deco and Renaissance Revival, but its siting on a bluff overlooking Rock Creek Park makes it feel a bit like a mountain resort in the heart of the city. In its heyday, this was one of those places that attracted countless famous performers and guests, from Rudy Vallee to the Beatles. As was often true for hotels of its era, the property initially included rental apartments, but here, somewhat unusually, apartments and hotel rooms were mixed together on most floors. The original plan above ground level was a double plus-sign, an arrangement that afforded good views from most every unit. The building was gradually converted to exclusive hotel use beginning in the mid-20th century, and numerous additions have changed the character of the campus.

S3

Wardman Tower

2660 Connecticut Avenue, NW

1928 — Mihran Mesrobian
Numerous alterations: various architects
2017 — Renovation: Deborah Berke Partners

The Wardman Tower was built as an apartment annex to the original Wardman Park Hotel, completed about 10 years earlier. Developer Harry Wardman tore down his own house to make way for the tower, which enjoyed a bucolic but still convenient setting that quickly made it one of the most prestigious addresses in Washington. The roster of famous residents remains unmatched by any other single structure in the capital save the White House, and includes former president Herbert Hoover, future president Lyndon Johnson, a bevy of cabinet officials, and more senators than you could shake a gavel at.

Beginning in 1973, the apartments were gradually converted to transient use, relegating the tower to secondary status as part of the larger complex. A few years later, the original Wardman Park Hotel next door was demolished and replaced by the current red-brick behemoth. Then, in recent years, things came full circle when the majority of space in the tower was split off, renovated, and reopened as a high-end condominium. (As of this writing, the huge hotel next door is closed indefinitely.)

The tower's design, by Mihran Mesrobian, skillfully diminishes the apparent bulk of the cross-shaped building while establishing a tone of posh domesticity. Subtle brick quoins modulate the scale of the tower at the corners, while vertical stacks of balconies balance the building's great breadth. Mesrobian's cleverest design move, though, was the incorporation of diagonal bays at the intersection of the two cross axes, thereby reducing the apparent length of each wing while providing prime spots for what are now, once again, grand parlors with spectacular views from the upper floors.

Characteristically Swiss in its no-nonsense modesty, this chancery could almost be confused with a relatively refined suburban elementary school. Designed late in William Lescaze's career, the structure suggests the influence of Ludwig Mies van der Rohe, with a simple office block of buff-colored brick and steel-and-glass pavilions housing more ceremonial spaces. Lescaze, who was born in Switzerland and immigrated to America in 1920, is best known for the Philadelphia Saving Fund Society (PSFS) Building (1932), which was designed in partnership with George Howe and widely acknowledged as the first International Style skyscraper in the United States.

S4a
Swiss Ambassador's Residence
Swiss Chancery grounds

2006 — Steven Holl Architects and Rüssli Architekten

The ambassador's residence, designed by a Swiss-American team led by Justin Rüssli and Steven Holl, may be just as reticent as the chancery, yet it is far more striking. In plan, the house is a slightly skewed and distorted Swiss cross set on a rectangular podium. Such apparently literal symbolism would be surprising in Holl's typically abstract work, but given the building's quasi-public function and the Swiss penchant for spending time outdoors, the shape has a certain logic to it. The building comfortably accommodates groups of different sizes, whether just a few people gathering in one wing or a large group spread throughout the public spaces on the first floor. The plan also allows each public room to be adjacent to at least one outdoor

S4
Embassy of Switzerland Chancery
2900 Cathedral Avenue, NW

1959 — William Lescaze
1975–2001 — Various renovations: architects unknown
2004 — Renovation: Leo Boeckl and Herbert Furrer
2008–15 — Minor renovations: architects unknown

terrace, while ensuring that all rooms have access to plenty of natural light.

The building's predominant materials — integrally colored gray concrete and sandblasted structural glass planks — abstractly evoke the wintry landscape of alpine Switzerland. Up close, one can see that the concrete, which appears smooth from a distance, is actually horizontally striated, in contrast to the verticality of the glass planks. Clear windows penetrate the sandblasted glass at irregular intervals; in some areas, the sandblasted glass continues across an opening in the wall, admitting filtered light to the interior.

S5

Woodley
(Maret School Main Building)

3000 Cathedral Avenue, NW

1801 — Philip Barton Key, owner-builder
1867, 1900 — Additions: architects unknown
1929 — Additions to front portico: Wolcott Waggaman
1952 — Renovation: architect unknown
1995, 1999 — Interior renovations: Charles E. Anthony

The oldest building on what is now the Maret School campus — and one of the oldest in the neighborhood — is a boxy Federal-style house built for Philip Barton Key. Ironically, given that his nephew, Francis Scott Key, would become a patriotic icon after a poem he wrote in 1814 was adapted as the lyrics of the national anthem, Uncle Philip was a loyalist who joined the British army during the Revolutionary War. He was captured and imprisoned by American forces and then fled to England upon being paroled. Key later returned to the United States, renounced his allegiance to the Crown, and eventually redeemed himself sufficiently in the eyes of his fellow Americans to get elected to Congress representing Maryland. He reportedly modeled this mansion on Woodley Lodge, an 18th-century manor house that he had visited in Reading, England. Key's estate went on to serve as the summer White House for several presidents, including Martin Van Buren and Grover Cleveland, and housed a number of prominent cabinet members. In 1946, then-owner Henry Stimson, former secretary of war, gave Woodley to the Phillips Academy Andover. The Maret School acquired the property in 1950.

S6

Smithsonian National Zoological Park

3001 Connecticut Avenue, NW

1890 — Initial layout based on plan by Frederick Law Olmsted, further developed by Frederick Law Olmsted Jr. and John Charles Olmsted
Various buildings and renovations by numerous architects

Established in 1889 and incorporated into the Smithsonian Institution the following year, the National Zoo was born of an initiative to create a "city of refuge" for bison and other endangered American species. The zoo's basic plan reflects the vision of landscape architect Frederick Law Olmsted, who worked with Smithsonian secretary Samuel P. Langley and animal curator William T. Hornaday on the project. Hornaday resigned in 1890 over disagreements with the secretary about the design, but Langley continued to develop the plan in collaboration with Olmsted, and later with Olmsted's sons, Frederick Jr. and John.

The earliest building on the zoo's grounds actually long predates the insti-

tution. It is the Holt House, believed to have been built in the 1810s as a suburban villa. The house was used by the zoo as administrative offices for many years but is now desperately in need of restoration. Many of the zoo's most interesting buildings date to the Great Depression, including the Reptile House (1931—Albert Harris), designed in a Byzantine-Romanesque manner; the Small Mammal House (1937—Edwin Hill Clark), inspired by Italian Renaissance precedents; and the Elephant House (1937—Edwin Hill Clark), recognizable for its great neoclassical arched entry portals. Other landmarks include the Great Flight Cage (1963—Daniel, Mann, Johnson & Mendenhall) and the Conservation Pavilion (2018—Quinn Evans Architects).

S7

Kennedy-Warren Apartments

3133 Connecticut Avenue, NW

1931—Joseph Younger
1935—Addition: Alexander Sonnemann, based on plans by Joseph Younger
2004—Restoration and addition: Hartman-Cox Architects; Interior design: Johnson-Berman, Hartman Design Group
2012—Renovation of original building: Hartman-Cox Architects

The Kennedy-Warren represents the zenith of Art Deco architecture in the nation's capital. Named after its developers, who, like so many of their cohort, went bankrupt during the Great Depression, the building is richly ornamented without seeming as frenzied as many other works of the same era and style. The welcoming forecourt, jazzy aluminum marquee, exuberant lobby, and ornate ballroom give the apartment house a decidedly theatrical air.

The building is even larger than it first appears. Taking advantage of the dramatic slope of the land at the northern and eastern sides of the site, there are six floors below the entrance level, including two floors of apartments, a ballroom, and several levels of parking and service spaces. In the days before air-conditioning was common, the building featured an innovative ventilation system that used giant fans at the lower levels to suck in cool air from the park floor and distribute it through the corridors.

More than 70 years after the building's opening, the owner obtained necessary approvals to build the unrealized south wing that had been part of the initial plan. The addition is remarkable in its impeccable replication of the original's buff brick, aluminum spandrel panels, and other details, though the apartments differ from the earlier ones in size and character.

expanses of glass and, on south-facing windows, solar shading devices. The sides are also less monumental than the front, incorporating elements that evoke the scale and proportions of neighboring houses.

S9
Highland Place

Between Newark Street and 34th Street, NW

Late 19th to early 20th centuries—Various architects

Romantic architecture, copious porches, and yards full of majestic, gnarled oaks make Highland Place one of the most picturesque streets in the city. Sequestered in the middle of a city block and easily overlooked, it is unknown even to many longtime Washingtonians. Several of the houses are interesting on their own, but the street warranted a collective entry in this book because of the houses' overall quality and intriguing variations on a similar architectural vocabulary.

S8
Cleveland Park
Neighborhood Library

3310 Connecticut Avenue, NW

2018—Perkins Eastman DC; Associate architects: Perkins Eastman

While Cleveland Park is renowned for its glorious turn-of-the-20th-century houses, the neighborhood's main commercial strip along Connecticut Avenue, NW, largely dates from the 1930s and boasts plenty of Art Deco and Art Moderne buildings to prove it. The design of the new DC Public Library branch at one end of the strip alludes to architectural motifs of that era with its tall portal-like windows and its rounded corner where the Connecticut Avenue and Newark Street façades meet. The side façades are more overtly contemporary, with large

Although Highland Place is called out here, nearby streets, including Newark, should not be overlooked. This portion of Cleveland Park is among the richest architectural troves in the city.

S10

Rosedale

3501 Newark Street, NW

ca. 1730s — Original cottage: builder unknown
1794 — Uriah Forrest, owner-builder
2003 — Addition and renovation: Muse Architects

Rosedale was the summer retreat of General Uriah Forrest and his wife, Rebecca, whose house in Georgetown was the site of the crucial dinner party at which George Washington convinced prominent area landowners to sell property to the government for the new capital city. When Forrest bought this property, it included a modest stone cabin that some historians believe may have been built before 1740, which, if so, would make it the oldest extant structure in DC. The cottage has been modified countless times, however, and was eventually incorporated into the new farmhouse that Forrest built in the 1790s.

In 1917, Chicago industrialist Avery Coonley and his wife, Queene Ferry Coonley, rented Rosedale from Forrest's descendants. The Coonleys asked Frank Lloyd Wright, who had designed a famous house for them in Riverside, Illinois, for his opinion of the Rosedale farmhouse, and he declared it to be "good for its time," endorsing its preservation. Queene bought the estate in 1920 after Avery's death and maintained the property for nearly four decades. Upon her death in 1958, the property passed to her daughter, Elizabeth, and son-in-law, architect Waldron Faulkner.

The estate's next owner was the National Cathedral School [see O30], which built dormitories for boarding students on the northern part of the site but maintained the southern part as a de facto park open to the community. When the subsequent owner, the nonprofit Youth for Understanding, put the property up for sale in 2002, neighbors worried that the green space they had long enjoyed might be rendered inaccessible — or, worse, fully developed — by a new owner, so a group of them got together and raised $12 million to buy the site. The historic farmhouse was renovated and returned to residential use, the dormitories were demolished, a portion of the property along Ordway Street was subdivided and developed as single-family houses, and the valued green space was placed in trust to be preserved in perpetuity.

Waldron / Winthrop Faulkner Houses at Rosedale

Ordway and 36th Streets, NW

1937–40 — Waldron Faulkner
1964–78 — Winthrop Faulkner

Waldron Faulkner, the son-in-law of Avery and Queene Ferry Coonley, designed two houses in the 1930s at the edge of his in-laws' Rosedale estate [see previous entry]: his own house, at 3415 36th Street, and another, at 3419 36th. The original houses were stylistic hybrids, essentially modern but incorporating ancient Greek and Art Deco motifs. Both have been greatly expanded since.

Waldron's sons Avery and Winthrop also became architects. Winthrop designed two clusters of houses bracketing those by his father, including 3530 and 3540 Ordway, built in the 1960s, and the triplets at 3403, 3407, and 3411 36th Street, built in the 1970s. The later three houses incorporated solar panels on their roofs—a very uncommon feature at the time, installed in response to the energy crisis that began earlier in the decade.

S12

Slayton House

3411 Ordway Street, NW

1960 — I. M. Pei & Associates; Associated architect: Thomas W. D. Wright
2003 — Renovation: Hugh Newell Jacobsen; Landscape architect: Jay Graham
2010 — Renovation: Maurice Walters Architect; Interior design: FORMA Design

A trio of barrel vaults peeks out impishly from behind a plain brick wall, inviting observant passersby to stop and investigate the unexpected form on an otherwise typical Cleveland Park street. Standing amid a well-landscaped garden is a modern pavilion rendered in concrete, brick, and glass. The house was one of a small number of private residences designed by the firm of I. M. Pei, architect of the National Gallery of Art's East Building. The client, urban planner William Slayton, managed this coup because he was a colleague of Pei's at the time (Slayton later served as commissioner of the Urban Renewal Administration, where he instituted rules to combat racial discrimination in housing, and as executive vice president of the American Institute of Architects, where he oversaw the construction

of the organization's new headquarters). He was locally renowned as the centerpiece of the "Slayton Irregulars," an amorphous group of architects and related professionals who often got together for conversation and lengthy meals.

The house is a zigzag in section—a sort of trilevel plus basement—with the main living space in front facing the street, two bedrooms on the upper level toward the rear, and a dining room, kitchen, and guest room below. As renovated by Hugh Newell Jacobsen, the house was remarkably improved while remaining true to Pei's fundamental intent. The top level of the central bay, for instance, which was originally enclosed, is now an open library and sitting area, allowing views from the front yard all the way through the house. Since then, a new owner has made additional changes while retaining the open layout.

S13

Sidwell Friends Middle School

3825 Wisconsin Avenue, NW (rear of Middle School is visible from 37th Street between Quebec and Tilden Streets)

1950 — Irwin S. Porter & Sons, Architects & Engineers; Associate architect: Arthur B. Heaton
1970 — Renovation and addition: Cope & Lippincott
2006 — Renovation and addition: KieranTimberlake

The Sidwell Friends Middle School, on the main campus of the prestigious, Quaker-run Sidwell Friends School, was the first building in DC—and the first K–12 educational facility in the United States—to be awarded LEED (Leadership in Energy and Environmental Design) Platinum certification. The project began with an existing two-story brick structure that was renovated—as minimally as possible, to avoid wasting energy and materials—and incorporated into the three-story addition. The addition is largely sheathed in reclaimed wood, including vertical slats on the main west-facing wall to reduce heat gain from the afternoon sun. Where the old and new structures meet, some of these wood slats extend down over the windows of the existing building, literally embracing it. On the south-facing wall of the new wing, horizontal louvers shield the interior from the sun's heat while allowing filtered light to enter the adjacent spaces. The building has a green roof, of course, as well as solar chimneys, which vent hot air from classrooms on multiple levels. Nestled between the old and new wings is a terraced courtyard that the architects describe as a "constructed wetland," which filters gray water for reuse in the building.

S14

International Chancery Center

Both Sides of Van Ness Street between Connecticut Avenue and Reno Road, NW

1970-present—Initial plan: Edward D. Stone Jr. and Associates; Landscape architects: Oehme, van Sweden & Associates

In the 1960s, as foreign governments were clamoring for more space for their Washington outposts and real estate pressures were making inner-city neighborhoods less viable for such facilities, the State Department began seeking a large tract of land to accommodate a number of completely new embassy buildings. The chosen site, formerly occupied by the National Bureau of Standards, was divided into 23 one-acre plots, plus one larger parcel that was set aside for Intelsat. The State Department decreed that each embassy must be of essentially domestic scale and somehow reflect the architectural character of the home country. The result is the International Chancery Center, though a better name for this suburban assemblage of disparate, detached buildings might be "Embassy Acres." Although a few buildings in the complex stand out, most are dreadful pastiches of pseudo-vernacular forms.

S14a

Embassy of Nigeria Chancery

3519 International Court, NW

2002—Shalom Baranes Associates

In approaching the Nigerian chancery, the visitor first passes alongside a sweeping limestone-clad wall that closely adheres to the curve of the street. Although this is the rear façade of the chancery, and it reflects the setback requirements common to all of the embassies in the International Center, its detailing, its fenestration pattern, and especially its respect for the street line make this one of the more urbane buildings in the complex. Around front, the primary façade, which is rectilinear and unpretentious, culminates in a modest, angular tower that houses a ceremonial "grand hall." In the middle of the building is a glass atrium that unites the curving wing and the rectilinear wing. The basic plan abstractly refers to a common West African building typology, in which separate structures surround a courtyard covered with a communal roof.

S14b

Embassy of Brunei Darussalam

3520 International Court, NW

1999—RTKL Associates

Brunei Darussalam is a tiny sultanate on the island of Borneo in the South China Sea, and both the country and its monarch virtually ooze wealth thanks to huge deposits of oil and gas. The design of this chancery draws not only on building strategies that are common in Southeast Asia, such as post-and-beam construction and steeply pitched roofs, but also on forms that are more particularly asso-

ciated with Brunei. The chancery's most direct antecedent is the "Kampung Ayer," or "Water Village," in Brunei's capital city, which is filled with simple gable-roofed houses on stilts.

S14c

Embassy of the People's Republic of China, Chancery Building

3505 International Place, NW

2008—Pei Partnership Architects with I. M. Pei Architect; Associate architects: China IPPR Engineering International

Famed Chinese American architect I. M. Pei collaborated with his sons' firm to design the new chancery of China. It is by far the largest building in the International Chancery Center, with more than 115,000 square feet of space. Clad in French limestone with relatively few windows and virtually no ornament, the building appears substantial but nondescript from most viewpoints. Along the Van Ness Street façade, the only sign that this structure is anything

out of the ordinary is a huge, open-air, diamond-shaped frame that emerges from the wall plane. This serves as a clue not only to the building's signature planning motifs but also to its authorship, since 45-degree angles and rotated squares have figured prominently in other works by the senior Pei, such as the Museum of Islamic Art in Qatar, and by his sons, such as the Suzhou Museum in China.

The main entrance is off International Place, a short L-shaped street entirely within the international compound. A circular transparent dome—the only hint of glitz in the entire project—is suspended over the driveway to create a partial *porte-cochère*. Immediately inside the door is the entrance hall, one of three circulation nodes with 45-degree chamfered corners and topped by square skylit towers that are also offset at 45 degrees. Public rooms, including a banquet hall and a 200-seat auditorium, occupy the central section of the building, with offices in the east and west wings. Several key rooms also have chamfered corners and light fixtures that recapitulate the rotated-square motif.

The chancery was built entirely by Chinese workers who were brought to the United States solely for this project. For years, they could be seen in unmarked vans being shuttled between the construction site and an anonymous motel where they were all housed for the duration.

S14d

Kuwait Cultural Office
(former Embassy of Kuwait Chancery)

3500 International Drive, NW

1982—Skidmore, Owings & Merrill

One of the first buildings in the new International Center enclave was the sleekly geometrical Kuwaiti chancery, which now houses the Kuwait Cultural Office. As with the new Chinese chancery, this building employs 45-degree angles as a compositional motif in both plan and elevation. Although relatively small, the structure has great presence thanks to the cantilever shielding its glassy corner entrance and the bold diagonal struts on the second floor. In certain light, an elaborate filigree screen in the lobby can be seen from the outside.

S14e
Embassy of Singapore Chancery
3501 International Place, NW

1993—RTKL Associates

With its cruciform plan, low-pitched roof, broad eaves, and horizontally striated façades, this chancery inevitably suggests a debt to Frank Lloyd Wright's Prairie Style houses, but the resemblance is accidental. Such forms are also characteristic of the vernacular buildings of Singapore (of course, Wright's work was strongly influenced by Asian architecture, so the correlation is understandable). The result, however, is a chancery that reflects certain building traditions of both the home and the host countries without resorting to hokey, superficial imitation.

S15
UDC Student Center
Northwest corner of Connecticut Avenue and Van Ness Street, NW

2016—CannonDesign in association with Marshall Moya Design

The new Student Center for the University of the District Columbia (UDC) demonstrates how a well-designed building can mend earlier architectural and planning mistakes. UDC's main campus, which opened in 1981, consists almost entirely of monotonous and forbidding Brutalist structures surrounding ill-defined outdoor spaces. The campus's original plan also virtually ignored Connecticut Avenue, leaving a prominent gap in the streetscape. The Student Center fills in that gap, reinforcing the built fabric of the neighborhood while creating a new gateway to the campus. The design also balances institutional and public aspects of the project: the clock tower and atrium clearly mark this as an academic building, for instance, but the broad staircase leading from the street-level plaza at the northern end of the site to the upper-level quadrangle invites the public to pass through the campus, thus maintaining a popular pathway long used by area residents walking to and from the adjacent Metro station. The copper-colored panels on the main façades complement the campus's prevailing beige concrete while adding a welcome warmth.

Whittle School and Studios
(former Intelsat Headquarters)

3400 International Drive, NW

1988 — John Andrews International;
Associated architects: Notter Finegold
+ Alexander
2020 — Renovation and expansion: Renzo
Piano Building Workshop

A rare example of high-tech architecture in Washington, this assemblage of steel-and-glass pods and cylindrical glass-block stair towers was built as the headquarters of Intelsat, a telecommunications satellite consortium. The building incorporates a number of environment-conscious features, including a network of atria that bring natural light to interior spaces, roof gardens that enhance insulation and minimize unnecessary water runoff, and shimmering sunscreens that reduce thermal gain. Without being overly literal about it, the precisely honed structure suggests a flotilla of spacecraft.

Intelsat moved its headquarters to northern Virginia in 2014, and the building was renovated by Italian architect Renzo Piano to serve as the DC campus of a for-profit private school.

S17

Sedgwick Gardens

3726 Connecticut Avenue, NW

1932 — Mihran Mesrobian
2018 — Renovation: Bonstra | Haresign
Architects

One of the great Depression-era apartment houses lining Connecticut Avenue, Sedgwick Gardens is an exotic concoction of Moorish, Byzantine, and Art Deco motifs, with a hint of Tudor Revival thrown in for good measure. In plan, it consists of two roughly U-shaped wings splayed to align with the avenue and with Sedgwick Street, respectively, and joined along an axis that bisects the street corner. That axis begins with the *porte-cochère*, composed of four octagonal columns crowned with light fixtures and supporting a flat canopy edged with decorative carvings (with complementary light fixtures masquerading as brackets below). Above the doorway is a large archway filled with stone tracery in a geometric pattern and framed by two slender, robed female figures. Marble-backed niches at the third-floor level and various sculptural panels along the rooftop parapet animate the main façades. The recently restored lobby is worth a peek if the building's security staff doesn't mind.

S18

Hillwood Estate, Museum, and Gardens

4155 Linnean Avenue, NW

1926 — John Deibert; Landscape architects: Willard Gebhart and Rose Greely

1955–65 — Landscape architects: Innocenti & Webel; Perry Wheeler

1957 — Renovation: Alexander McIlvaine with McMillan, Inc., French & Company, and Kapp and Nordholm; Outbuildings: Murphy and Locraft

1959 — Guesthouse and swimming pool: Arthur P. Davis

1969 — Dacha: Walter Peter Jr.

1978 — Greenhouse renovation: Lord & Burnham

1985 — Adirondack Building: O'Neil & Manion Architects

1986 — Café: O'Neil & Manion Architects

1988 — Conversion of chauffeur's house to library: Fisher Gordon Architects and John McKean Associates

1994 — Renovation of Dacha and Adirondack Building: Quinn Evans Architects

1998 — Visitor Center and renovation of Greenhouse: Bowie Gridley Architects; Visitor Center schematic design: Quinn Evans Architects; Restoration of Japanese Garden: Zen Associates

1999 — Renovation of French garden: Richard Williams Architect

2000 — Restoration of main house: Bowie Gridley Architects; Preservation architects: Oehrlein & Associates

2005 — Restoration of C. W. Post Center: Dynerman Whitesell Architects

2015–21 — C. W. Post Courtyard renovation, Visitor Center Conservatory, Collections and Research Center, and Dina Merrill Pavilion: EwingCole

This multifaceted museum complex is the legacy of cereal heir Marjorie Merriweather Post, who in 1955 bought what was then known as Arbremont, a red-brick, neo-Georgian mansion standing amid 25 acres of gardens and woods, and promptly changed the estate's name to Hillwood. She then embarked on what might be called, in contemporary parlance, an "extreme makeover" to create a showcase for her unparalleled collections of French and Russian art.

Post had begun collecting French decorative arts while she was in her 30s and still married to her second husband, financier E. F. Hutton, who took over her family's company and turned it into General Foods Corporation. She divorced Hutton in 1935 and soon married Joseph E. Davies, who became the American ambassador to the Soviet Union. While living in Moscow, Post developed a love of Russian imperial art, examples of which she was able to amass easily in exchange for the hard currency the Soviets then desperately needed. After divorcing Davies, Post (who eventually returned to using her maiden name after her fourth and final marriage to Herbert May) bought the estate that was to become her favorite project.

Mrs. Post, as she is still reverentially called by many Hillwood staff members decades after her death, terrorized workers for years, micromanaging the remodeling of the mansion to ensure that it would provide the perfect architectural complement to her collections. On the interior, the result is sort of a Beverly Hills take on the 18th-century French mode — the materials are impeccable, and most of the details quite credible, but one gets the (accurate) sense that the lavish rooms were fundamentally incompatible with the character and proportions of the Georgian-style house into which they were inserted. At any rate, meanwhile, Post was commanding various landscape designers and architects to add a French parterre, a Japanese garden, a rose garden, and so on to the rolling grounds. Once Hillwood finally met her standards, she began to fill it with her treasures, including an array of Russian Orthodox icons and a clutch of Fabergé eggs.

Upon her death in 1973, Post bequeathed Hillwood to the Smithsonian Institution along with a substantial endowment, but the Smithsonian deemed the funds insufficient to support the conversion of the estate to a museum, and in 1976 returned the property to the Post Foundation, which, fortunately, made a go of it. Additions to the estate since then include a building modeled after Post's camp in the Adirondacks, where she kept a significant collection of Indigenous American artifacts, and a Russian dacha.

S19

Peirce Mill

2401 Tilden Street, NW

ca. 1829 — Isaac Peirce, builder
1936 — Restoration: Thomas T. Waterman; Landscape architect: Malcolm Kirkpatrick
1960s — Restoration: architect unknown
2011 — Rehabilitation: Quinn Evans Architects

Rock Creek's formerly strong current once powered eight separate mills grinding corn, rye, oats, and wheat grown by local farmers. The 1932 *Washington Sketch Book*, in fact, observed that the creek "was originally a racing stream, deep enough where it flowed into the Potomac to anchor seagoing ships," but "gradually the little harbor filled up." Simultaneously, changes in land use spelled extinction for major local agricultural enterprises. Peirce Mill ceased operating after a machinery failure in 1897, but the building survived.

The mill and surrounding acreage were absorbed into Rock Creek Park in 1892, and for a time, the simple stone structure housed a tearoom. The Works Progress Administration restored the mill to working order in 1936, and flour and cornmeal produced here helped to stock government cafeterias of the 1930s and '40s. In 1993, the mill stopped working again, but in 2011 a citizen-driven restoration effort allowed basic milling operations to resume. Other survivors of the once-flourishing Peirce family compound include a distillery (ca. 1811), which is now private property, a stone springhouse (ca. 1801), and the adjacent Linnaean Hill / Klingle Mansion (1823).

Other Buildings of Interest

This chapter presents a selection of architecturally significant buildings scattered around the District's less-central neighborhoods, and in the case of the first entry, a network of structures that spans the entire metropolitan area.

This circa 1919 photograph shows typical stores in the Anacostia neighborhood.

Infrastructure

Often easily overlooked, works of infra-structure are vital to the character of any city. Washington's greatest such work is arguably L'Enfant's street plan, which, despite countless modifications over the centuries, still defines the city's monumental and commercial core. Also quintessential to Washington is the Metro system, which is surely as "DC" as any museum or monument.

T1

Metro System Stations
Throughout the City

1976–present — Harry Weese Associates; Silver Line: Dulles Transit Partners
2002–present — Exterior station canopies: Lourie & Chenoweth

To the typical American in the 1960s, the word *subway* would have evoked images of a stygian netherworld entered at one's peril. Conscious of such negative stereotypes, federal officials planning the new subway system for Washington, later named Metro, strongly advocated spending the money necessary to ensure that the system's stations were pleasant and inviting. Even President Lyndon John-son weighed in, sending a letter to the National Capital Transportation Agency in February 1966 directing the organization to "search worldwide for concepts and ideas that can be used to make the system attractive as well as useful. It should be designed so as to set an example for the Nation."

Chicago architect Harry Weese was hired to design the individual subway stations, and after a good deal of wran-gling with design review authorities, by 1967 his firm had developed a prototype that featured a coffered concrete barrel vault sheltering passenger platforms that appeared to float within the space. It was nearly a decade before the first of the airy stations opened, but when they finally did in 1976, they became instant icons of mod-ern public transportation. The cleverest aspect of Weese's design is the combina-tion of coffers and indirect lighting. Not only do the coffers make sense structur-ally — note how they grow shallower at the sides of the vault, where the forces acting on the tunnel are smaller — but when lit from below, they create a simple pattern of light and shadow that makes the scale of the space understandable and adds visual interest to what would otherwise be an undifferentiated expanse of concrete.

In 2001, the Washington Metropolitan Transit Authority conducted a competition for the design of a prototypical canopy to cover exterior escalators (which have long been prone to breakdowns) at many Metro stations. The winning design was a vault of glass and stainless steel — recall-ing the form of the stations themselves — supported by slim steel struts. Canopies based on this prototype have been built across the system. Meanwhile, the Metro system continues to grow, and while the station designs have evolved to meet changing needs, they reflect a continuing respect for Weese's original ideas.

T2

McMillan Sand Filtration Site
Southwest corner of Michigan Avenue and North Capitol Street, NW

1905 — Lieutenant Colonel Alexander M. Miller; Landscape architect: Frederick Law Olmsted Jr.

This former water filtration facility is now Washington's most intriguing ruin, and surely one of the most popular sites for local architecture school projects, thanks to the irresistible challenge of figuring out how to incorporate the facility's strange remnants into some sort of new devel-opment. The District of Columbia bought the decommissioned site from the federal government in 1987 and, in 2006, solicited proposals for a major mixed-use project that would preserve some of the property's

historic elements. The planned redevelopment has been repeatedly thwarted by a group of community activists, and as a result, as of this writing, the site remains vacant and fenced off.

Houses and Apartment Buildings

It is unfortunate, but perhaps inevitable, that architecture guidebooks tend to emphasize civic, institutional, and commercial buildings at the expense of smaller, privately owned structures, especially single-family residences. The reasons are simple: first, there are limits on the number of entries that may be included without compromising readability and portability; second, the vast quantity of distinct houses makes selection of representative examples difficult; and third, privacy concerns can complicate research into the history of residential buildings. The upshot is that DC's often fascinating houses and apartment buildings are underrepresented in these pages.

Washington is famous for its many historic row house neighborhoods, which can be easily explored on foot. Areas of particular interest in this regard include Capitol Hill, Logan Circle, Dupont Circle, and Georgetown, among others. Variations in scale, materials, and style reflect changing economics and tastes as the various areas were developed.

This section includes a smattering of residential buildings in the city's less-central neighborhoods that are especially noteworthy (and at least partially visible from public streets).

T3

Four Pavilions
2927 University Terrace, NW

1977 — Hugh Newell Jacobsen
2011 — Renovation: Richard Williams
    Architects

Local architect Hugh Newell Jacobsen became famous for his houses designed as assemblages of simple gabled pavilions, but this is the only example of such a project in DC. In this case, each pavilion is slightly offset from the next one, creating a serrated plan and making the house appear larger than it actually is. Jacobsen's trademark gutterless, eaveless roofs yield pure forms suggesting a child's archetypal drawing of a house.

T4

Hechinger / England Houses
2838/2832 Chain Bridge Road, NW

1952 — The Architects Collaborative
Numerous renovations and additions

This pair of houses was designed for John Hechinger, of the now-defunct Hechinger hardware store chain, and his sister, Lois England (and their respective spouses). Built on a dramatically sloping site, the two houses were articulated as a series of simple, taut geometric forms exemplifying the design philosophy of Walter Gropius, the founder of the Bauhaus who led The Architects Collaborative at the time these projects were built. Although the houses have

been modified since, the Bauhaus sensibility in each is still evident from the street.

The houses were constructed during an extraordinary era in American residential architecture. Ludwig Mies van der Rohe's Farnsworth House, Philip Johnson's Glass House, and even The Architects Collaborative's own noteworthy enclave of houses at Six Moon Hill in Lexington, Massachusetts, were all built around the same time. Perhaps inspired by such works, the Hechingers and Englands commissioned what were arguably the first revolutionarily modern houses in Washington.

T5
Cityline at Tenley
4101 Albemarle Street, NW, at Wisconsin Avenue

1941 — John S. Redden and John G. Raben
2005 — Renovation and addition: Shalom Baranes Associates

A classic Art Moderne former Sears store, with a swoopy canopy and soaring display window at the corner, now serves as the podium for a condominium apartment building with more than 200 units. The materials, fenestration patterns, and details of the new and old elements of the complex are dissimilar but aesthetically complementary. The striations of the aluminum panels on the apartment structure reinforce the characteristic horizontal emphasis of the original building, while the new structure's broad, gentle arc plays off against the more acute curves of the Art Moderne base.

T6
5333 Connecticut Avenue, NW

2016 — Eric Colbert & Associates PC;
Entrance canopy: Skidmore, Owings & Merrill

Sensitive planning and skillful façade composition combine to make this new apartment building a worthy counterpoint to the historic 20th-century apartment houses that line the inner stretches of Connecticut Avenue. Like many of its older cousins, the building is an irregular H-shape in plan, with two bars running parallel to the cross streets and linked by a narrow hyphen. The width of each wing is roughly equal to the depth of the typical single-family houses on adjacent streets, which helps to blend the new building into the fabric of the neighborhood. The plan allows for a circular entry driveway and welcoming entrance

T7

Brown House

3005 Audubon Terrace, NW

1968 — Richard Neutra
1993 — Renovation and addition: Cass
    and Associates

Richard Neutra helped to define the "California style" of residential architecture in the mid-20th century, which, in turn, influenced domestic design across the country. Open floor plans, asymmetrical compositions of simple forms, and large expanses of glass blurring the distinction between indoors and outdoors yielded houses that epitomized the informality that became a hallmark of American domestic life.

Donald and Ann Brown commissioned Neutra to design what turned out to be his last single-family house. To understand his clients' needs and desires, the architect instructed them to keep a diary of their activities and take an inventory of all their possessions, and he even insisted on living with them for two weeks. Though often frustrated by Neutra's notoriously difficult personality, the Browns were thoroughly pleased with the house he designed for them, which came in exactly on budget.

The house retains a remarkably pure silhouette thanks in part to the lack of railings at the edges of the balconies — the Browns simply did not let their children out onto the balconies until they were old enough to avoid tumbling over the edge. A large new music room, added under the direction of architect Heather Cass, seamlessly extends the structural and spatial character of this skillfully composed house.

canopy — elements also common to historic apartment houses.

The architects manipulated the composition of the sleek glass curtain wall to enhance the sense of depth and add variety. Broad projecting bays with relatively dense patterns of mullions contrast with the simpler, glassier planes behind them, a technique that also serves to diminish the apparent scale of the building. Shadowbox panels line the concrete floor slabs, adding another layer of depth to the skin. The balcony guardrails are of milky white semitranslucent glass, which mediates between the clear glass windows and white metal panels and rounds out the modern material palette.

T8

Hecht Company Warehouse

1401 New York Avenue, NE

1937—Abbott, Merkt & Co. (principal
   designer: Gilbert V. Steel)
1948, 1961—Additions: Abbott, Merkt &
   Co.
1992—Rehabilitation: architect unknown
2015—Renovation and addition:
   Antunovich Associates

The finest work of streamlined Art Moderne architecture in Washington, and one of the greatest such buildings anywhere in the United States, the Hecht Company Warehouse is a glistening layer cake of glazed brick and glass block. The ground floor, which originally incorporated large windows for displaying the department store chain's merchandise, is covered in glazed black bricks with jazzy white accents. The upper levels consist of alternating bands of buff bricks and glass blocks separated by thin black stripes. The glass-block bands are interrupted by clear glass windows, which are aligned vertically and thus provide an understated but crucial balance to the building's insistent horizontality. On the fifth floor is another subtle trick: the Hecht Company's name is spelled out in glazed black bricks, which, in certain light conditions, are barely distinguishable from the surrounding glass blocks. Of course, the pièce de résistance is the multifaceted glass-block

beacon that seemingly explodes from the top of the corner tower—a relatively inexpensive flourish at the time that secured the building's landmark status.

Local developer Douglas Jemal bought the former warehouse in 2011. A subsequent renovation and addition yielded 335 loft apartments and over 150,000 square feet of retail space. The repurposed building is now the cornerstone of a growing new mixed-use precinct.

T9

Langston Terrace Dwellings

**Between Benning Road and H Street, NE,
along 21st and 24th Streets**

1938—Hilyard R. Robinson; Associated
   architect: Paul R. Williams

The first federally financed public housing project in the District of Columbia, Langston Terrace was built under the auspices of the Public Works Administration expressly for low-income Black

families. The design by Hilyard Robinson, one of Washington's most prominent early Black architects, in collaboration with Los Angeles–based Paul R. Williams, was heavily influenced by the famed Karl-Marx-Hof housing estate in Vienna, Austria, and other avant-garde projects that Robinson had visited while touring Europe. In contrast to the drab, monolithic blocks widely associated with mid-20th-century housing projects in the United States, the buildings here are arranged as distinct units of two, three, or four stories offset from one another and situated on a terraced site. Although built on a very modest budget, the complex includes some relatively elaborate sculptural elements, including bas-reliefs, titled *The Progress of the Negro Race*, by Daniel Olney. The development was named after John Mercer Langston, a former congressman who also served as acting president of Howard University. Robinson and Williams also collaborated on a number of buildings on Howard University's campus.

Libraries

Over the past decade, the DC Public Library system has emerged as a patron of exceptional architecture, including both entirely new branch libraries and renovations of existing library buildings. Several of these projects have achieved international recognition. This section includes the most significant neighborhood branches built outside the city's core between 2010 and 2020.

T10

Tenley-Friendship Neighborhood Library

4450 Wisconsin Avenue, NW

2011 — The Freelon Group; Associate architects: R. McGhee & Associates

The Tenley-Friendship branch library is a dynamic composition of angular forms reflecting the irregular geometry of its polygonal site. In plan, the building is organized as two angled blocks separated by a skylit circulation zone, with book stacks and reading areas along the street and offices, meeting rooms, and support spaces to the rear. The section facing Wisconsin Avenue has a transparent base sheltered by an overhang lined with angled louvers, which modulate sunlight coming into the library but also add a welcome vertical emphasis to the low-rise building. The vertex of the oblique angle of the upper level directs visitors to the main entrance.

When the DC Public Library decided to demolish the bland, outmoded branch that previously stood on this site, city officials envisioned building a mixed-use complex here, with the library at the base and income-generating residential or commercial uses above. Some area residents were apoplectic, citing concerns about increased traffic and congestion, despite the fact that the site is across the street from a Metro station. Only the library portion was built, but at the request of the District government, the architects designed the structure so that it could accommodate an addition above should the development climate change in the future.

views over the adjacent Langdon Park [site of the Chuck Brown Memorial—see T25]. A broad staircase and circular opening between the main space and the third floor draw the eye upward. The best aspect of this library is the roof terrace, which offers views of the entire neighborhood from under the dappled shade of the canopy.

T11

Woodridge Neighborhood Library

1801 Hamlin Street, NE

2016—Design architects: Bing Thom Architects; Architects of record: Wiencek + Associates Architects + Planners

The Woodridge Neighborhood Library is the strangest of the recent DC Public Library branches. At first glance, it evokes the defensive urban American architecture of the 1960s and '70s, with its forbidding sloped concrete walls and vertical slit windows. At second glance, it can assume a futuristic aspect, thanks to its rounded corners and overscaled but gossamer louvered roof canopy. Fortunately, the interior is reassuringly airy and pleasant. The biggest surprise is a large window wall on the south façade, opposite the main entrance, affording excellent

T12

Dorothy I. Height / Benning Neighborhood Library

3935 Benning Road, NE

2010—Davis Brody Bond

The first of the new generation of DC neighborhood libraries to be completed, the Dorothy I. Height branch occupies a sloping site at the juncture between residential and commercial areas, right next to a decidedly non-pedestrian-friendly driveway leading to a shopping center. This challenging context gave rise to the building's signature element: an internal public stair, visible from the outside through a zigzag ribbon window, connecting the two levels at either end of the library. The staircase not only solves a micro-urban design problem but also encourages the public to enter the library and take advantage of its collections or services.

The library's side façades are mostly clad in vertically seamed copper panels, which add texture and visual warmth. A glass wall on the southwest façade, overlooking the shopping center, brightens the main reading room. Solar shading devices control glare and reduce heat gain.

distorted, with the individual panes gradually becoming taller toward the top. Meanwhile, a similarly warped diamond-pane grid appears in the horizontal canopy that hovers mysteriously over the core of the building as if completely detached from it.

From the inside, the building's envelope reads not as a wafer-thin curtain wall but as a tilted checkerboard of chunky, plywood-clad blocks alternating with clear glass. The warm-toned wood surfaces complement the views of surrounding trees. The second floor is set back from the outside walls so that the skylights around the perimeter can bring daylight to both levels.

T13
Francis A. Gregory Neighborhood Library
3660 Alabama Avenue, SE

2012 — Design architects: Adjaye Associates; Architects of record: Wiencek + Associates Architects + Planners

A harlequin fabric tailored into a crisp suit, the Francis A. Gregory branch library is almost a perfect rectangle in plan and elevation, yet its true shape, scale, and even its boundaries are difficult for passersby to discern at first. The main block of the building is sheathed in a most unusual curtain wall consisting of diamond-shaped panes of glass that are alternately reflective and transparent. Under certain lighting conditions, however, the façades are almost completely reflective, and the building practically disappears into the wooded parkland that surrounds it on three sides. Fooling the eye further, the diamond pattern is actually not a regular grid but is

T14
Anacostia Neighborhood Library
1800 Good Hope Road, SE

2010 — The Freelon Group; Associate architects: R. McGhee & Associates

The Anacostia branch library boldly announces itself with a long roof canopy of bright green perforated metal, the sides of which fold over the edges to provide shading for the glass walls below. The roof gently tilts upward toward the main street and projects beyond the front façade to create a shady civic porch. The main entrance, marked by a narrow translucent tower that glows at night, is off to one side.

The building's plan is a modified parallelogram with a few notches and protrusions that accommodate specialized activities. The main reading room is perhaps the most elegant of any of the new branch libraries thanks to its tall ceiling, linear skylights that admit abundant natural light,

low bookcases that allow for open views, and strips of exposed green roof decking that add color and visual texture. At the community's request, the architects placed the children's area at the front, facing the street—a gesture intended both to "celebrate" kids and encourage them to take advantage of this civic asset.

T15

William O. Lockridge / Bellevue Neighborhood Library

115 Atlantic Street, SW

2012—Design architects: Adjaye Associates; Architects of record: Wiencek + Associates Architects + Planners

Set into a sloping site, the Lockridge/ Bellevue branch library is an assemblage of four geometrically irregular blocks, the largest one containing the main book stacks and the three smaller ones accommodating dedicated program spaces for children, teens, and adults, along with conference rooms. This arrangement not only allows for a variety of more intimate spaces but also breaks down the building's apparent scale, helping it to fit better in its mostly residential neighborhood. While the largest block is set into the ground, the children's pod at the rear is elevated slightly, and the teen and adult pods are perched a full floor above grade on concrete piers, creating, in effect, covered porches that shelter the main entrance from the elements while providing places for outdoor events.

Academic and Museum Buildings

T16

Katzen Arts Center
American University

North corner of Massachusetts and Nebraska Avenues at Ward Circle, NW

2005—EYP Architecture & Engineering
2018—Renovation of Welcome Center:
  cox graae + spack architects

American University's Katzen Arts Center brought some much-needed architectural punch to Ward Circle, an otherwise undistinguished roundabout along this leafy stretch of Massachusetts Avenue. Occupying a long skinny site and incorporating several widely divergent functions, the building easily could have ended

up as either a monotonous fortress or a mishmash of competing forms. Instead, the architects successfully used dynamic curvilinear elements to break up the building's 660-foot length and to differentiate its myriad spaces. Although large expanses of the façades are windowless, the skin retains visual interest thanks to subtle variations in the color and pattern of the French limestone cladding.

In plan, the building looks a bit like a cubist painting of the human body, with the rounded "head," nearest the circle, housing the primary public exhibition space. In the "torso" are a recital hall, theater, and studio spaces, while the "legs" contain classrooms and other academic facilities for the university's visual and performing arts departments.

T17

Ben Murch Elementary School

4810 36th Street, NW

1929–32 — Albert L. Harris
2018 — Renovation architects of record: R. McGhee & Associates; Associate architects: Hord Coplan Macht

The historic portion of Murch Elementary School, built around the beginning of the Great Depression, is one of the finest remaining examples of DC's "extensible" school buildings, which were designed to be erected in stages as the student population grew and funds became available. In this case, the originally planned U-shaped structure was fully built out in just a few years, and it appears today as a cohesive work of architecture in an academic Colonial Revival style.

Charged with expanding this locally landmarked building in the late 2010s, R. McGhee & Associates and Hord Coplan Macht designed a sympathetic, modern addition to the rear of the original structure, running along Davenport Street. The new cafeteria at the corner was partially sunken so as to preserve the fundamental form of the historic building. A green roof over the cafeteria accommodates a microfarm, pollinator garden, and open-air teaching spaces supporting the school's flexible learning methodologies.

T18

United States National Arboretum Administration Building

3501 New York Avenue, NE

1963 — Albert G. Mumma Jr. of Deigert & Yerkes
1976 — National Bonsai & Penjing Museum: Masao Kinoshita of Sasaki Associates
1993, 1996 — Alterations: Sasaki Associates
2013 — Alterations: Richard F. Koehn
2017 — Japanese Pavilion in the National Bonsai & Penjing Museum: Hoichi Kurisu and Rhodeside & Harwell, Inc.

The National Arboretum comprises 446 hilly green acres, incongruously adjacent to a rather gritty stretch of New York Avenue. Lobbying for an arboretum in DC began at least as far back as 1901, and in 1927 Congress approved legislation to "establish

and maintain a national arboretum for purposes of research and education concerning tree and plant life." Since then, the institution has grown into one of the largest, most advanced of its kind in America.

The arboretum's Administration Building is a hidden mid-20th-century gem. The highlight is the folded-plate concrete roof supported on narrow piers—a modern take on the neoclassical colonnades that are common in DC. Visitors enter via a bridge over the shallow pool that surrounds the main wing on three sides. The complex's artful integration of architecture and landscape evokes traditional gardens in Asia.

the US Capitol during expansions in the 1950s. The columns, part of a portico designed by Benjamin Henry Latrobe and erected under the supervision of Charles Bulfinch, seemed, despite that pedigree, to be destined for some local landfill until arboretum benefactor Ethel Garrett intervened and rescued them. After years of negotiations, the columns finally were taken out of storage and placed in the arboretum, and landscape architect Russell Page designed a setting for them on a knoll. A small fountain adds gentle noise and movement to the composition and spills over to form a reflecting pool below.

T18a
National Capitol Columns

1990—Oehrlein & Associates Architects;
   Design concept: Russell Page;
   Landscape architects: EDAW

The arboretum is now the site of nearly two dozen, 34-foot-tall sandstone Corinthian columns that were removed from

T19
Frederick Douglass National Historic Site
(Cedar Hill)

1411 W Street, SE

1859—John Van Hook
1878–93—Various additions: architects
   unknown
1922—Restoration: architect unknown
1964, 1972, 2007—Restorations: National
   Park Service

Abolitionist, author, and editor Frederick Douglass moved to this house in 1877 when he became US marshal of the District of Columbia—the first Black presidential appointee ever confirmed by the Senate. He named the picturesque cottage after the cedar trees that once shaded the property but largely died off over the ensuing decades. The house's most distinctive architectural feature is the generously scaled front porch, lined with four fluted Doric columns supporting an unusual latticework entablature.

One evening in 1895, after returning from a women's rights meeting, Douglass suffered a heart attack (or possibly a stroke) and died in the house. His widow, Helen, successfully lobbied Congress to establish a nonprofit organization to care for Cedar Hill, and in 1903 the house was opened for public tours. The National Park Service acquired the property in 1962. The house has been faithfully restored to its appearance during Douglass's lifetime and thus provides an unusually vivid sense of domestic life in late 19th-century Washington.

T20

Smithsonian Anacostia Community Museum

1901 Fort Place, SE

1974—Original prefabricated building
1987—Renovation and addition: Keyes Condon Florance
2001—Renovation and new façade: architrave, p.c., architects / Wisnewski Blair & Associates
2019—Site and interior upgrades: cox graae + spack architects

African motifs give this museum—now a branch of the Smithsonian—its distinctive architectural character. The two cylindri-

cal towers bracketing the main entrance were inspired by the ruins of the ancient city of Great Zimbabwe in southern Africa, while the brick patterns in the undulating façade were drawn from woven Kente cloth. Diamond-shaped windows and decorative panels refer to elements common in West African adobe construction.

Religious Buildings and Memorials

T21

St. Paul's Episcopal Church, Rock Creek Parish

Rock Creek Cemetery
Rock Creek Church Road at Webster Street, NW

1775—Architect unknown
1810—Reconstruction: architect unknown
1868—Renovation: architect unknown
1922—Reconstruction: Delos H. Smith
2004—Restoration: Atelier Architects

The original chapel on this site, built around 1719, was the first church in what later became the District of Columbia. It was replaced in 1775; the replacement was then remodeled in 1868, but that version burned to the ground in 1921. The present one-story brick church, with its central entrance tower and projecting chancel, is a reconstruction incorporating surviving walls of the 1775 building.

T21a

Adams Memorial

Rock Creek Cemetery

1891 — Sculpture: Augustus Saint-
Gaudens; Base: Stanford White

Henry Adams commissioned this heavily
shrouded bronze as a memorial to his
wife, Marian, after her suicide, and it
almost immediately became one of the
most revered works of art in Washington.
Lorado Taft, who sculpted the Columbus
Fountain near Union Station, said that to
look on the figure's face was like "con-
fronting eternity"; its creator, Augustus
Saint-Gaudens, felt the sculpture "beyond
pain and beyond joy" and said, "It is the
human soul face to face with the greatest
of all mysteries." The figure sits on a
rough stone with a simple bench in front,
designed by the illustrious architect Stanford White.

T22

Saint John Paul II National Shrine

3900 Harewood Road, NE

2001 — LEO A DALY
2016 — Renovation and expansion: LSC
Design

Initially built as a cultural center and now
a shrine to Pope John Paul II, who was
canonized less than a decade after his

death (a decision that has since generated
substantial controversy), this is a startlingly modern building that eschews trite
symbolism and knee-jerk monumentality.
It is impressive without being overbearing, dignified without being stuffy.

The building is an asymmetrical but
balanced composition in both plan and
elevation. The primary façade is enlivened by the visual interplay between two
projecting forms — a stout cylinder, containing the main entrance at ground level,
and a rather enigmatic three-dimensional
puzzle of planes and volumes enclosing
a small chapel. Behind these foreground
elements is the main body of the building,
a long and solid bar offset by a wing-like
patinated copper roof, held aloft from
the main structure by slender struts. The
crowning touch is an attenuated gold-leaf
cross that engages a rectangular bay window before piercing the roof plane.

T23

Basilica of the National Shrine of the Immaculate Conception

400 Michigan Avenue, NE

1920–59 — Maginnis and Walsh (later
Maginnis, Walsh and Kennedy);
Associate architect (1920–32):
Frederick V. Murphy
1959–2017 — Ongoing work on interior
spaces and finishes: various designers
and artists

Washington is home to the largest collection of major Roman Catholic institutions
and facilities outside of Rome, many of

them concentrated in a section of the city's Northeast quadrant sometimes called the "Little Vatican" (which is funny, because it actually covers an area much larger than Vatican City). Noteworthy institutions in this area include the Catholic University of America, founded in 1887 and officially the national university of the American Catholic church, and Trinity University, the architectural star of which is the Notre Dame Chapel (1924—Maginnis & Walsh, with Frederick V. Murphy), visible from Michigan Avenue.

The centerpiece of DC's Little Vatican is the Basilica of the National Shrine of the Immaculate Conception. Despite being the largest Roman Catholic church in the country, and one of the largest churches in the world, with a main sanctuary accommodating up to 6,000 people, this is technically not a cathedral. It is, rather, a shrine dedicated to the Virgin Mary as patron saint of the United States. Designed and built over a period of 40 years, it is ostensibly a combination of the neo-Byzantine and neo-Romanesque styles, but the above-ground portions were mostly built in the 1950s, and the interiors do convey hints of a post–World War II *moderne* sensibility. The architects cited various rationales for the style of the church, including an explicit desire to contrast with the Gothic-style National Cathedral across town.

The church's bell tower, at 329 feet, is the second tallest occupiable structure in DC, after the Washington Monument. The slender spire complements the primary dome, which is distinctive for its colorful mosaic exterior shell. The main entrance is bracketed by bas-relief sculptures and a series of ultra-thin carved colonettes that rise to form a telescoping archway.

The main sanctuary, which was very loosely modeled after that of St. Mark's in Venice, is largely sheathed in a strongly striated travertine, which emphasizes the verticality of the space. The church is replete with colorful mosaics, including the one lining the Trinity Dome over the central crossing, composed of some 14 million Venetian glass tiles. The crypt level includes low domes built using the Guastavino structural tile vaulting system.

Just across Harewood Road from the church's spire is the Harewood Lodge, built around 1857 as a gatekeeper's house for the country estate of William Wilson Corcoran, founder of Riggs Bank. The lodge was designed by James Renwick Jr., who would later design the first Corcoran Gallery of Art (now the Renwick Gallery) for the same client.

T24

Franciscan Monastery of the Holy Land in America

1400 Quincy Street, NE

1899—Memorial Church of the Holy Sepulchre and Monastery: Aristide Leonori

1925—Ascension Chapel: John Joseph Earley, based on drawings by P. Ricci

1926—Rosary Portico and Portiuncula Chapel: Murphy & Olmsted; Concrete artist: John Joseph Earley

1942—Addition to Monastery: A. Hamilton Wilson

Various other renovations and additions: architects unknown

The Franciscan brothers who founded this monastery wanted nothing less than to create a "Holy Land in America." Their initial plan was to build a replica of Jerusalem's Church of the Holy Sepulchre on Staten Island, overlooking the entrance to New York Harbor. That project was never executed, but in 1897, they bought a 100-acre parcel of land (portions of which were subsequently sold off) in Northeast DC—a tract that, ironically, was known in the 17th century as "Cuckold's Delight"— and adjusted their plans to fit the new site. Within just two years, they had conducted a successful fundraising campaign, hired Italian architect Aristide Leonori, and built an impressive church and monastery according to his design. Over the next three decades, the monastery gradually added a number of peripheral structures inspired by, or directly replicating, historic sites in Italy and the Middle East.

The heart of the complex is the Memorial Church of the Holy Sepulchre, the design of which incorporates Byzantine, Romanesque, and even Renaissance elements (note, for instance, the Palladian window over the main entrance). The plan is in the shape of a modified Latin cross, with a tall nave and transept flanked by four shorter cubic elements nestled into the corners of the crossing. The exterior is relatively plain, in keeping with the Franciscan tenets of modesty and simplicity, but the sanctuary is surprisingly and spectacularly ornate, with vibrantly colored ceiling coffers, murals, and stained glass. At the center, beneath the dome, is an extraordinary *baldacchino*, with astonishingly slender posts supporting a delicate canopy.

Impressive though the church may be, some of the most significant architectural elements of the compound are the various artworks—including several full-scale structures—designed or executed by John Joseph Earley. Famed for his innovative concrete mosaics, Earley oversaw construction of the Ascension Chapel, which is a replica of the one erected by the Crusaders on Mount Olivet in Jerusalem. He also designed the mosaics in the Rosary Portico—the arcade that defines the church's forecourt—and the Portiuncula Chapel, which was copied from the small church in Assisi where St. Francis founded his eponymous order in 1209. To the south of the church is the Valley of the Shrines, featuring a series of grottos including more of Earley's characteristic mosaics.

T25

Chuck Brown Memorial Park

20th Street, NE, between Franklin and Hamlin Streets

2014—Marshall Moya Design; Landscape architects: Bradley Site Design

Chuck Brown was considered the "God-father of go-go," DC's homegrown brand of funk known for the use of call and response—a style that engages the audience in a performance. The core of this memorial is a curving, angled wall lined with photo-imprinted 12-by-12-inch tiles that form a mosaic of images from Brown's life. The most striking feature, though, is Jackie L. Braitman's sculpture composed of curving steel slivers and depicting Brown holding his guitar while extending his microphone toward dancing fans.

Notwithstanding the festive tone of the memorial, the designers were serious about making the site sustainable. Rain gardens help to manage storm water runoff, and the plant species selected do not require supplemental watering. The crape myrtle trees bloom in the summer and early fall, including the period around Brown's birthday in August.

Governmental and Community Buildings

T26

Armed Forces Retirement Home–Washington
(former US Soldiers' and Airmen's Home / US Military Asylum)
140 Rock Creek Church Road, NW

1843 — President Lincoln's Cottage (Anderson Cottage / Corn Riggs): John Skirving
1848, 1897, 1923 — Additions and alterations to President Lincoln's Cottage: architects unknown
1857 — Sherman Hall: Barton S. Alexander
1869 — Addition and alterations to Sherman Hall: Edward Clark
1912 — Grant Building: Baldwin and Pennington
2008 — Restoration of President Lincoln's Cottage: Hillier Architecture
Numerous other buildings, additions, and renovations

Lincoln slept here. Actually, several 19th-century presidents used what would come to be called the Old Soldiers' Home as a retreat from the White House, but Lincoln was especially fond of the place, and it is believed that he wrote the final draft of the Emancipation Proclamation in the cottage that was the institution's original building. Built in 1843 by banker George W. Riggs for his own use and soon expanded, that "cottage" is actually a rambling 34-room house designed in the fashionably picturesque Carpenter Gothic style. In 1851, Riggs sold the house and surrounding land to the government, which was looking for a large tract on which to build an "asylum for old and disabled veterans." Lincoln named the house in honor of Major Robert Anderson, the Union commander at Fort Sumter when the first shots of the Civil War were fired, and it was later renamed for the president himself.

The US Military Asylum, as it was officially known, was partially financed by General Winfield Scott, who donated part of the "tribute" he received in exchange for sparing Mexico City from pillaging during the Mexican-American War. Several significant structures were soon built on the huge campus, including Sherman Hall, a neo-Romanesque castle with a tall, central clock tower. Also noteworthy is the Grant Building, an elegant marble structure again in the Romanesque Revival style, which followed some 55 years later.

In 2020, the Armed Forces Retirement Home–Washington, as the institution is now known, announced an agreement with the DC government to lease a portion of its campus to a private developer with plans to build a mixed-use neighborhood there.

T27

The Commons at Stanton Square
2375 Elvans Road, SE

2018 — cox graae + spack architects; Concept design: Perkins Eastman

The first completed phase of a planned mixed-use development, the Commons at Stanton Square provides a new home for Martha's Table, a nonprofit focusing on food access and early childhood education, and Community of Hope, which combats homelessness through mental health and support services. The organizations' complementary but distinct purposes are evident in the contrasting designs of the

building's two main wings—one sheathed in colorful fiber-cement panels and the other primarily in brick. The two wings are joined at the Hub, a trapezoidal space that can accommodate live performances, community events, and other activities.

T28
THEARC

1901 Mississippi Avenue, SE

2005—Ayers Saint Gross
2018—THEARC West: Sanchez Palmer Architects

The Town Hall Education Arts Recreation Campus, better known as THEARC, accommodates a mixture of cultural and community facilities for various nonprofit agencies, such as Covenant House and the Boys & Girls Club. The main building, which includes a 375-seat theater, an art studio and gallery, and a gymnasium, is marked—appropriately enough—by an arc-shaped roof supported by slender steel struts. When the campus opened, some neighborhood children initially assumed that it was a fancy private club and were astonished to learn that it was intended to serve their own community.

THEARC is a project of Building Bridges Across the River, the organization behind

the eagerly anticipated 11th Street Bridge Park, designed by OMA with OLIN as landscape architects, which is expected to begin construction as early as 2022.

T29
St. Elizabeths Hospital, West Campus

2700 Martin Luther King Jr. Avenue, SE

1853–95—Center Building: Thomas U. Walter
1855–1979—Numerous other buildings: various architects
1902–1910—"Letter Buildings" and Hitchcock Hall: Shepley, Rutan and Coolidge
2009-present—West Campus reuse: Goody Clancy | HDR Joint Venture
2013—US Coast Guard Headquarters (Munro Building): Perkins+Will; Architects of record: WDG Architecture; Interior designers / landscape architects: HOK; Master planners: SmithGroup; Landscape architects: Andropogon Associates
2019—Rehabilitation and additions to Center Building: Shalom Baranes Associates; Bridging documents: Goody Clancy; Conservation architects: John Milner Associates
2020—West addition to Center Building: Shalom Baranes Associates; Bridging documents for addition: Goody Clancy; Rehabilitation of Hitchcock Hall: Perkins&Will

Outraged by the shameful neglect of the nation's homeless and mentally ill during the mid-19th century, Dorothea Dix lobbied the federal government to improve the condition of the "many persons from various parts of the Union, whose minds are more or less erratic," and who "find their way to the metropolis of the country [and] ramble about . . . poorly clad and suffering for want of food and shelter." Congress heeded her pleas and approved funds for what was initially known as the Government Hospital for the Insane but was later named St. Elizabeths (with no apostrophe). Working with the hospital's chief of staff, Dr. C. H. Nichol, architect Thomas U. Walter created the first build-ing: a burly red-brick structure with a crenellated roof parapet and buttresses at key corners. Called the Center Building, it was serrated in plan to maximize access to natural light and air. Subsequent build-ings include a series designed by the Bos-ton firm of Shepley, Rutan and Coolidge around the turn of the 20th century in a neoclassical style that brings to mind col-legiate campuses of the same era.

Over the years, thousands of people were treated in the original hospital. One of the most noted residents was the American-born poet Ezra Pound, who had lived in Italy for much of his life and was an ardent fascist. In the wake of Mussolini's execution in 1945, Pound was arrested by Italian partisans, turned over to American authorities, and later admitted to St. Eliz-abeths after he pled insanity in order to avoid a trial for treason. Released in 1958, Pound returned to Italy, declaring that "all America is an insane asylum."

The St. Elizabeths complex is divided into two major parts: the West Campus and the East Campus. In 2007, the federal government, which still owns the West Campus, announced plans to consolidate the Washington offices of the Department of Homeland Security (DHS) there. An entirely new headquarters for the US

Coast Guard opened on the campus in 2013, and in 2018 the renovated Center Building became the DHS headquarters. The East Campus is now owned by the District of Columbia government and is home to a new, modern mental hospital (2010 — EYP Architecture & Engineering). DC authorities are pursuing plans for the mixed-use redevelopment of the East Campus, where the new St. Elizabeths East Entertainment and Sports Arena by ROSSETTI and Marshall Moya Design opened in 2018.

T29a

St. Elizabeths East Gateway Pavilion
(G8WAY DC)

Martin Luther King Jr. Avenue, SE, at Pecan Street

2013 — Davis Brody Bond with KADCON
 Corporation; Landscape architects:
 Gustafson Guthrie Nichol

To generate excitement about the planned redevelopment of the St. Elizabeths East Campus, the DC government conducted a design competition for a temporary pavilion intended to begin drawing the broader community to the site. The winning scheme, completed in 2013, has become a neighborhood fixture, accom-modating food trucks, a farmers' market, and a range of cultural and recreational activities. The pavilion's sloping, chevron-shaped roof doubles as a ramp that invites pedestrians to climb up to the parapet and enjoy the view. Part architecture and part landscape, it is an inventive and unex-pected solution, and it sets an ambitious tone for what promises to be a major new development in a long-overlooked area of Washington, DC.

Index

Page numbers in **bold** *indicate map pages*

Abbott, Merkt & Co., 350
ABC News Washington Bureau (K4), **189**, 191
Abel, Joseph, 261, 331
Abel, Victor D., 105
Abel & Weinstein, 151
Abele, Julian, 250
Abner, Ed, 128
Acacia Building (A11), **26**, 38–39
Ackerman & Ross, 122
Adams, Abigail, 172, 176, 220
Adams, Henry, 10, 172, 181, 270, 358
Adams, John, 172, 176
Adams, John, Building (Library of Congress), 34
Adams Building, 124, 125
Adams Memorial (T21a), 358
Adas Israel congregation: Old Adas Israel Synagogue, 118–19; 6th & I Historic Synagogue (G12), 121
Adjaye Associates, 47, 48, 49, 353, 354
Adjmi, Morris, Architects, 307
AECOM, 46, 65, 80, 185
AEPA Architects Engineers, 111
AFL-CIO National Headquarters (J8), **174**, 180
African American Civil War Memorial (Q4), **300**, 303
Ai, 215
AIA. *See* American Institute of Architects
Air and Space Museum, National (B28), 15, **43**, 64–65
Akamu, Nina, 37
Alexander, Barton S., 361
Alexander, Robert, 93
Allen & Collins, 191
Allied Architects, 32
All Souls Church, Unitarian (R12), **318**, 326
Almas Temple, 160–61
Amateis, Edmond Romulus, 38
Amateis, Louis, 269
American Architectural Foundation, 208
American Coatings Association, 288

American Enterprise Institute, 285–86
American Geophysical Union Headquarters (P11), **272**, 280
American Institute of Architects (AIA): District Architecture Center (G23), **112**, 128–29; Headquarters (L5), **203**, 207; and the Octagon (L6), 7, 208
American National Red Cross (L8), **203**, 209–10
American Pharmacists Association (L14), **202**, 213–14
American Security Bank (J3), **174**, 178
American University, Katzen Arts Center (T16), 354–55
American Veterans Disabled for Life Memorial, 32
Ammann & Whitney, 27
Anacostia Community Museum, Smithsonian (T20), 357
Anacostia Neighborhood Library (T14), 353–54
Anacostia River: development of, 68, 80, 81; name, 1; neighborhood photo, 345; silting of, 8; Waterfront Initiative, 80
Andersen, Henry, 276, 277
Anderson, Marian, 54, 211
Anderson House, 11, 277–78
Andrews, John, International, 341
Andropogon Associates, 362
Anthem, The, 74
Anthony, Charles E., 333
Antunovich Associates, 107, 350
Apex Building (H4), **133**, 135–36
Apple Store at the Carnegie Library (G14), 110, **112**, 122–23
Arad, Ron, Architects, 216
Arboretum, National (T18), 31, 355–56
Arbremont, 342
Archetype, 256, 257, 259, 277, 320
Architectnique, 93
Architects Collaborative, The (TAC), 207, 265, 276–77, 347–48
architrave, p.c., architects, 46, 63, 76, 184, 206, 319, 357

Arena Stage at the Mead Center for American Theater (C8), **70**, 75–76
Argentine Naval Attaché Building, 136
Armed Forces Retirement Home–Washington (T26), 361
Armory, DC (E11), **91**, 96–97
Army-Navy Building, 166
Arrasmith, William S., 159
Art Museum of the Americas, 211
Arts and Industries Building (B25), **43**, 62–63, 115
Asbury Dwellings (Q20), **301**, 313
ASD, 153
Ashburton House, 179
Ashford, Snowden, 92, 232
Astore, P. T., 136
Atelier Architects, 357
Atlantic Building, 155
Atlantic Plumbing Apartments (Q13), **301**, 307–8
Atlas Building, 124, 125
Aubinoe, Alvin E., Sr., 294
Auchmutz, Robert T., 184
Auditors Main Building, 59
Aya, The (C15), **70**, 78–79
Ayers, Stephen T., 27, 31, 32, 33, 36
Ayers Saint Gross, 107, 362
Ayres, Louis, 143

Babcock, Orville, 185
Bacon, Henry, 54, 270
Bailey, Lance, & Associates, 232, 238, 308
Baker Cooper & Associates, 169
Baldwin and Pennington, 361
Balodemas Architects, 257
B and W Garage, 197–98
Banks, The (C7), **70**, 75
Banneker, Benjamin, 2, 5
Banneker Park and Circle, 73
Baranes, Shalom, Associates, 32, 33, 39, 103, 104, 109, 121, 125, 142, 151, 152, 155, 158, 159, 165, 166, 168, 176, 178, 182, 196, 209, 212, 239, 242, 263, 280, 303, 304, 314, 338, 348, 362
Barber, Amzi L., 311

Barclay House (K20), **188**, 199
Barlow, Joel, 252
Barnes, Edward Larrabee, Associates, 102
Barney, Alice Pike, Studio House (O3), **255**, 257
Barr Building (K1), **189**, 190
Bartholdi, Frédéric Auguste, 32
Basilica of the National Shrine of the Immaculate Conception (T23), 358–59
Baskin, Leonard, 56
Bass Architects, 216
Batley, The, 109
BBGM, 72, 74, 94, 145, 216, 331
Beale, Joseph, House, 257–58
Beckhard, Herbert, 57, 72
Beers, Albert H., 262
Belgian Ambassador's Residence (N4), **248**, 250
Bell, Alexander Graham, 191, 233, 288
Bell, Mabel, 191–92, 233, 288
BELL Architects, 95, 156
Bellevue Neighborhood Library (T15), 354
Bell Mansion, 288
Belmont, Perry, House, 280–81
Belmont-Paul Women's Equality National Monument, 36
Bennett, Edward, 135
Bennett, Parsons & Frost, 32, 135
Benning Neighborhood Library (T12), 352
Beresford, Robert S., 190
Berke, Deborah, Partners, 331
Berks, Robert, 213
Berla & Abel, 261
Beyer Blinder Belle Architects & Planners, 47, 49, 117, 122, 139, 140, 161
Bible, Museum of the (C1), **70**, 71
Biden, Joseph, 20, 138
Bikestation Washington DC (F3), **100**, 103–4
Blackburn and Associates, 210
Black Lives Matter Plaza, 173
Blaine, James G., 230, 276
Blaine Mansion (P5), **272**, 275–76
Blair, Francis Preston, 183
Blair-Lee House (J14), **174**, 183–84
Blanton, J. Brett, 36
Blatteau, John, 178
BLDG Architects, 304
Bleifeld, Stanley, 137
Bliss, Robert and Mildred, 231
Blodget's Hotel, 125
Blue Castle (D8), **82**, 86
BNIM, 218
Boardman House, 271, 284
Bodley, George Frederick, 268, 269

Boeckl, Leopold, 239, 332
Boilermaker Shops (D6), **82**, 85
Boleracz, Krisztina, 288
Bomford, George, 180, 241
Bond Building (I27), **148**, 166
Bonstra Architects, 291, 295
Bonstra | Haresign Architects, 34, 341
Borglum, Gutzon, 211, 257
Bossom, Alfred C., 164
Botanic Garden, United States (A2), **26**, 32
Bottomley, William Lawrence, 263
Bowen, Anthony, YMCA building, 303–4
Bowie Gridley Architects, 83, 179, 180, 235, 279, 342
Bowman, Smith, Jr., 258
Bowser, Muriel, 173
Bradley Site Design, 360
Brady, Mathew, 50, 95, 136, 154
Brady Building (H4), **133**, 135–36
Braitman, Jackie L., 360
Brauns, Henry F., 310
Brawer & Hauptman, Architects, 242
Brayton Hughes Design Studio, 285
Brazilian Ambassador's Residence (O24), **254**, 265–66
Brazilian Chancery (O25), **254**, 266
Bread for the City (Q21), **301**, 313–14
Breuer, Marcel, 16, 57, 72
Brewmaster's Castle, The, 275
Brewood Office Building (K11), **189**, 194–95
British Embassy (O26), **254**, 266–67
British Legation, 179
Brodhead-Bell-Morton Mansion, 288
Brooke, Frederick H., 55, 164, 230, 260, 266, 279, 284, 285
Brown, Arthur, Jr., 140
Brown, Bedford, IV, 256, 304
Brown, Chuck, Memorial Park (T25), 360
Brown, Glenn, 12, 154, 208, 256, 257
Brown House (T7), 349
Brumidi, Constantino, 30, 106
Brunei Darussalam, Embassy of (S14b), **330**, 338–39
Bryant & Bryant Architects, 71, 128
Bryant Mitchell Architects, 309
Bryant Street Pumping Station (Q15), **301**, 310–11
Buberl, Caspar, 62, 115
Buchart, Clair S., 289

Buckley, Davis, Architects and Planners, 37, 52, 114, 182, 208
Buffalo Bridge (O1), **255**, 256
Bulfinch, Charles, 27, 28, 49, 356
Bullock, E. L., Jr., 108
Bunshaft, Gordon, 16, 63, 64
Bureau of Alcohol, Tobacco, Firearms and Explosives Headquarters, 109
Burnap, George, 319
Burnham, Daniel H., 12, 18, 46, 54, 102, 103, 104, 168
Burnham Place, 103
Burt Hill Kosar Rittelmann Associates, 137
Busch Building, 128
Butler, Josephine, Parks Center (R4), **318**, 321
Butler Mansion, 281–82
Butzer Architects and Urbanism, 66

Cady's Alley (M29), **222**, 239
Caetani, Gelasio, 324, 325
Cahill, Duane, 106
Cairo, The (P36), 11, **273**, 294–95
Calder, Alexander, 44
CallisonRTKL, 144, 206. See also RTKL Associates
Calvert Street Bridge, 331
Camden Grand Parc Apartments (I32), **148**, 168
Cameroon, Embassy of (O7), **255**, 258–59
Canada, Embassy of (H2), **133**, 134–35
Canadian Embassy, Old, 286–87
Canal House, 241
Canal Lockkeeper's House, Old (B10), **42**, 52
Canal Square (M4), 17, **223**, 225
Cannon, Joseph, 33, 54
CannonDesign, 340
Cannon Faulkner, 234
Cannon House Office Building (A3), 25, **26**, 32–33
Canopy by Hilton, 74
Capital Jewish Museum, Lillian and Albert Small (G7), **113**, 118–19
Capital One Arena (G20), **112**, 127
Capital Yacht Club, 74
Capitol, Old Brick, 28, 36
Capitol, The (A1), 25, **26**, 27–31; burning of, 7, 28; construction and design, 5, 6, 7, 27–28; dome, 27, 28, 30, 31; East and West Fronts, 27, 30–31; expansion of, 9, 27, 28–30; Gatehouses (B7), **42**, 49; Grounds (A1a), 13, 31–32; January 6 attack on, viii, 31;

in L'Enfant Plan, 4, 24, 27; Old Hall of the House, 30; Old Senate Chamber, 27, 30; Old Supreme Court Chamber, 27, 30; Rotunda, 30; Summerhouse, 31; Visitor Center, 27, 31; waiting stations, 31

Capitol Hill: governmental (A), 24–39; residential (E), 88–97

Capitol Park (C16), **70**, 76, 79

Capitol Riverfront (D), 20, 80–87

Capitol Skyline Hotel, 290

Capitol Theatre Façade, Fox / Loew's (I2), **148**, 151

Capitol Traction Company Union Station (M30), **222**, 239–40

Cardinal, Douglas, 66–67

Carlhian, Jean-Paul, 61

Carlton Hotel, 170–71

Carnegie, Andrew, 110, 122, 211, 293

Carnegie Institution of Washington (P34), **273**, 293

Carnegie Library, Apple Store at the (G14), 110, **112**, 122–23

Carrère, John, 33

Carrère & Hastings, 32, 37, 145, 278, 293

Carroll, Grisdale, and Van Alen, 64

Carrollsburg Square Condominium (C10), **70**, 76

Carter, Darryl, 283

Cary, George, 284

Casey, Edward Pearce, 31, 33, 34, 210

Casey, Thomas Lincoln, 49, 185

Cass, Heather, and Associates, 349

Cassell, Albert I., 310

Cassell & Laws, 227

Castle, The. See Smithsonian Institution Building (B24)

Cataffo, Louis, 190

Cathedral Church of St. Peter and St. Paul, 268–69

Catholic University of America, 359

Cato Institute (I18), **149**, 160

Cavaglieri, Giorgio, 114

Cavanaugh, John, 283

Cedar Hill, 356–57

Ceglic, Jack, 239

Center for Strategic and International Studies (K7), **189**, 193

Center Market, 10, 108, 137

Central Heating Plant (B18), **43**, 58

Central Library. See DC History Center (G14)

Chagall, Marc, 46

Chamber of Commerce Building, US (J10), **174**, 181–82

Champalimaud Design, 331

Channel, The, 74

Chase's-Riggs (Keith-Albee) Building, 150

Chatelain, Gauger and Nolan, 181

Chatelain, Leon, 260, 289, 302

Chatelain, Samperton and Nolan Architects, 61

Cheatham, Benjamin Franklin, 55

Chesapeake and Ohio (C&O) Canal, 7, 220, 241

Chesapeake & Ohio Canal Warehouses (M34), **222**, 241–42

Chesapeake & Potomac Telephone Company Building, 163–64

Childs Restaurant Building (F5), **100**, 104–5

Chin, Perry Y., 44

China, People's Republic of, Embassy Chancery (S14c), **330**, 339

China IPPR Engineering International, 339

Chinatown, 111, 127

Chinese Community Church (G11), **112**, 120–21

Christ Church, Georgetown (M10), **223**, 227

Christ Church + Washington Parish (E5), **90**, 93–94, 95, 96

Church of Jesus Christ of Latter-day Saints, 326

Church of the Epiphany, The (I24), **148**, 164

Church of the Holy City (P38), **273**, 295–96

Church Place Condominium (P35), **273**, 293–94

Citadel DCA, 183

CityCenterDC (I15), **149**, 158–59

City Hall, Old (G4), 110, 111, **113**, 117–18

Cityline at Tenley (T5), 348

City Market at O (Q22), **301**, 314

City Post Office Building, 104

Civil War: African American Civil War Memorial (Q4), 303; and Bureau of Pensions, 10, 114–15; and Corcoran Gallery of Art, 184; defenses during, 8; and Georgetown, 220; and Lafayette Park, 172; and Old City Hall (G4), 117; and Old Patent Office, 124; and Pennsylvania Avenue, 130; Red Cross memorial, 210; and Scott-Grant House

(M17), 232; United States Colored Troops, 298, 303

Clark, Appleton P., Jr., 71, 151, 152, 178, 275

Clark, Edward, 31, 117, 123, 124, 125, 361

Clark, Edwin Hill, 334

Clark, William A., 209

Clarke, Edwin, 153

Clas, Riggs, Owens & Ramos, 277

Clas & Riggs, 206

Clemons, Albert Adsit, 236

Cleveland, Grover, 116, 328

Cleveland Park (S), 328–43

Cleveland Park Neighborhood Library (S8), **330**, 335

Clinton Building, William Jefferson (H13), **132**, 140–41, 144

Clorivière, Joseph Picot de, 233

Cluss, Adolf, 9, 10, 11, 59, 61, 62, 63, 92, 123, 124, 161, 162, 187, 192, 230, 269

Cluss and Kammerhueber, 156

Cluss & Schulze, 9, 62, 63, 123, 124

Cobb, Henry Ives, 12, 313

Codman, Ogden, Jr., 259

Codman-Davis House (O9), **255**, 259–60

Cogswell, Henry D., 136

Colbert, Eric, & Associates, 83, 109, 154, 167, 287, 292, 293, 306, 307, 312, 348

Cole, Frank W., 278

Cole & Denny / BVH, 60

Collins, Lester, 60, 64

Colorado Building, 166

Columbian College. See George Washington University (L1)

Commandants, Home of the (E7), **90**, 94–95

Commercial National Bank Building (I26), **148**, 165–66

Commons at Stanton Square (T27), 361–62

Commonwealth Architects, 323

Community of Hope, 361

Congo, Republic of the, Embassy, 296

Congressional Cemetery (E9), **90**, 95–96

Conklin & Rossant, 137

2100 Connecticut Apartments (O13), **255**, 261

800 Connecticut Avenue, NW (J12), **174**, 182

816 Connecticut Avenue, NW (J11), **174**, 182

1718 Connecticut Avenue, NW (P10), **272**, 279–80

2029 Connecticut Avenue, NW (O12), **255**, 261

2101 Connecticut Avenue, NW (O14), **255**, 261–62

5333 Connecticut Avenue, NW
(T6), 348–49
Connecticut Avenue Bridge, 256
Conrad Hotel, 159
101 Constitution Avenue, NW
(A12), **26**, 39, 214
Constitution Gardens, 52
Constitution Hall, Daughters of
the American Revolution, 54,
210–11
Consumer Financial Protection
Bureau (L3), **203**, 206
Convention Center, Walter E.
Washington (G13), **112**, 121–22
Conway Residence, John and
Jill Ker (F9), **100**, 106
Cooke's Row (M12), **223**, 228–29
Coolidge, Calvin, 284
Coolidge & Shat-
tuck / Coolidge, Shepley,
Bulfinch and Abbott, 326
Coonley, Avery and Queene
Ferry, 336
Cooper, Carl T., Jr., 289
Cooper, George S., 166, 205
Cooper, Kent, & Associates, 34
Cooper-Lecky Partnership, 52,
55
Cope & Lippincott, 337
Cope & Stewardson, 142
Corcoran, William W., 184, 230,
238, 359
Corcoran Gallery of Art, 184–
85, 208–9
Corcoran School of the Arts &
Design (L7), **203**, 208–9
CORE architecture + design,
198, 199, 225, 285
Core Group, 239
Corning, Moore, Elmore &
Fischer, 216
Cosmos Club (P8), 11, **272**, 278–
79
Cossutta, Araldo, 73
Council for Professional Recog-
nition, 320–21
Court of Appeals Building. See
City Hall, Old (G4)
Court of Claims, US, 179, 184
Cox, John, 237
cox graae + spack architects,
205, 231, 232, 234, 236, 279,
354, 357, 361. See also
KressCox Associates
Cox's Row (M24), **222**, 237
Cram and Ferguson, 268
Crane, C. Howard, 152
Crawford, Thomas, 30
Cret, Paul Philippe, 14–15, 35,
58, 211, 212, 256, 331
Crystal Heights, 15
518 C Street (E14), **90**, 97
Cuba, Embassy of (R7), **318**,
322–23

Cueva del Rio, Roberto, 326
Cummings, James, 294
Cunningham | Quill Architects,
74, 157
Curtis and Davis Architects and
Planners, 73
Customhouse, Georgetown
(M3), **223**, 224–25

Daly, Henry J., Building, 118
DALY, LEO A, 51, 78, 181, 208,
234, 264, 302, 358
Daniel, Mann, Johnson & Men-
denhall, 334
Daniel, Watha T., Library (Q19),
301, 312–13
Daughters of the American
Revolution (DAR) Headquar-
ters, National Society (L9),
203, 210–11
Davis, Alexander J., 123, 124
Davis, Arthur P., 342
Davis, Harry B., 232
Davis, Henry S., 290
Davis Brody Bond, 47, 49, 312,
352, 363
Davis House, 259–60
Dawson Design Associates, 125
DC Armory (E11), **91**, 96–97
DC Consolidated Forensic Lab-
oratory (C2), **70**, 71
DC Court of Appeals Building.
See City Hall, Old (G4)
DC Department of Parks & Rec-
reation, 327
DC Historical Society. See DC
History Center (G14)
DC History Center (G14), 110,
112, 122–23, 275
DC Public Library, 79, 122, 156–
57, 198–99, 312–13, 335, 351–
54. See also Carnegie
Library, Apple Store at the
(G14)
DCS Design, 325
DC Water Headquarters (D3),
82, 84
DC Water Main Pumping Station
(D4), **82**, 84–85
de Abreu, Ricardo, 266
Dearing, George, 169
Decatur, Stephen and Susan,
183
Decatur House (J13), **174**, 182–
83
Deibert, John, 342
Deigert & Yerkes, 355
Delano, William Adams, 175
Delano & Aldrich, 140, 263, 293
de la Roche, George, 230, 237
DEL Studio, 303
Demetriou, Angelos, & Associ-
ates, 267
De Nesti, Adolfo, 142

Denmark, Embassy of (O23),
254, 265
Department of Agriculture,
59–60
Department of Commerce
(H16), **132**, 143–44
Department of Energy, 73
Department of Homeland Secu-
rity, 363
Department of Housing and
Urban Development: HOPE
VI program, 94; Robert C.
Weaver Federal Building
(C3), **70**, 72
Department of Justice Building
(H8), **132**, 137–38
Department of Labor, 39, 140
Department of the Interior
Building (L11), **203**, 212
Department of the Treasury.
See Treasury Building (J2)
de Schweinitz, Dorothea, 224
de Sibour, Jules Henri, 150, 164,
167, 192, 285, 286, 324
Design for Business, 64
Designtech East, 46
Devore-Chase House (O18),
255, 263
Devrouax + Purnell Architects,
78, 83, 121, 122, 123, 127, 291,
303, 312
Dewberry & Davis / Habib, 160
DeWitt, Poor & Shelton, 27, 34
DeWitt, Roscoe, 27
Diamond + Schmitt Architects, 127
Didden, C. A., and Son, 84
Dillon and Abel, 331
Dirksen Senate Office Building,
37
District Architecture Center
(G23), **112**, 128–29
District Building, 142–43
District of Columbia War
Memorial (B14), **42**, 55
District Wharf (C6), 20, 68, **70**,
73, 74–75
di Valmarana, Mario, 216
Division1 Architects, 305
DLR Group, 106
DMJM Design, 32
Dodge, Anna Thomson, House,
250
Dodge, Francis, 243; House
(M13), **223**, 229
Dodge, Robert, House, 229
Dodge Center, 243
Donn, John Mahon, 291
Dorsey, William Hammond, 230
Douglass, Frederick, 170, 356–
57; Memorial Bridge, 80;
National Historic Site (T19),
356–57
Downing, Andrew Jackson
(A. J.), 8, 40, 173, 229, 230

Downing, Lewis K., Hall (Q14b), **301**, 309
downtown: East End (I), 146–71; West End (K), 186–99
Drake, The (P23), **272**, 287–88
Draper, Dorothy, 190
Dresden, The (O15), **255**, 262
Dreyfuss, John, 236, 237
Dudley, Henry, 164
Dulles Transit Partners, 346
Dumbarton Bridge, 256
Dumbarton House (M14), **223**, 229–30
Dumbarton Oaks (M16), **223**, 230–32; Pre-Columbian Collection Pavilion (M16a), 231–32
Dunbar, Paul Laurence, High School (Q25), **301**, 315
Dunlop House. See Laird-Dunlop House (M7)
Dunson, Edward D., Jr., 303
duPont, Stephen, Jr., 258
21 Dupont Circle, NW (P2), **272**, 274
Dupont Circle Building (P1), **272**, 274
Dupont / Logan (P), 11, 270–97
Durand, J.-N.-L., 62
Duveen, Joseph, 286
Dynerman Whitesell Architects, 342

Earle Theatre and Office Building, 152
Earley, John Joseph, 138, 167, 256, 319, 359, 360
East Capitol Street Car Barn (E12), **91**, 97
East End (I), 146–71
Eastern Branch. See Anacostia River
Eastern Market (E1), 11, **90**, 92
Eastman, Nat, 170
Eberson, John, 93
Eccles, Marriner S., Building, 212
Ecuador, Embassy of (R5), **318**, 322
EDAW, 32, 66, 268, 356
Edbrooke, Willoughby J., 11, 139
Edwards, Harry L., 294
Egbert & Houston, 237
Eggers & Higgins, 37, 44, 57, 210, 213
Egyptian Ambassador's Residence (O4), **255**, 257–58
Egyptian Ministry of Works, 264
Ehrenkrantz Eckstut & Kuhn Architects, 180, 184
Ehrenkrantz Group, 192
Eiermann, Egon, 249
1150 18th Street, NW (K10), **189**, 194
Einhorn Yaffee Prescott, 53, 57,

107, 143, 185, 205, 234, 235. See also EYP Architecture & Engineering
Einstein, Albert, Memorial, 213
Eisenhower, Dwight D., 124; Memorial (B29), **43**, 65–66
Eisenhower, Dwight D., Executive Office Building (J16), 10, **174**, 185
11th Street Bridge Park, 80, 362
Ellerbe Becket, 127, 141
Ellicott, Andrew, 2, 5
Ellicott, Benjamin, 5
Ellington, Duke, 302, 303
Ellington, Duke, Bridge (S1), 256, **330**, 331
Ellington, Duke, School of the Arts (M18), **222**, 232–33
Elliot, William P., Jr., 123, 124
Embassy Row, 252, 316. See also specific countries
Emori, Nahiko, 263
Ennead Architects, 62
Environmental Planning & Research, 234
Environmental Protection Agency, 141
Envision Design, 274
Erickson, Arthur, Architects, 134
ESI Design, 126
Esocoff, Phil, 199, 289
Esocoff & Associates | Architects, 76, 92, 120, 288, 289
Estern, Neil, 56
Etchison, Howard, 292
Euram Building, 274
Evans, Rudulph, 57
Evening Star Building (H10), **132**, 138–39
Everett, Edward Hamlin, 256
Everett House, 256
EwingCole, 44, 46, 47, 342
Executive Office Building, Old, 10, 185
Eylanbekov, Sergey, 65
EYP Architecture & Engineering, 354, 363

Fahnestock House, 258
Family Federation for World Peace and Unification–Family Church National Cathedral (R13), **318**, 326
Farmers and Mechanics Branch (M5), **223**, 225–26
Farragut Square, 187
Farrand, Beatrix, 230, 231
Faulkner, Fryer & Faulkner, 123
Faulkner, Fryer & Vanderpool, 320
Faulkner, Kingsbury & Stenhouse, 123, 320
Faulkner, Waldron, 183, 336
Faulkner, Waldron / Winthrop,

Houses at Rosedale (S11), **330**, 336–37
Faulkner, Winthrop, 336, 337
Faulkner & Kingsbury, 204
FBI Headquarters (H9), **132**, 138
Federal-American National Bank, 164–65
Federal Aviation Administration, 64
Federal Office Buildings 10A and 10B, 64
Federal Reserve Building (L12), 15, **203**, 212
Federal Trade Commission (H3), **133**, 135
Federal Triangle, 14, 15, 130, 131, 135, 137, 139–43
Fetterman, Marc, 296
Fetterman Associates, 216
900 15th Street, NW (I32), **148**, 168
Fillmore, Millard, 30
Finland, Embassy of (O27), 18, **254**, 267
First Congregational United Church of Christ (I14), **149**, 157
Fischer, Nora, Designs, 216
Fisher Gordon Architects, 342
Fitch Studio, The, 239
Flagg, Ernest, 208, 209, 268
Flagg Building, 208–9
Fleming, Edward, 93
Florance Eichbaum Esocoff King Architects, 104, 152, 159, 182, 293. See also Smith-Group
320 Florida Avenue, NE, 109
Floridian, The (Q12), **300**, 306–7
Flour Mill, The (M33), **222**, 241
Foggy Bottom (L), 200–219
Folger Building and Playhouse Theatre (I29), **148**, 167
Folger Shakespeare Library (A6), 14–15, **26**, 35
Ford's Theatre (I8), **149**, 153–54
Fordyce & Hamby Associates, 73
Forensic Laboratory, DC Consolidated (C2), **70**, 71
Forest Service, US, 59
FORMA Design, 337
Forrest, Uriah, 336
Forrestal Building, 73
Foster, Richard, 251
Foster, William Dewey, 105, 224
Foster + Partners, 122, 123, 124, 158, 159
Founders Library, Howard University (Q14e), **301**, 310
Foundry, The (M40), **223**, 245
Foundry Methodist Church, 246
Four Pavilions (T3), 347
1525 14th Street, NW (P31), **273**, 292

1270 4th Street, NE, 109
Foxall, Henry, 246
FOX Architects, 74, 166, 235
Foxhall (N), 246–51
Fox / Loew's Capitol Theatre Façade (I2), **148**, 151
Franciscan Monastery of the Holy Land in America (T24), 359–60
Franklin School (I20), 11, **149**, 161–62
Franklin Square, 160–61
Franzheim, Kenneth, 152
Fraser, John, 275, 276, 288
Freed, James Ingo, 59. See also Pei Cobb Freed & Partners
Freedom Plaza, 143
Freelon Adjaye Bond, 47
Freelon Group, The, 49, 351, 353
Freer, Charles Lang, 60
Freer Gallery of Art (B22), **43**, 60, 61
French, Daniel Chester, 53, 54, 270
French & Company, 342
French Embassy, Old (R3), **318**, 320–21
Fresnedo Siri, Román, 215
Friedberg, M. Paul, 80
Friedrich, E. S., 107
Friendship Arch, 111
Friends Meeting of Washington (O10), **255**, 260
Frohman, Philip Hubert, 268
Frohman, Robb & Little, 268
Fry, Louis E., Sr., 310
F Street, 14, 146, 147
Furrer, Herbert, 332

Gallaudet University (F11), 98, **101**, 107–8
Gallery Place, 111
Gallery Row (G24), **112**, 129
Gallup Organization, 156
Garner, John Nance, 145
Gauthier, Alvarado & Associates, 260
Gaylord, Frank, 55
GBQC Architects, 66
GBR Architects, 75, 249
GDG (Georgetown Design Group, Inc.), 288
Geare, Reginald, 302
Gebhart, Willard, 342
Gehry, Frank, 65, 209, 280
Gehry Partners, 65–66
Geier Brown Renfrow Architects, 135, 275
General Post Office, 125–26
Gensler, 85, 92, 109, 152, 160, 161, 243, 327
Geophysical Union Headquarters, American (P11), **272**, 280

Georgetown (M), 220–45
Georgetown Car Barn, 239
Georgetown Customhouse and Post Office (M3), **223**, 225
Georgetown Market (M28), **222**, 239
Georgetown Park Apartments, 241
Georgetown University (M21), 11, 119–20, **222**, 234–35, 240
Georgetown Visitation Preparatory School (M20), **222**, 233–34
George Washington University (L1), 200, **203**, 204–5, 208, 209, 246, 249–50. See also Corcoran School of the Arts & Design (L7)
German Ambassador's Residence (N2), **248**, 249
German Marshall Fund of the United States (P14), **272**, 281–82
Germany, Embassy of, Chancery (N1), **248**, 249
Gessford, George, 97
Getty, Robert, 224
Ghequier, T. Buckler, 34
Gifford, James J., 153
Gilbert, Cass, 36, 178, 181
Gilbert, Cass, Jr., 36
Gilman Building (H4), **133**, 135–36
Gilpin, Richard A., 206
Giuliani Associates Architects, 236
Godwin & Beckett, 268
Gonzaga College High School, 106
Goodhue, Bertram Grosvenor, 213, 214
Goodman, Charles M., Associates, 78
Goody Clancy, 362
Gordon, Tracy and Swartout, 150
Gordon & Greenberg Architects, 155
Government Publishing Office (F6), **100**, 105
Graae, Christoffer, 232. See also cox graae + spack architects
Grace Episcopal Church (M35), **223**, 242
Grad, Frank, and Sons, 73
Graham, Anderson, Probst and White, 104
Graham, Burnham & Company, 104
Graham, Jay, 337
Graham, Robert, 56
Graham Landscape Design, 236
Grant, Ulysses S., 32, 172, 232
Graves, Michael, & Associates, 49, 96, 134, 196

Greely, Rose, 260, 342
Greenberg, Allan, 183
Greenleaf, James, 68, 77
Greenleaf, James L., 55
Gregory, Francis A., Neighborhood Library (T13), 353
Gregory, Waylande, 118
Greyhound Bus Station, Old, 159–60
Grigg, Milton, 237
Grigg, Wood, and Browne, 326
Grimm + Parker, 217
Gropius, Walter, 347
Group Goetz Architects (GGA), 144, 180, 194
Gruzen Samton, 117
Guerin, Jules, 53
Gugler, Eric, 175
Guimard, Hector, 45
Gund, Graham, Architects, 128
GUND Partnership, 119
Gustafson, Kathryn, 123
Gustafson Guthrie Nichol, 47, 158, 363
GWWO Architects, 57

Hadfield, George, 6, 27, 28, 94, 95, 117, 208, 230
Haiti, Embassy of (O5), **255**, 258
Halcyon House (M23), **222**, 236–37
Hales, Georges P., 240
Halleck, Henry Walker, 232
Haller, Nicholas T., 124
Hallet, Stephen (Étienne) Sulpice, 27, 28
Hallett, Marcus, 325
Halprin, Lawrence, 56, 57
Hamilton, Alexander, 1
Hamilton, Ed, 303
Hammel, Green and Abrahamson, 46
Hand, Florence Hollis, Chapel (N3), **248**, 249–50
Handel, Gary Edward, + Associates, 240, 242
Handel Architects, 74
Hansen, Ramm, 326
Hansen, Tomas, 244
Hantman, Alan, 27, 32, 36
Harbaugh, Leonard, 235
Harbeson, Hough, Livingston & Larson, 27
Harbour Square (C12), **70**, 77–78
Hardenbergh, Henry, 144
Harding, Clarence L., 325
Harding and Upman, 262
Hardison, Fred L., 27
Hardy Holzman Pfeiffer Associates, 144
Harewood Lodge, 359
Harkness, John C., 164, 290
Harman, Sidney, Hall (G21), **112**, 127–28

Harman Center for the Arts, 127

Harris, Albert L., 205, 232, 334, 355

Harrison, Wallace K., 213

Harrison & Abramowitz, 213

Hart, Frederick, 269

Hart, Philip, 5

Hart, Philip A., Senate Office Building, 37

Hartman-Cox Architects, 35, 38, 44, 51, 53, 57, 105, 119, 120, 123, 124, 129, 135, 136, 137, 153, 160, 181, 192, 213, 217, 230, 237, 243, 249, 274, 283, 285, 297, 334

Hartman Design Group, 334

Hastings, Thomas, 33, 278

Hatton, Isaiah T., 303, 304

Hauge House, 258–59

Haussmann, William, 153

Hay, John, 10, 181

Hay-Adams Hotel (J9), 10, **174**, 181

Hayes Seay Mattern and Mattern, 44. *See also* HSMM

HCM, 55

HDR Architecture, Inc., 308, 362

Healy, Patrick, 234

Healy Hall, Georgetown University (M21a), 11, **222**, 234–35

Heaton, Arthur B., 155, 165, 191, 192, 205, 238, 268, 337

Hechinger/England Houses (T4), 347–48

Hecht Company Building, Old (G19), **112**, 126–27

Hecht Company Warehouse (T8), 350

Height, Dorothy I., Building, 135–36

Height, Dorothy I., Neighborhood Library (T12), 352

height limits, 11, 14, 294

Heikkinen-Komonen Architects, 267

Heins and La Farge, 194

Hellmuth, Obata + Kassabaum, 64, 160. *See also* HOK

Henderson, Mary Foote, 316, 319, 320, 321, 322, 323, 324, 325, 327

Henderson Castle, 316, 317

Herzog & de Meuron Architekten, 158, 159

Heurich, Christian, House Museum (P4), **272**, 275

Heurich Brewing Company, Christian, 200, 201

Hewlett, J. Monroe, 293

Hickok Cole, 39, 73, 109, 128, 191, 192, 193, 280, 292

Highland Place (S9), **330**, 335–36

Highline, The, 109

Hightowers, 294

Hill, James G., 59, 105, 136, 155

Hill Center at the Old Naval Hospital (E8), **90**, 95

Hillier Architecture, 36, 361

Hillwood Estate, Museum, and Gardens (S18), **330**, 342–43

Hintz, Berny, 93

Hirsch Bedner Associates, 139

Hirshhorn Museum and Sculpture Garden (B26), **43**, 63–64

Hisaka, Don, & Associates, 194

Hisaka & Associates Architects, 197–98

Historical Society of Washington, DC, 110, 122, 123. *See also* DC History Center (G14)

Historic Bank Buildings (J3), **174**, 178

Historic National Bank of Washington (I25), **148**, 164–65

HKS Architects, Inc., 38, 158

Hoban, James, 27, 28, 175, 176

Hoffman, William H., 93

Hoffmann Architects, 27

HOK, 71, 83, 241, 243, 362. *See also* Hellmuth, Obata + Kassabaum

Holabird & Root, 64

Holl, Steven, Architects, 218, 219, 332

Hollerith, Herman, 225

Holocaust Memorial Museum, US (B19), **43**, 58–59

Holodomor Memorial to Victims of the Ukrainian Famine-Genocide of 1932–3, 105

Holt House, 334

Holy Trinity Catholic Church (M22), **222**, 235–36

Hom, Kevin, 204

Homer Building (I4), **149**, 151–52

Honeymoon House, 77

Hooper, Robert "King," 262

Hoover, Herbert, 185, 260, 332

Hoover, Herbert Clark, Federal Building, 143–44

Hoover, J. Edgar, 95, 191

Hoover, J. Edgar, Building, 138

Hoover, Lou, 260

Hord Coplan Macht, 355

Hornaday, William T., 334

Hornblower & Marshall, 46, 62, 94, 191, 192, 260, 279, 284

Horsey & Thorpe, 233

Hotel Monaco (G18), **112**, 125–26

Hotel Washington (H18), **132**, 145

House of Sweden (M39), **223**, 244–45

House of the Temple, 297

Housing Studio, 168

Howard Hall (Q14c), **301**, 309

Howard Theatre (Q17), **301**, 311–12

Howard University (Q14), **301**, 308–10, 311

Howe, Foster and Snyder, 224

HPP Architekten GmbH, 249

HSMM, 46

1510 H Street, 167

HTB, 151

Hubbard, Gardiner Greene, 288

Hubbard Memorial Library, 191, 192

Huber, Charles H. and Hugo, 275

Hughes Design Associates, 216, 331

Hungary, Embassy of (P24), **273**, 288

Hunt, Jarvis, 126

Hunter and Bell, 261

Husted, Brie, 306

Hyatt House, 74

Hyde-Addison Elementary School (M27), **222**, 238

IA Interior Architects, 181, 216

Immaculate Conception, Basilica of the National Shrine of the (T23), 358–59

Independent Order of Odd Fellows Building, 128–29

Indonesia, Embassy of (P6), **272**, 276–77

Industrial Bank of Washington (Q3), **300**, 303

Innocenti & Webel, 342

Institute of Peace, US (L15), **202**, 214–15

INTEC Group, 86

Intelsat Headquarters, 341

Inter-American Defense Board (R6), **318**, 322

Inter-American Development Bank (I22), 17, **149**, 163

InterContinental Hotel: District Wharf (C6), 74; Willard (H17), **132**, 144–45

Interdisciplinary Research Building, Howard University (Q14a), **301**, 308–9

Internal Revenue Service Building (H12), **132**, 140, 141

International Chancery Center (S14), **330**, 338–40

International Finance Corporation Headquarters (K14), **188**, 196

International Inn, 289–90

International Spy Museum (C5), **70**, 73–74, 125

Interstate Commerce Commission, 140

Iraq, Chancery of (P18), **272**, 284

Islamic Center (O21), **255**, 264

1915 I Street, NW (K13), **189**, 195

ISTUDIO Architects, 281
Italy, Embassy of, Chancery (O22), **254**, 264–65
Italy, Embassy of, Old (R10), **318**, 324–25
Ives, Philip, 227

Jackson, Andrew, 172, 177
Jackson, Ed, Jr., 56
Jackson, Frank H., 290
Jackson, Samuel, 229
Jacobsen, Hugh Newell, 27, 62, 184, 227, 337, 347
James Corner Field Operations, 241
Japanese, Embassy (O19), **255**, 263
Jeckyll, Thomas, 60
Jefferson, Thomas, 1, 33, 130, 172, 238; and the Capitol, 27, 28; and the White House (J1), 172, 175, 176
Jefferson, Thomas, Building, Library of Congress (A4), 11, 25, **26**, 33–34
Jefferson, Thomas, Memorial (B17), **42**, 57–58
Jefferson Hotel, 192
Jennewein, C. Paul, 138
Jewish Historical Society of Greater Washington, 119
Jewish Museum, Lillian and Albert Small Capital (G7), **113**, 118–19
JMA Preservation, 278
Johnson, Andrew, 156
Johnson, E. Verner, and Associates, 60
Johnson, Lyndon, 332, 346
Johnson, Philip C., 16, 17, 217, 231, 251
Johnson & Boutin, 194
Johnson-Berman, 334
Jones, Johnpaul, 66
Jones & Jones Architects and Landscape Architects, 66
Judiciary Square (G), 110–29
Justement, Elam, Callmer & Kidd, 215
Justement, Louis, 134

KADCON Corporation, 363
Kahn, Louis, 35, 92
Kalorama. See Sheridan-Kalorama (O)
Kapp and Nordholm, 342
Karn Charuhas Chapman & Twohey (KCCT), 32, 114, 117, 139, 140, 215, 288, 324
Kaskey, Raymond, 51, 114
Katzen Arts Center (T16), 354–55
KCF-SHG Architects, 127. See also SmithGroup
Keck Center, 116–17

Keith-Albee Building, 150
Keith's Theatre, 150
Kelsey, Albert, 211
Kemnitzer, Reid & Haffler Architects, 185
Kendall Heaton Associates, 142
Kennedy, Jacqueline, 172, 179, 184
Kennedy, John F., 130, 136
Kennedy, John F., Center for the Performing Arts (L19), 201, **202**, 217–18; the REACH (L19a), 218–19
Kennedy, Robert F., Federal Building, 137–38
Kennedy-Warren Apartments (S7), **330**, 334–35
Kerns Group Architects, 195, 236, 290, 326
Key, Francis Scott, 238
Key, Philip Barton, 328, 333
Keyes, Lethbridge & Condon Architects, 17, 76, 77, 274. See also SmithGroup
Keyes Condon Florance, 44, 71, 114, 163, 165, 167, 199, 205, 278, 357. See also Florance Eichbaum Esocoff King Architects; SmithGroup
KGP Design Studio, 103
KieranTimberlake, 35, 337
Kiley, Dan, 44, 52, 73, 77, 79
Kimball, Fiske, 229
King, Frederic Rhinelander, 230
King, Martin Luther, Jr., 54, 56, 145
King, Martin Luther, Jr., Memorial (B15), **42**, 56
King, Martin Luther, Jr., Memorial Library (I13), 122, **149**, 156–57
King Greenleaf Recreation Center (C14), **70**, 78
Kinoshita, Masao, 355
Kirkpatrick, Malcolm, 343
Kleinman, Max, 118
Kling, Vincent, 206
Klingle Mansion, 343
Klingle Valley bridge, 256
Kluge, Russell O., 233
Koehn, Richard F., 355
Kohn Pedersen Fox (KPF) Associates, 74, 191, 205–6, 286
Konti, Isidore, 211
Koppel, Frank, 322
Korean War Veterans Memorial (B13), **42**, 55
Koubek, Vlastimil, 136, 144, 150, 190, 196, 245
Kreeger Museum (N6), **248**, 251
Kresge's, 128
KressCox Associates, 166, 205, 210, 234, 304. See also cox graae + spack architects

1999 K Street, NW (K12), **189**, 195
Kuhn Riddle Architects, 107
Kurisu, Hoichi, 355
Kurylas, Larysa, 105
Kuwait Chancery, Embassy of, 339–40
Kuwait Cultural Office (S14d), **330**, 339–40

Lacey, The (Q9), **300**, 305
La Farge, C. Grant, 194
Lafayette, Marquis de, 3, 172, 237
Lafayette Park, 172
Lafayette Square (J), 13, 17, 172–85
Lafayette Square Federal Buildings (J5), **174**, 179
Laird-Dunlop House (M7), **223**, 226
Landscape Architecture Bureau, 74
Langston Terrace Dwellings (T9), 350–51
Lankford, John A., 169, 302
Lansburgh, The (G22), **112**, 127, 128
Lantz, Michael, 135
Lapidus, Morris, 289–90
Lascaris, Carol, 163
Latrobe, Benjamin Henry, 6, 183; the Capitol (A1), 27, 28; Christ Church + Washington Parish (E5), 93; Congressional Cemetery cenotaphs (E9), 95, 96; Decatur House (J13), 182; National Capitol Columns (T18a), 356; St. John's Church, Lafayette Square (J7), 180; Van Ness mansion, 211; Washington Navy Yard (D9), 87; White House (J1), 175, 176
Latvia, Embassy of, 257
Laughlin, Irwin Boyle, 320
Lauinger, Joseph Mark, Memorial Library (M21c), **222**, 235
Lauritzen, Wilhelm, 265
Law, Thomas, 77
Law, Thomas, House (C11), **70**, 77
Lawrie, Lee, 213
Laws, Henry, 227
Law School, George Washington University (L1c), **203**, 205
Layman, Christopher and Rachael, 224
LeDroit Block (G17), **112**, 124–25
LeDroit Building, 124, 125
LeDroit Park (Q16), **301**, 311
Lee, Thomas Sim, Corner (M1), **223**, 224
Lee, Wanchul, Associates, 313

Lee and Associates, 158
Lee House, 183–84
Lehman Smith McLeish, 38. *See also* LSM
Leisenring, L. M., 290
Leiter Mansion, 271
LeMay Erickson Willcox Architects, 197
L'Enfant, Pierre Charles, 3–5, 8, 268
L'Enfant Plan: and the Capitol, 4, 24, 27; and Freedom Plaza, 143; and Hamburgh, 200; and Judiciary Square, 110, 111, 123; and the Mall, 4, 6, 9, 11–14, 40, 49; and Mount Vernon Square, 110; and National Archives Building (H7), 137; and National Portrait Gallery (G16), 123; outside of Historic Districts, 306; preparation for, 4–5; and President's House, 4, 172; street patterns in, 4, 5, 346; and Treasury Building (J2), 177
L'Enfant Plaza (C4), **70**, 73, 74
Leonori, Aristide, 359
Lescaze, William, 332
Lessig, Charles W., 153
Levi, Louis, 121
Liberty Plaza (L3), **203**, 206
Library of Congress (A4), 11, 25, **26**, 33–34
Lichtenstein, Roy, 46
Lin, Maya Ying, 52, 55
Lincoln, Abraham, 153, 214, 361
Lincoln Colonnade, 302
Lincoln Memorial (B12), **42**, 53–54, 211
Lincoln Square (I7), **149**, 153
Lincoln Theatre (Q1), **300**, 302
Lindens, The (O17), 224, **255**, 262–63
Linnaean Hill, 343
Linthicum, Edward, 230
Lippincott Architects, 260
Lisner Auditorium (L1b), **203**, 204–5
Lithuania, Embassy of, 323
Little and Browne, 277
Liu, Alfred H., 111
Livingston, Goodhue, 209
Lockman Associates, 241
Lockridge, William O., Neighborhood Library (T15), 354
Loew's / Fox Capitol Theatre Façade (I2), **148**, 151
Logan Circle (P29), 11, **273**, 290–91
Logan / Dupont (P), 270–97
Longworth House Office Building, 25, 33
Lord & Burnham, 32, 342
Lore Group, 155

Lothrop Mansion (O11), **255**, 260–61
Lourie & Chenoweth, 346
Lovering, William, 6, 77, 226
LSC Design, 358
LSM, 216
Lumber Shed, The (D5), **82**, 85
Lundy, Victor A., 118
Lutheran Church of the Reformation (A7), **26**, 35–36
Luther Place Memorial Church (P28), **273**, 290
Lutyens, Edwin, 266
Lyles Bissett / Carlisle & Wolff, 118
Lynn, David, 27, 32, 34, 37

Macklin, Jodi, Interior Design, 236
Macneil & Macneil, 322, 323
Macomber, Walter, 262
Macomber & Peter, 153
MacVeagh House, 325–26
Madison, James, Memorial Building, 34
Madison, James and Dolley, 1, 7, 176, 208
Maginnis and Walsh / Maginnis, Walsh and Kennedy, 358, 359
Magruder School, 192
800 Maine Avenue, SW, 74
1000 Maine Avenue, SW, 74
Maine Avenue Fish Market, 74
Malesardi + Steiner / Architects, 207–8
Mall, The (B), 40–58; and Grand Avenue in L'Enfant Plan, 4, 6, 9, 11–14, 40, 49
Manhattan Laundry Building (Q8), **300**, 304–5
Maret School Main Building, 333
Mariani & Associates, 46, 59, 145, 167, 235
Mariani Architects-Engineers, 121
Marine Barracks Washington (E7), **90**, 94–95
Market Square (H6), **133**, 136–37
Marshall, Thurgood, Center for Service and Heritage (Q5), **300**, 303–4
Marshall, Thurgood, Federal Judiciary Building (F1), **100**, 102
Marshall Moya Design, 311, 340, 360, 363
Marsh and Peter, 138, 210, 225, 235
Martha's Table, 361
Martin and Jones, 97, 199
Martinez + Johnson, 156, 168, 239, 311

Marvin Center, 204
Masonic Temple, Old (I12), **149**, 156
Masonic Temple, 163
Massachusetts Avenue (O), 252–69
400 Massachusetts Avenue, NW (G10), **113**, 120
Mathews, Arthur, 50
Matisse, Paul, 37
May, Maurice S., 275
Mayflower Hotel (K3), **189**, 190–91
McCormick Apartments (P20), **272**, 285–86
McCormick House (O24), **254**, 265–66
McGaughy, Marshall & McMillan, 139
McGhee, R., & Associates, 304, 351, 353, 355
McGill, James H., 124, 311
McIlvaine, Alexander, 342
McInturff Architects, 217, 239
McKean, John, Associates, 342
McKim, Charles Follen, 12–13, 46, 175
McKim, Mead & White, 12–13, 47, 175, 176, 180, 230, 279, 281, 283
McKinley, William, Manual Training School, 313
McKissack & McKissack, 53, 56, 57
McLean, Edward Beale and Evalyn, 277
McMahon, J. J., 105
McMillan, Inc., 342
McMillan, James, 12
McMillan Commission. *See* Senate Park Commission
McMillan Sand Filtration Site (T2), 346–47
Mead Center for American Theater (C8), **70**, 75–76
Mecanoo Architecten, 156, 157
Meière, Hildreth, 118, 213
Meigs, Montgomery C., 9–10, 27, 30, 50, 62, 114–15, 116, 125, 184
Mellon, Andrew, 14, 45, 135, 139, 286, 320
Mellon, Andrew W., Auditorium (H13), **132**, 140–41
Memorial Continental Hall, Daughters of the American Revolution, 210
Mendel Mesick Cohen Waite Hall Architects, 183
Meridian Hill (R), 316–28
Meridian Hill Park (R1), **318**, 319–20
Meridian House (R2), 316, **318**, 320

Meridian International Center, 320

Mesick Cohen Waite Architects, 208

Mesrobian, Mihran, 170, 171, 181, 274, 331, 332, 341

Metcalf and Eddy, 242

Metheny, Russell, 291

Metropolitan A.M.E. Church (I34), **148**, 169–70

Metropolitan Community Church of Washington (Q23), **301**, 314

Metropolitan Police Department, 118

Metropolitan Square (I1), **148**, 150

Metro System Stations (T1), 346

Mexican Cultural Institute (R11), **318**, 325–26

Mexico, Embassy of, Old, 325–26

Meyer, John G., 129

Meyers, J. G., 107

Michiels, J. A., 129

Midtown Center (I33), **148**, 169

Mies van der Rohe, Ludwig, 122, 156–57

Milken Center for Advancing the American Dream, 178

Miller, Alexander M., 346

Miller, William Henry, 296

Mills, Petticord & Mills, 46, 47, 180, 204, 205

Mills, Robert, 95; the Capitol (A1), 27; General Post Office / Tariff Commission Building (G18), 125–126; Old Patent Office, 7, 123, 124, 125, 126; St. John's Church, Lafayette Square (J7), 180; Treasury Building (J2), 7, 125, 126, 176, 177; Washington Monument (B8), 7, 49, 50

Mills + Schnoering Architects, 320

Milner, John, Associates, 53, 57, 135, 176, 209, 211, 362

Mindeleff, Victor, 205

Mitburne & Heister & Co., 128

Mitchell/Giurgola Architects, 207

MMM Design Group / PUDI, 62

Modera Sedici, 324–25

Monastery of the Visitation, 233–34

Moneo, Jose Rafael, 251

Moneo Brock Studio, 251

Monroe, James, 28

Moody Nolan, 315

Moore, Arthur Cotton, 17, 244

Moore, Arthur Cotton / Associates, 33, 139, 176, 225, 239, 243, 244, 245, 279, 294

Moore, Clarence, House, 286–87

Moran House (O6), **255**, 258

Moretti, Luigi, 216, 217

Morgan, Gick, McBeath and Associates, 181

Morison, George, 256

Morris*Architects, 136

Morsell, Samuel, 169

350 Morse Street, NE, 109

Morton, Levi, 288

Morton Mansion, 288

Mount Vernon Square (G), 110, 121–23

Mount Zion United Methodist Church (M9), **223**, 227

Moynihan, Daniel Patrick, 137

MTFA Architecture, 74, 114

MTFA Design + Preservation, 35, 86

Mullett, A. B., and Company, 128, 167, 312

Mullett, Alfred B., 135, 151, 176, 177, 185

Mumma, Albert G., Jr., 355

Municipal Building (G5), **113**, 118

Murch, Ben, Elementary School (T17), 355

Murphy, C. F., & Associates, 138

Murphy, Frederick V., 358, 359

Murphy and Locraft, 342

Murphy & Olmsted, 291, 359

Murphy/Jahn, 195

Muse Architects, 336

Museum of the Bible (C1), **70**, 71

Muse-Wiedemann Architects, 34

Mushinsky Voelzke Associates / MV+A, 292

Myer, Don, 49

Myers, John Granville, 275

Nägele Hofmann Tiedemann und Partner, 205

National Academies Building (G3), **113**, 116–17

National Academy of Sciences (L13), **203**, 213

National Air and Space Museum (B28), 15, **43**, 64–65

National Arboretum (T18), 31, 355–56

National Archives Building (H7), 10, 14, 15, **133**, 137

National Association of Realtors Building (G8), **113**, 119

National Bank of Washington: Historic (I25), **148**, 164–65; Washington Branch (H5), **133**, 136

National Baptist Memorial Church, 326

National Building Museum (G2), 10, 110, **113**, 114–16

National Bureau of Standards, 328, 338

National Capitol Columns (T18a), 356

National Cathedral of African Methodism. See Metropolitan A.M.E. Church (I34)

National Cathedral School, 336; Hearst Hall (O30), **254**, 269

National Center for White House History, 183

National City Christian Church (P26), **273**, 289

National Community Church–Capitol Hill, 86

National Council of Negro Women, 136

National Galleries of History and Art (proposed), 11, 12

National Gallery of Art, 65, 208, 286, 320; East Building (B1), **43**, 44, 55; Sculpture Garden (B3), **43**, 45–46; West Building (B2), **43**, 44–45

National Garden, 32

National Geographic Society Headquarters (K5), **189**, 191–92

National Japanese American Memorial (A10), **26**, 37

National Law Enforcement Museum, 114

National Law Enforcement Officers Memorial (G1), **113**, 114

National Metropolitan Bank, 150

National Museum. See Arts and Industries Building (B25)

National Museum of African American History and Culture (B6), 19, **43**, 47–49

National Museum of African Art, 60

National Museum of American History, Behring Center (B5), **43**, 47

National Museum of Natural History (B4), **43**, 46

National Museum of the American Indian (B30), **43**, 66–67

National Museum of Women in the Arts (I21), **149**, 163

National Native American Veterans Memorial, 66, 67

National Park Service, 49, 52, 55, 95, 96, 140, 154, 183, 224, 241, 356–57

National Portrait Gallery (G16), **112**, 123–24

National Postal Museum (F4), **100**, 104

National Press Building, 151

National Savings and Trust Company (I28), **148**, 166

National Society of the Colonial Dames of America, 229–30

Nationals Park (D1), **82**, 83
National Swedenborgian
 Church (P38), **273**, 295–96
National Trust for Historic
 Preservation, 183, 259, 286
National Union Building (I9),
 149, 154–55
National Woman's Party, 36
National Zoo. *See* Smithsonian
 National Zoological Park
 (S6)
Native American Design Col-
 laborative, 66
Naval Hospital, Old (E8), **90**, 95
Navy, Marshall, Gordon, 192
Navy Memorial, 137
Navy Yard, Washington (D9),
 82, 87
Near Southwest (C), 68–79
Neer and Graef, 290
Nelson Architects, 289
Neutra, Richard, 349
Neville-Stent, Edward J., 164
New Executive Office Building,
 179
Newseum, 135
1100 New York Avenue (I16),
 149, 159–60
1099 New York Avenue, NW
 (I17), **149**, 160
Nigeria, Embassy of, Chancery
 (S14a), **330**, 338
9:30 Club, 155
Nolen-Swinburne & Associ-
 ates, 72
NoMa (F), 98–109
Norten, Enrique, 198
800 North Capitol Street, NW
 (F7), **100**, 105–6
Northern Liberty Market, 110
Notre Dame Chapel, Trinity
 University, 359
Notter Finegold + Alexander,
 58, 59, 269, 341

Oak Hill Cemetery (M15), **223**,
 230
Oakwood Suites & Studios
 (P17), 11, **272**, 283–84
Obata, Gyo, 65
Octagon, The (L6), 7, 176, **203**,
 208
ODA Architecture, 83
Oehme, van Sweden & Associates, 51, 56, 213, 338
OEHME, van SWEDEN | OvS,
 84, 92
Oehrlein & Associates Architects, 31, 36, 49, 55, 61, 62,
 104, 116, 123, 125, 126, 128, 129,
 134, 137, 138, 142, 144, 151, 153,
 156, 160, 161, 168, 192, 194,
 231, 262, 283, 293, 302, 309,
 342, 356

Ohev Sholom synagogue, 120,
 121
Old Brick Capitol, 28, 36
Oldham and Seltz, 274
Old Naval Hospital (E8), **90**, 95
Old North Hall, Georgetown
 University (M21b), **222**, 235
Old Stone House (M2), **223**, 224
OLIN, 80, 85, 362
Olin Partnership, 45, 49
Olmsted, Frederick Law, 31, 107,
 108, 333, 334
Olmsted, Frederick Law, Jr., 12,
 102, 333, 334, 346
Olmsted, John Charles, 333, 334
Olmsted, Vaux and Co., 107
Olmsted Brothers, 268
Olney, Daniel, 351
OMA, 80, 122, 362
Oman, Ambassador's Resi-
 dence and Embassy of, 263
O'Marah & Benulis, 291
Omni Shoreham Hotel (S2),
 330, 331
One Franklin Square (I19), **149**,
 160–61
O'Neil & Manion Architects,
 278, 342
OPX, 109, 281
Order of the Eastern Star, Inter-
 national Headquarters (P12),
 272, 280–81
Organization of American
 States (L10), **203**, 211
Osinski, Tomas, 65
OTJ Architects, 156, 157, 217
Owen, Robert Dale, 8, 20
Owings, Nathaniel, 17, 130, 138

Page, Harvey L., 282
Page, Russell, 356
Page, Thomas Nelson, House
 (P13), **272**, 281
Pakistan, former Chancery of,
 258
Palmer Alley, 158
Pan American Health Organiza-
 tion (L16), **202**, 215
Pan-American Union. *See*
 Organization of American
 States (L10)
Parker Torres Design, Inc., 74
Parks, Josephine Butler, Center
 (R4), **318**, 321
Parks & Recreation, Depart-
 ment of, 327
Patent Office, Old, 7, 111, 123–24,
 125, 126
Patterson House (P17), 11, 271,
 272, 283–84
Patton, George E., 143
Peabody and Stearns, 233
Peaslee, Horace W., 55, 93, 94,
 179, 180, 229, 278, 279, 319

Peck, G. Byron, 303
Pedersen and Tilney, 57
Pei, I. M., 16, 44, 55, 76, 337, 339
Pei, I. M., & Associates, 337
Pei, I. M. & Partners, 44, 73, 76
Pei Cobb Freed & Partners, 58,
 141, 152
Pei Partnership Architects, 339
Peirce, Isaac, 343
Peirce Mill (S19), **300**, 343
Pelz, Paul J., 11, 12, 33–34, 167,
 295, 316. *See also* Smith-
 meyer & Pelz
Pelz and Carlisle, 295
Penn Quarter (G), 111
Pennsylvania Avenue (H), 130–
 45
660 Pennsylvania Avenue (E3),
 90, 93
1001 Pennsylvania Avenue, 153
1501 Pennsylvania Avenue, NW,
 174, 178
1503 Pennsylvania Avenue, NW,
 174, 178
2401 Pennsylvania Avenue, NW
 (K19), **188**, 199
Pennsylvania Avenue Development Corporation (PADC),
 131, 134, 145
700 Penn (E2), **90**, 92
Penn Theater Project (E4), **90**,
 93
Pension Building, 10, 110, 114–16
Pepco Headquarters (G15), **112**,
 123
Perkins&Will / Perkins+Will,
 49, 79, 362
Perkins Eastman, 74, 155, 314,
 315, 335, 361
Perkins Eastman DC, 74, 335
Perry, Roland Hinton, 256
Peruvian Chancery, 287
Peter, Walter, Jr., 342
Peter, Walter G. (Gibson), 144,
 167, 228
Petersen House, 154
Peterson Institute for Interna-
 tional Economics (P21), **272**,
 286
Pettit, Richard, 233
Pheasant, Thomas, 181
Phifer, Thomas, and Partners,
 160
Philadelphia Row (E13), **91**, 97
Phillips Collection (P9), **272**,
 279
Piano, Renzo, Building Work-
 shop, 341
Pier 4, 74
Pierson, F., 235
Pierson & Wilson, 34
Pink Palace, 322
Pittman, William Sidney, 303,
 304

Plager, W. S., 128

Planet Word, 11, 161–62

Platt, Charles Adams, 60, 208

Playhouse Theatre (I29), **148**, 167

Plowman, Thomas, 242

PNC Bank, 225–26

Poland, Embassy of, 323

Polshek Partnership Architects, 66, 67, 217

Poor, Alfred, 27

Pope, John Russell, 54, 185; American Pharmacists Association (L14), 213, 214; Brodhead-Bell-Morton Mansion, 288; Daughters of the American Revolution Headquarters (L9), 210, 211; McCormick House (O24), 265–66; Meridian House (R2), 320; National Archives Building (H7), 137; National City Christian Church (P26), 289; National Gallery of Art, West Building (B2), 44, 45; Scottish Rite Temple (P40), 297; Thomas Jefferson Memorial (B17), 57, 58; White-Meyer House, 320

Populous, 83

Porter, Irwin, and Sons, 35, 264, 337

Porter & Lockie, 35, 167, 168

Post, Marjorie Merriweather, 342–43

Postal Square (F4), **100**, 104

Post Massachusetts Apartments (P25), **273**, 288–89

Post Office, General, 125–26

Post Office, Georgetown Customhouse and (M3), **223**, 225

Post Office Building, City, 104

Post Office Building, Old (H11), 11, **132**, 139–40

Post Office Building, William Jefferson Clinton Building, 141, 144

Potomac River, 1, 5, 7–8, 40, 68, 69, 74, 217

Potter, William, 185

Potts, Allen Hussell, 161

Poynton, Arthur M., 95, 313

Pratt, Harvey, 66

Pre-Columbian Collection Pavilion (M16a), **223**, 231–32

Prettyman, E. Barrett, Courthouse (H1), 39, **133**, 134

Price, Bruce, 167

Price, Walter F., 260

Price & de Sibour, 167, 286

Proctor, A. Phimister, 256

Progression Place (Q18), **301**, 312

Pullman House, 170

Quadrangle Museums Project (B23), **43**, 60–61

Quincy Park, 289

Quinn Evans Architects, 46, 60, 65, 92, 104, 176, 185, 210, 213, 217, 250, 258, 334, 342, 343

Raben, John G., 348

Rainbow Lofts (P32), **273**, 292

Rankin, Andrew, Memorial Chapel (Q14d), **301**, 309–10

Rankin, Kellogg & Crane, 59

Rapp & Rapp, 151

Ray, George N., 260, 275

Rayburn Building, 33

REACH, The (L19a), **202**, 218–19

Reagan, Ronald, Building and International Trade Center (H14), **132**, 141–42, 144

Reatig, Suzanne, Architecture, 314, 315

Red Cross, American National (L8), **203**, 209–10

Redden, John S., 348

Redevelopment Land Agency, 76

Redig de Campos, Olavo, 266

Reinsen, Peter, 197

Renwick, Aspinwall and Russell, 216

Renwick, James, Jr., 7, 8, 12, 61, 62, 180, 184, 216, 230, 359

Renwick Gallery of the Smithsonian American Art Museum (J15), **174**, 184–85, 209

Republic Theatre, 299

Residences at Eastern Market, The (E2), **90**, 92

Revere, John, 326

Revery Architecture Inc., 76. See also Thom, Bing, Architects

Reynolds, Donald W., Center for American Art and Portraiture (G16), **112**, 123–24

1701 Rhode Island Avenue, NW (K8), **189**, 193

Rhodeside & Harwell, 117, 355

Rhodes Tavern, 150

Ricci, P., 359

Ricci Architects & Planners, 134

Richardson, Henry Hobson, 10, 105, 181, 323

Richter Cornbrooks Gribble, 217

Ridge Place Co-Living (Q24), **301**, 314–15

Riggs Library, Georgetown University, 234, 235

Riggs National Bank Building (Riggs Washington DC Hotel) (I11), **149**, 155; Historic Bank Buildings (J3), **174**, 178

Rill Architects, 236

Rios, Ariel, Federal Building (F13), **100**, 109

Ripley, S. Dillon, 63, 64

Ripley, S. Dillon, Center, 60

Rippeteau Architects, 120, 293

Ritchie, Matthew, 160

Ritter Norton Architects, 78

Ritz-Carlton Georgetown (M36), **223**, 242–43

River Park (C13), **70**, 78

Riverside Baptist Church (C7), **70**, 75

RJShirley & Associates Architects, 216

RKK&G Museum and Cultural Facilities Consultants, 122

Roberts & Schaefer, 107

Robinson, Hilyard R., 309, 350–51

Rockart, John R., 36

Rock Creek Cemetery, 357–58

Rock Creek Park, 221, 328, 343

Rockwell Group, 74, 170, 242, 283

Rogers, Isaiah, 176, 177

Rogers, Richard, 38

Rogers Krajnak Architects, Inc, 164

Rogers Stirk Harbour + Partners, 38, 73

ROMA Design Group, 56

Roosevelt, Eleanor, 183–84, 211, 283

Roosevelt, Franklin Delano, 58, 183; Memorial (B16), **42**, 56–57

Roosevelt, Theodore, 59, 176, 269

Root, Walter C., 86

Rosedale (S10), 224, 262, **330**, 336

Rosenblum, Martin, 229

Ross, Andrew, 224

ROSSETTI, 363

Rossi, Mario, 264

Rottet Studio, 158

RTKL Associates, 27, 59, 140, 163, 192, 233, 239, 338, 340. See also CallisonRTKL

Russell Senate Office Building (A9), 25, **26**, 33, 37

Russian Embassy (I35), **148**, 170

Russian Trade Representation, 260–61

Rüssli Architekten / Rüssli, Justin, 332

Saarinen, Eero, 15, 16

Saarinen, Eliel, 15, 16

Sackler Gallery, Arthur M., 60, 61

Sadler & Whitehead Architects, 323

Safdie Architects, 109, 214

Saint-Gaudens, Augustus, 13, 358

Saint-Gaudens, Louis, 102
Saint John Paul II National Shrine (T22), 358
Samperton, John S., 181
Sanchez Palmer Architects, 362
S & R Foundation, 237
Sanson, Paul-Ernest Eugène, 280
Santmyers, George T., 261
Sartogo Architetti Associati, 264
Sasaki Associates, 206, 245, 355
Satterlee, Nicholas, 282
Satterlee & Smith, 79
SCAPE Studio, 169
Scharnberg, Hans-Ullrich, Architects, 92, 266
Scheimgarten, Milton, 320
Schlesinger, Frank, Associates, 239, 240
Schneider, Thomas Franklin, 282, 294
Schneider Row Houses (P15), **272**, 282
Schoen, Eugene, and Sons, 170
Schuler Shook, 217
Schulze, Paul, 9, 62, 123, 124
Schwartz, Martha, 72
Schwarz, David M. / Architectural Services, 93, 232, 279
Scott-Grant House (M17), **222**, 232
Scottish Rite Temple (P40), 137, **273**, 297
Sears House, 135–36
Sedgwick Gardens (S17), **330**, 341–42
Segal, George, 56, 57
Senate: Old Senate Chamber, 27, 30. *See also* Hart, Philip A., Senate Office Building; Russell Senate Office Building (A9)
Senate Park Commission: formation of, 13; influence of, 13–14, 46, 85, 139; and Lafayette Square, 172, 178; and Lincoln Memorial (B12), 53–54; and the Mall, 32, 40, 46, 59, 62; and Union Station (F2), 102–3
Sestini, Benedict, 106
1200 17th Street, 193
7th Flats Apartments, 312
7th Street Park and Recreation Pier, 74
Shakespeare Library. *See* Folger Shakespeare Library (A6)
Shakespeare Theatre Company, 127–28
Shaw Junior High School, 298, 313

Shaw Library (Q19), **301**, 312–13
Shaw / U Street (Q), 298–315
Shepherd, Alexander Robey "Boss," 11, 187, 270
Shepherd's Row, 187
Shepley, Bullfinch, Richardson & Abbot, 60
Shepley, Rutan and Coolidge, 362, 363
Sheridan Circle, 257
Sheridan-Kalorama (O), 252–69
Shinberg.Levinas, 238
SHoP Architects, 169
Shrady, Henry M., 32
Shreve, Lamb & Harmon, 38
Sidwell Friends Middle School (S13), **330**, 337–38
Signal House, 109
Sills Huniford, 170
Simmons, B. Stanley, 150, 151, 190
Simmons & Cooper, 312
Simon, Louis A., 105, 140
Singapore, Embassy of, Chancery (S14e), **330**, 340
3149 16th Street, NW (R14), **318**, 327
6th & I Historic Synagogue (G12), **112**, 121
1000/1100 6th Street, SW (C9), **70**, 76
SK&I Architectural Design Group, 304
Skidmore, Owings & Merrill, 45, 47, 52, 63, 138, 150, 163, 191, 206, 267, 339, 348
Skirving, John, 361
Slayton House (S12), **330**, 337
Small, Lillian and Albert, Capital Jewish Museum (G7), **113**, 118–19
SMB Architects, 119
Smith, Chloethiel Woodard, and Associates, 17, 19, 77, 79, 190, 241
Smith, Delos, 34, 93, 357
Smith, Franklin Webster, 11, 12
Smith, John, 1
Smith, Segreti, Tepper, McMahon & Harned, 170
Smith, Walter and Clement, 237
SmithGroup, 32, 45, 46, 47, 49, 62, 66, 74, 84, 107, 116, 119, 123, 126, 127, 134, 152, 153, 185, 204, 268, 362. *See also* Florance Eichbaum Esocoff King Architects; KCF-SHG Architects; Keyes, Lethbridge & Condon Architects; Keyes Condon Florance
SmithGroupJJR, 47, 49, 71, 74, 144
Smithmeyer, John L., 11, 33–34
Smithmeyer & Pelz, 11, 33–34, 234

Smith Row (M25), **222**, 237
Smith Segreti Tepper Architects and Planners, 268
Smithson, James, 61, 62
Smithsonian: Arts and Industries Building, 9; Gallery of Art design, 15, 16; grounds design, 8; Visitor Center, 62
Smithsonian American Art Museum, National Portrait Gallery and (G16), **112**, 123–24
Smithsonian American Art Museum, Renwick Gallery of the (J15), **174**, 184–85
Smithsonian Anacostia Community Museum (T20), 357
Smithsonian Institution Building (B24), 7, 8, **43**, 61–62
Smithsonian National Zoological Park (S6), 328, 329, **330**, 333–34
Society of the Cincinnati (P7), 11, **272**, 277–78
Soldiers' and Airmen's Home, US, 361
Sonnemann, Alexander, 334
Sorg, Suman, 106
Sorg and Associates, 225, 239, 302, 311
SORG Architects, 106
Southern Building (I31), **148**, 168
Spain, Former Residence of the Ambassadors of (R9), **318**, 324
Spain-USA Foundation, 324
Spanish Ambassador's Residence (N5), **248**, 251
Spanish Steps, 260
Speck House (Q11), **300**, 306
Speiden & Speiden Architects, 278
Spy Museum, International (C5), **70**, 74
Square 37 / Squash on Fire Building (K16), **188**, 197
St. Albans School, Marriott Hall (O28), **254**, 267–68
St. Aloysius Catholic Church (F8), **100**, 106
Stanton, Michael, Architects, 125
Stanton Architecture, 125
Starkweather, Norris G., 233, 237
Starkweather and Plowman, 228
State, War, and Navy Building, 10, 185
St. Augustine's Episcopal Church, 74
Staunton, Francis, 235
Stavropoulos Associates, 236
St. Coletta of Greater Washington (E10), **91**, 96

Steel, Gilbert V., 350
Steinman, Cain & White, 47
St. Elizabeths East Gateway
Pavilion (T29a), 363
St. Elizabeths Hospital, West
Campus (T29), 362–63
Stenhouse, Douglas, 263
Stenhouse, John W., 164
Stevens, Ernest D., 326
Stewart, J. George, 27, 34
St. Florian, Friedrich, 51
St. John's Church, Lafayette
Square (J7), **174**, 180
St. John's Episcopal Church,
Georgetown (M26), **222**,
237–38
St. John's Parish Building (J6),
174, 179
St. Mark's Episcopal Church
(A5), **26**, 34–35
St. Mary's Church, Foggy Bot-
tom (L17), **203**, 216
St. Matthew the Apostle,
Cathedral of (K9), **189**, 194
Stoddert, Benjamin, 236, 238;
House, 236–37
Stoiber + Associates, 321
Stone, Edward Durell, 120, 191,
192, 218
Stone, Edward Durell, Associ-
ates, 217
Stone, Edward Durrell, Jr., 217,
338
Stoneleigh Court Apartments,
187
Storck, J. Edward, 311
St. Paul's Episcopal Church,
Rock Creek Parish (T21), 357
Strauss, Jacu, 155
Streetsense, 154
St. Regis Hotel (I36), **148**, 170–71
Studio GAIA, 145, 190
StudioMB, 74
STUDIOS Architecture, 75, 85,
161, 167, 191, 227
Studio Theatre, The (P30), **273**,
291–92
Studio Twenty Seven Architec-
ture, 78, 107
Sugimoto, Hiroshi, 64
Sulgrave Club (P19), **272**, 284–
85
Sullivan, Francis P., 27, 37
Summer School and Summer
Square (K6), **189**, 192
Sun Building, The (I3), **148**, 151
Sunderland Building (P3), **272**,
274–75
SunTrust Bank: Childs Restau-
rant Building (F5), 104–5;
National Savings and Trust
Company (I28), 166
Supreme Court Building (A8),
24, 25, **26**, 36–37

Swanke, Albert, 27
Swanke Hayden Connell, 140
Swanson, J. Robert F., 15, 16
Swartout, Egerton, 326
Swartzell, Rheem & Hensey
Company Building, 167
Sweden, House of (M39), **223**,
244–45
Swiss Ambassador's Residence
(S4a), **330**, 332–33
Switzerland, Embassy of,
Chancery (S4), **330**, 332

Taft, Lorado, 102
Taft, William Howard, 36, 261
Taft, William Howard, Bridge,
256
Tapies Apartments, The (P37),
273, 295
Tariff Commission Building, 111,
125–26
Tax Court Building, US (G6),
113, 118
Tayloe, John, III, 7, 144, 208
Taylor, James Knox, 59
Temperance Fountain, 136
TEN Arquitectos, 197, 198
Tenley-Friendship Neighbor-
hood Library (T10), 351
10th & G Offices (I14), **149**, 157
Terrell Place, 126–27
Thai Ambassador's Residence,
259–60
THEARC (T28), 362
Theatre Projects Consultants,
217
1001/1101 3rd Street, SW (C9),
70, 76
Thom, Bing, Architects, 75, 76,
352
Thomas, Leuterio, 84
Thompson, Benjamin, & Asso-
ciates, 102
Thompson, Ventulett, Stain-
back & Associates, 121
Thornton, William, 6, 27, 95,
208, 228, 237
Tiber Island Cooperative
Homes (C10), **70**, 76
Tiffany, Louis Comfort, 34, 210
Titanic Memorial, Women's, 78
Tobey Davis, 217
Tod Williams Billie Tsien Archi-
tects, 157
Totten, George Oakley, Jr., 168,
256–57, 258–59, 320–21, 322,
323–24, 327
Toutorsky Mansion (P39), **273**,
296
Town, Ithiel, 123, 124
Town Center Plaza, 76
Town Hall Education Arts Rec-
reation Campus (THEARC)
(T28), 362

Townhomes on Capitol Hill
(E6), **90**, 94
Townsend House, 11, 278–79
Treasury Annex (J4), **174**, 178–
79, 181
Treasury Building (J2), 7, 125,
174, 176–78
Trentman House (M8), **223**, 227
Trevillian, Howard B., Jr., 268
Trinity University, Notre Dame
Chapel, 359
Trowbridge, A. Breck, 209
Trowbridge, Alexander Buel,
34, 35
Trowbridge and Livingston, 209
True Reformer Building (Q2),
300, 302–3
Truman, Harry, 184
Trumbauer, Horace, 250, 280
Trumbull, John, 30
Trump, Donald, 20, 138, 140, 173,
180
Trump International Hotel, 139–
40
Tudor Place (M11), **223**, 228
Turkish Ambassador's Resi-
dence (O2), **255**, 256–57
Turkish Chancery (O20), **255**,
263–64
Turner Memorial AME Church,
121
Turpin, Wachter and Associ-
ates, 104
555 12th Street, NW (I6), **149**,
152–53
1250 24th Street, NW (K17), **188**,
197–98

Udall, Stewart Lee, Department
of the Interior Building (L11),
203, 212
UDC Student Center (S15), **330**,
340
Uline Arena (F10), **100**, 107
Underwood, Bayard, 123
Ungers, O. M., 249
Unification Church (R13), **318**,
326
Union Bethel A.M.E. Church, 170
Union Market (F12), 20, 98, **101**,
108–9
Union Row (Q7), **300**, 304
Union Station and Plaza (F2),
98, 99, **100**, 102–3
Union Trust Building (I30), **148**,
167–68
Unitarian All Souls Church
(R12), **318**, 326
United Mine Workers of Amer-
ica Building, 168
United Negro College Fund
Building, 312
United States Colored Troops,
303

University Club, 168–69
University of the District of Columbia, 122, 328; Student Center (S15), **330**, 340
University Student Center, George Washington University (L1a), **203**, 204
Urbahn, Max O., Associates, 206
Urban, James, 37, 63, 191, 236
US Court of Claims, 179, 184
US Military Asylum, 361
US National Arboretum (T18), 31, 355–56
US Soldiers' and Airmen's Home, 361
U Street / Shaw (Q), 14, 298–315
Uzbekistan, Embassy of (P22), **272**, 286–87

Valtchev, Ivan, 145
Van Alen, William, 104, 105
Van Buren, Martin, 183, 333
Van Dresser Company, 331
Van Dusen Architects, 275
Van Hook, John, 336
Van Ness (S), 328–43
Van Ness mansion, 211
Van Ness mausoleum, 230
Vaughan, Henry, 268
Vaux, Calvert, 107, 108, 229
Ventana, The (I10), **149**, 155
Venturi, Rauch & Scott Brown, 143
Venturi, Robert, 17
Venturi, Scott Brown and Associates, 231
Vercelli, Peter, 241
Vergason, Michael, Landscape Architects, 32, 74, 268
Verizon Building (I23), **149**, 163–64
Victims of Communism Memorial Foundation, 168
Vietnam Veterans Memorial (B11), **42**, 52–53, 55
Villareal, Leo, 44
VIO/Incanto, 74
Vitale, Brinckerhoff & Geiffert, 319
Vitetta / Vitetta Group, 44, 55, 159
VOA Associates, 141, 156, 244, 265
Voghi, Peter, 262
Vogt, Oscar, 84
Volta Bureau (M19), **222**, 233
von Ezdorf, Richard, 185
Voorhees, Gmelin & Walker, 163, 164
Voorhees, Walker, Smith and Smith, 180

Wadsworth House, 284–85
Waggaman, Clarke, 281

Waggaman, Wolcott, 333
Waggaman & Ray, 281
Wah Luck House, 111
Walker Building, 167
Walsh, Thomas, 276–77
Walsh-McLean House, 276–77
Walter, Thomas U., 9, 129; and the Capitol, 27, 30; Chinese Community Church (G11), 120; General Post Office / Tariff Commission Building (G18), 125; National Portrait Gallery (G16), 123; Old Patent Office Building (G16), 123, 124; St. Elizabeths Hospital (T29), 362–63; St. John's Parish Building (J6), 179; and Treasury Building (J2), 176, 177
Walters, Maurice, 283, 337
Warder Building, 124, 125
Warder-Totten Mansion (R8), **318**, 323–24
Wardman, Harry, 14, 171, 332
Wardman Park Hotel, 332
Wardman Tower (S3), **330**, 331–32
Warnecke, John Carl, 17, 179; & Associates, 37, 179, 184, 235
Warner Theatre / Office Building (I5), **149**, 152
War of 1812, 6, 7, 28, 95, 176, 208, 246
Warren, Herbert Langford, 295
Warren & Wetmore, 190, 324, 325
Washburn, Sharon, 262
Washington, George, 2, 4, 7, 47, 224, 278, 336; and the Capitol, 27–28; and establishment of District of Columbia, 2–5; Monument (B8), 7, 13, 40, 41, **42**, 49–51
Washington, Walter E., Convention Center (G13), **112**, 121–22
Washington and Georgetown Railroad Car House, 86
Washington Aqueduct, 9
Washington Canal Park (D7), **82**, 85–86
Washington Canoe Club (M31), **222**, 240
Washington Channel Bridge, 19
Washington Club, The, 284
Washington Coliseum, 107
Washington Design Center, 71
Washington Harbour (M38), **223**, 243–44
Washington Hilton Hotel, 15
Washington Metropolitan Area Transit Authority, 346
Washington Monument (B8), 7, 13, 40, 41, **42**, 49–51
Washington National Cathedral (O29), **254**, 268–69

Washington Navy Yard (D9), 80, **82**, 87
Washington Parks & People, 321
Washington Plaza Hotel (P27), **273**, 289–90
Washington Square (K2), **189**, 190
Washington Technical Institute, 328
525 Water Condominium, 74
Waterfront Center (M37), **223**, 243
Watergate, The (L18), **203**, 216–17
Water Headquarters, DC (D3), **82**, 84
Water Main Pumping Station, DC (D4), **82**, 84–85
Waterman, Thomas T., 49, 182, 230, 343
3303 Water Street (M32), **222**, 240
W. B. Hibbs & Co. Building, 167
WDG Architecture, 74, 139, 169, 197, 198, 199, 362
Weaver, Robert C., Federal Building (C3), **70**, 72–73
Weese, Harry, & Associates, 75, 102, 346
Weihe Partnership, 290. See also WDG Architecture
Weinman, Adolph A., 57
Weinstein, Amy, 94, 97
Weinstein Associates Architects, 93, 94, 97
Weinstein Studio, 92
Weller, Lou, 66
22 West Condominium (K15), **188**, 196
West End (K), 186–99
West End Neighborhood Library (K18), **188**, 198–99
Western High School, 232
West Half (D2), **82**, 83–84
Westlake Reed Leskosky, 184
Westlight (K18), **188**, 197, 198–99
Wetzell-Archbold Farmstead, 247
Wheatley, Francis, 226
Wheatley Houses (M6), **223**, 226
Wheat Row (C12), 68, **70**, 77–78
Wheeler, Perry, 342
Whistler, James McNeill, 60
White, Clifton B., 128
White, Frank Russell, 195
White, George, 27, 33
White, Lawrence, 230
White, Stanford, 281, 283, 358
White House, The (J1), 5–6, 7, 8, 144, 172, **174**, 175–76
White House Historical Association, 183

White House / Lafayette Square (J), 172–85
Whitelaw Hotel (Q6), **300**, 304
White-Meyer House, 320
Whitney, Gertrude Vanderbilt, 78, 211
Whittemore House, 282–83
Whitten, Jamie L., Federal Building (B21), **43**, 59–60
Whittle School and Studios (S16), **330**, 341
Whole Foods Market (P33), **273**, 292–93
Wiebenson & Dorman Architects, 313
Wiencek + Associates Architects + Planners, 352, 353, 354
Wilkes & Faulkner, 194, 212
Wilkins House, 287
Willard InterContinental Hotel (H17), **132**, 144–45
Williams, Edward Bennett, Law Library (G9), **113**, 119–20
Williams, Paul Revere, 309, 350–51
Williams, Richard, Architect, 231, 342, 347
Wilson, A. Hamilton, 359
Wilson, Ellen, Complex, 94
Wilson, James, 59
Wilson, Jesse B., 314
Wilson, John A., Building (H15), **132**, 142–43
Wilson, Woodrow, 210, 259
Wilson, Woodrow, House (O8), **255**, 259
Winder Building (L4), **203**, 206–7
Windrim, James T., 166

Wingårdh, Gert, 244
Winslow, Lorenzo S., 175
Winstanley Architects & Planners, 102
Winter, Lumen Martin, 180
Wischmeyer, Arrasmith & Elswick, 159
Wisnewski Blair & Associates, 357
Wiss, Janney, Elstner Associates, 49
Withers, Frederick C., 107
Woman's National Democratic Club (P16), **272**, 282–83
Women's Equality National Monument, Belmont-Paul, 36
Women's *Titanic* Memorial, 78
Wonder Bread Bakery, 312
Wong, Dianna, Architecture & Interior Design, 145
Wood, Donn & Deming, 163, 167
Wood, Waddy B., 97, 165, 166, 185, 208, 212, 239, 242, 257, 259
Woodley (S5), 328, **330**, 333
Woodley Park (S), 328–43
Woodridge Neighborhood Library (T11), 352
Woods, Elliott, 32, 37, 117, 297
Woodward & Lothrop department store, 147, 260
Woodward Condominium (O16), **255**, 262
World Bank Headquarters (L2), **203**, 205–6
World War I Memorial. *See* District of Columbia War Memorial (B14)

World War II Memorial (B9), **42**, 51–52
Wright, Frank Lloyd, 15, 58, 192, 336
Wright, Orville and Wilbur, Federal Buildings (B27), **43**, 64
Wright, Thomas W. D., 337
W Street Residence (Q10), **300**, 305–6
Wyeth, Nathan C., 37, 55, 96, 118, 170, 175, 176, 258, 325
Wyeth and King, 230, 279

Yards, The, 20, 80
Yards Park, 80
Yates, Sidney R., Federal Building (B20), **43**, 59
Yellin, Samuel, 212
Yerkes, Pappas and Parker, 285
Yixin, Lei, 56
YMCA, 193, 303–4
York, Judson, 290
York & Sawyer, 143, 176, 178
Yoshimura, Junzo, 60
Young, Ammi B., 95, 164, 176, 177, 225
Young, Don Carlos, Jr., 326
Younger, Joseph, 334

Zantzinger, Borie & Medary, 137
Zapatka, Christian, Architect, 228
Zen Associates, 342
ZGF Architects, 193
Zink, Atkins and Craycroft, 152
Zoo. *See* Smithsonian National Zoological Park (S6)

Photo Credits

3, Library of Congress

4, Library of Congress

5, Maryland Historical Society

6, Library of Congress

7, Library of Congress

9, Library of Congress

10, Library of Congress

12, Library of Congress

13, Courtesy of the U.S. Commission of Fine Arts

15, National Archives

16, Smithsonian American Art Museum

19, Courtesy of the National Building Museum

20, Visualization by Interface Multimedia, courtesy of Hoffman Madison Waterfront

25, Library of Congress

27, Alan Karchmer

28, Architect of the Capitol

29, Library of Congress

30, Architect of the Capitol

31, Boris Feldblyum

32, Dan Cunningham (*left*); Alan Karchmer (*right*)

33, Boris Feldblyum

34, Alan Karchmer

35, Alan Karchmer

36, Boris Feldblyum (*top*); Alan Karchmer (*bottom*)

37, © Robert C. Lautman Photography, National Building Museum (*top*); Boris Feldblyum (*bottom*)

38, Boris Feldblyum

39, © Maxwell MacKenzie

41, Library of Congress

44, Esto

45, Alan Karchmer (*left*); G. Martin Moeller, Jr., Assoc. AIA (*right*)

46, Alan Karchmer

47, Alan Karchmer

48, Smithsonian Institution

49, Alan Karchmer

50, Library of Congress

51, Boris Feldblyum

52, Photography, Michael Ventura

53, Boris Feldblyum

54, Boris Feldblyum

55, Boris Feldblyum

56, Photo credit: Hoachlander Davis Photography, Courtesy: Bonnie Fisher and Boris Dramov ROMA Design Group

57, Boris Feldblyum (*left*); Alan Karchmer (*right*)

58, G. Martin Moeller, Jr., Assoc. AIA (*top*); Alan Karchmer (*bottom*)

59, Alan Karchmer

60, Alan Karchmer

61, Bob Lautman (*top*); Alan Karchmer (*bottom*)

62, Boris Feldblyum

63, Alan Karchmer

64, Library of Congress (*left*); George A. Cott (*right*)

65, © Alan Karchmer/OTTO

66, © Maxwell MacKenzie

69, Smithsonian Institution

71, © Alan Karchmer/OTTO (*left*); Alan Karchmer (*right*)

72, Boris Feldblyum

73, Library of Congress (*top*); The International Spy Museum, Photo by Nic Lehoux (*bottom*)

74, Copyright Jeff Goldberg-ESTO Courtesy Perkins Eastman

75, The Banks, Washington, DC. Photography © Alan Karchmer (*left*); Photo by Nic Lehoux, courtesy of Bing Thom Architects (*right*)

76, Philip A. Esocoff (*left*); Alan Karchmer (*right*)

77, Alan Karchmer

78, Boris Feldblyum (*left*); Devrouax & Purnell (*top right*); © Anice Hoachlander (*bottom right*)

79, Alan Karchmer

81, Library of Congress

83, Photograph by Scott Frances (*top*); Kenneth M. Wyner (*bottom*)

84, © Alan Karchmer/OTTO

85, © Alan Karchmer/OTTO (*top left*); Prakash Patel (*bottom left* and *right*)

86, Canal Park, Washington, DC. Photography © Bruce Damonte (*top*); Boris Feldblyum (*bottom*)

87, Boris Feldblyum

89, Library of Congress

92, Alan Karchmer (*left*); © Maxwell MacKenzie, Architectural Photographer (*right*)

93, © Maxwell MacKenzie (*left*); Michael O. Houlahan (*right*)

94, Alan Karchmer (*top left* and *right*); Anice Hoachlander (*bottom left*)

95, Boris Feldblyum (*left*); Alan Karchmer (*right*)

96, © Maxwell MacKenzie (*left*); Boris Feldblyum (*right*)

97, Boris Feldblyum (*left*); Alan Karchmer (*top right*); © Maxwell MacKenzie (*bottom right*)

99, Library of Congress

102, Boris Feldblyum

103, Donald Paine

104, Alan Karchmer (*top*); Boris Feldblyum (*bottom*)

105, Boris Feldblyum

106, Boris Feldblyum (*top left*); Library of Congress (*bottom left*); © Robert Benson Photography (*right*)

107, Photo courtesy of Dana Bowden Photography

108, Alan Karchmer (*top*); EDENS (*bottom*)

109, Tim Hursley

111, Library of Congress

114, © Robert C. Lautman Photography, National Building Museum

115, Boris Feldblyum

116, Library of Congress (*top*); Prakash Patel (*bottom*)

117, Alan Karchmer

118, Boris Feldblyum (*left* and *bottom right*); Alan Karchmer (*top right*)

119, Boris Feldblyum

120, Boris Feldblyum

121, Boris Feldblyum (*left*); Kenneth M. Wyner (*right*)

122, Boris Feldblyum

123, Kenneth M. Wyner (*left*); Alan Karchmer (*right*)

125, Alan Karchmer (*left*); Boris Feldblyum (*right*)

126, Boris Feldblyum

127, Boris Feldblyum

128, Alan Karchmer (*top*);
G. Martin Moeller, Jr., Assoc.
AIA (*bottom*)

129, G. Martin Moeller, Jr.,
Assoc. AIA

131, Library of Congress

134, Boris Feldblyum (*left*);
Alan Karchmer (*right*)

135, Alan Karchmer (*left*);
Carol M. Highsmith (*right*)

136, Alan Karchmer

137, Alan Karchmer

138, Alan Karchmer

139, Skidmore, Owings & Merrill (*left*); Boris Feldblyum
(*right*)

140, Boris Feldblyum

141, Alan Karchmer

142, Boris Feldblyum

143, Carol M. Highsmith (*top*);
Alan Karchmer (*bottom*)

144, Alan Karchmer

145, Alan Karchmer

147, Library of Congress

150, Boris Feldblyum

151, Alan Karchmer (*left and top
right*); Carol M. Highsmith
(*bottom right*)

152, Courtesy of Shalom
Baranes Associates

153, Prakash Patel (*left*); Bryan
Becker (*right*)

154, Alan Karchmer (*left*); Boris
Feldblyum (*right*)

155, © Maxwell MacKenzie
(*left*); Boris Feldblyum
(*right*)

156, Boris Feldblyum (*top*);
Robert Benson Photography
(*bottom*)

157, © Michael Moran Photography, Inc.

158, © Maxwell MacKenzie

159, Michael Dersin

160, Boris Feldblyum (*left*);
© Maxwell MacKenzie (*right*)

161, Boris Feldblyum

162, Boris Feldblyum

163, Dan Cunningham (*left*);
© Maxwell MacKenzie (*right*)

164, Boris Feldblyum (*left*);
Alan Karchmer (*right*)

165, Boris Feldblyum

166, Carol M. Highsmith (*left*);
Alan Karchmer (*right*)

167, Boris Feldblyum

168, Courtesy of Shalom
Baranes Associates (*left*);
© Maxwell Mackenzie Archi-
tectural Photographer (*right*)

169, © Ty Cole/OTTO (*top*);
Boris Feldblyum (*bottom*)

170, Boris Feldblyum

171, Boris Feldblyum

173, Library of Congress

175, Alan Karchmer (*top*);
Maryland Historical Society
(*bottom*)

177, Quinn Evans Architects

178, Alan Karchmer

179, Alan Karchmer

180, Alan Karchmer (*left*); Ron
Solomon (*right*)

181, Boris Feldblyum (*left*); Alan
Karchmer (*right*)

182, Courtesy of Shalom
Baranes Associates (*left*);
© Maxwell MacKenzie (*top
right*); Alan Karchmer (*bottom right*)

183, Alan Karchmer

184, © Kevin G Reeves Photographer

185, Alan Karchmer

187, Library of Congress

190, Boris Feldblyum (*top left*);
Alan Karchmer (*bottom left
and right*)

191, Alan Karchmer (*left*); Esto
(*right*)

192, Esto

193, Center for Strategic and
International Studies, Photo
by Anice Hoachlander (*top*);
1701 Rhode Island Avenue,
Photo by Alan Schindler
(*bottom*)

194, Boris Feldblyum

195, Boris Feldblyum

196, Boris Feldblyum (*left*);
© Maxwell MacKenzie (*right*)

197, © Alan Karchmer/OTTO

198, Alan Karchmer (*top*);
© Alan Karchmer/OTTO
(*bottom*)

199, © Maxwell MacKenzie
(*left*); Boris Feldblyum
(*right*)

201, Library of Congress

204, Prakash Patel (*top*); Boris
Feldblyum (*bottom*)

205, Boris Feldblyum (*top*); Tim
Hursley (*bottom*)

206, Alan Karchmer

207, Alan Karchmer

208, Boris Feldblyum

209, Alan Karchmer

210, © Maxwell MacKenzie
(*left*); Alan Karchmer (*right*)

211, Alan Karchmer

212, Alan Karchmer (*top*); Boris
Feldblyum (*bottom*)

213, Alan Karchmer (*left*); Bryan
Becker (*right*)

214, Boris Feldblyum

215, Boris Feldblyum

216, Alan Karchmer (*top*); Boris
Feldblyum (*bottom*)

218, Boris Feldblyum (*top*);
Richard Barnes / JBSA (*bottom*)

221, Library of Congress

224, Alan Karchmer

225, Alan Karchmer (*left*); Boris
Feldblyum (*right*)

226, Boris Feldblyum (*top left*);
Alan Karchmer (*bottom left
and right*)

227, Alan Karchmer

228, Alan Karchmer

229, Alan Karchmer

230, Alan Karchmer

231, Alan Karchmer (*left*);
© Dumbarton Oaks, Pre-
Columbian Collection,
Washington, D.C. (*right*)

232, Alan Karchmer

233, Photo © Chris Ambridge /
Ambridge Photography (*top*);
Alan Karchmer (*bottom*)

234, Alan Karchmer

235, Alan Karchmer

236, Alan Karchmer

237, Alan Karchmer

238, Alan Karchmer (*top*);
© Alan Karchmer (*bottom*)

239, Boris Feldblyum (*left*);
Julia Heine (*right*)

240, Boris Feldblyum (*top left*);
Alan Karchmer (*bottom left*);
© Maxwell MacKenzie
(*right*)

241, Alan Karchmer

242, Boris Feldblyum

243, © Maxwell MacKenzie
(*top*); Hartman—Cox Architects (*bottom*)

244, Arthur Cotton Moore

245, Boris Feldblyum (*top*);
Alan Karchmer (*bottom*)

247, DC Preservation League
Archives

249, Alan Karchmer (*left*); Boris
Feldblyum (*right*)

250, Alan Karchmer (*top*); Robert Creamer (*bottom*)

251, Boris Feldblyum

253, Library of Congress

256, Alan Karchmer

257, Boris Feldblyum (*left*);
Ronald O'Rourke (*right*)

258, Alan Karchmer (*left*); Boris
Feldblyum (*right*)

259, Alan Karchmer

260, Alan Karchmer

261, Boris Feldblyum (*left and
top right*); Sean Shanahan
(*bottom right*)

262, Boris Feldblyum (*left*); Alan Karchmer (*right*)

263, Alan Karchmer

264, © Maxwell MacKenzie (*left*); Alan Karchmer (*right*)

265, Boris Feldblyum (*top*); Alan Karchmer (*bottom*)

266, Alan Karchmer (*top left*); Boris Feldblyum (*bottom left* and *right*)

267, Boris Feldblyum (*left*); Robert Polidori (*right*)

268, Boris Feldblyum

269, Boris Feldblyum

271, Library of Congress

274, Boris Feldblyum (*left*); Alan Karchmer (*top right* and *bottom right*)

275, Boris Feldblyum

276, Boris Feldblyum

277, Alan Karchmer

278, Boris Feldblyum

279, Boris Feldblyum

280, Dana Tautfest for Fred Sons Photography (*top*); The American Geophysical Union Headquarters, Photo by Devon Perkins (*bottom*)

281, Alan Karchmer

282, Boris Feldblyum (*top*); Alan Karchmer (*bottom*)

283, Alan Karchmer (*top*); Anice Hoachlander (*bottom*)

284, Boris Feldblyum

285, Alan Karchmer (*top*); Anice Hoachlander (*bottom*)

286, Michael Dersin

287, Boris Feldblyum (*top*); Photo by Anice Hoachlander (*bottom*)

288, Image courtesy of the American Coatings Association (*top*); © Maxwell MacKenzie (*bottom*)

289, Alan Karchmer

290, Boris Feldblyum (*left*); Alan Karchmer (*top right* and *bottom right*)

291, Boris Feldblyum

292, Photograph by Maxwell MacKenzie (*left*); Boris Feldblyum (*top right*); Dan Cunningham (*bottom right*)

293, Alan Karchmer

294, Alex Jamison (*left*); Boris Feldblyum (*right*)

295, Cunningham, Dan (*left*); Alan Karchmer (*right*)

296, Boris Feldblyum

297, Alan Karchmer

299, © Robert H. McNeill, courtesy of Susan McNeill

302, Boris Feldblyum (*left*); Nicole Sorg (*right*)

303, Boris Feldblyum

304, Boris Feldblyum

305, Anice Hoachlander (*top left*); Boris Feldblyum (*bottom left*); Debi Fox (*right*)

306, Boris Feldblyum

307, Boris Feldblyum (*top*); Photograph by Alan Karchmer (*bottom*)

308, Photo courtesy of HDR © 2015 Dan Schwalm

309, Boris Feldblyum (*left*); Hoachlander Photography Associates (*right*)

310, Courtesy of Howard University (*top left* and *top right*); Library of Congress (*bottom*)

311, Alan Karchmer (*left*); Boris Feldblyum (*right*)

312, Photograph by Anice Hoachlander (*left*); Paúl Rivera (*right*)

313, Boris Feldblyum (*left*); Photograph by John Cole (*right*)

314, © Maxwell MacKenzie (*left*); Suzane Reatig Architecture (*right*)

315, © Alan Karchmer (*top*); Copyright Joseph Romeo Courtesy Perkins Eastman (*bottom*)

317, Library of Congress

319, Boris Feldblyum

320, Alan Karchmer

321, Boris Feldblyum

322, Alan Karchmer (*left* and *top right*); John DeFerrari (*bottom right*)

323, Boris Feldblyum

324, Boris Feldblyum

325, © DavidMadisonPhotography.com (*top*); Boris Feldblyum (*bottom*)

326, Alan Karchmer

327, G. Martin Moeller, Jr., Assoc. AIA

329, Library of Congress

331, Alan Karchmer

332, Alan Karchmer

333, Bill Lebovich (*top*); Alan Karchmer (*bottom*)

334, Alan Karchmer (*top*); Bryan Becker (*bottom*)

335, Copyright Joseph Romeo Courtesy Perkins Eastman (*top*); Alan Karchmer (*bottom*)

336, Boris Feldblyum (*left*); Alan Karchmer (*right*)

337, Boris Feldblyum (*left*); Esto (*right*)

338, © Maxwell MacKenzie

339, Boris Feldblyum (*top left*); Paul Warchol Photography (*bottom left*); Esto (*right*)

340, Alan Karchmer (*top*); © Sam Kittner (*bottom*)

341, Alan Karchmer (*top*); © Judy Davis, Architectural Photographer (*bottom*)

342, Alan Karchmer

343, Alan Karchmer

345, Library of Congress

346, WMATA photo by Larry M. Levine

347, Bob Lautman (*left*); CORE Group, PC (*right*)

348, Boris Feldblyum (*top*); © Maxwell MacKenzie (*bottom*)

349, Photograph by Maxwell MacKenzie (*top*); Bob Lautman (*bottom*)

350, Photo courtesy of Dana Bowden Photography (*top*); Boris Feldblyum (*bottom*)

351, Boris Feldblyum

352, Bellevue Library, Francis Gregory Library, Woodridge Library (*top*); Copyright Paúl Rivera (*bottom*)

353, Bellevue Library, Francis Gregory Library, Woodridge Library (*top*); © Mark Herboth Photography, LLC (*bottom*)

354, Esto (*top*); Bellevue Library, Francis Gregory Library, Woodridge Library (*bottom*)

355, Ken Wyner

356, Boris Feldblyum (*top*); Alan Karchmer (*bottom left* and *bottom right*)

357, Boris Feldblyum (*left*); Alan Karchmer (*right*)

358, Alan Karchmer (*top left* and *right*); Boris Feldblyum (*bottom left*)

359, Alan Karchmer

360, Courtesy of Michael Marshall Design

361, Alan Karchmer (*left*); Photo © Chris Ambridge / Ambridge Photography (*right*)

362, Image Courtesy of Ayers Saint Gross, Photography by Ron Solomon (*left*); Alan Karchmer (*right*)

363, Copyright Eric Taylor